SOCIAL STUDIES
Building Our Country

Pearson

Boston, Massachusetts   Chandler, Arizona
Glenview, Illinois   New York, New York

Pearson would like to extend a special thank you to all of the teachers who helped guide the development of this program. We gratefully acknowledge your efforts to realize the possibilities of elementary Social Studies teaching and learning. Together, we will prepare students for college, careers, and civic life.

Cover: Dann Tardif/Getty Images

Credits appear on pages R74–R77, which constitute an extension of this copyright page.

ISBN-13: 978-0-328-97312-5
ISBN-10: 0-328-97312-2

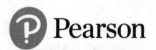 **Pearson**

Program Authors

Dr. Linda B. Bennett
Faculty, Social Studies Education
College of Education
University of Missouri
Columbia, MO

Dr. James B. Kracht
Professor Emeritus
Departments of Geography and
  Teaching, Learning, and Culture
Texas A&M University
College Station, TX

Reviewers and Consultants

Program Consultants

ELL Consultant
Jim Cummins Ph.D.

Professor Emeritus,
Department of
  Curriculum, Teaching,
  and Learning
University of Toronto
Toronto, Canada

Differentiated Instruction Consultant

Kathy Tuchman Glass
President of Glass
  Educational Consulting
Woodside, CA

Reading Consultant
Elfrieda H. Hiebert Ph.D.

Founder, President and
  CEO, TextProject, Inc.
University of California
Santa Cruz

Inquiry and C3 Consultant

Dr. Kathy Swan
Professor of Curriculum
  and Instruction
University of Kentucky
Lexington, KY

Academic Reviewers

Paul Apodaca, Ph.D.

Associate Professor,
  American Studies
Chapman University
Orange, CA

Warren J. Blumenfeld, Ed.D.

Former Associate
  Professor, Iowa State
  University, School
  of Education
South Hadley, MA

Dr. Albert M. Camarillo

Professor of History,
  Emeritus
Stanford University
Palo Alto, CA

Dr. Shirley A. James Hanshaw

Professor, Department
  of English
Mississippi State
  University
Mississippi State, MS

Xiaojian Zhao

Professor, Department
  of Asian American
  Studies
University of California,
  Santa Barbara
Santa Barbara, CA

Teacher Reviewers

Mercedes Kirk
First grade teacher
Folsom Cordova USD
Folsom, CA

Julie Martire
Teacher, Grade 5
Flocktown Elementary School
Long Valley, NJ

Kristy H. Spears
K-5 Reading Specialist
Pleasant Knoll Elementary School
Fort Mill, SC

Kristin Sullens
Teacher, Grade 4
Chula Vista ESD
San Diego, CA

Program Partner

Campaign for the Civic Mission of Schools is a coalition of over 70 national civic learning, education, civic engagement, and business groups committed to improving the quality and quantity of civic learning in American schools.

CAMPAIGN FOR THE CIVIC MISSION OF SCHOOLS
Educating for Democracy

🌐 Geography Skills Handbook

✏️ Writing Workshop

🔍 Using Primary and Secondary Sources

GO ONLINE FOR
DIGITAL RESOURCES

 ETEXT

 VIDEO

- **Field Trip Video**
  Ancient Farmers:
  Builders in Stone
- **Digital Skill
  Practice**
  Interpret Cultural
  Data on Maps
  Compare and
  Contrast

 AUDIO

Rap About It! lyrics
and music

INTERACTIVITY

- **Big Question
  Activity**
  How does
  geography
  influence how
  people live?
- **Quest
  Interactivities**
  Quest Kick Off
  Quest Connections
  Quest Findings
- **Lesson
  Interactivities**
  Lesson Introduction
  Key Ideas
  Lesson Review

GAMES

Vocabulary Practice

 **ASSESSMENT**

Lesson Quizzes and
Chapter Tests

The **BIG** **How does geography influence**
Question **how people live?**

GO ONLINE FOR
DIGITAL RESOURCES

 ETEXT

 VIDEO

- **Field Trip Video**
  Coronado
  National Memorial:
  Searching for Cities
  of Gold
- **Digital Skill Practice**
  Sequence
  Interpret Timelines

🔊 AUDIO

Rap About It! lyrics
and music

👆 INTERACTIVITY

- **Big Question Activity**
  Why do people
  explore?
- **Quest Interactivities**
  Quest Kick Off
  Quest Connections
  Quest Findings
- **Lesson Interactivities**
  Lesson Introduction
  Key Ideas
  Lesson Review

🎮 GAMES

Vocabulary Practice

☑ ASSESSMENT

Lesson Quizzes and
Chapter Tests

The BIG Question Why do people explore?

Chapter 3

Settling the Colonies in North America

GO ONLINE FOR DIGITAL RESOURCES

ETEXT

VIDEO

- **Field Trip Video** Jamestown Settlement: Three Cultures Meet
- **Digital Skill Practice** Ask and Answer Questions Distinguish Fact From Opinion

AUDIO

Rap About It! lyrics and music

INTERACTIVITY

- **Big Question Activity** Why do people leave their homelands?
- **Quest Interactivities** Quest Kick Off Quest Connections Quest Findings
- **Lesson Interactivities** Lesson Introduction Key Ideas Lesson Review

GAMES

Vocabulary Practice

ASSESSMENT

Lesson Quizzes and Chapter Tests

The BIG Question Why do people leave their homelands?

Chapter 4 Life in the Colonies

GO ONLINE FOR DIGITAL RESOURCES

 ETEXT

 VIDEO

- **Field Trip Video**
  Children in Colonial Times
- **Digital Skill Practice**
  Main Idea and Details
  Read Circle Graphs

 AUDIO

Rap About It! lyrics and music

 **INTERACTIVITY**

- **Big Question Activity**
  What does it take to build a new society?
- **Quest Interactivities**
  Quest Kick Off
  Quest Connections
  Quest Findings
- **Lesson Interactivities**
  Lesson Introduction
  Key Ideas
  Lesson Review

 GAMES

Vocabulary Practice

ASSESSMENT

Lesson Quizzes and Chapter Tests

The BIG Question What does it take to build a new society?

Chapter 5 The American Revolution

The BIG Question What is worth fighting for?

Chapter 6 A New Nation

GO ONLINE FOR
DIGITAL RESOURCES

📖 ETEXT

▶ VIDEO

- **Field Trip Video**
Capitol Visitor
Center: At the
Nation's Legislature
- **Digital Skill
Practice**
Summarize
Compare Points
of View

🔊 AUDIO

Rap About It! lyrics
and music

👆 INTERACTIVITY

- **Big Question
Activity**
What is the purpose
of government?
- **Quest
Interactivities**
Quest Kick Off
Quest Connections
Quest Findings
- **Lesson
Interactivities**
Lesson Introduction
Key Ideas
Lesson Review

🎮 GAMES

Vocabulary Practice

☑ ASSESSMENT

Lesson Quizzes and
Chapter Tests

The BIG Question

What is the purpose of government?

GO ONLINE FOR
DIGITAL RESOURCES

 ETEXT

▶ VIDEO

• **Field Trip Video**
Cherokee Heritage
Center: A Trail of
Tears

• **Digital Skill Practice**
Draw Inferences
Use and Interpret
Evidence

◀)) AUDIO

Rap About It! lyrics
and music

👆 INTERACTIVITY

• **Big Question Activity**
How do leaders
shape a nation?

• **Quest Interactivities**
Quest Kick Off
Quest Connections
Quest Findings

• **Lesson Interactivities**
Lesson Introduction
Key Ideas
Lesson Review

🎮 GAMES

Vocabulary Practice

✓ ASSESSMENT

Lesson Quizzes and
Chapter Tests

The **BIG**
Question How do leaders shape a nation?

GO ONLINE FOR
DIGITAL RESOURCES

 ETEXT

▶ VIDEO

- **Field Trip Video**
  Lowell: An Early
  Industrial Town

- **Digital Skill
  Practice**
  Distinguish Fact
  From Fiction
  Analyze Costs and
  Benefits

◀» AUDIO

Rap About It! lyrics
and music

👆 INTERACTIVITY

- **Big Question
  Activity**
  What are the costs
  and benefits of
  growth?

- **Quest
  Interactivities**
  Quest Kick Off
  Quest Connections
  Quest Findings

- **Lesson
  Interactivities**
  Lesson Introduction
  Key Ideas
  Lesson Review

 GAMES

Vocabulary Practice

☑ ASSESSMENT

Lesson Quizzes and
Chapter Tests

The **BIG** Question: What are the costs and benefits of growth?

Quests

Ask questions, explore sources, and cite evidence to support your view!

Maps

Where did this happen? Find out on these maps in your text.

Chapter 9 Civil War and Reconstruction

Maps continued

Maps continued

Graphs and Charts

Find these charts, graphs, and tables in your text. They will help you pull it together.

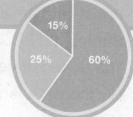

Graphs and Charts continued

Graphs and Charts continued

Primary Sources

Read primary sources to hear voices from the time.

Primary Sources continued

Primary Sources continued

People to Know

Read about the people who made history.

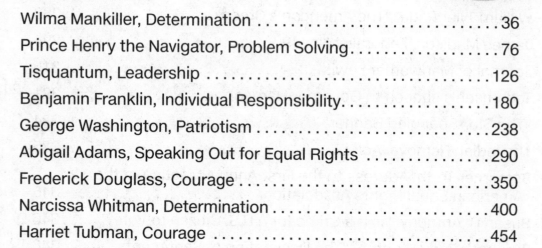

Citizenship

Biographies Online

Abigail Adams

John Adams

Samuel Adams

Elsie Allen

James Armistead

Benedict Arnold

Clara Barton

Delilah Beasley

James Beckwourth

William Bradford

Chaz Bono

Sergey Brin

Jerry Brown

Edmund Burke

Juan Rodriguez Cabrillo

Tani Gorre Cantil-Sakauye

Chirstopher "Kit" Carson

César Chávez

Louise Clappe

Thomas Clifford

Christopher Columbus

Hernán Cortés

Juan Crespi

Charles Crocker

Hallie M. Daggett

Juan Bautista de Anza

Pedro Menéndez de Avilés

Samuel de Champlain

Gaspar de Portolá

Antonio Lopez de Santa Anna

María Angustias de la Guerra

Bartolomeu Dias

John Dickinson

Walt Disney

Frederick Douglass

Ralph Waldo Emerson

William Fargo

First Lady Pat Nixon

Wong Chin Foo

Benjamin Franklin

John C. Fremont

Eric Garcetti

John Gast

Nathan Hale

Alexander Hamilton

John Hancock

Kamala D. Harris

Patrick Henry

Mark Hopkins

Henry Hudson

Dolores Huerta

Collis P. Huntington

Anne Hutchinson

Daniel Inouye

Joseph James

Thomas Jefferson

Hiram Johnson

Billie Jean King

Martin Luther King, Jr.

King Charles III

King George III

Dorothea Lange

Lewis and Clark

Abraham Lincoln

Henry Wadsworth Longfellow

Mary Ludwig Hays

Lord Dunmore

Wilma Mankiller

James Wilson Marshall

John Marshall

Biddy Mason

Ferdinand Magellan

Louis B. Mayer

Sylvia Mendez

Metacom

Harvey Milk

James Monroe

Samuel Morse

John Muir

José Nicolás

Thomas Paine

Charley Parkhurst

William Penn

William Pitt

James K. Polk

Prince Henry the Navigator

Edmund Randolph

Ronald Reagan

Paul Revere

Sally Ride

People to Know continued

Jackie Robinson
Eleanor Roosevelt
Sarah Royce
Bernarda Ruiz
Sacagawea
Haym Salomon
Deborah Sampson
José Julio Sarria
Dalip Singh Saund
Junípero Serra
Roger Sherman
Sir Francis Drake
John Drake Sloat
Jedediah Smith
John Smith
Leland Stanford
John Steinbeck
Levi Strauss
John A. Sutter
Mary Tape
Archie Thompson
Tisquantum
Harriet Tubman
Mariano Guadalupe Vallejo
Earl Warren
Mercy Otis Warren
George Washington
Henry Wells
Phillis Wheatley
Narcissa Whitman
Mary Williams
Roger Williams
Sarah Winnemucca
John Winthrop
Jerry Yang

Skills

Practice key skills in these skills lessons.

Literacy Skills

Critical Thinking Skills

Map and Graph Skills

Skills continued

Skills Online

Gold found at Sutter's Mill.

Cali becc

348 1849 1850

Analyze Cause and Effect

Analyze Costs and Benefits

Analyze Images

Ask and Answer Questions

Classify and Categorize

Compare and Contrast

Compare Viewpoints

Conduct Research

Create Charts

Deliver an Effective Presentation

Distinguish Fact From Opinion

Distinguish Fact From Fiction

Draw Conclusions

Draw Inferences

Evaluate Media Content

Generalize

Generate New Ideas

Identify Bias

Identify Main Idea and Details

Interpret Cultural Data on Maps

Interpret Economic Data on Maps

Interpret Graphs

Interpret Physical Maps

Interpret Timelines

Make Decisions

Predict Consequences

Resolve Conflict

Sequence

Solve Problems

Summarize

Use and Interpret Evidence

Use Latitude and Longitude

Use Primary and Secondary Sources

Use the Internet Safely

Work in Cooperative Teams

Welcome to Your Book!

Your Worktext is made up of chapters and lessons.
Each lesson starts with pages like this.

Look for these words as you read.

Words with yellow highlight are important social studies words. The sentence with the word will help you understand what the word means.

Lesson 2 — Explorers for Spain

INTERACTIVITY
Participate in a class discussion to preview the content of this lesson.

Vocabulary
patron
conquistador
expedition
empire
colony
epidemic

Academic Vocabulary
organized
demolish

Unlock The **BIG** Question
I will know why Spain sent explorers to new lands.

 Jumpstart Activity

With a partner, discuss reasons why you would travel to a new place. What risks are involved? Make a list of the reasons and risks, and then choose one example of each to act out for the class.

Columbus and his crew set sail from Spain in 1492, hoping to discover a new route to Asia.

Christopher Columbus was a man who made bold plans. He was from the Genoa region of Italy. Columbus wanted to find a new route to Asia by sailing west across the Atlantic Ocean. Columbus had a lot of courage but not much money for the voyage. He had to find someone to pay for this dangerous trip.

Christopher Columbus

Columbus asked Portugal's king to pay for his voyage. The king turned down Columbus's request. Columbus did not give up. He decided to ask Spain's rulers. Columbus told them that he would bring Christianity to the people of Asia, and he would bring back riches for Spain. It took several requests, but King Ferdinand and Queen Isabella finally agreed to become Columbus's patrons. A **patron** gives money to support another person or cause.

The Spanish rulers hoped to earn money from the gold and spices that Columbus expected to trade for in Asia. They needed money to pay for a war that Spain had recently fought. Spain was a Catholic country. Ferdinand and Isabella had just restored Christianity to their lands after the *Reconquista*. During the *Reconquista* ("reconquering"), the Spanish had pushed Muslims out of the southern part of the Iberian Peninsula after a struggle that lasted more than 700 years.

Columbus sailed from Spain with about 90 men on three different ships. The crew started off very hopeful and excited for their new journey, but after five weeks at sea, they became tired and weak. After traveling close to 4,500 miles, they spotted land and reached shore on October 12, 1492. Wanting to document the discovery, Columbus wrote:

Primary Source

The crew . . . saw signs of land, and a small branch covered with berries. Everyone breathed afresh and rejoiced at these signs.

–Christopher Columbus, *Journal of the First Voyage of Christopher Columbus*, 1492

INTERACTIVITY
Explore the key ideas of this lesson.

1. ☑ Reading Check
Turn and Talk with a partner about why you think Columbus wrote that "everyone breathed afresh and rejoiced." Ask your partner other questions about Columbus's journal.

Reading Checks will help you make sure you understood what you read.

Your Turn!

Flip through your book with a partner.

1. Find the start of another lesson.
   What do you see on the page?

This book will give you a lot of chances to figure things out. Then you can show what you have figured out and give your reasons.

The Quest Kick Off will tell you the goal of the Quest.

Watch for Quest Connections all through the chapter.

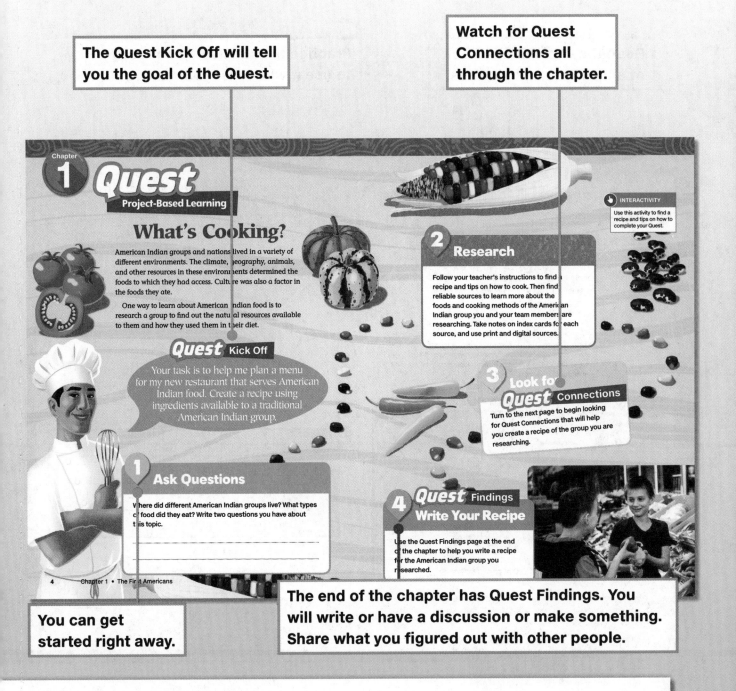

Chapter 1

Quest

Project-Based Learning

What's Cooking?

American Indian groups and nations lived in a variety of different environments. The climate, geography, animals, and other resources in these environments determined the foods to which they had access. Culture was also a factor in the foods they ate.

One way to learn about American Indian food is to research a group to find out the natural resources available to them and how they used them in their diet.

Quest Kick Off

Your task is to help me plan a menu for my new restaurant that serves American Indian food. Create a recipe using ingredients available to a traditional American Indian group.

1 Ask Questions

Where did different American Indian groups live? What types of food did they eat? Write two questions you have about this topic.

_____

_____

2 Research

Follow your teacher's instructions to find a recipe and tips on how to cook. Then find reliable sources to learn more about the foods and cooking methods of the American Indian group you and your team members are researching. Take notes on index cards for each source, and use print and digital sources.

INTERACTIVITY

Use this activity to find a recipe and tips on how to complete your Quest.

3 Look for Quest Connections

Turn to the next page to begin looking for Quest Connections that will help you create a recipe of the group you are researching.

4 Quest Findings
Write Your Recipe

Use the Quest Findings page at the end of the chapter to help you write a recipe for the American Indian group you researched.

You can get started right away.

The end of the chapter has Quest Findings. You will write or have a discussion or make something. Share what you figured out with other people.

2. Find two words with yellow highlight. What page are they on?

3. Find another Reading Check. What does it ask you to do?

4. Find another Quest. What is it called?

Learn to use important skills.

> **Read the explanation. Look at all the text and pictures.**

> **Practice the skill. You'll be ready to use it whenever you need it.**

Map and Graph Skills

Interpret Cultural Data on Maps

VIDEO
Watch a video about interpreting cultural data on maps.

Many different American Indian cultural groups lived in the Americas before Europeans arrived in the late 1400s. They all had their own culture, or way of life.

When you examine data on maps, you look at the map key, or legend, to help you understand what you see. Colors, shading, and symbols on a map help you to interpret, or understand, the information that it shows.

What does the legend tell you on this map? _____

_____

Look at the geographic features on the map. These also can help you interpret information. For example, what can you interpret about American Indian groups that lived on the coasts or near lakes? You could determine that living near water affected their way of life. It likely influenced other resources they used in their environment to survive.

American Indian Cultural Groups

Your Turn!

1. Locate and circle these American Indian cultural groups on the map. Then choose one group that lived near a body of water and one that did not. Write about how their environment affected the way they lived. Think about how their environment affected their relations with other American Indian groups.

   - Pueblo
   - Iroquois
   - Huron
   - Crow
   - Navajo
   - Creek
   - Hopi
   - Algonquin
   - Lakota (Sioux)
   - Chinook
   - Nez Perce
   - Pawnee

   _____

   _____

   _____

   _____

   _____

2. In which regions did the cultural groups listed in question 1 live? Complete the chart.

Woodlands				
Great Plains				
Pacific Northwest				
Southwest				

Your Turn!

Work with a partner.

1. Find another skill lesson. What skill will you learn? Talk about another time you might need that skill.

Every chapter has primary source pages. You can read or look at these sources to learn right from people who were there.

Find out what this source is about and who made it.

These questions help you think about the source.

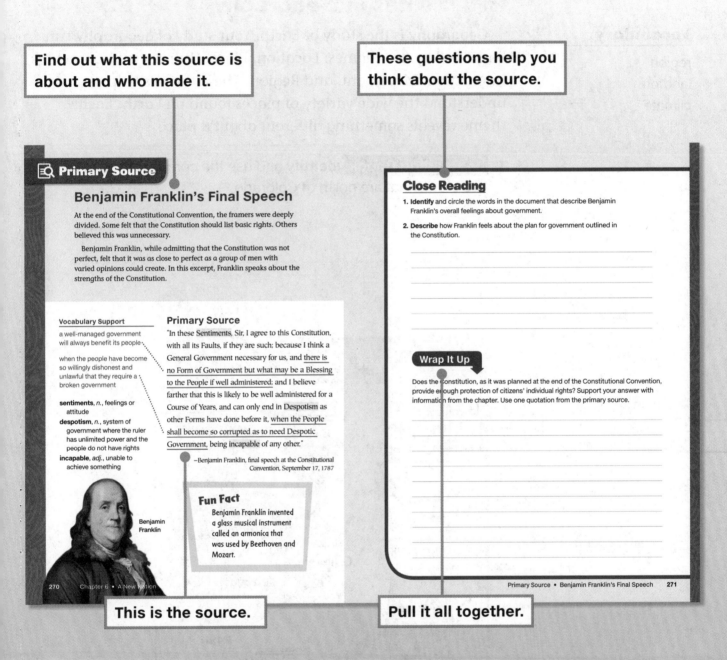

🔍 Primary Source

Benjamin Franklin's Final Speech

At the end of the Constitutional Convention, the framers were deeply divided. Some felt that the Constitution should list basic rights. Others believed this was unnecessary.

Benjamin Franklin, while admitting that the Constitution was not perfect, felt that it was as close to perfect as a group of men with varied opinions could create. In this excerpt, Franklin speaks about the strengths of the Constitution.

Vocabulary Support

a well-managed government will always benefit its people

when the people have become so willingly dishonest and unlawful that they require a broken government

sentiments, *n.,* feelings or attitude
despotism, *n.,* system of government where the ruler has unlimited power and the people do not have rights
incapable, *adj.,* unable to achieve something

Benjamin Franklin

Primary Source

"In these Sentiments, Sir, I agree to this Constitution, with all its Faults, if they are such; because I think a General Government necessary for us, and there is no Form of Government but what may be a Blessing to the People if well administered; and I believe farther that this is likely to be well administered for a Course of Years, and can only end in Despotism as other Forms have done before it, when the People shall become so corrupted as to need Despotic Government, being incapable of any other."

–Benjamin Franklin, final speech at the Constitutional Convention, September 17, 1787

Fun Fact
Benjamin Franklin invented a glass musical instrument called an armonica that was used by Beethoven and Mozart.

270   Chapter 6 • A New Nation

Close Reading

1. **Identify** and circle the words in the document that describe Benjamin Franklin's overall feelings about government.

2. **Describe** how Franklin feels about the plan for government outlined in the Constitution.

Wrap It Up

Does the Constitution, as it was planned at the end of the Constitutional Convention, provide enough protection of citizens' individual rights? Support your answer with information from the chapter. Use one quotation from the primary source.

Primary Source • Benjamin Franklin's Final Speech   271

This is the source.

Pull it all together.

2. Find another primary source lesson in your book. What is the source about?

Five Themes of Geography

Vocabulary

region
landform
climate

Geography is the study of Earth. Your study of geography can be guided by five themes: Location, Place, Human/Environment Interaction, Movement, and Region. These themes help you understand the wide variety of places found on Earth. Each theme reveals something different about a place.

1. ☑ **Reading Check** **Identify** and use the compass rose to list two states that are north of Colorado.

_____

_____

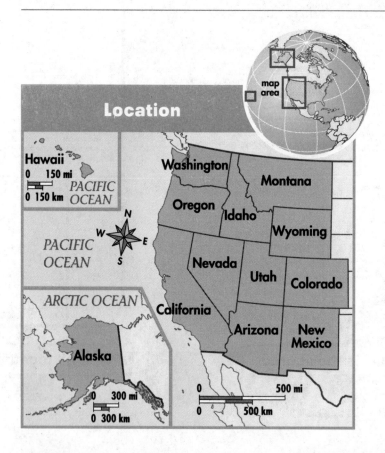

Where can Washington be found within the West region?

A **region** is an area that shares physical or human characteristics. Washington is located in the northern and western part of the West region. It is next to the Pacific Ocean.

| Place | Human/Environment Interaction |

How is this area different from others?

The United States includes a variety of landforms and bodies of water. A landform is a natural feature of the Earth. Many people enjoy time at beaches and coastal areas such as this beach in Georgia.

How have people changed the place?

In the 1800s, people built canals to connect cities to rivers or lakes. Canals changed the land and made it easier to move people and goods. The Indiana Central Canal helped Indianapolis, Indiana, grow. Today, canals may be used to enjoy the outdoors.

| Movement | Region |

How has movement changed a region?

Movement describes how and why people move from one place to another. The highways around New York City are often clogged with cars and trucks. People drive cars to get to work, school, and other places. Trucks deliver food and other goods from one place to another.

What else is special about a region?

California's redwood trees can grow to over 320 feet tall. They are the tallest trees on Earth and are found near the coast in northern California. The climate in northern California is cool and wet. Climate is the usual weather pattern in a place over a period of time.

2. ☑ Reading Check Discuss with a partner the place where you live. Describe each of the themes of geography in your discussion.

Using Maps and Globes

People use globes and maps to learn about the world. A **globe** is a model of Earth, so it is shaped like a sphere. It is useful for looking at the entire world. A globe shows the continents and the oceans as they really are.

Flat maps, such as those in this text, offer a different view of Earth. Flat maps of Earth are less accurate than globes because they need to stretch out some parts of the world to make them flat. This is called distortion. Still, there are advantages to flat maps. Flat maps fold or can be mounted to walls. They are also useful for looking at smaller areas such as a single country, state, or city.

The **equator** is the imaginary line that extends around the center of Earth. It is marked as 0 degrees latitude. **Latitude** lines are evenly spaced and extend around the globe both north and south of the equator. **Longitude** lines are evenly spaced lines that extend north and south between the North Pole and the South Pole. The **prime meridian** is the line of longitude marked as 0 degrees. Other lines of longitude are measured in degrees east or west of the prime meridian. Longitude and latitude are used to tell a place's absolute location. The **absolute location** is the exact location of a place, and it does not change. For example, Los Angeles is 34 degrees north of the equator and 118 degrees west of the prime meridian. The absolute location of Los Angeles is written as 34° N, 118° W.

The equator divides Earth into northern and southern hemispheres. The prime meridian and the 180-degree line opposite it, divide Earth into eastern and western hemispheres. Each **hemisphere** is half of the sphere.

Relative location describes where a place is in relation to another place. For example, you might say that the library is across from the police station. A city may grow based on its relative location to a river or trade route.

Latitude

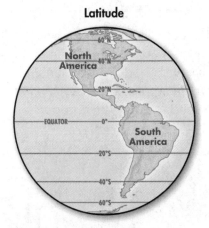

Longitude

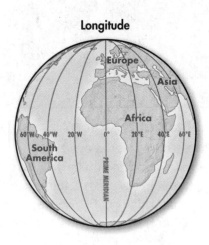

3. 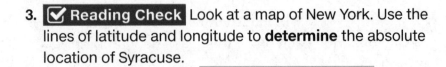 **Reading Check** Look at a map of New York. Use the lines of latitude and longitude to **determine** the absolute location of Syracuse. _____

Different kinds of maps give different kinds of information. Political maps show information such as the location of state capitals and other cities. Look at the political map of the United States and find each of these map tools.

Title: The title tells you what the map shows.

Map legend: The map legend defines the symbols used on the map.

Symbol: A symbol is a mark or color that represents something.

Scale: The scale on the map shows distance. There are three scales on this map. Think about why that is so.

Compass rose: A compass rose shows directions on a map.

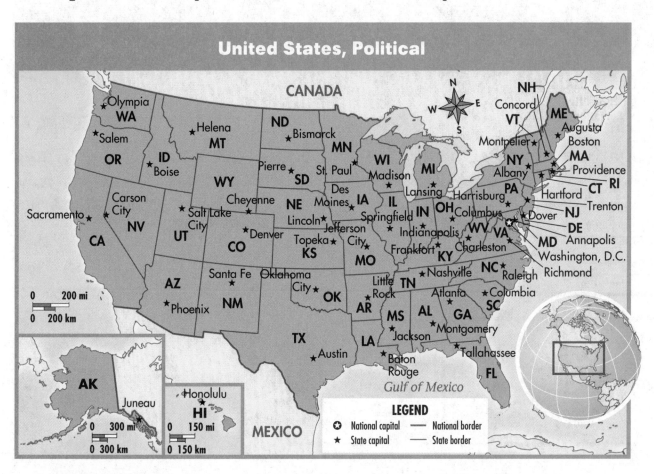

United States, Political

4. ☑ **Reading Check** **Locate** the states that share a border with Mexico. Circle these on the map.

5. ☑ **Reading Check** Work with a partner. **Ask** each other questions about the location of the 50 states and the names of their capitals.

Physical Maps

A **physical map** shows information such as landforms and bodies of water. A **landform** is a physical feature such as a mountain, desert, or valley. Bodies of water can include rivers, lakes, and oceans.

A physical map also shows the **relief** of an area. Relief shows high and low places by using different colors and shading. The elevation or height of the land above sea level is shown in color on the map. Shading is used to show landforms, such as mountain peaks. A **plain** is an open area of flat land.

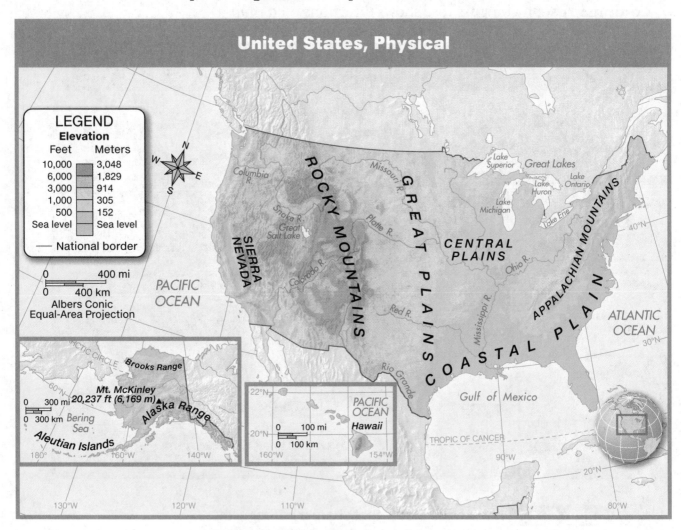

United States, Physical

6. ✅ **Reading Check** What mountain range shown on the map would people have to cross when traveling from the Great Plains to California?

Elevation Maps

Elevation is the distance or height of land above sea level. An **elevation map** allows you to compare and contrast the elevations of different areas. For example, you can compare the elevation of a mountain range to the elevation of a valley or plain. This map uses different colors to show changes in elevation in the state of New York.

Vocabulary

physical map
landform
relief
plain
elevation
elevation map

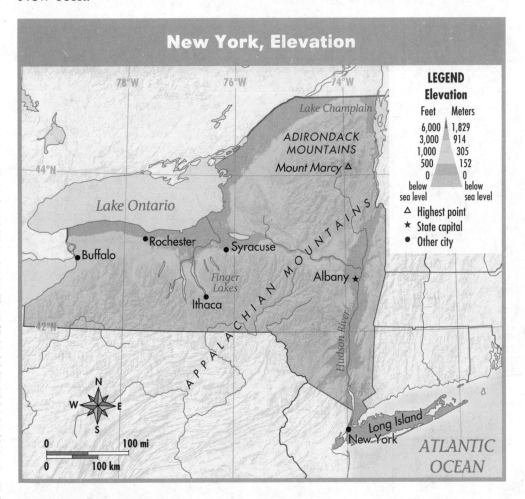

New York, Elevation

LEGEND
Elevation

Feet	Meters
6,000	1,829
3,000	914
1,000	305
500	152
0	0
below sea level	below sea level

△ Highest point
★ State capital
● Other city

7. ☑ **Reading Check** **Identify** which landform in New York has the highest elevation. Then **identify** an area of the state that has one of the lowest elevations.

_____

_____

Human and Physical Characteristics of Regions

A **regions map** shows areas that share similar physical or human characteristics. Regions may result from patterns of human activity, such as population or economic activity. They might be areas that share similar physical characteristics, such as vegetation, landforms, or climate. The map below shows five regions of the United States.

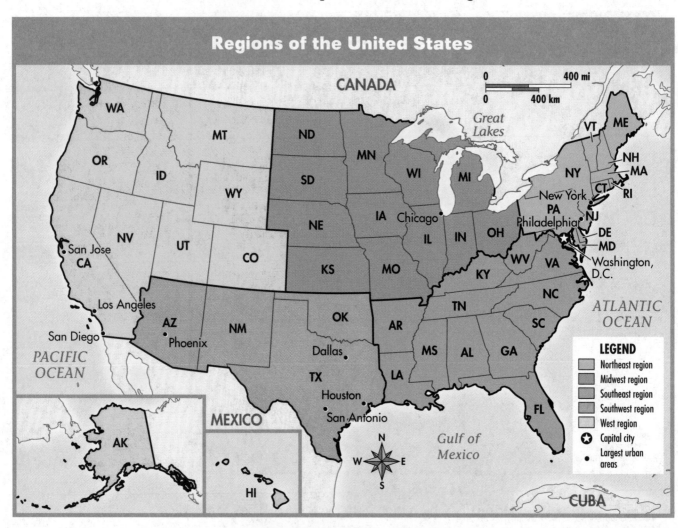

Regions of the United States

8. ☑ **Reading Check** **Identify** which states are in the same region as Utah. Circle them on the map.

9. ☑ **Reading Check** Make a list of the physical and human characteristics that make your state unique.

_____

_____

_____

Historical Maps

A **historical map** shows a particular time from the past. It is important when studying a historical map to notice the date or dates on the map. Historical maps can help you understand how places have changed over time.

This map shows the United States in 1850. During this time, the United States had expanded from the East Coast to the West Coast. Notice that the map also shows free and slave states. The balance between states that allowed slavery and those that did not, divided the U.S. Congress.

Vocabulary

regions map
historical map

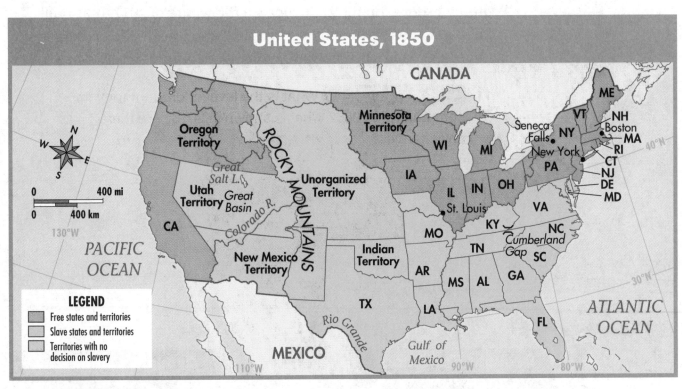

United States, 1850

10. ☑ **Reading Check** **Summarize** the location of the slave states and the location of the free states.

_____

_____

_____

_____

_____

Special-Purpose Maps

A special-purpose map gives information related to a certain theme. For example, a drought map, like the maps of California on this page, shows if there is a drought and how severe it is. A **drought** is a long period of low rainfall. In a drought, plants and animals can suffer. People may have to take extra steps to save water. Drought maps change over time as rainfall increases and decreases. The two maps below show how drought levels have changed between the years 2006 and 2016.

A map of drought conditions in 2017 would look very different from drought shown on the 2016 map. In the winter of 2017, unusually large amounts of rainfall in parts of California caused flooding and mudslides. Dams overflowed as rain filled lakes and reservoirs.

11. ☑ **Reading Check** What is the level of drought for your community in 2006? What is shown in 2016? Are there any changes?

_____

_____

_____

_____

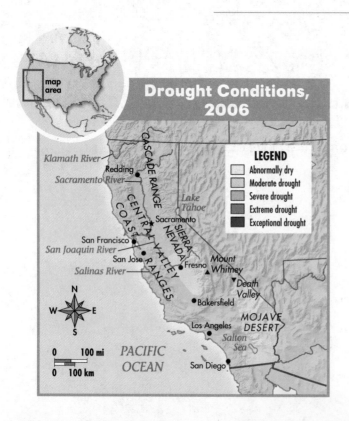

Drought Conditions, 2006

map area

LEGEND
- Abnormally dry
- Moderate drought
- Severe drought
- Extreme drought
- Exceptional drought

Klamath River
Redding
Sacramento River
CASCADE RANGE
Lake Tahoe
Sacramento
CENTRAL VALLEY
SIERRA NEVADA
COAST RANGES
San Francisco
San Joaquin River
San Jose
Salinas River
Fresno
Mount Whitney
Death Valley
Bakersfield
MOJAVE DESERT
Los Angeles
Salton Sea
PACIFIC OCEAN
San Diego

N W E S

0   100 mi
0   100 km

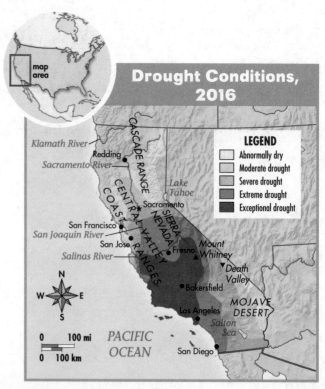

Drought Conditions, 2016

map area

LEGEND
- Abnormally dry
- Moderate drought
- Severe drought
- Extreme drought
- Exceptional drought

Klamath River
Redding
Sacramento River
CASCADE RANGE
Lake Tahoe
Sacramento
CENTRAL VALLEY
SIERRA NEVADA
COAST RANGES
San Francisco
San Joaquin River
San Jose
Salinas River
Fresno
Mount Whitney
Death Valley
Bakersfield
MOJAVE DESERT
Los Angeles
Salton Sea
PACIFIC OCEAN
San Diego

N W E S

0   100 mi
0   100 km

Some special-purpose maps are related to current events. **Current events** are events that are in the news. The outcome of a current event such as an election can more easily be seen on a map such as the one below. The map legend helps you know what the colors represent.

Vocabulary

drought
current events

12. ☑ Reading Check **Summarize** what is shown on the election map.

_____

_____

_____

_____

Writing Workshop

Keys to Good Writing

Good writers follow five steps when they write.

Plan	• Think about how to write about a topic.
	• Find details about the topic.
	• Take notes from sources.
	• Write down your sources.
	• Plan how to use the details.
Draft	• Write down all of your ideas.
	• Think about which ideas go together.
	• Put ideas that go together in groups.
	• Write a sentence for the introduction and write a sentence for the conclusion.
Revise	• Review what you wrote.
	• Check that your ideas and organization make sense.
	• Add time-order words and transitions (words and phrases such as *because* or *for example*).
	• List any more sources that you used.
Edit	• Check for correct grammar, spelling, and punctuation.
	• Make a final copy.
Share	• Use technology to print or publish your work.
	• Make sure that you list all of your sources.

1. **✓ Reading Check Sequence** How might completing these steps out of order affect your writing?

_____

_____

Christopher Columbus

There are three main writing genres—opinion, informative, and narrative. They all have a different purpose for writing.

Opinion Writing

When you write an opinion piece, you are sharing your point of view on a topic. Your goal should be to make your viewpoint clear and to support it with evidence, or facts. Read the steps and sample sentences below to see how to write effective opinion pieces.

1	**Introduce the topic.** *Christopher Columbus landed in the Americas in 1492 after thinking he had reached Asia.*
2	**State your opinion.** *I think Christopher Columbus made a good decision when he chose to leave Spain in search of a western route to Asia.*
3	**Support your opinion with reasons and evidence.** *The trade routes on land were long and dangerous. Columbus sailed across the Atlantic Ocean in 1492 in search of a shorter and faster route to Asia.*
4	**Make sure that your ideas are clear, organized, and written in a logical way to support your purpose.**
5	**Support your opinion statement with a conclusion.** *Columbus did not find the western route to Asia he had hoped for. Yet he made history by being one of the first Europeans to land in the Americas.*

2. ☑ **Reading Check** **Analyze** Answer this question with a partner: Why must you use evidence to support a point of view in opinion writing?

Informative Writing

Informative writing is also called explanatory writing, because you are writing to explain a topic to your reader. Reliable sources are important to use in this kind of writing. Make sure to avoid plagiarism. This means using someone else's words without giving that person credit. Take notes on your sources, including what they say and where you found them. Keep in mind that your reader may know nothing about the topic. Try to be clear and thorough in your writing. Read the steps and sample sentences below.

Pilgrims' landing of the *Mayflower*

1	**Introduce the topic.** *The 13 British colonies were started for different reasons.*
2	**Develop the topic with facts, details, definitions, and concrete details.** *The 13 British colonies were set up in North America between the early 1600s and the early 1700s. A colony is a settlement that is far away from the country that rules it.*
3	**Support your writing with a quotation if possible.** *Some colonies were founded so that people could worship freely. As William Penn explained, "No people can be truly happy . . . if abridged [shortened] of the freedom of their conscience [inner voice]."*
4	**Use precise language and content words.** *In contrast, other colonies were founded for economic reasons. John Rolfe discovered that tobacco grew well in Virginia's soil and it soon became a cash crop for the colony.*
5	**Write a conclusion that supports your introduction.** *Britain's 13 colonies were settled for religious, economic, and political reasons.*

3. ☑ **Reading Check** **Infer** Discuss with a partner why it is important to use facts and details from reliable sources.

Narrative Writing

When you write a narrative piece, you are telling a story, whether it is about a real or imagined event or experience. In this type of writing, you want to show, rather than tell, what happened. You can do this by using sensory words, which describe what a person sees, hears, touches, tastes, or smells. You want the reader to be able to visualize, or see, what you are describing. The events in your narrative should be clear, connected, and unfold in a natural way. Read the steps and sample sentences below.

1	**Introduce the story and characters.** *Kai hid behind the willow tree and watched as the settlers chopped down trees. She ran back to the village to tell her father that people were cutting down their trees.*
2	**Use dialogue and descriptive words.** *Kai asked, "Father, why did the settlers come here? They aren't sharing the land." The settlers looked weary and weakened, as they had been traveling in a rickety wagon for four long weeks.*
3	**Strengthen your writing with sensory words.** *Kai breathed in the freshness of the cool, autumn air and held on tightly to the straw that she was using to weave a basket.*
4	**Write a strong conclusion to close the narrative.** *Kai knew that her life would change once more settlers moved to the area. But for now she focused on the traditions that she had learned so that she could keep them alive.*

4. ☑ **Reading Check** **Summarize** Answer this question with a partner: Why do you think the events or experience of a narrative need to unfold in a natural way?

Using a Library Media Center to Write a Research Paper

When you are writing a research paper, it is helpful to use the resources available in your Library Media Center. To use them effectively, make sure that you:

- use different kinds of print and digital sources and make sure they are reliable.

- compare the information you find in sources.

- take notes by summarizing or paraphrasing content from your sources.

- ask a librarian for help if you are unsure what sources to use for your topic.

Follow these steps to write a research paper:

1. Write down two or three questions to guide your research.

2. Use reliable sources to do your research and answer the questions. Revise the questions if needed.

3. Based on the answers to your questions, organize your topic. If your topic is broad, narrow it or consider focusing on different aspects of the topic.

4. Write a thesis statement based on your research and evidence. This will become your introduction.

5. Use evidence in the form of details, examples, and quotes to support your thesis statement.

6. Use transitions and clauses to connect your ideas.

7. Write a strong conclusion that relates back to your thesis statement.

8. Make a list of your sources.

Researching on the Internet

Not all sites are safe to use for research on the Internet. Look for Web sites with .org, .edu, or .gov, which have reliable content. Content from sites that end in .com cannot necessarily be trusted. If you do use them, check one or two other sources from reliable sites. Just like you should look for credible sources when using library books, you should use the same type of inquiry when you look for information on the Internet.

5. ☑ **Reading Check**
Draw Conclusions Why is it important to check more than one source when you are gathering information to write a research paper?

_____

_____

_____

_____

Using Primary and Secondary Sources

Vocabulary

primary source
autobiography
artifact
secondary source
biography

Primary Sources

Have you ever used a journal or diary to write down something you witnessed? Perhaps you saw an exciting sporting event or went on a trip with your family. If you wrote about those events or took pictures, then you have created a primary source based on events in your life. Read to find out what a primary source is and how historians use primary sources.

A **primary source** is one made or written by a person who witnessed an event. Primary sources help us learn about events or historical periods from people who lived during that time. Primary sources can be written, visual, or oral (spoken).

A historical document, like the United States Constitution, is an example of a written primary source. Letters, journals, and photographs are also primary sources. An **autobiography** is an account of a person's life written by that person. Because it is a firsthand, eyewitness account, an autobiography is a primary source.

Visual primary sources include artwork, maps, and architecture, which show us what people, places, and buildings look like now and in the past. An artifact is another visual primary source. **Artifacts** are objects made and used by people, like a soldier's uniform from the American Revolution. Oral primary sources include speeches, interviews, and recordings of events.

1. ☑ **Reading Check** If you have visited a museum, you have seen artifacts. **Identify** an artifact you saw at a museum.

_____

_____

_____

This uniform is a primary source. It is an artifact from the American Revolution.

Secondary Sources

Have you ever written a research report for school? If you have, you very likely used primary and secondary sources. A **secondary source** is material that was written or created by someone who did not witness or experience an event firsthand. A **biography** is a book about a person's life written by someone else. For example, if a historian today writes a biography on Abraham Lincoln, it is a secondary source since the writer was not present during Lincoln's life.

Secondary sources are important because they often analyze events, sometimes long after they have taken place. Some secondary sources offer readers new ideas or facts about people and events. This textbook is a secondary source. Encyclopedias, online or in print, are also secondary sources. Most reference materials, such as dictionaries and instruction manuals, are secondary sources. Books and magazine articles that were not written firsthand are secondary sources.

Like primary sources, secondary sources can be oral or visual. A radio program about Martin Luther King, Jr., or a historical film about the American Revolution are secondary sources. A painting created today showing a battle during the American Revolution is also a secondary source. Charts and graphs that interpret information are secondary sources because they are made from original data after events occur.

Encyclopedias are secondary sources.

2. ☑ **Reading Check** **Describe** the difference between primary and secondary sources.

_____

_____

_____

_____

How to Interpret Primary Sources

One way to interpret, or understand, a primary source is to study the material or object, think about it, and then answer questions. It can also be helpful to compare and contrast primary sources that are about the same subject or event.

The next document is a primary source because it was written by Hernán Cortés, a Spanish explorer who defeated the Aztec empire and claimed a vast area in what is today Mexico for Spain. Moctezuma is the Aztec emperor.

Primary Source

...the inhabitants of this province would often caution [warn] me not to trust these vassals [servants] of Moctezuma for they were traitors, . . . and they warned me as true friends, and as persons who had long known those men, to beware of them.

–Hernán Cortés to King Charles V of Spain, *Second Letter*, 1520

Hernán Cortés

3. ☑ **Reading Check** Why do you think Cortés wrote this letter? If Cortés had written a letter to a friend how might it be different than one he wrote to the king?

_____

_____

_____

_____

4. **Apply** Explain why this document is a primary source and not a secondary source.

_____

_____

_____

The next document is also a primary source. Bernal Díaz del Castillo, a soldier who was with Cortés during the conquest of Mexico, wrote an account of the event. Díaz del Castillo's account is considered the most complete description of these events that exists. Unlike the letters of Cortés, the book by Díaz was not written until 1568 when Díaz was 72 years old.

Primary Source

They replied that they were the tax collectors of the great Moctezuma and . . . they now demanded twenty men and women to sacrifice to their god, Huitzilopochtli, so that he would give them victory over us, for they said that Moctezuma had declared that he intended to capture us and make us slaves.

-Bernal Díaz del Castillo,
The True History of the Conquest of New Spain, 1576

5. ☑ **Reading Check** **Compare** and **contrast** the similarities and differences between the authors' writings.

_____

_____

_____

_____

_____

_____

_____

_____

_____

_____

How to Interpret Secondary Sources

Your textbook has information about the Lewis and Clark expedition, but the information was not written by someone who was there in real time, like Cortés. This makes it a secondary source. The authors did not see or live through the events that are described. They learned their information by reading other people's writings or looking at other primary sources, like photographs, diaries, and artifacts. You can answer questions to interpret secondary sources just as you did with primary sources. Read the passage below from your textbook and answer the question that follows.

Lewis and Clark took along medals like this one to present to American Indian leaders along their route. The medal is a primary source.

Soon after the Louisiana Purchase, Jefferson finalized plans for an expedition to explore the new lands. He asked Meriwether Lewis to lead the expedition. Lewis had worked as Jefferson's secretary. He was also an explorer and frontiersman.

Lewis asked a fellow frontiersman William Clark to go with him. Together, they put together the Corps of Discovery, a group of capable men who would take the nearly two-year journey to the Pacific Ocean. Jefferson was hoping that they would find a water route that would link the Mississippi with the Pacific Ocean. Such a route would provide access to the western part of the United States. Jefferson also wanted Lewis and Clark to learn about the American Indians who lived in the west, as well as bring back information about the land itself.

6. ☑ **Reading Check** **Compare** the Cortés letter on the previous page to the textbook excerpt. How do they differ?

_____

_____

_____

_____

_____

GO ONLINE FOR
DIGITAL RESOURCES

▶ VIDEO

👆 INTERACTIVITY

🔊 AUDIO

🎮 GAMES

☑ ASSESSMENT

📖 eTEXT

The BIG Question

How does geography influence how people live?

▶ VIDEO

JumpStart Activity

👆 INTERACTIVITY

Look out the window or walk outside of the school with your teacher and classmates. Make a list of the natural resources you see and the ways people use each resource.

_____

_____

_____

_____

_____

_____

_____

The Power of Geography

Preview the chapter **vocabulary** as you sing the rap:

American Indian folk were spread all over the land

And stayed in one place for most of the year

Finding food, fishing, and hunting for deer

Sometimes they would **migrate** or move around
in a year.

The land and bodies of water that you find in a place

Is the **geography** and can create challenges to face.

But it also can provide the means to flourish and grow

Like when Indians farmed and grew the seeds they
would sow.

Some groups had fertile land and would plant and
grow food

Which is **agriculture** and each year their stock
was renewed

In the summer months when temperatures started
to climb.

The **climate** is the weather in a place over time.

PACIFIC
NORTHWEST

Missouri River

Mississippi River

Ohio River

DESERT
SOUTHWEST

GREAT
PLAINS

EASTERN
WOODLANDS

Where did pre-Columbian groups in North America emerge?

Over time, American Indian peoples settled in various regions of North America. The geography and climate influenced how they lived.

Locate the Mississippi River and identify the American Indian regions it is in.

What happened and When?

Read the timeline to find out the history of some American Indian nations and civilizations.

2000 BC

1000 BC

2000 BC
Mayan civilization rises in Central America.

1000 BC
Mound Building people live near the Ohio and Mississippi rivers.

TODAY
You can learn about many early American Indian groups at the National Museum of the American Indian in Washington, D.C.

Who will you meet?

People of the Southwest
Farming in the dry desert Southwest was a challenge.

People of the Northwest
Fishing on nearby oceans and rivers, and hunting in forests provided food.

People of the Great Plains
As they hunted bison on the Great Plains, these Indian groups often lived in tepees.

People of the Woodlands
Forests provided food and shelter, including houses made from tree bark.

 INTERACTIVITY

Complete the interactive map digital activity.

AD 100

AD 100
Ancestral Puebloans live in what is today the Southwest.

TODAY
Ancestral Pueblo cliff dwellings can be seen in Mesa Verde National Park in southwest Colorado.

AD 1000

AD 1000
Aztec civilization rises in what is today Mexico City.

AD 2000

AD 1500
A constitution is likely first used in North America by the League of the Iroquois.

3

Quest
Project-Based Learning

What's Cooking?

American Indian groups and nations lived in a variety of different environments. The climate, geography, animals, and other resources in these environments determined the foods to which they had access. Culture was also a factor in the foods they ate.

One way to learn about American Indian food is to research a group to find out the natural resources available to them and how they used them in their diet.

Quest Kick Off

Your task is to help me plan a menu for my new restaurant that serves American Indian food. Create a recipe using ingredients available to a traditional American Indian group.

1 Ask Questions

Where did different American Indian groups live? What types of food did they eat? Write two questions you have about this topic.

....

....

INTERACTIVITY

Use this activity to find a recipe and tips on how to complete your Quest.

2 Research

Follow your teacher's instructions to find a recipe and tips on how to cook. Then find reliable sources to learn more about the foods and cooking methods of the American Indian group you and your team members are researching. Take notes on index cards for each source, and use print and digital sources.

3 Look for Quest Connections

Turn to the next page to begin looking for Quest Connections that will help you create a recipe of the group you are researching.

4 Quest Findings
Write Your Recipe

Use the Quest Findings page at the end of the chapter to help you write a recipe for the American Indian group you researched.

Ancient American Indian Civilizations

INTERACTIVITY

Participate in a class discussion to preview the content of this lesson.

Vocabulary

migrate
hunter-gatherer
geography
climate
nomad
agriculture
technology
irrigation
civilization

Academic Vocabulary

influence
distribute

Unlock The BIG Question

I will know how geography and climate influenced the way different ancient American Indian nations lived in North America.

JumpStart Activity

In small groups, discuss and put on a short skit showing what it would be like to cross a desert, mountain, river, or lake. As you read this lesson, think about how American Indian groups used land and water features where they lived.

People have lived on the continents of North America and South America for thousands of years. Scientists and historians do not agree about when the first people arrived. They continue to study the past to learn more about this. However, many believe that the first people traveled from Asia to North America about 15,000 years ago.

Ancient people crossed over land from Asia to North America.

Early People Arrive in the Americas

Many scientists and historians agree that the first people arrived in North and South America over time and in several large groups. They have found evidence that early arrivals **migrated**, or moved, to the Americas in several different ways. Some early arrivals traveled by boat, while others traveled over land. Many of the first Americans may have crossed over to North America from Asia on what is today the Bering Strait. A strait is a narrow body of water.

The Bering Strait was not a narrow body of water thousands of years ago when some of the first Americans may have crossed it. It was a dry bridge of land that people today call Beringia.

Thousands of years ago, the temperatures were very cold, much colder than today. There were thick sheets of ice that covered much of the land. Many scientists and historians think that the first people crossed the land bridge from Asia because they were tracking animals to hunt. They lived in North America as **hunter-gatherers**, traveling from place to place in search of animals to hunt, fish to catch, and fruit and nuts to collect.

INTERACTIVITY

Explore the key ideas of this lesson.

1. ☑ **Reading Check** Look at the map. **Describe** the directions of the routes and **analyze** why people might have migrated in those directions.

_____

_____

_____

_____

_____

_____

Possible Routes of First People from Asia to the Americas

ASIA

Bering Strait

Beringia Land Bridge

NORTH AMERICA

ATLANTIC OCEAN

PACIFIC OCEAN

SOUTH AMERICA

N W E S

0   2,000 mi
0   2,000 km

LEGEND
Dry land
Ice cap
→ Route of first people

Using Resources to Live

Over thousands of years, people moved to different areas of North and South America to live. They found that the **geography**, or land and bodies of water of a place, varied. The **climate**, the weather in a place over time, was also different in each region. Often, the geography and climate **influenced** where people decided to settle and how they used the resources of an area. Resources are **distributed** differently across continents. They also affect how people live—what they use to build their homes, what they eat, the clothing they wear, and the tools they create.

Areas with mountains are often colder and wetter than low-lying areas with dry, hot deserts. They have different resources, but both areas pose different challenges for survival. People had to adapt, or adjust, to their environment in order to live in it. Sometimes, they had to modify it, or change it. Early peoples were hunter-gatherers and often roamed a region in search of food. They were **nomads**, people who move within a specific region to follow herds of animals and collect food.

When people began practicing **agriculture** about 10,000 years ago, they modified their environment. Agriculture is the practice of planting and raising food. People who were living then in what is present-day Mexico were the first farmers in North America. The area where they lived was dry and hot. They needed to bring water from nearby rivers to their crops. This kind of **technology**, or the use of scientific knowledge or tools to do work, is called **irrigation**. Groups that farmed stayed in one place. Indian groups in the Southwest and east of the Mississippi built permanent settlements and often built their villages in areas that were near water.

Groups in the Pacific Northwest had little need for agriculture. They lived on coastal land between present-day California and Alaska. The region's oceans and rivers provided fish. Groups hunted deer and gathered nuts and berries in the forests.

Academic Vocabulary

influence • *v.*, to help produce an effect

distribute • *v.*, to spread out

Primary Source

Hand-carved harpoons made from ivory or bone were used by Northwest Inuit peoples to hunt sea mammals.

Some groups on the large, flat grasslands of the Great Plains were nomads, while others established villages and farmed the rich soil near rivers. All Plains groups depended on the buffalo as their primary food source.

Lifestyles of Ancient American Peoples	
Nomadic	Stationary
hunting and gathering	agriculture
limited agriculture	limited hunting and gathering
limited fishing	fishing
no irrigation	irrigation

2. ☑ Reading Check **Explain** how geography and climate affected the resources that American Indian groups used.

_____

_____

_____

_____

Mayan and Aztec Civilizations

Wherever agriculture developed, it helped to feed more people, and populations began to grow. Growing settlements needed rules for living together and making decisions that affected everyone. Eventually, something called **civilizations** developed. In civilizations, there are organized systems of government, religion, and learning.

Aztec "floating gardens," called *chinampas*, provided most of the food for the people of Tenochtitlán.

3. ☑ **Reading Check** **Describe** to a partner how the picture of the Aztec floating gardens shows people modifying the environment.

Central America was home to advanced civilizations, including the Maya and later the Aztec. The Maya rose about 3,500 years ago. They developed a writing system, made a very accurate calendar, charted movements of the moon and stars, and created a system for advanced math. Yet Mayan civilization faded by about the year 900.

Aztec civilization began to thrive throughout southern Mexico and Central America. The Aztec built their main city center in what is today Mexico City. It was called Tenochtitlán (tay nawch tee TLAHN). Hundreds of thousands of people lived there at one point.

The Aztec modified their environment in order to live in it. Beds were made out of reeds, tall grasses that grow in lakes. They built "floating gardens" to grow their crops on the shores of lakes outside the dry land of Tenochtitlán.

Other North American Groups

Other Indian cultures emerged in North America thousands of years ago. These included the Inuit, the Mound Builders, and the Ancestral Puebloans. They lived in very different climates and had a variety of resources available to them.

The Inuit (IHN oo iht) live in the far northern part of North America where it is frozen much of the year. They had to adapt to a harsh environment where there are few plants and land animals. The Inuit relied on the sea for whales, seals, and other sea animals. They developed and used the kayak, a small canoe that is watertight, to fish in the sea. Homes were built out of blocks of snow.

About 3,000 years ago, the Mound Builders developed a civilization that started around the Ohio River. They had resources such as trees and earth for building. They built large mounds made of earth. Some scientists believe that the mounds were used for religious ceremonies or as graves. By digging in the mounds, they know that the Mound Builders traded with other groups because they found materials that are not available in the environment where the mounds were built.

The Ancestral Puebloans first appeared about 2,000 years ago. They lived in the desert Southwest that includes the present-day states of Arizona, Colorado, New Mexico, and Utah. The Puebloans lived in a dry environment, but they were successful farmers because they used irrigation. They dug canals to bring water to fields of crops, such as corn, beans, and squash.

The cliff dwellings that the Ancestral Puebloans left behind are an example of their great skill in building and modifying the environment. They built homes inside cliffs to stay cool in the hot climate and to get shelter from the sun. The Puebloans left their cliff dwellings in about the year 1300 and did not return. After this period, the Navajo and other people migrated to the Southwest. When they discovered the cliff dwellings, they called these ancient people by the Navajo word *Anasazi* (ah nuh SAH zee).

Quest Connections

Highlight words that describe the foods available to early peoples.

 INTERACTIVITY

Learn more about the foods available to American Indians long ago.

The Serpent Mound in southern Ohio is in the form of a snake. It was built by American Indian peoples at least a thousand years ago.

Adapting to the Environment

These North American groups, and later, American Indian nations such as the Iroquois, Huron, Cherokee, Navajo, Creek, Hopi, Algonquin, and Lakota (Sioux), adapted to their environment. Many modified it as needed to survive and to support their ways of life.

The Chumash, who lived in present-day southern California, used fire to burn shrubs and grasslands. When they cleared the land, they could better hunt animals such as deer. They would use the deer for food and use the skins for shelter and clothing. They used the antlers for tools. Woodland peoples used deer in the same way. They used the wood from forests to build their homes, canoes for travel and fishing, and tools and utensils.

A group called the Calusa lived on the Florida coast and used shells as a resource. They even built an island made of shells. Other American Indians also had shells available to them in some coastal areas. Groups like the Chumash used seashells to make many items, including jewelry, tools, and decorations for clothing.

Snow shoes like these helped the Algonquin Indians travel and hunt in the northern woodlands area.

4. ☑ **Reading Check**
Compare and Contrast
Fill in the chart to **compare** and **contrast** how two different groups of American Indians used the same resource.

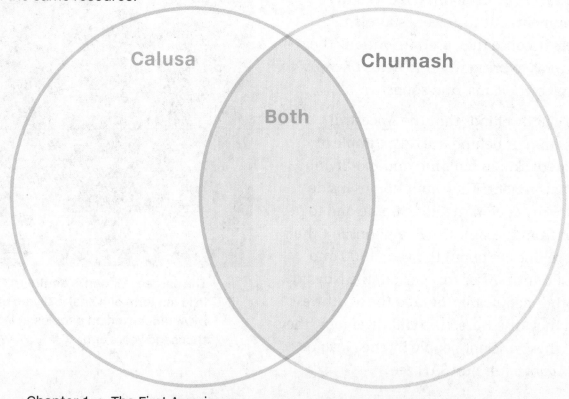

Calusa   Chumash

Both

☑ Lesson 1 Check

5. **Compare and Contrast Describe** how geography and climate influenced the way that different American Indians lived and adapted to their environment.

_____

_____

_____

_____

_____

_____

6. **Identify** resources that American Indians used in their environment to live.

_____

_____

_____

_____

7. **Quest Connections Analyze** the factors that affected the foods that American Indian groups had available to them. Explain how at least two groups got food.

_____

_____

_____

_____

Interpret Cultural Data on Maps

VIDEO

Watch a video about interpreting cultural data on maps.

Many different American Indian cultural groups lived in the Americas before Europeans arrived in the late 1400s. They all had their own culture, or way of life.

When you examine data on maps, you look at the map key, or legend, to help you understand what you see. Colors, shading, and symbols on a map help you to interpret, or understand, the information that it shows.

What does the legend tell you on this map? _____

_____

Look at the geographic features on the map. These also can help you interpret information. For example, what can you interpret about American Indian groups that lived on the coasts or near lakes? You could determine that living near water affected their way of life. It likely influenced other resources they used in their environment to survive.

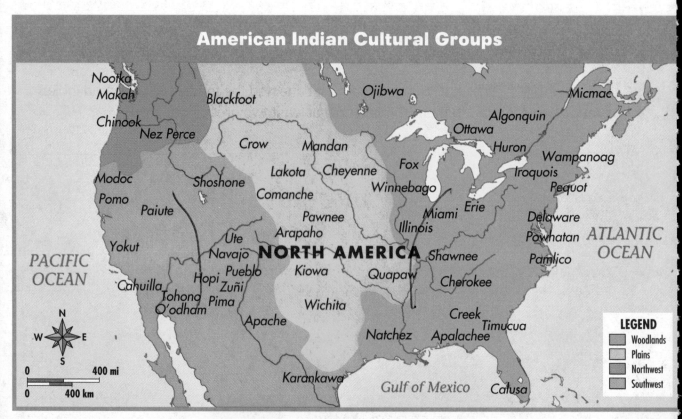

American Indian Cultural Groups

Your Turn!

1. Locate and circle these American Indian cultural groups on the map. Then choose one group that lived near a body of water and one that did not. Write about how their environment affected the way they lived. Think about how their environment affected their relations with other American Indian groups.

- Pueblo
- Iroquois
- Huron
- Crow

- Navajo
- Creek
- Hopi
- Algonquin

- Lakota (Sioux)
- Chinook
- Nez Perce
- Pawnee

_____

_____

_____

_____

_____

_____

2. In which regions did the cultural groups listed in question 1 live? Complete the chart.

Woodlands			
Great Plains			
Pacific Northwest			
Southwest			

American Indian Culture

INTERACTIVITY

Participate in a class discussion to preview the content of this lesson.

Vocabulary

custom
tradition
folklore
ancestor

Academic Vocabulary

aspect
maintain

Unlock The BIG Question

I will know that cultures varied widely among American Indian peoples.

Jumpstart Activity

Take an opinion poll about what your favorite fruit is. Your teacher will call out different kinds of fruit. Stand up when you hear the fruit of your choice. Keep a tally at your desk of the different "tastes" in your class.

Bison were a rich resource to the Plains Indians and became an important part of their culture.

American Indian cultural groups had their own ways of life. They made homes and raised their families. They formed villages and governments. Ceremonies and religious practices were important to them. They played music and created artwork. They also shared stories and passed customs along to family members.

👆 **INTERACTIVITY**

Explore the key ideas of this lesson.

What Is Culture?

Culture is the way of life of a group of people. It includes their art, language, ideas, beliefs, and history. Tools and skills are also part of a group's culture. The ideas that they have and live by form part of their culture. Sometimes groups share culture or aspects of culture. For example, many American Indian groups farmed the land, which is a similar cultural trait. However, others relied more on hunting, such as the groups that lived on the Great Plains. In the Pacific Northwest, fishing became part of the culture of many groups that lived in that region.

Language is also part of a group's culture. American Indian groups spoke their own languages. Before Europeans came to North America, hundreds of different American Indian languages were spoken. Today, American Indian languages are still spoken throughout the present-day United States. The Southwest, where many descendants of the Pueblo and Navajo live, has the most native speakers. A descendant is someone who is related to a person or group of people who lived in the past.

Customs, or ways of life that are repeated on a regular basis, are a part of a group's culture. They relate to actions or practices among group members that are based on tradition. **Tradition** is a custom or belief that is passed on from one generation to the next.

An Apache man tells a story to a group of Apache girls wearing traditional dresses.

Dancers dressed in traditional clothing perform in a Tlingit potlatch ceremony in Alaska.

The hairstyle that we call a mohawk today was a custom of some American Indian groups in the Eastern Woodlands. The hairstyle was seen as fierce and was a warning to enemies not to dare cut off the Mohawk during battle. Other groups, such as the Sioux in the Great Plains, wore special feathered headdresses. A Green Corn Ceremony was held by many groups, including those in the Southeast and Northeast Woodlands, because a good harvest was very important to their culture. In the Pacific Northwest, groups held potlatches, big feasts that showed a person's wealth and rank in the community.

1. ☑ **Reading Check** **Identify** three characteristics or traits that define culture. Discuss with a partner how these traits were similar and different among American Indian groups.

_____

_____

_____

_____

Daily Life

Daily life for American Indians was different than what you experience today. Adults would be busy with hunting, planting, gathering, making clothing, craftwork, and cooking.

There was much work to do in the morning, so adults rose very early to get all of the chores down. Men might leave before dawn to go on a hunt after a meal of some meat and nuts. Women might carry water and gather wood for the fire and to cook. Young children would stay with their mothers and help with some of the chores. Older boys might join their fathers on a hunt.

When men and boys returned from the hunt in the afternoon, women would prepare a meal. After a meal there was still work to do, but sometimes American Indians played ball games or did craftwork. In the Southwest, groups such as the Pueblo created beautiful but useful pottery that could be used as food storage.

Some evenings, American Indians gathered around an elder family member to listen to folktales, or traditional stories. Folktales were and still are important to American Indian custom and tradition. They are part of **folklore**, or traditional customs, beliefs, and stories. Through folklore, American Indians could pass on **aspects** of their culture that are still practiced by some descendants today.

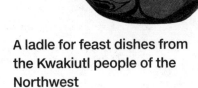

Primary Source

A ladle for feast dishes from the Kwakiutl people of the Northwest

Academic Vocabulary

aspect • *n.*, a part of something

2. ✅ **Reading Check** **Infer Explain** how daily life for ancient American Indians might be similar to daily life for American Indians today? How might it be different? Use evidence from the text to draw your inference.

_____

_____

_____

_____

_____

Family Roles

Much of American Indian life was based on traditions. In that way, men and women had traditional roles. Everyone's roles were important to the livelihood and survival of the group.

Maintaining a steady food supply was a major focus of everyday life. American Indian men did the hunting and fishing for their family and village and kept the village safe. Women often cleaned and prepared the meat and fish.

Both men and women shared in the farm work. Women planted and tended to the crops while the men were away, but men also helped with clearing the land for planting. In most regions, women also gathered nuts, seeds, and berries to provide a well-rounded diet.

Family life and home life were often under the care of men and women. Women not only cared for the children but also made clothing and household goods, cleaned, and cooked. Men often took care of religious and social tasks.

On the Great Plains, where the bison was so important to survival, women made sure that every part of the animal was used. They often had the task of butchering the bison. When moving from place to place, American Indian women on the Plains would be in charge of packing the tepee and then setting it up when the group arrived at a new place. In the Pacific Northwest, women would make clothes out of deerskin or tree bark. In the Southwest, where water was scarce, women may have had to carry water long distance to their home. In the Woodlands and in other regions where forests were nearby, women would carry wood that men cut down for the campfire.

Academic Vocabulary

maintain • v., to keep something going or continuing without changing

Many centuries ago, Woodlands Indians began the game of lacrosse, in which a ball is shot from a stick into a goal. It is still played today, with some modern changes.

Children also had important roles in the family. Yet childhood was short. Children would leave the protective care of their mothers by the time they were in their teens. They would then begin training for their roles as adults. Children also listened to storytellers to learn about their group's customs and traditions.

Teen boys would learn from their fathers and other men in their village. They had to prove that they were strong and brave. One test that they had to pass to show these traits was spending time alone in the wilderness. Girls would learn wilderness skills, too.

Some games and activities for children helped teach them the skills they needed as they got older. For example, children would learn how to fish. This skill would later help them provide food for the family and village. In the Woodlands, the ball game of lacrosse was played. This game helped prepare young men to be hunters and warriors. Girls might learn how to weave a basket or make a clay pot. Those skills were needed as they got older and such containers were needed for food storage.

3. ☑ **Reading Check** Fill in the chart to **identify** examples of family roles in American Indian life.

Traditional Family Roles		
Men	**Women**	**Children**
	planted crops	
	gathered seeds, nuts, fruit	
	cared for children	
	cooked, cleaned, made clothing	

Word Wise

Multiple-Meaning Words
When you see a word that has more than one meaning, reread the sentence. Think about the different meanings of the word and which meaning makes the most sense in the sentence. Which meaning of *force* fits best in the sentence that includes "natural forces such as sun, wind, and storms"?

Most American Indian groups had religious customs and traditions. Each American Indian group, tribe, and nation had its own religious beliefs. Some groups believed that animals and the earth had spirits. This belief is called animism.

American Indian beliefs were often tied to daily tasks. For example, before men went on a hunt, it was a common custom for them to ask permission from the spirits before killing an animal or catching fish. As you read before, traditions such as the Green Corn Ceremony were religious festivals in which Eastern Woodland groups celebrated the harvest and gave thanks. They joyfully danced, sang, and prayed because the land had provided the harvest they needed to live.

Kachina dolls are presented to young Puebloan girls. The spirits the dolls represent are shown in the masks, feathers, and clothing.

Pueblo groups in the Southwest like the Hopi sought help and advice from kachinas (kuh CHEE nuhs). These are the spirits of natural forces such as sun, wind, and storms. The kachinas could also represent ancestors. An **ancestor** is a relative who lived in the past. Hopi artists created decorative kachina dolls that they used to help children learn important traditions and customs. Sometimes the Hopi would perform special dances to call forth the kachinas to join the group.

In some American Indian groups, there were a few men and women who were believed to have special religious powers. Historians call them *shamans*. Other special individuals were called *two-spirits* and were believed to contain both male and female spirits. People believed that these individuals had special knowledge or skills, such as the ability to heal the sick or to pray to the forces they felt guided them.

4. ☑ **Reading Check** **Describe** how the Hopi people used *kachina* dolls as part of their religion.

_____

_____

_____

● **INTERACTIVITY**

Check your understanding of the key ideas of this lesson.

☑ Lesson 2 Check

5. **Compare and Contrast** **Describe** how the roles of American Indian adults were similar to and different than those of children.

_____

_____

_____

_____

_____

6. **Identify** customs and traditions that many American Indian groups share.

_____

_____

7. **Describe** how family roles contributed to the supply of food and the meals American Indian groups ate.

_____

_____

_____

American Indian Folktales

Customs and traditions such as storytelling were and still are important to American Indian groups. Most American Indian groups did not have a written language. Therefore, oral, or spoken, traditions were an important way to pass folklore from one generation to the next. Folktales, or traditional stories, are one way that American Indians share their group's history, customs, and traditions. The following folktale originated in the Pacific Northwest.

Trickster Becomes a Dish

Two brothers lived on a river near the mountains. One brother became ill, and the other tried to cure him. There were no fish there so he threw sticks into the water. They turned into fish, but they didn't cure his sick brother.

The brothers set off down the river in a canoe. Eventually they reached the sea and rowed to the land of the salmon. There the strong brother hid and the sick brother turned himself into a beautiful wooden dish. He set himself afloat in an area where people had caught all the salmon behind a dam. A man found the dish and gave it to his daughter. Whenever she ate salmon from the dish, her leftovers always disappeared. The sick brother disguised as the dish was eating her salmon.

Soon the sick brother grew well. As he and his brother left, they broke the dam and made the salmon follow them back across the sea and up the river to where they lived. Now every year the salmon swim from the sea up into the rivers and streams where the two brothers and their people can eat them.

Fun Fact

In trickster tales, there is usually a character such as an animal or person who plays a trick. Can you guess who the trickster is trying to trick?

Close Reading

1. Identify six events in the folktale and list them in the correct sequence.

_____

_____

_____

_____

_____

_____

2. Describe the connection between the title of the folktale and what happens in the story.

_____

_____

_____

_____

Wrap It Up

How is this folktale an example of an American Indian tradition?

_____

_____

_____

_____

American Indian Government and Economy

Lesson 3

 INTERACTIVITY

Participate in a class discussion to preview the content of this lesson.

Vocabulary

government
council
confederacy
league
economy
commodity
trading network

Academic Vocabulary

adviser
establish

Unlock The BIG Question

I will know that American Indian groups had varied systems of government and economies.

Jumpstart Activity

Divide into small groups. Select a leader within your group. Follow your teacher's instructions to figure out how best to make a decision that involves all your group members. Once your group decision is made, have your leader share it with the class.

American Indian groups had to make decisions about many different things. They needed to decide where they would live, what resources they would use, and what actions would best support the group. They believed that individuals were responsible for acting properly and making good choices. Some developed a **government**, a system for making rules and decisions. Many American Indian groups did not form traditional governments. They were largely bands of people who were related to each other. Leadership was made up of family leaders.

American Indian Government

A group's government often fits its way of life. You have read about American Indian groups that were nomadic and others that were stationary. Nomadic groups, such as some on the Great Plains, often were smaller bands of American Indians, and they moved in small family units. Usually a male was the leader, such as a father or grandfather. Other family members could challenge the male leader's decisions, but that did not mean that the decision would change.

Stationary groups often included larger bands of American Indians. Sometimes they had more formal systems of government, such as a government run by a council. A **council** is a decision-making body that could be made up of a group's single leader or a small group of leaders. A single leader, or chief, often led a council.

In general, the chief was chosen by the group's family members. The chief did not rule on his own. He would work with the other leaders in the council to make decisions. Eventually, the chief might give his power as chief to another member of the band or group who had been helpful to the group and had shown leadership skills.

👆 **INTERACTIVITY**

Explore the key ideas of this lesson.

1. ☑ **Reading Check** **Identify** different types of governments that American Indians had in the past.

_____

_____

_____

A Sioux chief leads a group of council and family members.

Governments Past and Present

Small groups often combined with other groups to form large nations. Sometimes the groups were forced to join the larger nation, often through warfare. The Powhatans in the Woodlands region are an example of a larger group made up of smaller groups. They formed a **confederacy**, a group whose members share the same goals. The Powhatan Confederacy formed to share resources and protect each other.

In the Southwest, a religious leader led the Pueblo people's government. This leader was called a cacique (kah SEEK). Today, the Pueblo have a group of leaders called the All Pueblo Council of Governors that makes decisions for the entire Pueblo community. Different Pueblo groups each send a governor to represent them on the council. These groups also have their own tribal governments.

The Navajo Nation is also located in the Southwest. In the past, a tribal council governed the Navajo, and each band of Navajo had its own chief. The tribal council selected the chief, but the chief did not make decisions for the group. He acted more as an **adviser**. The tribal council made decisions. Today, the Navajo Nation Council governs the Navajo people in the Southwest. Council members are elected, and they make and enforce tribal laws.

Academic Vocabulary

adviser • *n.*, a person who gives advice or guidance
establish • *v.*, set up or organize something permanent

The Navajo Nation Seal contains images important to their way of life.

GREAT SEAL OF THE NAVAJO NATION

Around 1600, in what is today New York State, five different nations joined to **establish** a **league** or a confederacy. Both of these terms refer to a group whose members share the same goals. In a confederacy, there is usually a written or oral form of an alliance or agreement.

The members of the League of the Iroquois called themselves the People of the Longhouse, or Haudenosaunee (haw duh noh SAW nee). They were also called the Iroquois Confederacy. This league was made up of five American Indian nations—the Cayuga, Mohawk, Oneida, Onondaga, and the Seneca. Later, a sixth member nation joined, the Tuscarora.

Chief Hiawatha, of the Onondaga group, was a founder of the original Iroquois League of five nations.

Annie Dodge Wauneka was the second woman   cted to the Navajo Nation Council. Her work in impro   ] the education, health, and housing of the Navajo ea   d her a Presidential Medal of Freedom in 1963.

The League had rules that made sure its members worked together to make decisions and to remain in peace. A council made up of 50 men led this group. Leading women in the member nations chose these men. Women also had the power to remove leaders that had been chosen to serve in the council. All of the decisions that the League made had to be agreed upon by the leaders in the council.

The League had a constitution, or a plan of government, that was likely the first used in North America. The main principles of the constitution were peace, equity, and justice.

2. ☑ **Reading Check** **Use Evidence From Text** Explain why decision making is important, both in the past and in the present, in organized groups such as American Indian groups.

_____

_____

_____

_____

_____

American Indian Economies

Word Wise

Context Clues

When you are reading and come to an unfamiliar word, you can look for context clues. Read the words and phrases around or in the same sentence as the unfamiliar word to see if you can figure out its meaning. Based on its context, what do you think *robust* means?

In the 1600s, trade with Europeans began to affect the economies of some Woodland Indian groups.

American Indians made decisions through different forms of government. Groups often had to make decisions related to their economy. An **economy** is the system by which a group makes, shares, and uses goods.

How American Indians settled on land was part of their economy. In the Plains, American Indians relied heavily on the buffalo, so they settled on land near buffalo. They could use the buffalo as a resource to make the things that they needed to live. They could also trade items that they made or got from buffalo, such as skins.

American Indians of the Woodlands, such as the Iroquois, had a robust economy. They farmed, hunted, and gathered food. The types of houses they built from available resources were part of the economy. They had trees and animal skins as resources and used them to build longhouses and wigwams.

a canoe made from birch tree bark by the Woodland Cree people

Plank houses and totem poles of the Pacific Northwest Haida people show how resources in the forest are used.

Groups that lived by the sea and other bodies of water had different resources. American Indians in the Pacific Northwest were skilled at catching fish, seals, and whales. They used these resources for food but also to make tools and clothing. Tall trees in the forests nearby provided wood for homes, canoes, and totem poles. Totem poles are sculptures carved from tall trees. They display symbols of the natural world that tell part of a story or event.

In the Southwest, where water was limited, the Pueblo were still able to farm crops. They also figured out how to weave cloth from plant fibers to make clothing. They could wear the clothing but also trade it. For groups such as the Cahuilla (kuh WEE uh) in what is now Southern California, food was hard to find. They had to travel long distances in search of wild plants and animals. They built simple homes made from brush that they could set up quickly in different places.

3. ☑ **Reading Check**
Main Idea and Details
With a partner, **describe** some factors that contributed to American Indian economies.

American Indian Trade

As part of their economy, American Indians traded with each other. Trade was an important way for American Indians to obtain the goods that they wanted and needed. They also traded with Europeans after they arrived in the Americas. American Indians often traded items that they made from the resources in their environment. They traded for items they did not have the resources, skills, or knowledge to make.

Some key trade items that American Indians exchanged included jewelry, pots, baskets, conch shells, shark teeth, clothing, animal skins, copper, turquoise, and beads. Trade items also included food. Being able to trade for food that was not available enabled a group to have a more varied diet. Some food items that American Indians traded included dried fish and buffalo meat.

In the Woodlands, American Indians often traded animal furs, because there was an abundance of animals to hunt where they lived. After Europeans arrived, furs would become a key **commodity**, or a trade good that is a raw material and not manufactured, for American Indians. European traders would then send them back to Europe to sell them.

Groups in this region set up **trading networks**, or systems of trade routes that connected different areas. Larger trade networks often resulted in being able to trade more goods and to obtain trade goods that were difficult to find.

Examples of American Indian trade items (from top to bottom): bison hide dress with beadwork; beaver pelt; jewelry made from turquoise, silver, pipe stone, and beads. What questions do you have about these artifacts? Share them with the class.

4. ☑ **Reading Check** **Identify** goods that might have been traded between American Indian groups on the Great Plains and in the Desert Southwest by filling in the chart.

Trade Goods	
Great Plains	**Desert Southwest**

Quest Connections

With a partner, discuss what kinds of meals could be made with the food items Indian groups traded.

 INTERACTIVITY

Take a closer look at the connections between food and trade.

 INTERACTIVITY

Check your understanding of the key ideas of this lesson.

☑ Lesson 3 Check

5. **Compare and Contrast** **Compare** American Indian governments from the past and present.

_____

_____

_____

_____

6. **Explain** the importance of trading networks in American Indian economies.

_____

_____

_____

7. **Quest** Connections **Identify** foods that contributed to the economy of American Indian groups in different regions.

_____

_____

Compare and Contrast

▶ VIDEO

Watch a video about comparing and contrasting.

When you **compare** things, you look for similarities. When you **contrast** things, you look for differences. As you study American Indian groups and other social studies topics, comparing and contrasting can help you organize information. In this chapter, you are reading about the resources American Indians used, where they lived, and their ways of life. Their similarities and differences will be revealed by comparing and contrasting.

Using a chart, called a Venn diagram, can help you organize details to compare and contrast two or more things. Look at the Venn diagram that compares and contrasts the resources that Woodlands and Desert Southwest peoples used to live. In the left circle are resources used only by Indians of the Woodlands region. In the right circle are resources used only by Indians of the Desert Southwest. In the middle section are resources used by both groups.

Resources Used by Woodlands and Desert Southwest Indians

Woodlands

- trees
- fur from animals
- fish
- rivers

- made tools out of stone and rocks
- gathered wild plants

Desert Southwest

- dried clay
- land to grow corn, beans, squash
- cliffs

Your Turn!

Use the information in the Venn diagram to write one paragraph about how the resources used by the two American Indian groups were similar. Then write a second paragraph about how the resources that the two groups used were different.

1. Write two paragraphs about the Woodlands and Desert Southwest peoples to compare and contrast the resources they used to live.

_____

_____

_____

_____

_____

_____

_____

_____

2. Reread the description of children's roles under the heading "Family Roles." Write some of the roles of children in American Indian culture below. On a separate sheet of paper, create a Venn diagram comparing and contrasting the roles of Indian children in the past to children in the U.S. today. What do you think has changed? What has remained the same?

_____

_____

_____

Quality:
Determination

Wilma Mankiller (1945–2010)
A Cherokee Chief

Wilma Mankiller was a Cherokee woman who grew up in the 1940s and 1950s in Oklahoma but later moved to California. She returned to Oklahoma in the 1970s and began to work with the Cherokee Nation to help make its economy stronger. By the late 1980s, she was the first female chief of the Cherokee Nation, one of the largest American Indian nations in the country.

Mankiller worked to help many Cherokee find jobs and to improve healthcare for them. She also made advancements in education in Cherokee schools. Mankiller was determined to keep the Cherokee traditions and culture alive among her people. She started the Institute for Cherokee Literacy to preserve Cherokee language and traditions. In 1998, she received the Presidential Medal of Freedom for her work helping the Cherokee people.

Primary Source

"I have always known that Cherokee people—particularly those in more traditional communities—have retained [kept] a great sense of interdependence [support for each other], and a willingness to pitch in and help one another."

—Wilma Mankiller, *Mankiller: A Chief and Her People*, 1993

Find Out More

1. How does the quote from Wilma Mankiller support the idea that she and other Cherokee have determination?

_____

_____

_____

2. How are other American Indian leaders today working to help make a difference? Research American Indians who have helped improve the lives of other American Indians. Write about your findings on a separate sheet of paper.

Visual Review

Use this graphic to review some of the key terms and ideas from this chapter.

Features of American Indian Cultural Regions

Region	Resources	Home	Food	Clothing
Northwest wet, cool climate	ocean, rivers, lakes, forest		fish, seals, whales, deer, nuts, berries	cloth from tree bark, seal skin
Southwest very dry, hot climate	some rivers, shrubs, earth, cliffs		corn, beans, squash	cloth from plant fibers
Plains dry, limited rain, warm and cold climate	some rivers and lakes, tall grasses, some trees		bison meat, deer, fish, beans, squash	bison skin, deer skin
Woodlands moderate rain, warm or cool climate	ocean, rivers, lakes, forests		deer, fish, nuts, berries	deer skin, cloth from tree bark

☑ Assessment

 GAMES

Play the vocabulary game.

Vocabulary and Key Ideas

1. Draw a line to match the definitions with the correct terms.

a body that makes decisions for a group   **culture**

a relative who lived in the past   **ancestor**

a system by which a group makes, shares, and uses goods   **government**

a system for making rules and decisions   **economy**

a way of life of a group of people   **council**

2. **Define** What does **migrate** mean? _____

_____

3. **Define agriculture**. _____

_____

4. **Identify** The Pueblo people used _____ to grow crops in a dry land.

5. **Identify** a religious custom practiced by an American Indian group.

_____

_____

_____

6. **Identify** Which was a key role of American Indian women in feeding their families?

- Ⓐ taking down and setting up tepees
- Ⓑ planting and harvesting crops
- Ⓒ hunting and fishing for food
- Ⓓ trading with other groups

Critical Thinking and Writing

7. **Make Inferences** Why were the Maya and Aztec considered advanced civilizations?

_____

_____

_____

8. **Draw Conclusions** Why did people who settled in different regions of North America develop different cultures?

_____

_____

_____

_____

9. **Apply** What kinds of decisions would American Indian groups make in the past that American Indian governments might also have to make today?

_____

_____

_____

_____

10. **Revisit the Big Question** How does geography influence how people live?

_____

_____

_____

_____

11. **Writing Workshop: Write Informative Text** On a separate sheet of paper write two short paragraphs about American Indian economies. Identify the different aspects of their economies and give examples.

Analyze Primary Sources

"The object of these laws is to establish peace between the numerous nations of Indians. Hostility will be done away with, for the preservations and protection of life, property, and liberty."   —Constitution of the Iroquois Nations

12. Why do you think the Iroquois Constitution explains that hostility will be "done away with"?

_____

_____

_____

_____

_____

_____

_____

Compare and Contrast

13. Fill in the chart and identify the types of settlements used by the three different native peoples.

Inuits	Mound Builders	Ancient Puebloans

Quest Findings

What's Cooking?

You've read the lessons in this chapter and researched American Indian food resources and cooking methods. Now you're ready to help me with a recipe for my menu.

👆 **INTERACTIVITY**

Use this activity to help you complete your recipe and learn more about American Indian foods and recipes.

1 Describe the Food

Use your notes to write down the kinds of foods available to the American Indian group you researched. Include the types of crops, fish, or meat they ate.

2 List Ingredients

Use your notes and the evidence from your Quest Connections to list ingredients available from the foods available to your American Indian group.

3 Write Your Recipe

Use your notes and your ingredients list to write a recipe that your American Indian group might have cooked. Make sure your recipe follows these criteria:

- Includes resources in the American Indian group's environment
- Uses ingredients that these resources provide
- Includes the correct measurements of each ingredient in your recipe
- Provides a meal that is delicious and healthy

Then, exchange recipes with another group to provide suggestions.

4 Revise

Make changes to your recipe based on your meeting with the other group. Correct any grammatical, mathematical, and spelling errors.

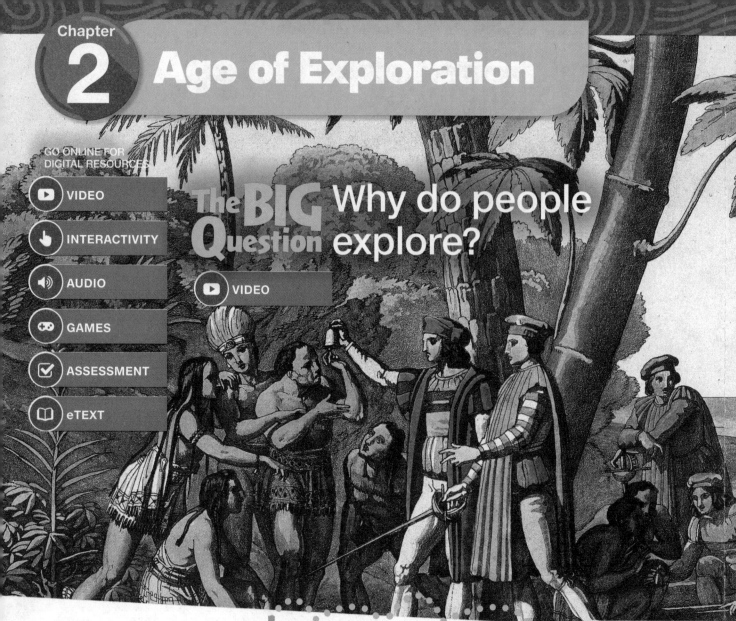

GO ONLINE FOR
DIGITAL RESOURCES

▶ VIDEO

👆 INTERACTIVITY

🔊 AUDIO

🎮 GAMES

☑ ASSESSMENT

📖 eTEXT

The BIG Question Why do people explore?

▶ VIDEO

Lesson 1
Early Explorers
and Advances in
Technology

Lesson 2
Explorers for Spain

Lesson 3
The Columbian
Exchange

JumpStart Activity 👆 INTERACTIVITY

Stand up and walk to a large world map on the classroom
wall or a screen or study a globe. Take turns calling out
different places that you would like to visit. Discuss as a class
why it might be interesting to visit and explore each of these
locations. How are the reasons for visiting these locations
alike and different?

_____

_____

_____

_____

Exploring the World

Preview the chapter **vocabulary** as you sing the rap:

The Portuguese had set out first to find a new route

To get to Asia using water, sailed day in and day out.

They set up trading posts along the way, so some of them stayed

They wanted to be first to Asia and control all the trade.

A distant journey over seas in search of riches and land

Was impossible without somebody lending a hand.

A **patron** was the one who gave financial support

To ensure that their voyages would not be cut short.

The tools had improved that they used for **navigation**

Which is charting a ship's course or finding one's exact location.

These tools were being used by the explorers from Spain

Who were looking for new lands and other things for their gain.

Age of Exploration

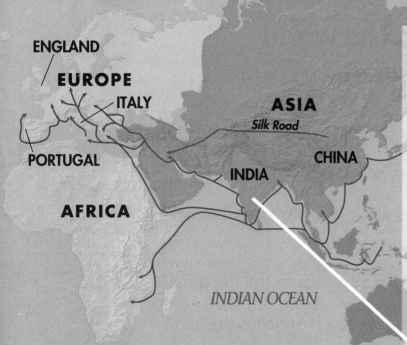

ENGLAND

EUROPE

ITALY

ASIA

Silk Road

PORTUGAL

CHINA

INDIA

AFRICA

INDIAN OCEAN

What trade routes connected the continents of Europe, Asia, and Africa?

Trade allows people to exchange goods near and far. Red lines on the map show some trade routes between parts of the world in the 1400s. Europeans traded for silks from China and spices from India. Locate the Silk Road and trace a route from China to Italy. Then, find a water route from Portugal to India.

TODAY
You can purchase Indian spices at U.S. supermarkets.

What happened and When?

Read the timeline to find out about the early explorers' adventures.

1400

1450

1419
Prince Henry opens a navigation school.

Today
People can find silks from Asia in many stores all over the world.

Who will you meet?

Bartolomeu Dias
A Portuguese sailor who sailed around the tip of Africa

Hernán Cortés
A Spanish conquistador who led a journey to Mexico

Christopher Columbus
Explorer who sailed for Spain to find a new route to Asia by crossing the Atlantic Ocean

Ferdinand Magellan
A Portuguese explorer whose fleet sailed completely around the globe

 INTERACTIVITY

Complete the interactive digital activity.

1500

1550

1487
Bartolomeu Dias rounds the Cape of Good Hope.

1492
Christopher Columbus reaches North America.

1535
New Spain is founded in North America.

1565
Spain founds St. Augustine.

Today
You can visit the old Spanish fort Castillo de San Marcos in St. Augustine.

2 Quest
Project-Based Learning

Ahoy, Sailors!

Early explorers traveled for long distances on their journeys. They needed strong, capable sailors to assist them. Knowing what items were needed to bring along was important.

You are the captain of a ship or ships about to sail west from Europe and cross the Atlantic Ocean. What type of people and provisions, or items, do you need? How many ships will you take?

Quest Kick Off

Your mission is to take on the role of an early European ship captain who is looking for good sailors. Create an advertisement to attract sailors. Write a list of provisions for your journey.

1 Ask Questions

What makes a good sailor? What are important items you need for your journey? Write two questions that will help you in your research.

....

....

....

....

2 Research

Follow your teacher's instructions to find examples of the qualities a good sailor should have, as well as items that are needed on a long journey.

....

....

....

....

....

INTERACTIVITY

Analyze the parts of an advertisement and see some examples.

3 Look for *Quest* Connections

Turn to the next page to begin looking for Quest Connections that will help you create your advertisement.

4 *Quest* Findings
Create an Advertisement

Use the Quest Findings page at the end of the chapter to help you create your advertisement.

Early Explorers and Advances in Technology

INTERACTIVITY

Participate in a class discussion to preview the content of this lesson.

Vocabulary

merchant
slave trade
navigation
astrolabe
caravel

Academic Vocabulary

examine
accurately

Unlock The BIG Question

I will know how advances in technology helped European explorers sail to and settle in new places.

Jumpstart Activity

Work with a partner to think of three technologies that you use almost every day. Share your ideas with the class. Now you will learn about technology during the age of exploration.

Because the sea surrounds Europe on three sides, Europeans long ago learned to travel the ocean. At first, most European sailors stayed close to land. Once new types of ships and new sailing instruments were introduced, travel by sea became more common. Brave sailors set out for new lands and riches. Most looked for routes to trade with Asia. A few explorers found their way to North America.

INTERACTIVITY

Explore the key ideas of this lesson.

Early Explorers

The Vikings were from Scandinavia. This region in northern Europe includes Norway, Denmark, and Sweden. Beginning in the 800s, the Vikings sailed the northern seas. They raided European towns while exploring and settling new lands. One of these Vikings was called Eric the Red because of his red hair. Leif Ericsson, his son, was an explorer and was likely one of the first Europeans to land in North America.

Early Viking explorers were experienced sailors. Their slender boats often had a dragon's head at the front.

In 1001, Leif Ericsson founded a settlement in what is now Canada. The Vikings did not stay at this location very long. Europeans lost interest in sailing west from Europe or any long distance. However, hundreds of years later, Europeans would return to North America. They would return because they were motivated by trade.

By the 1400s, trade between Europe and Asia was brisk. European **merchants**, or people who buy and sell goods, bought goods from Asia, such as silk and spices. Traders then shipped these goods over dangerous roads. Traders sometimes faced thieves who stole the traders' property. However, trade with Asia made many people rich. This attracted more European nations to compete for control of trade routes. Some European rulers wanted to find a sea route to Asia to obtain its riches more easily.

1. ☑ **Reading Check** **Draw Conclusions** Examine the chart and fill in the conclusion based on the facts given.

New Routes to Asia

Fact
Goods from Asia were in demand in Europe.

Fact
Land routes to Asia were long and dangerous.

Conclusion

_____

_____

_____

_____

Portuguese Explorers

Finding a sea route to Asia became important for many European leaders. Portugal led this search to find a way to reach Asia by water. Its relative location on the western coast of Europe made it a perfect place for sailors to start their journeys. Also, Portuguese rulers encouraged exploration. They often provided the money sailors needed to make expensive sea voyages.

The son of Portugal's king, Prince Henry, opened a school to teach navigation and mapmaking in about 1419. He wanted to know more about the world around him and to make money by sending fleets to capture African gold and slaves. At Henry's school, sailors, scholars, mapmakers, and shipbuilders **examined** information and worked together to improve sea travel and invent new tools.

Word Wise

Root Words When you see an unfamiliar word, try using root words to figure out the meaning. For example, you will see the word *exploration* in this lesson. Inside the word is a root word you already know, *explore*. What do you think *exploration* means?

Academic Vocabulary

examine • *v.*, to inspect or look carefully

Portuguese and Spanish explorers sailed in ships like this caravel.

The sailors Henry hired explored the west coast of Africa. They explored the region and established settlements where goods could be bought and sold. They also searched for a route to Asia around the southern tip of Africa. They wanted to be the first Europeans to reach Asia by sea in order to control trade there.

The Portuguese traded more than gold and ivory. They also took part in the **slave trade**. Slave traders bought and sold humans as property. In fact, the Portuguese made the slave trade an important business activity. This caused the slave trade to grow. Continuing for many centuries, this cruel practice expanded to European colonies across the Atlantic Ocean.

2. ☑ Reading Check Fill in the chart with details about Portuguese exploration.

Facts About Portuguese Exploration

What made Portugal a good place for sea exploration?	Why did Prince Henry open his school?	What were the main accomplishments of Henry's voyages?
• _____ _____ _____ • _____ _____ _____ _____ _____ _____	• to learn about the world • to gain wealth through trade • to improve sea travel	• _____ _____ _____ • _____ _____ _____ _____ _____ _____ _____

Water Routes

Prince Henry spent nearly 40 years providing money for voyages to Africa's western coast. However, his sailors never made it all the way around the tip of Africa. Other Portuguese sailors continued searching for a sea route to Asia even after Henry's death in 1460.

One such explorer was Bartolomeu Dias (bar toh loh MAY oh DEE as). In 1487, he led an expedition of three ships to explore Africa's western coast. An expedition is a trip that is made for the purpose of exploration. Making his way through a fierce storm, his ships were successful in sailing around the tip of Africa. The Portuguese named the tip of Africa the Cape of Good Hope.

Ten years later, Vasco da Gama followed Dias's route around Africa. He crossed the Indian Ocean and reached India, which was farther than Dias had reached. Landing in India allowed Portugal to take a leading position in India's rich spice trade.

Vasco da Gama
Vsco

Portuguese explorers used sea routes that were long and dangerous in order to reach India.

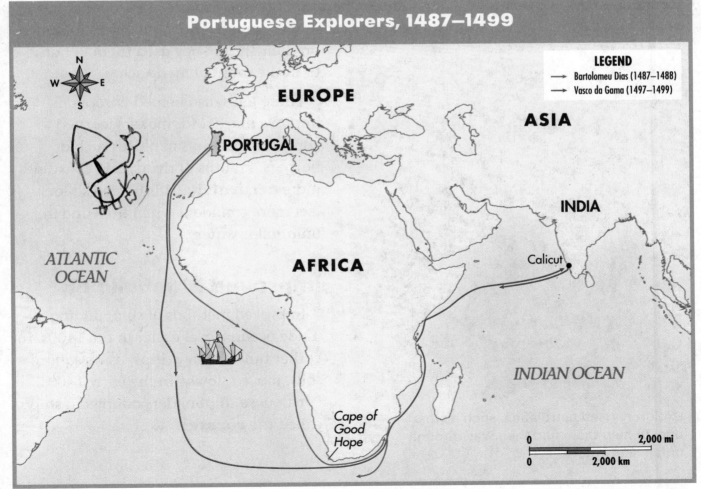

Portuguese Explorers, 1487–1499

LEGEND
→ Bartolomeu Dias (1487–1488)
→ Vasco da Gama (1497–1499)

EUROPE

ASIA

PORTUGAL

INDIA

ATLANTIC OCEAN

AFRICA

Calicut

INDIAN OCEAN

Cape of Good Hope

0   2,000 mi
0   2,000 km

Highlight some words and phrases in the text that contributed to a successful journey for the explorers and their crew.

INTERACTIVITY

Learn more about the journeys of early explorers.

Academic Vocabulary

accurately • *adv.*, without errors or mistakes

Explorers used astrolabes, such as this one, to help them find their way through unfamiliar waters.

Technology in Exploration

Although a sea route from Europe to Asia would be longer than the land route, traveling by sea was faster. Navigation tools helped improve sea travel. **Navigation** is the process sailors use to plan their course and find their location far from land.

Centuries earlier, the Chinese invented the magnetic compass. European sailors relied on it to know in which direction they were headed. The needle of a compass always points north so sailors could know their direction. The **astrolabe** (AS truh layb) was a tool from North Africa. It measured the height of the sun or a star above the horizon. Astrolabes helped sailors tell how far north or south of the equator they had sailed. Other useful navigational tools were the sextant, which was used to tell latitude and longitude at sea, and the chronometer (kroh NAH muh tur), which provided latitude at sea and exact measurement of time. Gunpowder, also an invention of the Chinese, became useful to explorers. Europeans used gunpowder in their guns and cannons that were mounted on their ships. They used them in battle or in the event of an attack.

These tools also helped Europeans improve maps. Mapmakers learned to chart the locations of places such as harbors, mouths of rivers, and coastlines more **accurately**. This helped sailors feel more confident when traveling in unfamiliar waters.

Improved Shipbuilding

Improved methods of shipbuilding made ocean travel easier in the 1400s. In earlier times, heavy ships, using square sails, moved slowly. In the early 1400s, Portuguese shipbuilders adapted a ship called the **caravel**.

The caravel was smaller and lighter than other ships. It had triangular sails to better control the wind. Other improvements included wooden decks without gaps and waterproofed wood. The Portuguese shipbuilders braided stronger ropes and made long-lasting sails from canvas. Larger cargo areas in the ship could carry enough supplies for longer voyages.

3. ☑ **Reading Check** How do you think Chinese and Arab technologies reached Europe?

_____

INTERACTIVITY

Check your understanding of the key ideas of this lesson.

☑ Lesson 1 Check

4. **Analyze** why Portuguese rulers paid for the exploration of new lands. How did Portugal benefit from Vasco da Gama's voyage to India?

_____

_____

5. **Describe** the technological contributions that Prince Henry made to navigation.

_____

_____

_____

_____

6. **Understand the** *Quest* **Connections** Based on the text, why do you think technology for navigation is important on your journey?

_____

_____

Sequence

What European explorers came to North America first?

First, the Vikings landed in North America. Then, other explorers came about 400 years later.

When you **sequence**, you place events in the order in which they happened. Something happens first, then second, and so on. Words that help you determine the sequence include *first, second, third, then, when, after,* and *since.* You can also look at dates to help you identify sequence.

The ability to sequence is important because it helps you understand when important events happened. Events can be from the past, present, or future. They can occur within a year, a decade (ten years), a generation (time between the birth of parents and the birth of the parents' children), a century (100 years), or longer. Read the paragraph. Pay attention to details and words that tell when important events occurred. The words that can help you understand sequence have been underlined.

▶ VIDEO

Watch a video about sequencing.

Portuguese sailors searched for a sea route to Asia even <u>after</u> Prince Henry's death in <u>1460</u>. <u>In 1487</u>, Bartolomeu Dias led an expedition of three ships to explore Africa's western coast. Making his way through a fierce storm, his ships were successful in sailing around the tip of Africa. <u>Ten years later</u>, Vasco da Gama followed Dias's route around Africa. <u>When</u> he crossed the Indian Ocean and reached India, he traveled farther than Dias had ever reached.

1. What important events happened in the paragraph? Fill in the graphic organizer to show the sequence of events.

2. Using the information from the paragraph, rewrite the sequence of events from the death of Prince Henry to Vasco da Gama's crossing of the Indian Ocean. Use the term *decade, generation, or century* in your statement.

_____

_____

_____

_____

Lesson 2 Explorers for Spain

INTERACTIVITY

Participate in a class discussion to preview the content of this lesson.

Vocabulary

patron
conquistador
expedition
empire
colony
epidemic

Academic Vocabulary

organized
demolish

Unlock The BIG Question

I will know why Spain sent explorers to new lands.

Jumpstart Activity

With a partner, discuss reasons why you would travel to a new place. What risks are involved? Make a list of the reasons and risks, and then choose one example of each to act out for the class.

Columbus and his crew set sail from Spain in 1492, hoping to discover a new route to Asia.

Christopher Columbus was a man who made bold plans. He was from the Genoa region of Italy. Columbus wanted to find a new route to Asia by sailing west across the Atlantic Ocean. Columbus had a lot of courage but not much money for the voyage. He had to find someone to pay for this dangerous trip.

INTERACTIVITY

Explore the key ideas of this lesson.

Christopher Columbus

Columbus asked Portugal's king to pay for his voyage. The king turned down Columbus's request. Columbus did not give up. He decided to ask Spain's rulers. Columbus told them that he would bring Christianity to the people of Asia, and he would bring back riches for Spain. It took several requests, but King Ferdinand and Queen Isabella finally agreed to become Columbus's patrons. A **patron** gives money to support another person or cause.

The Spanish rulers hoped to earn money from the gold and spices that Columbus expected to trade for in Asia. They needed money to pay for a war that Spain had recently fought. Spain was a Catholic country. Ferdinand and Isabella had just restored Christianity to their lands after the *Reconquista*. During the *Reconquista* ("reconquering"), the Spanish had pushed Muslims out of the southern part of the Iberian Peninsula after a struggle that lasted more than 700 years.

Columbus sailed from Spain with about 90 men on three different ships. The crew started off very hopeful and excited for their new journey, but after five weeks at sea, they became tired and weak. After traveling close to 4,500 miles, they spotted land and reached shore on October 12, 1492. Wanting to document the discovery, Columbus wrote:

1. ☑ **Reading Check**
Turn and Talk with a partner about why you think Columbus wrote that "everyone breathed afresh and rejoiced." Ask your partner other questions about Columbus's journal.

Primary Source

The crew . . . saw signs of land, and a small branch covered with berries. Everyone breathed afresh and rejoiced at these signs.

–Christopher Columbus, *Journal of the First Voyage of Christopher Columbus*, 1492

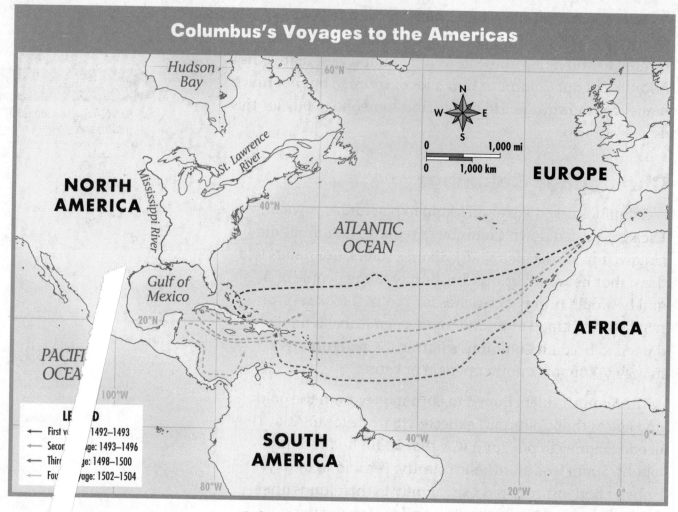

Columbus's Voyages to the Americas

Hudson Bay

60°N

NORTH AMERICA

St. Lawrence River

Mississippi River

40°N

Gulf of Mexico

20°N

PACIFIC OCEAN

100°W

ATLANTIC OCEAN

EUROPE

AFRICA

SOUTH AMERICA

40°W

80°W

20°W

0°

0   1,000 mi
0   1,000 km

LEGEND
- First voyage: 1492–1493
- Second voyage: 1493–1496
- Third voyage: 1498–1500
- Fourth voyage: 1502–1504

Columbus believed they had reached Asia. Instead, his ships had landed on an island in the Caribbean Sea, which is part of North America. Because he thought they were near India, Columbus named the region the "West Indies" and called its people "Indians." The people he met had a different name for themselves. They were the Tainos (TY nohz), and many looked fearful when they saw him and his crew.

Columbus made three additional voyages to the Americas, traveling close to a total of 30,000 miles. On each of these trips, Columbus was convinced that he was in India. He conquered the Tainos and took many captive, as well as claimed land for Spain to start settlements. Like many explorers, he did not always think about the consequences of his actions. In 1494, he founded La Isabela in what is now the Dominican Republic. This settlement became the first European town in North America.

2. ☑ **Reading Check** On the map, trace each of Columbus's routes from Spain to North America.

The Spanish Conquest of the Americas

The discovery of a land between Europe and Asia spread quickly throughout Europe. Soon, other Europeans set sail for the Americas. In the early 1500s, a group of Spanish soldiers, later called **conquistadors** (kahn KEES tuh dorz), or Spanish conquerors of the Americas, arrived.

Hernán Cortés (er NAHN kor TEZ) was a conquistador who led an **expedition**, or **organized** journey, to Mexico in 1519. Cortés wanted to go to this land because he had heard of the Aztec empire and its riches. An **empire** is a group of nations or peoples ruled by a single group or leader. Cortés planned to conquer the Aztec and claim the Aztec riches for Spain.

He gathered an army of Spanish soldiers and Indians, who resented Aztec rule. Cortés led them into the grand city of Tenochtitlán (tay noch tee TLAHN), the Aztec capital. Cortés was impressed by the city and the Aztec leader, Moctezuma (mahk teh ZOO muh). He wrote to the Spanish king:

Academic Vocabulary

organized • *adj.*, formal or arranged

demolish • *v.*, destroy

Primary Source

". . . Of Moctezuma, and the wonderful grandeur and state that he maintains, there is so much to be told."

–Hernán Cortés, "Letter to King Charles V of Spain," 1520

Moctezuma was welcoming to Cortés and his crew and gave them gifts because the monarch thought Cortés was a god. However, relations between the Aztec and Spaniards soon grew strained. Following through with his plan, Cortés took Moctezuma prisoner. This caused fighting that lasted for nearly two years. In 1521, in a brutal struggle, Cortés and his Indian allies captured and **demolished** Tenochtitlán. The Spanish later built Mexico City on the ruins of Tenochtitlán.

This painting shows a battle between Cortés's soldiers and Aztec warriors in Tenochtitlán. The Aztec used spears and wore quilted cotton armor. The conquistadors used guns and swords.

Ferdinand Magellan

In 1519, Ferdinand Magellan, another explorer, set sail from Spain. He was an expert navigator who commanded five ships. He followed in Columbus's path, with hopes of reaching Asia by sailing west. Magellan traveled south along the coast of South America until he found a strait, or narrow waterway, leading to the Pacific Ocean. From there, he thought the journey to Asia would be a short one, but he was wrong. He and his crew sailed for over four months before reaching land. His exhausted men were weak when they finally landed in the Philippines, off the east coast of Asia.

Magellan's journey on land did not last long. Weeks after his landing, he was killed in a battle with the people of the Philippines. His crew continued their journey back to Spain, but only one of his ships made it back home. This ship was the first ship to sail completely around the world.

3. ☑ Reading Check Use the diagram to **compare and contrast** the explorations of Cortés and Magellan.

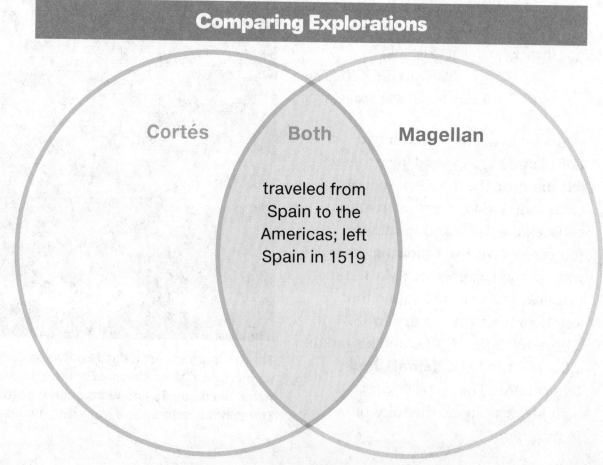

Comparing Explorations

Cortés

Both

Magellan

traveled from Spain to the Americas; left Spain in 1519

More Spanish Explorers

Another Spanish explorer, Francisco Vásquez de Coronado, wanted to gain riches by searching for treasures in the Americas. He had experience as a leader in Mexico and, while there, he heard rumors of a rich kingdom that was supposed to be filled with gold, silver, and jewels. He was told that others had looked for this treasure, but no one had found it.

Coronado was determined to find this land. So in 1540, he, along with hundreds of American Indian soldiers and servants and Spanish soldiers, set off to find these riches. During his travels, he claimed land for Spain in the southwestern states, including present-day New Mexico and Arizona. Coronado never found the treasures he sought, so he returned to Mexico very disappointed.

Juan Ponce de León was another Spanish explorer. He settled the island of Puerto Rico in 1508. Tradition tells us that he was told about a magical spring that could turn old people young. He wanted to find this fountain of youth, but he was also motivated to explore new lands. So in 1513, he led an expedition to present-day Florida and may have become the first European to visit Florida.

Other Spanish explorers came to Florida, including Hernando de Soto. He sailed to the area with 10 ships and 700 men. He also led an expedition through what is now the southeastern United States.

During his land travels, Coronado traveled around 2,700 miles. De Soto traveled close to 2,400 miles throughout North America.

Francisco Vásquez de Coronado

Spanish Exploration, 1513-1542

Map showing:
- N, W, E, S compass
- PACIFIC OCEAN
- NORTH AMERICA
- ATLANTIC OCEAN
- Gulf of Mexico
- Havana, Cuba
- Puerto Rico
- San German
- Hispaniola
- Caribbean Sea
- 0 — 600 mi
- 0 — 600 km

LEGEND
- Ponce de León, 1513
- De Soto, 1539–1542
- Coronado, 1540–1542

4. ☑ **Reading Check**
Analyze the map and discuss with a partner which expedition seemed the longest and most difficult.

Spain's New Territory

Word Wise

Suffixes Suffixes are word parts that are added to the end of a word. Suffixes change the meaning of the word. For example, in the word *settlement*, the suffix *–ment* is added to the end of the verb *settle*. When *–ment* is added to the end of *settle*, it becomes a noun, *settlement*.

Quest Connections

Think about the Spanish explorers' journeys. Why were they successful? Remember your thoughts as you complete your Quest.

👆 **INTERACTIVITY**

Learn more about the expeditions of Spanish explorers.

After a time of exploration, Spain was ready to settle in the Americas. So in 1535, Spain established the colony of New Spain in North America. A **colony** is a settlement or area far from the country that rules it. New Spain, now known as Mexico, became an important part of the Spanish Empire. Over time, New Spain would expand to include many islands in the Caribbean, as well as large parts of North America and Central America.

Towns began to emerge throughout New Spain. In 1565, St. Augustine was founded in what is today Florida. It is the oldest town established by Europeans in the United States.

Over time, Spain imposed its culture, language, religion, and way of life on Indians who had lived in the region long before the Spanish arrived. The Spanish built new Spanish-style cities on top of the ruins of American Indian cities. Spanish officials moved to the colony to set up a government. Catholic priests came to teach American Indians about Christianity. They built missions in American Indian villages where they encouraged American Indians to adopt Christianity as their religion. Many American Indians were influenced to live and work on missions. Some Indians were tempted by steady food and shelter. But many were forced to work in the field. Others ran away from the missions.

The Spanish takeover of New Spain brought harsh changes to American Indians. The Spanish would set various Indian groups against each other in an attempt to form alliances with some of them. Then, many Indians were killed battling the conquistadors. Many more died from diseases, such as smallpox, brought unknowingly to the Americas by the Spaniards. American Indians had never been exposed to smallpox and other European diseases. They had no natural immunity. Epidemics occurred among peoples. An **epidemic** is an outbreak of disease that spreads quickly and affects many people.

This church was built in the 1620s as part of a Spanish mission. Today, it is part of the Salinas Pueblo Missions National Monument in Salinas Valley, New Mexico.

American Indians who survived often lost their lands and property. Many Spanish missionaries also forced American Indians to adopt European culture.

To make the empire profitable, Spain closely controlled its economic activities, especially trade. Laws forbade colonists from trading with other European nations or even with other Spanish colonies.

5. ☑ **Reading Check** What was the effect of the founding of Spanish colonies on the American Indians?

_____

_____

INTERACTIVITY

Check your understanding of the key ideas of this lesson.

☑ **Lesson 2 Check**

6. **Cause and Effect** After Europeans arrived in the Americas, how did epidemics destroy much of the American Indian population?

_____

_____

_____

7. **Describe** what life was like for American Indians in New Spain.

_____

_____

_____

8. **Understand the** *Quest* **Connections** Based on what you read in the text, what conclusion can you make about the characteristics of a good sailor?

_____

_____

Journal of Christopher Columbus

As you have read, Christopher Columbus kept a journal while he searched for a shorter route to Asia. Instead of arriving in Asia, he landed in North America. During his journey, Columbus described the challenges that he and his crew faced and the sights they encountered.

Columbus's journal was a valuable resource to other explorers. Never before had anyone traveled the route that Columbus had taken. Even though Columbus continued to believe he had landed in Asia, his discovery changed history. In the passage below, Columbus describes what happened when his crew first saw land in the Americas. Note that in his writings, Columbus referred to himself as "The Admiral."

Primary Source

Vocabulary Support

yelled happily ┄┄┄┄┄┄

told Columbus ┄┄┄┄┄┄

dropped to his knees ┄┄┄┄

thanked God ┄┄┄┄┄┄

vessel *n.*, a ship
intelligence *n.*, knowledge
declare *v.*, say

At sunset Martin Alonzo <u>called out with great joy</u> from this <u>vessel</u> that he saw land, and <u>demanded of the Admiral</u> a reward for his <u>intelligence</u>. The Admiral says, when he heard him <u>declare</u> this, he <u>fell on his knees</u> and <u>returned thanks to God.</u>

- Christopher Columbus, *Journal of Christopher Columbus, 1492*

Fun Fact

Columbus made four voyages to the Americas, but he never became wealthy as a result of his voyages.

Close Reading

1. **Identify** and circle the words that describe how Columbus's crew member felt when land was first sighted.

_____

_____

2. **Describe** the importance of Columbus's voyage.

_____

_____

_____

_____

_____

Wrap It Up

Why did Columbus and his men set out for new land? What might have kept them going after such a long voyage? Support your answer with information from the chapter. Use one quotation from the passage shown here to support your response.

_____

_____

_____

_____

_____

_____

_____

Lesson 3

The Columbian Exchange

INTERACTIVITY

Participate in a class discussion to preview the content of this lesson.

Vocabulary

Columbian Exchange
plantation

Academic Vocabulary

enormous
distinct

Unlock The BIG Question

I will know that the Columbian Exchange resulted in the exchange of useful crops and animals, as well as deadly diseases.

JumpStart Activity

Your teacher has assigned a resource to you that you must trade with another student. Try to convince another student to trade with you. Think about what makes certain goods more attractive than others.

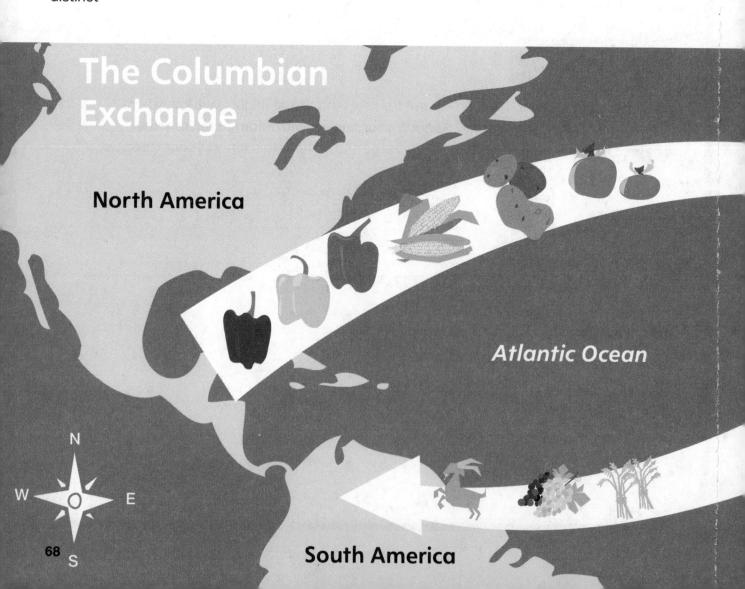

The Columbian Exchange

North America

Atlantic Ocean

South America

When Columbus returned to Spain, he did not bring back spices and silk to Europe, which may have been expected. Instead, he brought a little gold and some American Indians. He also brought plants and animals. Many Europeans were amazed by what they saw. His arrival in the Americas the previous year set something that is called the **Columbian Exchange** in motion. The Columbian Exchange was a movement of people, animals, plants, and cultures between the Eastern and Western hemispheres. When Columbus returned to the Americas from Spain, he brought over 1,200 men and a collection of European animals and plants. In this way, Columbus began a vast global exchange that would affect much of the entire world.

INTERACTIVITY

Explore the key ideas of this lesson.

1. ☑ **Reading Check** **Identify** the foods and animals that were sent from the Americas on one side of the map and those from Europe, Africa, and Asia on the other side of the map. Circle the ones that traveled west in red and the ones that traveled east in blue.

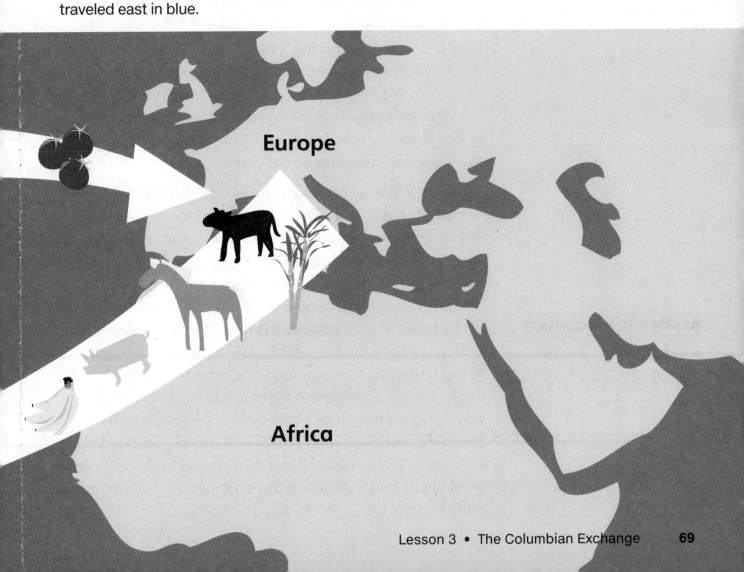

Europe

Africa

Horses brought by the Spanish to the Americas in the 1500s changed how many American Indian groups lived.

A Powerful Exchange

In the Americas, Europeans found a variety of foods that were new to them, including tomatoes, pumpkins, and peppers. They transported these foods to Europe. Two of these new foods, corn and potatoes, became important foods in Europe. Potatoes were easy to grow and store. They helped feed Europe's rapidly growing population. Corn spread across Europe and to Africa and Asia. It became one of the world's most important cereal crops.

In the exchange of goods, Europeans carried a wide variety of plants and animals to the Americas, including wheat and grapes from Europe and bananas and sugar cane from Africa and Asia. Cattle, pigs, goats, and chickens became part of the American Indian diet. Horses and donkeys transported people and goods quickly. The arrival of the horse had an **enormous** impact on some American Indian cultures. On horseback, American Indians could travel farther in search of food and hunt their prey more easily. Horses also allowed them to use bigger sleds and carry heavier loads than they could before. American Indians became experts at riding horses and moving quickly to hunt or to fight. The introduction of horses, and later, gunpowder, would both make warfare between American Indian groups more violent.

Academic Vocabulary

enormous • *adj.*, very large or great in size

Effects on American Indians

When sugar cane was introduced into the West Indies and elsewhere, it quickly became a profitable resource. Sugar cane grew well in the warm, moist climate of the Caribbean. The crop, however, had to be grown on plantations, large estates run by an owner or the owner's overseer. These plantations changed the land and caused the need for many workers to be profitable.

At first, the Spanish forced American Indians to work the **plantations** under the most brutal conditions. Diseases, which you read about in Lesson 2, caused a massive number of deaths of American Indians. The Spanish did not know that American Indians had no immunity to these diseases, such as measles and smallpox. However, once they saw the effects of the diseases they could use them as a threat.

By the early 1600s, plantations in the Caribbean and else where in the Americas stopped relying only on American Indian labor. By this time, the Europeans started forcing enslaved Africans do the work.

These American Indians are shown suffering from smallpox, a disease that was brought to the Americas by Europeans.

Cultures Collide

Plants, animals, and diseases were not the only things shared during the Columbian Exchange. People from the Western and Eastern hemispheres also exchanged culture.

Europeans, Africans, and American Indians had very different cultures. They wore different clothing and practiced different religions. Each culture had its own **distinct** styles of music, dance, and celebrations.

The movement of people to different parts of the world led to the transfer of ideas and technologies. In Europe, Asia, Africa, and the Americas, people adapted ideas and inventions from distant lands. Language also traveled through exploration and trade. Words such as *pajama* (from India) and *hammock* or *canoe* (from the Americas) were adopted and became words in European languages, which is evidence of this global exchange.

Even today, the exchange between cultures continues to affect people around the world. People eat foods and use goods from across the globe every day. Most places on Earth possess a mixture of cultures.

This modern-day canoe was influenced by American Indian culture.

2. **☑ Reading Check** As this chart shows, many words in English began in other cultures that came together in the Americas. Reflect on other words you know that come from a different language and share them with a partner.

Sharing Language		
European Words	**Native American Words**	**African Words**
coffee (Arabic)	canoe	banjo
guitar (Spanish)	hurricane	jazz
mosquito (Spanish)	moose	yam
sugar (French)	skunk	

INTERACTIVITY

Check your understanding of the key ideas of this lesson.

☑ Lesson 3 Check

3. **Sequence** Which event started the Columbian Exchange, and why did it happen?

_____

_____

_____

4. **Explain** how the introduction of horses changed the way that many American Indians lived.

_____

_____

_____

5. **Analyze** how the Columbian Exchange changed the way Europeans traded.

_____

_____

_____

_____

Interpret Timelines

A timeline is a diagram that shows the sequence, or order, of a group of events. You can use a timeline to understand whether events happened before or after each other. Timelines also help you see whether events happened at almost the same time or far apart in time.

Timelines are divided into sections. Each section shows an equal period of time. This timeline covers more than a century, or 100 years. Its subject is "European Exploration." Fill in the missing events on the timeline. One event has been filled in on the timeline as an example. A line is drawn from each event to its correct location on the timeline.

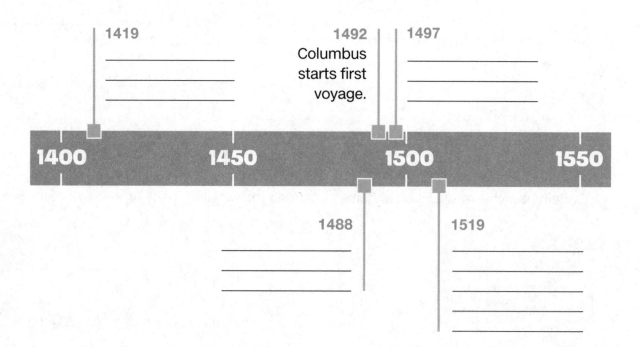

1419 _____

1492 Columbus starts first voyage.

1497 _____

1400   1450   1500   1550

1488 _____

1519 _____

Your Turn!

Read the paragraph about Christopher Columbus's first three voyages. Then, use the information to answer the questions.

 VIDEO

Watch a video about interpreting timelines.

Christopher Columbus sailed from Spain on his first voyage in August 1492. He made landfall later that year on an island in the Caribbean Sea. Columbus made a second voyage in September 1493 to explore more of the region. In 1494, Columbus founded La Isabela in the present-day Dominican Republic. He returned to Spain in 1496.

1. List the four dates mentioned in the paragraph. Then write a short description of the event that happened on each date.

Date: _____

_____

_____

Date: _____

_____

_____

Date: _____

_____

_____

Date: _____

_____

_____

2. Based on the information in the timeline and in the paragraph, how would you explain Spanish and Portuguese exploration in the late 1400s?

_____

_____

_____

_____

Quality:
Problem Solving

Prince Henry the Navigator (1394–1460)
Patron of Exploration

Prince Henry was the son of King John I of Portugal. He was called Henry the Navigator because he sponsored voyages of exploration. He also established a school of navigation to develop new technologies to make exploring and traveling by ship easier and faster.

Prince Henry and his father wanted to explore Africa and wanted to make use of its trade in gold and slaves. The ships they used were too slow and heavy to make these voyages. Prince Henry's fleet adapted the caravel, a newer and much lighter ship that could sail farther and faster. It also was easy to steer. With this new ship, sailors were able to explore all types of seas in their quests.

Find Out More

1. Would you consider Prince Henry the Navigator a good citizen? Why or why not?

_____

_____

_____

_____

2. People today use problem-solving skills on a daily basis. Think of some tools and strategies that you use today to help you solve problems. Share your ideas with the class.

_____

_____

_____

Visual Review

Use these graphics to review some of the key terms, people, and ideas from this chapter.

Early European Explorers

Explorer	Accomplishment
Leif Ericsson	one of the first Europeans to land in North America
Prince Henry	early supporter of exploration and navigation
Bartolomeu Dias	sailed around the Cape of Good Hope
Vasco da Gama	crossed the Indian Ocean and reached India
Christopher Columbus	searched for a western route to Asia; landed in North America
Hernán Cortés	led an expedition to Mexico and conquered the Aztec
Francisco de Coronado	claimed land for Spain in the present-day Southwest
Juan Ponce de León	settled the island of Puerto Rico and explored Florida
Hernando de Soto	led an expedition through the present-day Southeast
Ferdinand Magellan	led the first expedition to sail all the way around the world

Motivations and Results of Early Explorations

Reason for Exploration	Result
The Vikings wanted to settle new lands.	raided European towns; were the first Europeans to sail to North America
The Portuguese wanted to find a sea route to Asia to control trade there.	sailed around the tip of Africa; took part in the slave trade; took the lead in India's spice trade
The Spanish wanted to find a new route to Asia by sailing west and wanted to find riches such as gold.	claimed land in North America; settled the first European town in North America
The Spanish wanted to explore and conquer land in North America.	invaded and conquered the Aztec Empire; sailed the first ship around the world; destroyed the population of American Indians

☑ Assessment

 GAMES

Play the vocabulary game.

Vocabulary and Key Ideas

1. Draw a line to match the definitions with the correct terms.

an instrument that measured the height of the sun or a star   **merchant**

outbreak of disease that spreads quickly   **astrolabe**

one who buys goods from others   **conquistador**

a trip made to explore   **expedition**

a Spanish conqueror   **epidemic**

2. Define What is a **caravel**?

_____

_____

_____

_____

3. Define What is **navigation**?

_____

_____

4. Define Why did some European rulers agree to be **patrons** for explorers?

_____

_____

_____

5. Identify Fill in the blanks in the paragraph below. Choose from these words: potatoes, grapes, corn, horses, wheat.

Europeans introduced crops such as _____ and animals such as _____ to the Americas. They returned to Europe with vegetables such as _____ and _____.

6. **Interpreting a Map** Write the answer to each question about the Spanish explorers.

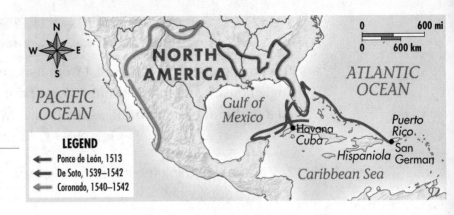

a. Where did Ponce de Leon begin his journey?

_____

b. Which explorer started his expedition near the Pacific Ocean?

_____

Critical Thinking and Writing

7. **Analyze** What did people learn and do at Prince Henry's school?

_____

_____

_____

8. **Analyze** What was the significance of Ferdinand Magellan's voyage?

_____

_____

9. **Apply** What technological advances do we still use today?

_____

_____

10. **Revisit the Big Question** Why do people explore?

_____

_____

11. **Writing Workshop: Write Informative Text** Write two paragraphs on a separate sheet of paper explaining the effects the Columbian Exchange had on Africa the Americas, and Europe.

Analyze Primary Sources

After having dispatched a meal, I went ashore, and found no habitation save a "single house", and that without an occupant; we had no doubt that the people had fled in terror at our approach, as the house was completely furnished.

-Christopher Columbus, *Journal of Columbus*, October 21, 1492

12. Why do you think the people might have "fled in terror" at Columbus and his men's approach?

_____

_____

_____

_____

Sequence

13. Why were European rulers willing to pay for expensive explorations?

_____

_____

14. Sequence Using the correct sequence, write a paragraph about how American Indians were affected by the Europeans' arrival in the Americas.

_____

_____

_____

_____

_____

_____

Quest Findings

Ahoy, Sailors!

You've read the lessons in this chapter and now you're ready to create your advertisement. Remember that the goal of your ad is to find good sailors to help you on your voyage and to decide what items you will need. Follow these steps:

INTERACTIVITY

Use this activity to help you prepare your advertisement.

1 Prepare Your Lists

List the qualities that you want your sailors to have. Use adjectives to describe these qualities. Then, write a list of the items that you will need for your voyage, not items that you just want. Use these lists to help you create your ad.

2 Create a Draft

Use your notes and the information collected from your Quest Connections to create a descriptive ad. Make sure your ad addresses the following questions:

- What makes a good sailor?
- What items are needed for a long voyage? How will they be useful?
- Why must people need to be able to work together to solve a problem?

3 Share With a Partner

Exchange your draft advertisement with a partner. Tell your partner what you like about the ad and what could be improved. Be polite when you provide suggestions.

4 Revise

Make changes to your ad after meeting with your partner. Correct any grammatical or spelling errors.

Settling the Colonies in North America

GO ONLINE FOR
DIGITAL RESOURCES

▶ VIDEO

👆 INTERACTIVITY

🔊 AUDIO

🎮 GAMES

☑ ASSESSMENT

📖 eTEXT

The BIG Question

Why do people leave their homelands?

▶ VIDEO

JumPstart Activity

👆 INTERACTIVITY

Choose a location on a world map or a globe. Imagine that you are going to visit that place. List the items you would pack, including those that would remind you of home. Share your location, list, and reasons for choosing those items with a partner.

AUDIO

Going to North America

Preview the chapter **vocabulary** as you sing the rap:

Spanish explorers left home to colonize a New Spain

The king sent **viceroys** to rule the colonies that they'd gained.

Some **missionaries** came along hoping to achieve

Changes to the local religion and what people believe.

The English had soon heard of the Spanish success

And so they set out to get themselves a brand new address.

A **Royal Charter** was provided to the men on this mission

To govern the new colonies with the Queen's permission.

The **Pilgrims** left home seeking religious freedom

The Wampanoag Indians were there to greet 'em.

The men had agreed before they made this contact

That they'd govern themselves and signed the **Mayflower Compact**.

Settling the Colonies in North America

Quebec, Canada
(France)•

Massachusetts Bay Colony
(England)
•Plymouth, Massachusetts
(England)
New Netherlands
(Netherlands)
New Sweden
(Sweden)

Jamestown, Virginia•
(England)

St. Augustine, Florida
•(Spain)

Where was the first successful English colony in North America settled?

In 1607, English colonists led by John Smith arrived in North America. They create a settlement at Jamestown.

Locate Jamestown on the map and identify the state it is now in.

TODAY
The Jamestown colony established the House of Burgesses, the first representative government in North America. Today, you can visit Williamsburg, Virginia, and see where the House of Burgesses met.

What happened and When?

Read the timeline to find out about important events in founding colonies in North America.

1560	1580	1600	

1565
The Spanish found St. Augustine.

1607
The English establish Jamestown.

TODAY
Historic Jamestown is a part of the Colonial National Historical Park in Virginia.

1608
The French settle Quebec.

Who will you meet?

Pedro Menéndez de Avilés
A Spaniard who established St. Augustine

John Smith
Jamestown colony's leader who brought them through hard times

Samuel de Champlain
French explorer who founded Quebec in New France

Henry Hudson
British explorer who claimed the Hudson River Valley for the Netherlands

 INTERACTIVITY

Complete the interactive timeline and learn more about people and places during colonial times.

1620   1640

1620
English colonists land in Massachusetts; write and sign Mayflower Compact.

1630
Puritans establish Massachusetts Bay Colony.

Quest
Document-Based Writing

Live It! Write It!

Some of the explorers and colonists who settled in North America kept journals. They described their journey across the Atlantic Ocean and what life was like in their new home. William Bradford was governor of the Plymouth Colony and kept a journal that described the Pilgrims' lives.

Today, people can write about their lives in a journal or on a blog. On a blog, they write on a Web site instead of on paper.

Quest Kick Off

I wrote about what I saw around me. Your task is to combine imagination and facts. Create journal entries or blogs in the voice of someone who is leaving Europe to settle in North America.

William Bradford

1 Create a Character and Setting

Who are you? Where is your homeland? Which colony are you going to? Why are you leaving your old home for a new one?

....

....

....

....

2 Describe Events

INTERACTIVITY

Analyze what a narrative journal or blog includes and see some examples.

Describe your new surroundings. Share your thoughts about what you are seeing and hearing.

....

....

....

....

....

....

3 Look for Quest Connections

Turn to the next page to begin looking for Quest connections that will help you write your journal or blog.

4 Quest Findings
Write Your Journal Entry

Use the Quest Findings page at the end of this chapter to help you write your journal entry or blog.

Spanish Colonies in the Americas

INTERACTIVITY

Participate in a class discussion to preview the content of this lesson.

Unlock
The **BIG**
Question

I will know why Spain explored and settled in the Americas.

Vocabulary

viceroy
encomienda
class system
missionary

Academic Vocabulary

rigid
convince

JumpStart Activity

Divide into two teams. Look at an object in the classroom. Discuss with your team why you should claim that object. Then present the reasons for the team's claim. Listen as the other team presents their reasons. Decide as a class whether both teams could share the objects. What are the benefits and drawbacks of competing for the same resource?

Christopher Columbus and other explorers and conquistadors claimed land in North and South America for Spain. This land was called New Spain. Acquiring this land was important. Any country that claimed the land could also claim its resources, including gold and silver. These valuable resources made Spain a wealthy and powerful nation.

Spanish soldiers, priests, and settlers began to arrive in New Spain. The soldiers protected the priests and colonists. The priests were sent by the Spanish king. They helped settle the land by building missions. The missions used American Indians as laborers and, in addition, wanted to convert them to Christianity.

A number of early missions grew into very large ranches with many church buildings. Towns grew around the missions and set up local governments. As you will read, on missions and elsewhere in New Spain, many American Indians were forced to work for the Spanish.

Competition in the Americas

Other European countries quickly became interested in North and South America. Like Spain, they wanted to acquire more land and resources. Spain, England, France, Portugal, and the Netherlands competed with one another for wealth and power. These countries were often at war with one another in Europe and in the Americas.

In 1493, the Treaty of Tordesillas (tohr day SEE yuhs) divided North and South America between Spain and Portugal. An imaginary line was drawn from the North Pole to the South Pole across the Atlantic Ocean. Spain could claim all the land west of this line. Portugal could claim all the land east of it. Portugal wanted the line changed so they could have more land. The next year, the line was moved. This allowed Portugal to claim what is now Brazil in South America. None of the other European countries agreed to follow the treaty.

The image shows Mexico City, the capital of New Spain. The dotted lines on the map show how Spain and Portugal divided North and South America.

INTERACTIVITY

Explore the key ideas of this lesson.

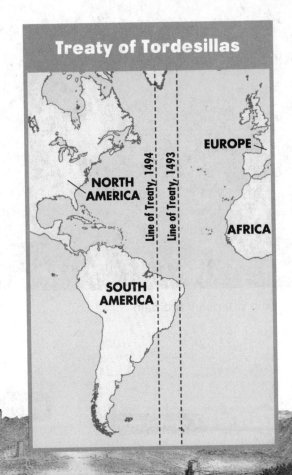

Treaty of Tordesillas

King Charles V of Spain

For example, France established colonies in Florida in 1562. Jean Ribault (ree BOW) led 150 French colonists on three ships. Spain was troubled to find out that the French were in Florida. Spanish ships sailed along the Florida coast on their way from Mexico to Europe. The ships were filled with gold and silver. It would be easy for the French to try to capture the ships and their valuable cargo.

Changes in New Spain

King Charles V ruled Spain, and so he ruled New Spain, too. The king not only worried about the French in Florida, but also about the loyalty of Hernán Cortés. Was Cortés keeping some of the riches from Mexico? Was he planning to set up his own kingdom in Mexico? Cortés protested these ideas in a letter to the king:

Quest Connection

Highlight details in the letter that reveal the writer's feelings about working for the king.

 INTERACTIVITY

Study the letter and use it to take a closer look at events in this lesson. Then go online to create a news story and blog about it.

Primary Source

. . . having consumed [used] very large sums, not indeed in buying lands, . . . or acquiring any sort of property for myself and heirs, but in extending and enlarging your Highness's . . . rights in these parts through conquest and acquisition of so many kingdoms and empires, achieved at my own peril.

–Hernán Cortés, *fifth letter to the Emperor Charles V*, 1526

After King Charles V chose a **viceroy** to act for him in Mexico, Cortés went back to Spain. A viceroy is a person who rules a country or territory as a representative of the king or queen. The Spanish viceroy's duties included collecting money for the royal treasury, selecting other officials, enforcing laws, and converting American Indians to Christianity.

Then King Charles V set up a new practice. It was called the **encomienda** system. Under this new system, Indians were supposed to be treated better. Spaniards in New Spain could still make American Indians work for them. In return, they had to protect their workers and teach them about Christianity. Often, the Spaniards took the American Indians' land and refused to protect them.

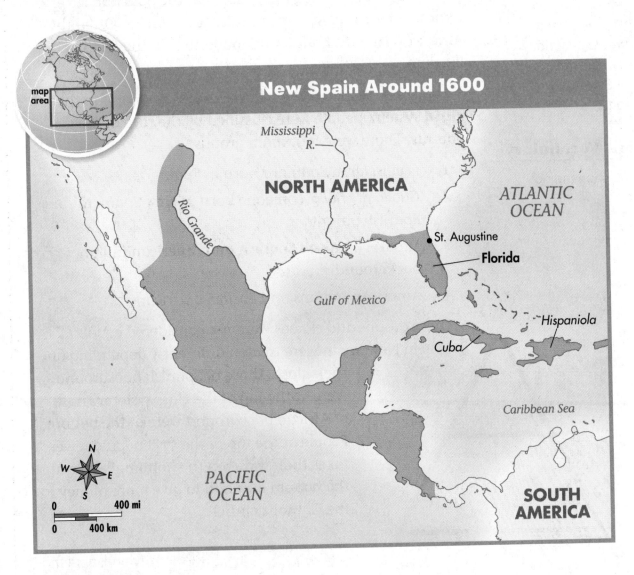

New Spain Around 1600

map area

Mississippi R.

NORTH AMERICA

Rio Grande

ATLANTIC OCEAN

St. Augustine
Florida

Gulf of Mexico

Cuba

Hispaniola

Caribbean Sea

PACIFIC OCEAN

0   400 mi
0   400 km

SOUTH AMERICA

1. ☑ **Reading Check**   Use the labels on the map to **explain** where New Spain is located.

_____

_____

_____

Class Structure in New Spain

Gold and silver mining was important to the economy of New Spain, but most of that treasure was sent to Spain. At one time, silver mined in the colony made up 20 percent of Spain's budget. Ranching and farming were also important in New Spain. Under the *encomienda* system, some American Indians had to work for the Spanish in the gold and silver mines. Others had to work on ranches or farms. Often the American Indians had to work on land that they had once lived on.

Spain established a **class system** in New Spain. In this **rigid** system, people were classified by the race of their parents. There were four main groups:

1. *Peninsular*: a Spaniard born in Spain
2. *Criollo* or *criolla*: someone born in New Spain, to Spanish parents
3. *Mestizo*: of mixed Spanish and American Indian background
4. American Indians and enslaved Africans

These groups and classes were not considered equal. People in New Spain were treated differently depending on their class. Those of Spanish background were at the top of the class system. Those of African background were at the bottom. People at the top of the system paid fewer taxes than those on the bottom. People at the bottom also had to give more money to the Catholic church.

2. ☑ **Reading Check** **Identify** and label the missing classes of society in New Spain to complete the diagram.

mestizos

The Spanish Missions

The Spanish built settlements in what is now Texas, New Mexico, Arizona, Utah, Nevada, and Florida. These settlements were often built inside missions. Missionaries governed these settlements instead of soldiers or civilians. A **missionary** is a person who is sent to another country to **convince** others to believe in a particular religion. The Spanish government sent missionaries to New Spain to make American Indians work on the very large ranches and farms the missions owned and to convert them to the Catholic religion. The government also wanted the American Indians to become a part of New Spain, instead of fighting it.

Academic Vocabulary

convince • *n.*, to make another believe something is true

The American Indians were forced to do the hard work of building the missions. Then, they were expected to live in the missions and learn about the Spanish way of life, including its religion. Life inside the mission followed a daily routine: prayer, work, training, eating meals, and time off for relaxing and religious celebrations. Most of the American Indians moved within the region to hunt and trade. They often left the missions to continue these activities and then returned.

Because distances between settlements in New Spain were so great, travelers stopped and rested at missions. They might see crops such as grain, vegetables, and fruit from Spain growing alongside native corn. The workers built irrigation ditches to water the fields.

3. ☑ **Reading Check** **Analyze** the distances on the map. Circle the missions farthest from one another and **identify** the distance between them.

_____

Spanish Missions, 1600–1650

NORTH AMERICA

Florida

ATLANTIC OCEAN

Gulf of Mexico

Hispaniola

New Spain

Cuba

Trinidad

Caribbean Sea

PACIFIC OCEAN

SOUTH AMERICA

map area

LEGEND
- New Spain, 1600
- • Spanish mission, 1600–1650

0   400 mi

0   400 km

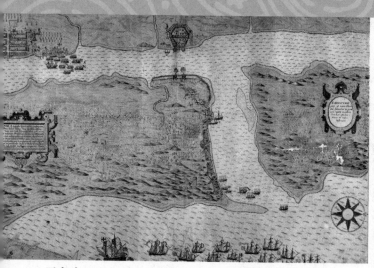

This is an early map of St. Augustine.

This is what St. Augustine looks like today.

St. Augustine

More settlements were being built in New Spain, so it seemed unlikely that another European country would try to take control of this area. Still, Spain worried about the French. France had built Fort Caroline along the Florida coast. Ships loaded with resources from New Spain sailed close to the Florida coast. What would stop French soldiers or pirates from trying to steal those valuable resources? What would stop the French from trying to gain control of more land in North America?

Spain sent Pedro Menéndez de Avilés to make the French leave Florida. He was also ordered to begin a Spanish settlement there. In 1565, he arrived in Florida and founded St. Augustine. This became the first permanent European settlement in the United States. Avilés succeeded in getting rid of the French. The troops at St. Augustine protected the ships sailing along the main trade route between New Spain and Europe. Their presence kept other European countries from invading Florida, protecting Spain's claim to it.

4. ✅ **Reading Check** **Draw Inferences** Analyze both photos of St. Augustine. How has the city's relative location helped it to endure?

_____

_____

_____

Cooperation and Conflict

Before any Europeans arrived, the Timucuan (tee MOO quan) Indians had lived in Florida for thousands of years. They grew crops and hunted and fished for food. The Timucuans had friendly relations with the French in the beginning. For instance, they offered to share their food with the French and assisted them in building a village and Fort Caroline.

When the Spanish arrived and attacked the French, the Timucuans did not help the French. They stayed out of the fight between the two European powers. After the French left, the Spanish began building missions in Florida. They forced the Timucuan Indians into these missions. As at other settlements in New Spain, the Indians were expected to convert to Christianity and to adopt the Spanish way of life. A Spanish priest translated some Catholic teachings into the Timucuan language in 1612. This was the first time a European text had been translated into an American Indian language.

This illustration shows a typical Timucuan village at the time of first contact with Europeans. A protective wall surrounded about 30 family houses and a council house in the center, where all of the people in the village could meet.

Throughout New Spain, the Spanish relied on American Indians to provide food and labor. In return, Spanish leaders offered gifts to Indian leaders and did not challenge their right to govern their own people. At the missions, however, the Spanish sometimes used force to change the way American Indians lived, worked, and worshiped in New Spain. At St. Augustine and many other missions, many Indians suffered from harsh treatment and died of overwork and from illnesses carried by the Spanish.

From 1585 to 1586, Sir Francis Drake sailed from England and began attacking Spanish possessions in North and South America. Spain and England were at war. Drake and his men raided and looted Spanish settlements in the Caribbean Sea. In May 1586, English ships attacked and burned down St. Augustine. Spain rebuilt the city. Then, in the early 1600s, the residents of St. Augustine heard about new threats from England. The English were establishing colonies to the north in what is now North Carolina and Virginia.

5. ☑ Reading Check **Describe** examples of cooperation and conflict between the Spanish colonists and American Indians in Florida by completing the chart.

Cooperation	Conflict
Indians help provide food and labor for Spanish	Indian land taken by Spanish

☑ Lesson 1 Check

6. Analyze Why did Spain establish colonies in the Americas?

_____

_____

_____

7. Distinguish Fact From Opinion Explain what Sir Francis Drake did to St. Augustine. Do you think he was right or wrong to do this? Use evidence from the text to support your opinion.

_____

_____

_____

_____

_____

8. Understand the  **Think about the European settlers and events you learned about in this lesson. What details could you use to describe them?**

_____

_____

_____

_____

Lesson 2 The English Colonies in Virginia

INTERACTIVITY

Participate in a class discussion to preview the content of this lesson.

Vocabulary

royal charter
indentured servant
Anglican
cash crop
House of Burgesses
representative

Academic Vocabulary

finance
assemble

Unlock The BIG Question

I will know why England explored and settled in North America.

JumpStart Activity

Work with a partner and try to convince your partner to move and switch desks or spaces with you. Explain why your desk is better and why your partner should move. Think about how this relates to settling North America. Why did people want to move there? How did countries such as England try to convince people to move?

English colonists land at Roanoke Island.

In the late 1500s, England and Spain were bitter rivals. They fought over land, resources, and trade. They fought over religion, too. People in Spain followed the Roman Catholic Church. The Roman Catholic leader was the pope in Rome, Italy.

Many English people were Christian Protestants, who followed the teachings of Martin Luther and others. Luther started a movement called the Protestant Reformation in 1517. Followers of Luther became known as Protestants because they protested some practices of the Catholic Church. Protestants translated the Bible from Latin into German or English, the languages people spoke. They believed that everyone should be able to read the Bible.

The Catholic Church was angry at Luther and others because they challenged the Church's authority. However, the pope tried to reform the Catholic Church in a movement that became known as the Counter-Reformation. The Reformation and Counter-Reformation influenced European Protestants and Catholic missionaries to explore and colonize North America.

England envied Spain's vast and rich American colony, New Spain. England's Queen Elizabeth I supported English colonization in North America. She agreed to let Sir Walter Raleigh (RAW lee) send an exploring party to North America. The goal was to find the best locations for setting up colonies in North America. The queen hoped to find gold and silver, as the Spanish had.

INTERACTIVITY

Explore the key ideas of this lesson.

The First Colony Fails

Queen Elizabeth gave a **royal charter** to Raleigh. This was a document that gave him the right to set up and govern colonies. In return, he promised the colonies would belong to England.

Raleigh sent scouts to North America to look for good locations in 1584. One group landed in what is now North Carolina. They reported that the American Indians living on this land were friendly and the land was good for growing crops.

Raleigh sent about 100 settlers to establish a colony in North Carolina. These men landed on Roanoke (ROH uh nohk) Island in 1585. They built a fort, but soon ran into trouble. The colonists' supplies ran out and they relied on the Roanoke Island Indians for food. The Indians, however, stopped helping the colonists. Discouraged, the colonists returned to England in 1586.

John White and others return to Roanoke Island and find only a carving on a tree.

The Lost Colony of Roanoke

The next year, in 1587, Sir Walter Raleigh sent another group of over 100 settlers to Virginia. This group included men, women, and children on three ships. The colony would grow its own food and make its own products to use and to sell across the Atlantic. Instead of settling on Roanoke Island, the plan was to set up a colony farther north on Chesapeake Bay. The bay was deeper, which was better for large ships.

This group of colonists faced problems, too. First they landed at Roanoke Island. Then the pilot refused to take them to Chesapeake Bay. The colonists had no choice but to stay on Roanoke Island. This did not please the Roanoke Island Indians because of their relationships with the earlier colonists. John White was in charge of the colony. He tried to make peace with the Indians, but neither side trusted each other.

There was some good news. White's granddaughter, Virginia Dare, was born in August. She was the first English child born in North America. There was more bad news, however. The colonists were running out of supplies. White knew they could not depend upon the Indians for help. He decided to return to England for more supplies.

At this time, England and Spain were still at war. White reached England, but the war prevented him from returning to Roanoke Island. He returned two years later, in 1590. There were no English colonists left on Roanoke Island. All that remained was the name of a nearby island carved on a post: CROATOAN. Currently, historians and scientists do not know exactly what happened to the lost colony of Roanoke Island.

Quest Connection

Think about the people and events in the Roanoke Island colony. How can you use both the text and illustrations to help you complete your Quest?

INTERACTIVITY

You can make your blog or journal entry more powerful by creating or using images. Go online to play a sorting game with images.

1. ☑ **Reading Check** **Analyze** the illustration of John White upon his return to Roanoke Island. **Talk with a partner** about how it supports the text.

The Virginia Company

The failure of the colonies on Roanoke Island made England reluctant about settling North America. Then, after more than a decade, in 1606, the Virginia Company received a royal charter from James I, the new king of England. The Virginia Company would pay to establish and supply a new colony in North America. In return, the company would make money for England by exporting and selling natural resources in Europe. Because of Spain's success in mining silver and gold, the Virginia Company hoped to find those precious metals in North America, too. The company also expected to make money by selling goods that the colonists would produce.

To raise money, the Virginia Company sold shares. People could buy part of the company and become shareholders. That money **financed** the ships and supplies for the new colony. When the Virginia Company sold resources and products from the colony and made money, they would give part of those profits to the shareholders.

In December of 1606, the Virginia Company sent three ships with over 100 men and boys to North America. Their destination was Jamestown.

Academic Vocabulary

finance • v., to provide money for something

2. ☑ **Reading Check** **Analyze** the diagram. Circle the steps that show how the Virginia Company expected to make money.

How the Virginia Company Worked

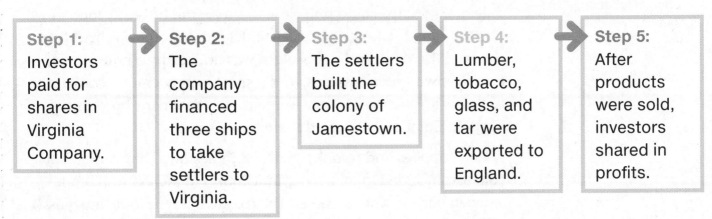

Step 1:	Step 2:	Step 3:	Step 4:	Step 5:
Investors paid for shares in Virginia Company.	The company financed three ships to take settlers to Virginia.	The settlers built the colony of Jamestown.	Lumber, tobacco, glass, and tar were exported to England.	After products were sold, investors shared in profits.

A New Beginning: Jamestown

Many of these first settlers were **indentured servants**. An indentured servant is someone who agrees to work without pay for someone else for a set time. Indentured servants agreed to work for the Virginia Company for seven years. In exchange, the company paid for their trip to North America and for food, shelter, and clothing after they arrived. After seven years, the settlers received their own land.

Most colonists were **Anglican**. They followed the Church of England, which was a Protestant religion. At that time, it was illegal to practice any other religion in England.

The Virginia Company had specific rules and instructions for the colonists. They had to find a good location, build a safe settlement, find gold, make a profit, and look for an all-water route to the Pacific Ocean. The company chose the leaders for the Jamestown colony. One of them was Captain John Smith.

Primary Source

You must take [special] care that you choose a seat for habitation [settlement] that shall not be over burthened [overrun] with woods near your town; for all the men you have, shall not be able to cleanse [clear] twenty acres a year; besides that it may serve for a [cover] for your enemies round about.

—Instructions for the Virginia Colony, 1606

These kitchen tools have been dug up at the original location of the Jamestown colony.

In April 1607, the ships arrived in Chesapeake Bay. By mid-May, they had found a site for their settlement. The location had a deep bay. Ships could pull close to shore and be easily loaded and unloaded. The site was easy to defend. No one was living on the land. Unfortunately, this place was unhealthy. That summer, bad river water, mosquitoes, and a short supply of food caused the colonists to become ill. They were unable to work as hard as the Virginia Company expected them to.

New supplies and colonists reached Jamestown that winter. The colonists included tailors, a perfume maker, a person who made wooden barrels, and a jeweler. The colonists were producing glass and lumber to export, but these products were not making enough money.

The Starving Time

Powhatan Indians lived in the area of Jamestown, but their relationship with the Jamestown colonists was difficult. John Smith became the leader of Jamestown. He worked to improve relationships with the Powhatan. Food was scarce at Jamestown, so Smith traded goods to the Indians for food. During this time, in 1608, the first English women arrived in Jamestown. This was important, as the colony viewed family as important to its survival.

Smith was a tough leader. He said that if people did not work, then they would not eat. The colonists worked hard. They planted crops, dug a well for good water, and made products to send to England.

The next year, John Smith was hurt in an accident and had to return to England. With winter approaching, Chief Powhatan, leader of the Indians, stopped trading with Jamestown. The Indians began to attack colonists who left the fort at Jamestown to hunt for food. The amount of food supplies dropped. This harsh winter of 1609 to 1610 became known as the Starving Time. Almost 400 of the English colonists died. That left only about 100 people at Jamestown.

Help arrived that spring. A ship loaded with supplies and more settlers sailed into Chesapeake Bay.

3. ☑ Reading Check **Sequence** Which important event is missing from the timeline? Add it to the timeline in the correct **sequence**.

Jamestown, Early 1600s

1606
Virginia Company receives a royal charter from King James I.

1608
The first English women arrive at Jamestown.

1610
The Starving Time continues.
Supply ships and new colonists arrive.

1619
The House of Burgesses meets for the first time.

| 1600 | | 1610 | | 1620 |

1607
English colonists reach Chesapeake Bay.

1609
_____
_____
The Starving Time begins.

1613
John Rolfe exports first crop of tobacco.

A Cash Crop Saves Jamestown

A man named John Rolfe was on the ships that arrived in Jamestown in the spring of 1610. He brought with him tobacco seeds for Spanish tobacco. Tobacco grew well in Virginia, and American Indians had been harvesting it for hundreds of years. Rolfe decided to plant the Spanish tobacco seeds. His experiment turned out to be a success.

Rolfe shipped some of his tobacco to England in 1613 and it sold well. In 1617, England received 20,000 pounds of tobacco from Jamestown. The next year, the colony sent twice as much tobacco for sale. The Virginia Company was making money at last.

Other colonists began planting tobacco. It became the Virginia colony's most successful **cash crop**. A cash crop is a crop that a farmer raises only to sell. The fields grew so large that more workers were needed to plant, tend, and harvest tobacco. More indentured servants came to Virginia, including Europeans and Africans. This was the start of a plantation economy in the South, in which large farms produced a single crop.

Then, in 1614, Rolfe married Pocahontas, who was also called Mataoaka. She was Chief Powhatan's daughter. Their marriage helped create peace between Jamestown and the Powhatans. This peace allowed the English colony in Virginia to expand and grow stronger.

More Changes in Jamestown

To attract more workers to Jamestown, the Virginia Company offered land to settlers. In England, people who owned land could take part in the government. The Virginia Company promised this right to settlers, too. In 1618, the company ordered the colony to create "just laws for the happy guiding and governing of the people."

Harvesting tobacco at the Virginia colony

4. ☑ **Reading Check**
Main Idea and Details
Talk with a partner about how John Rolfe affected the English colonies in Virginia.

The company created the **House of Burgesses**. In England, a burgess represented a town. The House of Burgesses included a governor and 22 **representatives**. A representative is someone who is chosen by voters to speak for them. By this time, there were 11 towns in Virginia. Each town elected two representatives. The House of Burgesses was the first representative government that **assembled** in English North America.

Academic Vocabulary

assemble • *v.*, to meet together

 INTERACTIVITY

Check your understanding of the key ideas of this lesson.

☑ Lesson 2 Check

5. **Sequence** Describe how the Virginia Company worked.

_____

_____

_____

_____

_____

6. **Compare and Contrast** the Roanoke colony and the Jamestown colony.

_____

_____

_____

_____

7. **Understand the** *Quest* Connections Think about how information is presented in this lesson. How can you use text and graphic features to provide details for your journal entry or blog?

_____

_____

_____

Ask and Answer Questions

Reading a textbook, a primary source, or a novel can be difficult. Authors may use unfamiliar words or discuss people or events you have not learned about yet. One strategy you can use is asking and answering questions.

VIDEO

Watch a video about asking and answering questions.

Follow the steps below to learn how to ask and answer questions.

1. **What do you know? What do you need to know?**
   Before reading, ask yourself what you already know about the topic. Then scan the reading to see if there are people and events that do not seem familiar to you. This is what you need to know.

2. **Ask questions** As you read, you can ask questions about unfamiliar words or difficult parts of the text.

3. **Find answers** Reread the text to find answers to your questions. Asking and answering questions about key ideas and details will also help you remember the most important information in the text.

Read the paragraphs. What questions can you ask to better understand the text?

In 1541, France decided to establish a colony in New France. Rival Spain was already claiming land in North America. Jacques Cartier traveled with the French colonists. They built a settlement near what is now Quebec. Cartier found the winter was too cold and returned to France. The gold and silver Cartier thought he had found in New France turned out to be worthless.

This first French colony eventually failed, too. What survived, though, was the beginning of a fur trade with the North American Indians. Beaver and other kinds of fur were greatly prized in Europe.

Use the organizer on the facing page to ask and answer questions about this text.

1. Fill in the organizer to answer questions based on the passage.
   Then write your own question and answer.

Question	Answer
Why did France want a colony in North America?	
How might France establish a successful fur trade?	

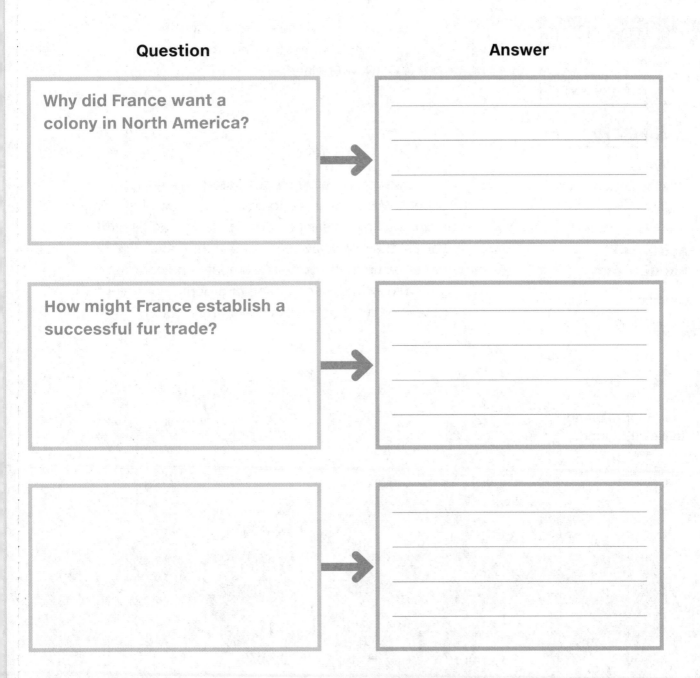

2. Read the last paragraph under the heading "The Growth of New Netherlands" in Lesson 4. On a separate sheet of paper, write a question based on the text. Then write the answer to the question.

Lesson 3
Pilgrims and Puritans in New England

INTERACTIVITY

Participate in a class discussion to preview the content of this lesson.

Vocabulary

pilgrim
Mayflower Compact
Puritan

Academic Vocabulary

condition
responsible

Unlock The BIG Question

I will know the key events in the establishment of English colonies in New England.

JumPstart Activity

Suppose you were in charge of starting a new school. Work in a group to create rules for the school, including how to select a principal and teachers. After you list the rules, have everyone in the group sign his or her name at the bottom. Compare and contrast your rules with those from other groups. How might governing a school be like governing a colony?

The Pilgrims land in New England.

Some groups in England wanted the freedom to practice their religion. The Separatists were one of these groups. They were called Separatists because they wanted to separate from the Church of England. At this time, everyone in England had to belong to this church. Another group known as the Puritans wanted to purify, or change, the Church of England. Both groups were influenced by the Protestant Reformation, which encouraged equality among worshipers. The Separatists and the Puritans left Europe hoping for freedom to practice their religion.

INTERACTIVITY

Explore the key ideas of this lesson.

The Pilgrims

Some Separatists went to jail in England because of their religious beliefs. Many moved to the Netherlands where they could worship more freely. For about 12 years, these Separatists lived in the Netherlands. Eventually, the group decided to go to the northern part of the Virginia colony. Although the Virginia colony belonged to England, the Separatists thought they would be able to worship freely there.

The Separatists did not have enough money to finance their journey. They made an agreement with a company of investors, similar to the Virginia Company. In exchange for paying for the trip, shelter, food, tools, and other supplies, the Separatists would work for the company for seven years. They would send natural resources, such as lumber, fish, and furs, back to England.

1. ☑ **Reading Check** **Draw Inferences** **Describe** some of the risks and sacrifices of the Pilgrims boarding the *Mayflower*.

_____

_____

_____

_____

The Mayflower Compact

The Separatists left from England. They were joined by English colonists who belonged to the Church of England. On September 16, 1620, 102 passengers on board the *Mayflower* headed for New England. All of the colonists became known as Pilgrims. A **pilgrim** is a person who goes on a long journey, usually for a religious purpose. Shortly before their departure, one of the colonists, William Bradford, wrote:

Primary Source

They knew they were pilgrims, and looked not much on those things, but lifted up their eyes to the heavens, their dearest country; and quieted their spirits.

—William Bradford, journal entry, 1620

Academic Vocabulary

condition • *n.*, physical state of something

Plymouth Colony

ATLANTIC OCEAN

Poor soil

Original Mayflower landing site

Plymouth

Cape Cod

Better farmland

N W E S

LEGEND
- Wampanoag land
- ◄ - - Route of Mayflower

0   20 mi
0   20 km

Before leaving the *Mayflower*, most of the men aboard gathered to sign an important agreement. This document, the **Mayflower Compact**, explained how the Pilgrims would govern themselves. They promised to work together and hold meetings to talk about important issues. This was the beginning of town meetings in New England. It was another step in self-government in the English colonies.

The Pilgrims were supposed to land near the mouth of the Hudson River. Bad weather and dangerous water **conditions** forced them north to what is today Cape Cod. But Cape Cod had poor soil and the Pilgrims moved west.

2. **Reading Check** **Talk with a partner** about how town meetings in New England are similar to the House of Burgesses in Virginia.

The Pilgrims and the Wampanoag People

After exploring the area, a group chose a spot on a hill to settle on. It had water, a good harbor, and fields. Wampanoag (wahm puh NOH ag) Indians had once lived there. The Pilgrims called their new home Plymouth and began to build a settlement. The first winter was harsh and many colonists fell ill and died.

In the spring, William Bradford became governor of Plymouth. The Pilgrims also met the Wampanoag people in the area. They learned that a series of epidemics had killed a great number of Wampanoag. Massasoit (MAS uh soit), the Wampanoag chief, made an agreement with the Pilgrims through Bradford. The two groups would trade with and protect one another.

Quest Connection

What important agreement is described on this page? Think how you would write about it if you were a settler or an American Indian in the area.

INTERACTIVITY

Images are important in a journal or blog entry. What images will you choose for your Quest?

Life in Plymouth

Everyone at the Plymouth colony worked. The Pilgrims had to cut down trees to build houses and to clear fields. They had to grow their own food to eat and to trade with the Wampanoag for furs, which were sold in England. Money from the sales helped pay back the company. It would be years before they would be able to own their land and supplies. Besides the fur trade, the economy at Plymouth was based on self-sufficient family farms. The Pilgrims did not export large amounts of goods overseas as at Jamestown.

Between work and worship, there was little time to relax or to play. After their first year, though, the Pilgrims did celebrate. The harvest in the fall of 1621 had been good. They invited the Wampanoag to a feast of thanksgiving. For three days, the Plymouth colonists and Wampanoag Indians relaxed and ate together.

3. ☑ **Reading Check** **Analyze** the information in the graph. With a partner, ask and answer two questions about the information.

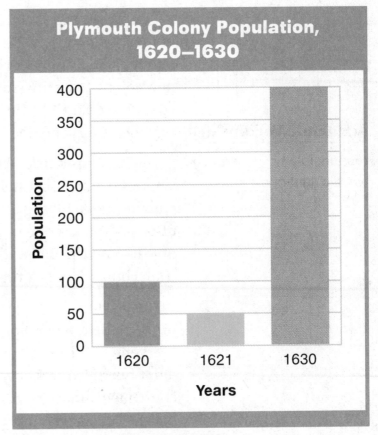

Plymouth Colony Population, 1620–1630

Source: Dept. of Anthropology, UIUC

Public punishment for breaking laws in the Massachusetts Bay Colony often included standing in a pillory in a town square.

The Puritans

In 1629, the Massachusetts Bay Company received a charter from King Charles I of England to settle in New England. Many of the company's members were **Puritans**. Like the Separatists, the Puritans left England to start a community where they could worship freely. Unlike the Virginia Company located in England, the Massachusetts Bay Company moved to New England. This meant that England had less control over the company and the colony's government.

John Winthrop was the leader of the Puritans, and a member of the Massachusetts Bay Colony. In 1630, he led a group of about 1,000 Puritans to New England. Winthrop wanted the new colony to be an example for others to follow, and called it "a City upon a Hill." He believed that the colonists had to work together. Everyone had to be **responsible** for his or her actions.

Academic Vocabulary

responsible • *n.*, able to do what is right or expected

The Puritans quickly began building towns including Boston, Charlestown, Dorchester, and Lynn. Each town had its own church, which all the townspeople had to attend. The Puritans also believed in education. They felt that all colonists should be able to read the Bible, so they also built schools and libraries. To train church leaders, the Puritans founded Harvard College.

The Puritans had moved to New England so they could practice their own religion without fear. However, they expected everyone in the Massachusetts Bay Colony to worship as they did. Church leaders governed and all colonists had to obey church teachings. No one was allowed to question the Puritans' beliefs. People who did speak out were punished. Some people were thrown out of the colony because of their beliefs.

The Pilgrims did not try to convert the American Indians to their religion. The Puritans, however, felt it was their duty to convince the Indians to become Christians. They considered most American Indian traditions and practices as savage or devilish. The Puritans had some success in converting Indians to Christianity. By 1650, they began setting up villages called Praying Towns. Indians living there promised to give up their native language, ceremonies, beliefs, and customs. Young Indian men were trained as missionaries.

4. ☑ **Reading Check**
Summarize Talk with a partner about what kind of behavior was expected of the Puritans at their "City upon a Hill."

INTERACTIVITY
Check your understanding of the key ideas of this lesson.

☑ Lesson 3 Check

5. **Compare and Contrast** What were some similarities and differences between the way the Pilgrims and Puritans governed?

_____

_____

_____

_____

6. **Summarize** why the Separatists wanted to establish their own colony in New England.

_____

_____

_____

7. **Understand the Quest Connections** Pretend you are William Bradford and writing a journal entry about the agreement with the Wampanoag people. What kinds of details would you include?

_____

_____

_____

The Mayflower Compact

As you have read, nearly all of the men on board the *Mayflower* signed an agreement before any of the Pilgrims left the ship. The *Mayflower* had landed north of where they were supposed to land. Their charter from the king did not cover this part of New England. Some of the Pilgrims were worried about this and wanted to leave to start their own settlement. But the compact, or agreement, William Bradford and others had written helped keep everyone together. The compact promised that they would work together to govern themselves.

Vocabulary Support

fair·······················

proper·······················

acceptance of authority···········

. . . to **enact**, **constitute** and **frame** such just and equal Laws, **Ordinances**, **Acts**, Constitutions and Offices from time to time, as shall be thought most meet and convenient for the general good of the Colony, unto which we promise all due submission and obedience.

–from the Mayflower Compact, November 11, 1620

enact, *v.*, to make a law
constitute, *v.*, to create
frame, *v.*, to produce
ordinances, *n.*, laws made by a government
acts, *n.*, laws made by a group

Fun Fact

The original copy of the Mayflower Compact has been lost. William Bradford and Edward Winslow included the text in *Mourt's Relation*, which they wrote in 1622 about the Plymouth settlement.

William Bradford

Close Reading

1. **Identify** and circle in the Mayflower Compact text what the signers promise to do.

2. **Describe** the importance of the Mayflower Compact.

_____

_____

_____

_____

Wrap It Up

Why was it important for colonists in North America to work together and to have rules about governing themselves? Support your answer with information from the chapter. Use one quotation from the Mayflower Compact.

_____

_____

_____

_____

_____

_____

_____

_____

The French and Dutch in North America

INTERACTIVITY

Participate in a class discussion to preview the content of this lesson.

Vocabulary

Northwest Passage
monopoly
royal province

Academic Vocabulary

eventually
relationship

European explorers searched for a northern route from North America to Asia by sailing through the icy waters of Baffin Bay.

Unlock The BIG Question

I will know the key events surrounding the establishment of French and Dutch colonies in North America.

Jumpstart Activity

Look at a globe or world map. Locate France and the Netherlands. Find the shortest route to travel by ship west across the Atlantic Ocean to the Pacific Ocean. Explain how you chose the route and what problems that route might have.

France and the Netherlands first sent explorers to North America to find the **Northwest Passage**. They were searching for a westward sea route across the Atlantic Ocean to the Pacific Ocean. Sailing above North America would be quicker than traveling around South America. They hoped to find a faster trade route from Europe to Asia. Explorers from many European countries tried for hundreds of years to find a Northwest Passage. Although these explorers failed, some realized the value of North America's natural resources.

INTERACTIVITY

Explore the key ideas of this lesson.

The French Explore North America

Giovanni da Verrazano (jaw VAHN nee dah ver uh ZAH noh) was Italian, but he explored North America for France. In 1524, he sailed along the coastline from what are now North and South Carolina up to Nova Scotia in Canada. He claimed this region for the French king, Francis I. Verrazano's brother made a map of the area and called it New France.

Ten years later, Jacques Cartier (zhahk kar tee AY) went to the northern part of New France in what is today Canada. His task was to search for gold, spices, and the Northwest Passage. Iroquois Indians in the area told Cartier that he would find gold, silver, and spices if he traveled west. Cartier and his crew explored the Canadian coast. They then sailed west up the Saint Lawrence River as far as the area that is now the city of Quebec. The French explorer had to turn back there, however. He had angered the Iroquois, and the winter was too cold.

1. ☑ Reading Check **Analyze** the image. **Explain** why explorers had difficulty in finding the Northwest Passage.

_____

_____

_____

_____

_____

In 1541, France decided to establish a colony in New France. Rival Spain was already claiming land in North America. Cartier traveled with a group of French colonists and again reached the Quebec area. The colonists built a settlement there. Cartier thought he had found gold and silver and returned to France. His find, however, turned out to be worthless rocks.

Although the first French colony **eventually** failed, the fur trade with the North American Indians began. Beaver and other kinds of fur were greatly prized in Europe. Fur hats were a very popular style in Europe at this time. Some companies in France held a **monopoly** on the North American fur. They were the only companies that had permission to trade with the Indians for the furs. The fur trade was not a free-market system in New France, as the tobacco trade was in Jamestown, for example.

Samuel de Champlain (sham PLAYN) worked for some of these companies. In 1608, Champlain traveled to New France. He helped establish a trading post called Port Royal. Champlain also worked hard to gain the trust of the Huron Indians he traded with. Because of the success of the fur trade, this became the first successful French settlement in North America. Then, Champlain established a fort and named it Quebec.

2. ☑ **Reading Check**
Work with a partner to complete the chart. Decide who will be Cartier and who will be Champlain. **Summarize** the information in the chart to help you act out the role of each man.

Jacques Cartier	Samuel de Champlain
explored for French king	worked for French fur trading companies
established a colony that failed	
	remained in New France

Wars and Settlement in New France

The colony of New France grew slowly. War between France and England began in 1627 and discouraged more settlers from moving there. War between the Iroquois Indians and the French and their American Indian trading partners also discouraged settlement. The Iroquois Indians had acquired firearms through trade with Europeans along the Hudson River. They fought with France and their Huron Indian fur trade partner to the north for control of the fur trade in New France. After a major attack on the Hurons by the Iroquois in 1648, the Hurons moved to land further north. As Iroquois territory expanded, other woodland Indian groups were pushed west. The Lakota (Sioux) moved across the Mississippi onto the Great Plains.

By the 1660s, just a few thousand French people lived in New France. Some French settlers built farms and villages, and raised families. Others roamed the land trading for furs. Missionaries arrived to try to convert American Indians to Christianity.

In 1663, the French king, Louis XIV, took control of the colony. He made New France a **royal province**. The king selected a governor of the colony who followed the king's commands. Unlike the self-governing systems in the British colonies, New France, as well as New Spain, were ruled more strictly by monarchs in Europe. The settlers in these colonies did not have a voice in the government. Louis XIV sent soldiers to New France to fight the Iroquois. After peace was made with the Iroquois, more settlers began moving to New France.

The French continued to explore North America. Robert de La Salle claimed the Mississippi River and its valley for France in 1682. He named the area Louisiana after Louis XIV. La Salle returned two years later to set up a French colony at the mouth of the Mississippi River. This location would allow French ships to attack Spanish ships sailing to and from Mexico. It could also stop the English from moving into the area. Finally, furs could be shipped down the river from the north. Unfortunately, La Salle and his boat, *La Belle,* sailed past the Mississippi River and was shipwrecked off the coast of what is now Texas.

Word Wise

Homonyms The word *roam* means to travel over a large area without a definite direction. It is a homophone of the word Rome, the city in Italy. Homophones are words that sound the same but have different meanings and spellings.

La Salle's shipwrecked boat, *La Belle*, is being reassembled following its discovery on the seafloor of the Gulf of Mexico in 1995.

The Dutch Arrive in North America

Henry Hudson was English, but he explored for the Dutch East India Company in the Netherlands. He had hoped to find a Northeast Passage, a shortcut by water from Europe to Asia. The Dutch East India Company hired Hudson to search north of Scandinavia and Russia. A storm kept Hudson from traveling east, so he decided to sail west to look for the Northwest Passage.

Sailing along the North American coast in 1609, Hudson found a promising path. A great river entered the Atlantic Ocean. Hudson sailed his ship, the *Half Moon*, up the river. After about 150 miles, the river became too shallow to navigate. This river is now called the Hudson River. Hudson claimed the river and its valley for the Netherlands.

The Dutch government gave the West Indian Company the right to manage the territory. The company also received a monopoly on the rich fur trade there. In 1634, thirty Dutch families arrived in the colony of New Netherlands.

3. ☑ **Reading Check**
Identify and circle one settlement or colony of each European power. **Discuss** with a partner each location in relation to the other settlements.

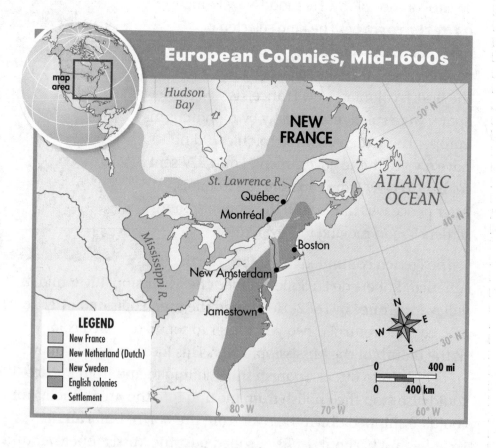

European Colonies, Mid-1600s

map area

Hudson Bay

NEW FRANCE

St. Lawrence R.

Québec

Montréal

Boston

New Amsterdam

Jamestown

Mississippi R.

ATLANTIC OCEAN

50° N

40° N

30° N

80° W   70° W   60° W

LEGEND
- New France
- New Netherland (Dutch)
- New Sweden
- English colonies
- • Settlement

N E W S

| 0 | 400 mi |
| 0 | 400 km |

New Amsterdam had a canal that led to a harbor where ships could dock.

The Growth of New Netherlands

The Dutch West India Company built a trading post at the south end of what is now Manhattan. The settlement of New Amsterdam quickly grew up around it. The shareholders of the company hoped they would get rich. New Netherlands traded in furs, timber, and tobacco. The colony also participated in the trade of enslaved Africans.

The population of New Netherlands grew steadily and was diverse. The Dutch West India Company encouraged the arrival of settlers from all over Europe, including Germany, Sweden, Denmark, and elsewhere. New Netherlands was home to a small number of Jews, or people who practiced the Jewish religion.

Peter Stuyvesant (STY vuh sahnt) was governor of New Netherlands from 1647 to 1664. During this time, the colony grew in wealth and its population increased. Settlers in the southern part of the colony wanted to take over land from the Indians living there. In the north, the settlers relied on the Indians to supply furs for trade. They worked hard to build good relationships with the Indian groups. During this period and in the 1700s, many white fur traders married American Indian women. This helped improve trade partnerships.

New Sweden

Academic Vocabulary

relationship • *n.*, way in which people or things are connected

4. ☑ **Reading Check**
Draw Inferences Analyze the drawing. What can you infer about the relationships between the Algonquin people and the Swedish colonists? Label the illustration with your ideas.

One nearby colony that Peter Stuyvesant worried about was New Sweden. In 1637, a group of Dutch, German, and Swedish investors formed the New Sweden Company. Sweden wanted to profit from the rich tobacco and fur trade in North America.

The company hired Peter Minuit to find land in North America that had not yet been claimed. He found available land between the English colony in Virginia and the Dutch colony in New Amsterdam.

Minuit and the Swedish settlers arrived in 1638. Minuit bought the land from the local Algonquin Indians, who were settled on large farms. The **relationship** between the two neighbors was peaceful. The colonists built a settlement and named it Fort Christina after the Swedish queen. Soon farms and other small settlements grew up.

In 1655, Peter Stuyvesant attacked New Sweden and the Dutch captured the colony. Stuyvesant allowed New Sweden to remain a "Swedish Nation." Despite the capture, the colonists could choose their own government, hold on to their land, and continue to trade with the local Indian groups.

Changes Ahead

Throughout the 1600s, France and England continued to fight over territory in New France and New England. England would take land in New France, and France would push into the New England colonies.

Wars in Europe also affected the colonies. For instance, war broke out between England and the Netherlands. England won the war. As a result, the Netherlands was forced to give up its rich colony in North America.

INTERACTIVITY

Check your understanding of the key ideas of this lesson.

✓ Lesson 4 Check

5. **Compare and Contrast** How were New France and New Netherlands similar? How were the two colonies different? Complete the graphic organizer.

New France and New Netherlands

Alike	Different
_____	_____
_____	_____
_____	_____

6. **Describe** the relationship between the American Indian groups and the European settlers in the New Sweden colony.

_____

_____

_____

7. **Explain** the role of explorers in founding European colonies. Focus on one explorer or one colony.

_____

_____

_____

Distinguish Fact From Opinion

How can you tell the difference between a fact from an opinion when you are reading? A **fact** is a statement that can be proved true or false. An **opinion** is someone's belief. It cannot be proved true or false.

Being able to distinguish between fact and opinion allows you to judge a text. Is the writer using facts to inform readers? Is the writer using feelings and beliefs to persuade readers? Read the paragraph. The words that can help you distinguish facts from opinions have been underlined.

> **VIDEO**
>
> Watch a video about distinguishing fact from opinion.

The year was 1609, and two famous explorers in North America almost met each other. It is too bad that Henry Hudson and Samuel de Champlain never got that chance. Hudson was English, but he was exploring North America for the Netherlands. Champlain was seeking land for his home country of France. Hudson and Champlain probably had a lot in common. Both men were explorers, so they had to be brave, smart, and adventurous. Where did they almost meet? While Hudson was sailing up the river now named for him, Champlain was exploring about 100 miles away.

My explorations in North America led to a successful fur trade between France and the Huron Indians at Quebec.

Champlain

But I am the greatest explorer, for I found what became New York City!

Hudson

Use the graphic organizer on the facing page to distinguish between the facts and opinions in this paragraph.

Your Turn!

1. What facts appear in the paragraph? What opinions does the writer express? Fill in the organizer to distinguish between the facts and opinions in the journal entry.

Facts Versus Opinions

Facts	Opinions

2. Champlain helped start the French settlement at Quebec by gaining the trust of the Huron Indians. Write a short paragraph explaining how you think Champlain worked successfully with the Huron Indians. Use both facts from your reading and your own opinion to describe the peace.

Quality:
Leadership

Tisquantum (about 1580–1622)
A Bridge Between Peoples

Tisquantum (ti SKWON tum) (also known as Squanto) was a Pawtuxet Indian. He lived in what is now Massachusetts and Rhode Island. Because of Tisquantum, the Pilgrims at Plymouth Colony were able to solve important problems. He taught the Pilgrims how to plant crops. Tisquantum also helped the Pilgrims negotiate trade deals and peace treaties with Indian groups.

Tisquantum had to learn how to solve problems at a young age. He was kidnapped by one of Captain John Smith's men and taken to Spain. Before he could be sold as a slave, Tisquantum escaped to England. There, he learned to speak English.

On his return to North America, Tisquantum discovered that all his people had died. Illness had spread from the English colonists and killed them. Tisquantum went to live with the nearby Wampanoag Indians. Massasoit (MA suh soit), leader of the Wampanoag, wanted to make peace with the Pilgrims so they could help protect the Wampanoag against other Indian groups. Massasoit sent him to talk to the Pilgrims at Plymouth. Tisquantum helped create a treaty of peace between the two groups, He then stayed to help the Pilgrims.

Find Out More

1. What problems did Tisquantum help solve at Plymouth colony? How did Tisquantum solve these problems?

_____

_____

_____

_____

2. Determine a problem in your community and find out who can help you solve the problem. Then research what needs to be done to solve the problem. Report your findings to the class and suggest how you can take action.

Use these graphics to review some of the key terms, people, and ideas from this chapter.

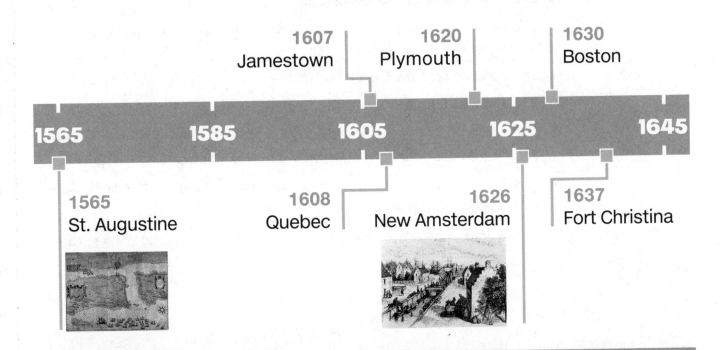

| 1607 Jamestown | 1620 Plymouth | 1630 Boston |

1565 | **1585** | **1605** | **1625** | **1645**

| 1565 St. Augustine | 1608 Quebec | 1626 New Amsterdam | 1637 Fort Christina |

European Colonies in North America

Settlement	Date	Country
St. Augustine	1565	Spain
Jamestown	1607	England
Quebec	1608	France
Plymouth	1620	England
New Amsterdam	1626	Netherlands
Boston	1630	England
Fort Christina	1637	Sweden

GAME

Play the vocabulary game.

Vocabulary and Key Ideas

1. Complete the sentences below. Choose from these words: missionaries, Puritan, monopoly, *encomienda* system.

   (A) The Company of New France had a _____, so no one else could buy and sell furs.

   (B) The _____ meant that Spanish settlers could take Indians' lands and make them work for free.

   (C) _____ governed and tried to convert American Indians to Catholicism in New Spain.

   (D) John Winthrop was a _____ because he wanted to change the Church of England.

2. **Define** What is a **royal province**? _____

   _____

3. **Explain** What is an **indentured servant**? _____

   _____

   _____

4. **Interpreting a Line Graph**
   Analyze the line graph. What happened to the price of tobacco in the Virginia colony from 1720 to 1740?

   _____

   _____

   Describe on a separate piece of paper how the price of tobacco in the Virginia colony changed from 1700 to 1760.

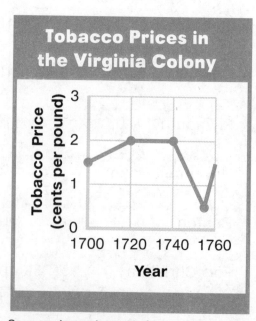

Tobacco Prices in the Virginia Colony

Source: Jamestown-Yorktown Foundation

Critical Thinking and Writing

5. **Analyze** How did competition among European countries affect the settlement of North America?

_____

_____

_____

6. **Identifying Points of View** How did the Separatists feel about the Church of England? How did the Puritans point of view about the Church of England differ from the Separatists?

_____

_____

_____

7. **Apply** Why was the formation of the House of Burgesses important? How does its formation affect American life today?

_____

_____

_____

8. **Revisit the Big Question** Why did people in Europe leave their homelands?

_____

_____

_____

_____

9. **Writing Workshop Informative Text** On a separate sheet of paper, write two short paragraphs about the cooperation between the Wampanoag Indians and the Pilgrims at Plymouth.

Analyze Primary Sources

Vines here are in suche abundance [large quantity], as where soever a man treads [walks], they are ready to embrace [cling to] his foote. I have tasted here of a great black grape as big as a Damascin [different type of grape], that hath a true Muscatell-taste; the vine whereof now spending itselfe to the topps of high trees, if it were reduced into a vineyard, and there domesticated, would yield incomparable [excellent] fruite.   —John Pory, letter dated September 30, 1619, to Sir Dudley Carleton

10. John Pory worked for the Virginia Company. He wrote this letter about how the Jamestown colony was doing. What is Pory describing? Why do you think Pory included this description in his letter? Explain whether this letter would encourage or discourage the Virginia Company shareholders.

_____

_____

_____

_____

_____

Distinguish Fact From Opinion

11. Suppose you were going to write historical fiction, or a story based on history, about the relationship between American Indians and Spanish missionaries in New Spain or Florida. What facts would you include? How would you show the opinions of the characters? How would you make sure that your readers were able to tell the difference between facts and fiction?

_____

_____

_____

_____

Quest Findings

Write Your Journal or Blog Entry

Now you're ready to write your own journal or blog entry about one of the events you read about in this chapter. Remember that the goal of your entry is to show readers who was involved, what happened, and why. Include facts and give details about your character and the setting. Follow these steps.

INTERACTIVITY

Use this activity to help you write your journal or blog entry.

1 Prepare to Write

Record the facts about the people and event you want to include. Make notes about where your character lives and how he or she will respond to the event. Use these notes to help you write your entry.

2 Write a Draft

Use your notes and the evidence from your Quest Connections to write the most descriptive, yet factual, entry that you can. Make sure your entry answers the following questions:

- Who is the character? Who is writing the entry?
- Where is the character?
- What is happening?
- Why is it happening?
- What does the character think and feel about the event?

3 Share With a Partner

Exchange your draft journal entry or blog with a partner. Tell your partner what you like about the journal entry or blog and what could use improvement. Be polite when you provide suggestions.

4 Revise

Make changes to your journal entry or blog after meeting with your partner. Correct any grammatical or spelling errors.

Chapter
4 Life in the Colonies

GO ONLINE FOR
DIGITAL RESOURCES

▶ VIDEO

👆 INTERACTIVITY

🔊 AUDIO

🎮 GAMES

☑ ASSESSMENT

📖 eTEXT

The BIG Question

What does it take to build a new society?

▶ VIDEO

Jumpstart Activity

👆 INTERACTIVITY

Imagine you are going on a long trip. What would you need for your journey to help you survive? Think of three items that you need. Write your items on the lines. Then take turns coming to the board to write them to share with others.

Building a Life in the Colonies

Preview the chapter **vocabulary** as you sing the rap:

The **climate** was important when a region was chosen

What good is a farm if the ground is always frozen?

The weather patterns in a place over a lengthy duration

Is the climate that if not ideal can cause devastation.

A **proprietor** was someone who owns land,

And farmed it to grow food to sell and meet the demand.

And, when someone didn't have something they wanted they would **barter**,

Which is when someone is trading one good for another.

In order to succeed without financial support,

The new colonies would need products for them to **export**.

Exports are goods they'd sell to other countries they knew

Creating more stability as their economy grew.

Life in the Colonies

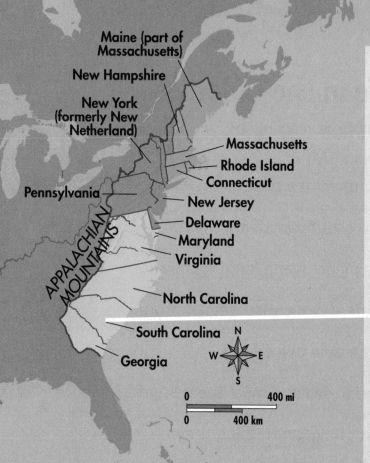

Maine (part of Massachusetts)

New Hampshire

New York (formerly New Netherland)

Massachusetts

Rhode Island

Connecticut

Pennsylvania

New Jersey

Delaware

Maryland

Virginia

APPALACHIAN MOUNTAINS

North Carolina

South Carolina

Georgia

N
W   E
S

0   400 mi
0   400 km

Where were the 13 English colonies established?

The 13 colonies were founded along the coast of the Atlantic Ocean. Describe where South Carolina is located.

TODAY
You can visit Magnolia Plantation, the most widely visited plantation in South Carolina.

What happened and When?

Read the timeline to find out about colonial America.

1600

1650

1636
Roger Williams founds Rhode Island.

1637
The Pequot War and King Philip's War break out.

1664
England takes over New Amsterdam and establishes New York.

Who will you meet?

Roger Williams
A church leader who believed in freedom of religion

Anne Hutchinson
She offended Puritan leaders by disagreeing about religious matters

William Penn
A Quaker, he believed in each person's right to practice his or her religion

Metacom
A Wampanoag leader who led a war against New England colonists

 INTERACTIVITY

Complete the interactive map to learn more about the 13 British colonies.

1700

1750

1682
William Penn founds Pennsylvania.

1733
Georgia becomes the thirteenth colony.

1754
The French and Indian War begins.

TODAY
You can visit the French and Indian War Museum in Fort Ligonier, Pennsylvania.

Quest

Project-Based Learning

You're Home!

Each of the 13 colonies are unique. Choosing which one to live in is a tough decision.

You think your colony is the best! You want to convince people to move there. What makes your colony better than others?

One way you can reach many people is through the use of media. An infomercial is one way to present your information. An infomercial is like a commercial. It tries to convince viewers to feel or think in a certain way.

Quest Kick Off

Your mission is to take the role of children who live in one of the 13 colonies and make an infomercial convincing others to move to your colony . . . because it's the best!

1 Ask Questions

Why is your colony the best one? What is the geography like in your assigned area? How do people earn money? Write two questions of your own.

....

....

2 Research to Learn More

Follow your teacher's instructions to learn more about the colonies so that you can write an effective infomercial. Write some of your thoughts below.

INTERACTIVITY

Go online to learn more about the colonies so you can write your infomercial.

3 Look for *Quest* Connections

Turn to the next page to begin looking for Quest Connections that will help you create your infomercial.

4 *Quest* Findings
Create an Infomercial

Use the Quest Findings page at the end of the chapter to help you create your infomercial.

New England, Middle, and Southern Colonies

INTERACTIVITY

Participate in a class discussion to preview the content of this lesson.

Unlock **The BIG Question**

I will know the role of geography in the settling and development of the English colonies.

Vocabulary

region
proprietor
diverse

Academic Vocabulary

interact
coordinate

JumpStart Activity

Look around the room. Think about which desk you would like to sit in. When your teacher says "go," switch desks. Why did you choose the desk you switched to? Think about what made immigrants want to live in one place over another place.

Colonists settled in New England's coastal region because its seaports supported the fishing and shipping industries.

The geography of North America greatly affected the early colonists. Settlers in Jamestown were swarmed by mosquitoes from nearby swamps. The Pilgrims suffered through harsh and cruel winters. The Dutch in New Amsterdam used their location to become a center for trade. Geography shaped where colonists settled and how they made a living.

INTERACTIVITY

Explore the key ideas of this lesson.

Geographic Regions of the Colonies

Throughout the 1600s, English settlers came to North America. The colonies stretched along the Atlantic coast from present-day Maine to what is now Georgia. The colonies can be divided into three different regions. A **region** is an area that shares physical or human characteristics. The original 13 colonies were divided into the New England, Mid-Atlantic, and Southern regions.

By the 1730s, there were 13 English colonies covering a narrow strip between the coast and the Appalachian Mountains.

The geography of this region in the present is much like it was in the past. In New England, the soil was thin and so it could only support small farms. Merchants traded goods with England and other colonies. The dense forests in certain regions allowed other colonists to cut timber. Colonists built ships, fished, and hunted whales on the coast.

The English Colonies

0   200 mi
0   200 km

map area

N W E S

Maine (part of Massachusetts)

New York (formerly New Netherland)

New Hampshire

Massachusetts

Rhode Island
Connecticut

Pennsylvania

New Jersey

40° N

Delaware
Maryland

APPALACHIAN MOUNTAINS

Virginia

ATLANTIC OCEAN

North Carolina

35° N

South Carolina

Georgia

80° W   75° W

LEGEND
New England Colonies
Middle Colonies
Southern Colonies

In New England, the summers were warm, but winters were long and cold. The growing season was only about five months long.

The Middle Colonies had rich soil and a warmer climate. Climate is the pattern of weather in a place over a long period of time. This made the region good for growing wheat. There was more sun and lots of rain. Colonists used riverboats on long, wide rivers to ship products. Colonists also hunted deer and beaver for food and fur.

The best climate and land for farming was in the Southern Colonies. In the Southern Colonies, the climate was warm all year long. The soil was rich and the growing season lasted for seven or eight months. In the rich soil along the coastline, farmers planted cash crops, or crops they could sell, such as tobacco and rice. Large farms, called plantations thrived there.

Bodies of water were present in all three regions. Rivers and the coast were vital for travel and trade. Most settlements were built along rivers and the coast. Seaport cities grew in New England and the Middle Colonies.

While the land shaped how the settlements grew, the settlers also changed the land. They cleared trees to make way for farms and harvested the timber to sell. Growing crops every year changed the soil. To make transportation easier, settlers built roads and bridges.

1. ☑ **Reading Check**
Compare Complete the chart with information about the characteristics of each of the colonies.

Geographic Features of the Colonies

New England Colony	Middle Colony	Southern Colony

The New England Colonies

The Puritans set up towns and farms in New England on land that looked empty to them. This was not true, however, as local American Indians did not use fences to separate land and did not use land the same way English people did. Such differences sometimes led to conflict.

New England towns had a meetinghouse. These structures were usually the largest buildings in the town. Government decisions and actions were decided at town meetings. However, only church-going men who owned property could vote at these meetings.

Although the Puritans came to Massachusetts to practice their religion freely, they did not believe in freedom of religion. Puritan leaders punished any type of dissent, or disagreement, from colonists and also brought charges against suspected witches. They did not believe that women were equal to men or should challenge men in any way. Roger Williams, a church leader, disagreed with some of these ideas. He argued that community leaders did not have the right to require everyone to worship in exactly the same way.

Puritan leaders were afraid that Williams's ideas were "new and dangerous." So, in 1636, he was put on trial and forced to leave the colony. He then started a new settlement that he called Providence, in which settlers were free to practice religion in their own way. This was the beginning of the colony of Rhode Island.

In each New England town, houses were clustered around a common area as shown in this photograph of Plimouth Plantation.

Quest Connection

As a colonist in one of the New England colonies, you need to get to the meetinghouse for a government meeting. How is your town laid out? Is it easy to get to the meetinghouse?

 INTERACTIVITY

Learn more about how New England towns are organized by going online.

Anne Hutchinson was another Puritan dissenter. She moved from England to the Massachusetts Bay Colony in 1634. Hutchinson spoke with other women about her religious beliefs. She felt that church leaders held too much power, and that having a personal relationship with God was more important than following church rules. Many people in Boston agreed with her. One person did not. That was John Winthrop. No one was allowed to question Puritan beliefs—especially not a woman. Women were to obey their husbands and fathers. Like Roger Williams, Hutchinson was put on trial for her beliefs and was banished from Massachusetts. In 1638, she and some of her followers went to Rhode Island to spread her teachings.

Thomas Hooker was a Puritan minister. He, like Williams and Hutchinson, wanted more political freedom. He felt that all men should be allowed to vote, not just church members or property owners. His ideas led him to leave Massachusetts in 1636 to start a colony that would become Connecticut.

2. ☑ **Reading Check** **Main Idea and Details** Fill in the missing details to describe what happened to Hutchinson and Hooker.

Dissent in the Puritan Colonies

Main Idea

_____

_____

_____

Supporting Detail

Williams was banished for having different ideas.

Supporting Detail

_____

_____

_____

Supporting Detail

_____

_____

_____

The Middle Colonies

The Dutch founded New Netherland in the 1620s. It soon became a thriving trade center where people **interacted**. In the 1630s, the Middle Colonies included a Swedish settlement in the New Jersey area.

After England's new king, Charles II, came to power, a fleet was sent to capture New Netherland. Governor Peter Stuyvesant surrendered to the English when the colonists refused to fight. Later, the Dutch tried to take back the colony with no success. By 1674, England was in control of the colony.

King Charles II gave the colony to his brother, the Duke of York, who renamed it New York. The Duke of York gave some land to two friends, and this land became the colony of New Jersey. The Duke of York and his two friends were known as proprietors (pruh PRYE uh turz). A **proprietor** is someone who owns land or property. Because New York and New Jersey were owned by individuals, they were called proprietary colonies.

New York and New Jersey had **diverse** populations. That is, there were people from many different countries and backgrounds living there. These people belonged to many different religious groups, too.

The colony of Pennsylvania was founded on religious freedom. The king of England gave the land that became the colony of Pennsylvania to William Penn. A Quaker, Penn founded the colony in 1681. Quakers were against war, said people could pray in their own way, and that women could be preachers. Many people disagreed with these beliefs. Quakers thought that all people had an "inner light" and women could be church leaders. Penn also believed in the rights of American Indians and paying them a fair price for their land.

Academic Vocabulary

interact • *v.*, to talk or work with one another

A colonial home in Philadelphia

3. ☑ **Reading Check** **Use Evidence From Text** When and how were the colonies of New Jersey and Pennsylvania created?

_____

_____

The Southern Colonies

In the South, the Virginia Company controlled the colony of Virginia. In 1624, King James I of England took control of the colony. He chose a leader to govern the colony, making Virginia a royal colony. Yet this brought little change as the governing body, the House of Burgesses, continued to meet.

One big change did occur in the Southern Colonies in 1632. When Charles I became England's new king, he gave part of Virginia to Lord Baltimore, one of his followers. This new colony was named Maryland. Lord Baltimore belonged to the Catholic Church. Maryland welcomed Catholics, who were not always accepted in other colonies.

Carolina began as a proprietary colony. In 1663, King Charles II gave the land to eight of his supporters. The colony was split in 1712 and became North Carolina and, later, in 1729 South Carolina became a royal colony. Rich soil made the land good for growing crops. In South Carolina, plantations grew valuable crops, especially rice. They relied on enslaved Africans to farm and act as servants. Charleston, with its fine harbor, became a key trading center.

Georgia was founded in 1732. King George II allowed James Oglethorpe to start a colony there for English people who had been sent to jail for debt, which meant they owed money.

When he arrived in Georgia, Oglethorpe immediately started a friendship with the Yamacraw chief, Tomochichi (toh moh chee CHEE). Oglethorpe **coordinated** good relations between colonists and the Yamacraw for many years. It also served a key military role, standing between Spain's Florida colony and the other English colonies.

Academic Vocabulary

coordinate • *v.*, to make sure two or more groups can work well together

4. ☑ Reading Check **Compare and contrast** the colonies of Virginia, Maryland, North Carolina, and South Carolina.

_____

_____

_____

Large plantations in the South relied on enslaved Africans to farm and act as servants.

INTERACTIVITY

Check your understanding of the key ideas of this lesson.

✅ Lesson 1 Check

5. **Define** region.

_____

_____

6. **Explain** how early colonial government worked in the Middle Colonies.

_____

_____

7. **Understand the** *Quest* Connections Based on the text, in what ways did the geography of each colony differ? How did geography influence settlement?

_____

_____

_____

_____

Main Idea and Details

The **main idea** of a written passage is its most important idea. **Details** are the pieces of information that help the writer support, or explain, the main idea.

You can analyze information more easily by finding the main idea. To find the main idea in a paragraph, ask, "What idea do most sentences in the paragraph describe?" To find the details, ask, "Which sentences give information about the most important idea?

You can often find the main idea in the first or last sentences of a paragraph. A main idea may also be implied, or not stated for the reader in the text. If this happens, ask yourself, "What are the details in this paragraph about?

Read the following paragraph about Benjamin Franklin. The main idea has been highlighted in the paragraph. The details that support the main idea have been underlined.

VIDEO

Watch a video about main ideas and details.

Benjamin Franklin was a remarkable man with a wide range of talents. As a printer and writer, he helped to shape the ideas of American colonists. As a scientist and inventor, he conducted important experiments and created useful tools, such as bifocals and the Franklin stove. As a civic leader, he set up America's first public library and fire department.

Use the graphic organizer on the facing page to list the main ideas and details from a paragraph in the lesson.

Bifocals

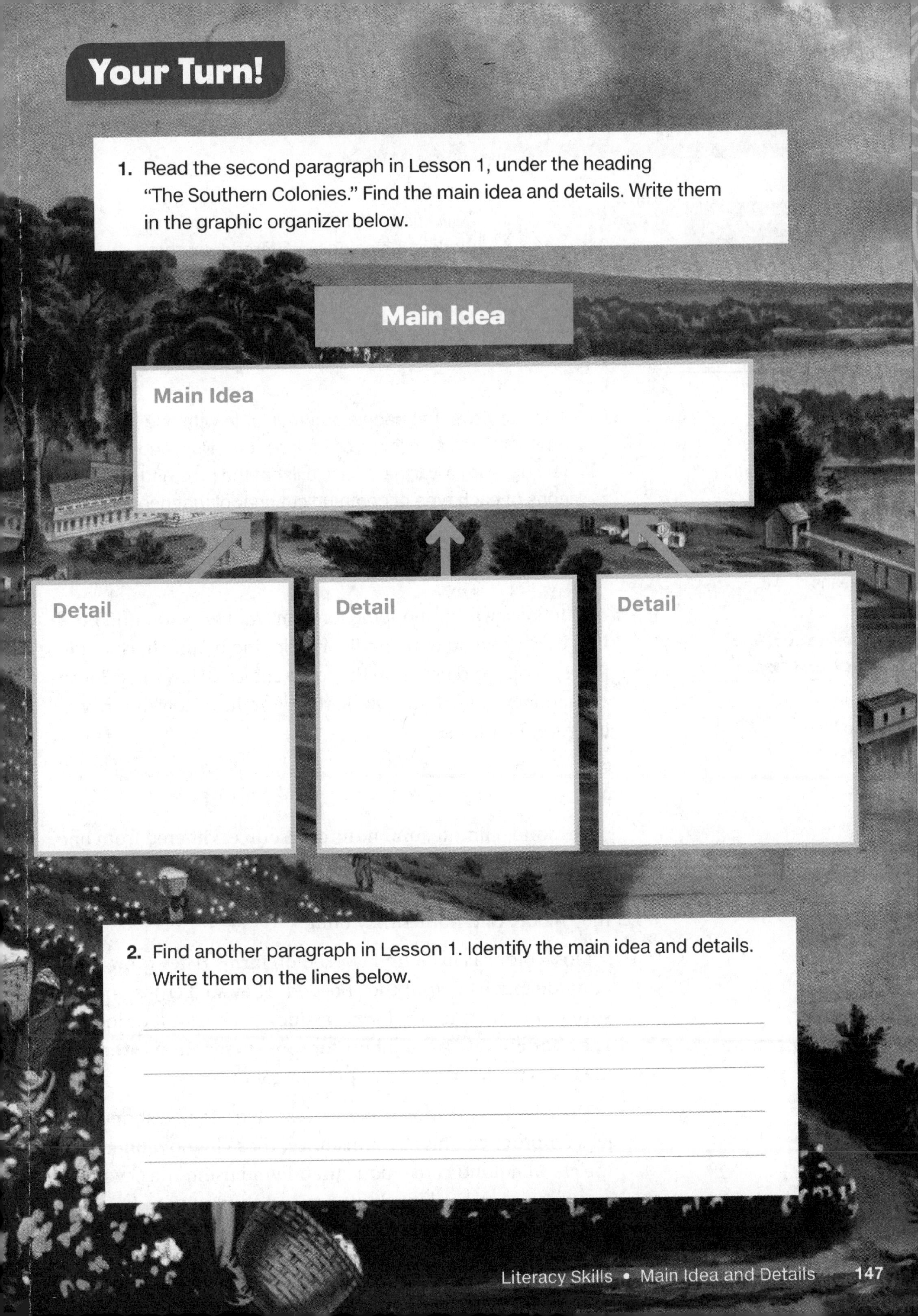

Your Turn!

1. Read the second paragraph in Lesson 1, under the heading "The Southern Colonies." Find the main idea and details. Write them in the graphic organizer below.

Main Idea

Main Idea

Detail

Detail

Detail

2. Find another paragraph in Lesson 1. Identify the main idea and details. Write them on the lines below.

Lesson 2 Daily Life in the Colonies

INTERACTIVITY

Participate in a class discussion to preview the content of this lesson.

Vocabulary

barter
export
import
raw materials
mercantilism
triangular trade
classes
artisans

Academic Vocabulary

insert
display

Unlock The BIG Question

I will know how the patterns of life and work in the colonies differed from the patterns today.

Jumpstart Activity

Think of ways that people communicate with one another, such as using a cell phone, e-mailing and texting. With a partner, make a list of the pros and cons of each type of communication tool that people use today.

In today's world, shopping for items that we want and need is as easy as going to the mall or shopping online. In colonial times, people did not have the same choices. How did colonists earn money to feed and clothe their families? How did they improve their lives?

Resources of the Early Colonies

The land, climate, and natural resources differed from one colony to another, which made living in each one unique. The environment affected the food colonists ate, clothing they made, and homes they built.

Most colonists lived and worked on farms. They grew or made much of what they needed. They sold crops and various products to pay for necessities, such as salt or tools. They bartered with neighbors for some items. To **barter** means to trade one good or product for another.

The colony's location, land, or resources helped shaped jobs for other colonists. For instance, those living along the New England coast made their living using the ocean's resources, such as whale hunting, and shipbuilding.

The Middle Colonies' sheltered harbors and deep rivers, made traveling and trading easier. Because of this, some cities became thriving ports. Many colonists in cities such as New York and Philadelphia worked as merchants and traders. Others worked as sailors or dockworkers, or people who loaded and unloaded cargo from ships.

People changed the land to suit their needs. For example, some colonists built dams blocking rivers and streams to create power from the rushing water. Millers often set up their businesses next to a river or stream. They used the water power for their gristmills. Gristmills were machines used for grinding wheat into flour. Millers would **insert** the wheat or corn between two stones. As the power from the moving water crushed the wheat or corn, it would produce a fine grain.

INTERACTIVITY

Explore the key ideas of this lesson.

Academic Vocabulary

insert • *v.*, to put inside

Gristmills used flowing water on a water wheel, so the moving wheel would turn the grinding stones inside the mill.

Products of the 13 Colonies

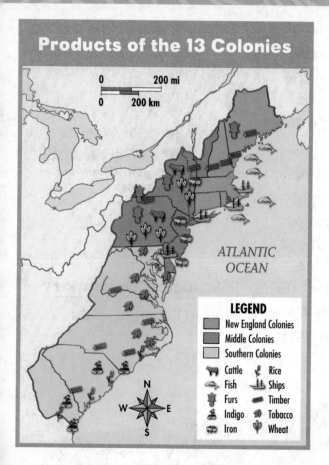

0 ——— 200 mi
0 ——— 200 km

ATLANTIC OCEAN

LEGEND
New England Colonies
Middle Colonies
Southern Colonies

Cattle   Rice
Fish   Ships
Furs   Timber
Indigo   Tobacco
Iron   Wheat

N W E S

Colonists had to work long, hard days to make and provide all of the things that they needed to live. They did not have much time for luxury items that were not valuable to their everyday lives.

Benjamin Franklin, a printer and writer who lived in the 1700s, wrote of a time when he was young and made the mistake of buying an unnecessary item (a whistle) that did not benefit the rest of his family. In "The Whistle," he explained, "In short, I conceive [think] that great part of the miseries [unhappiness] of mankind are brought upon them by false estimates they have made of the value of things, and by their giving too much for their whistles."

1. ☑ **Reading Check** **Identify** Circle the industry that was found in every region. Then place a checkmark next to those industries found in more than one region.

Trade Routes and the Location of the Colonies

American colonists traded goods with other colonists. The colonies also traded with other countries, selling exports and buying imports. An **export** is a product sold to another country. An **import** is a product bought from another country. The colonies provided England with **raw materials**, or resources that can be made into other products. The English sold manufactured goods, such as furniture and pottery, to the colonies, which merchants **displayed** for sale to customers.

Academic Vocabulary

display • v., to show

To control trade and protect its industries, England passed laws limiting trade between its colonies and other countries. This practice is known as protectionism. As a result, colonists had to rely on England for many necessities. These restrictions made many colonists angry. They felt that England was treating the colonies unfairly to increase England's profits from trade.

The trade laws that England created were largely based on the system of **mercantilism**. This was an economic idea popular in the 1600s and 1700s, which suggested that governments should limit imports but increase manufacturing and exports. A country would earn more money from products it sold to other countries than it spent buying products from other countries.

Over time colonial trade developed into a pattern known as **triangular trade**. It was called *triangular* because it had three stages that roughly formed the shape of a triangle when viewed on a map. The locations of these areas were significant. They were located on coasts and on major trade routes. Trade began in Europe. Goods such as metals and cloth were loaded onto ships. These ships sailed to the West African coast. There the goods were exchanged for slaves. The enslaved people were then brought to the Americas where they were sold. The cycle then started again.

2. ☑ **Reading Check**
Describe Trace the route on the map with your finger. Then discuss with a partner who benefited most and least from this trade. How did the location of each trading partner affect it?

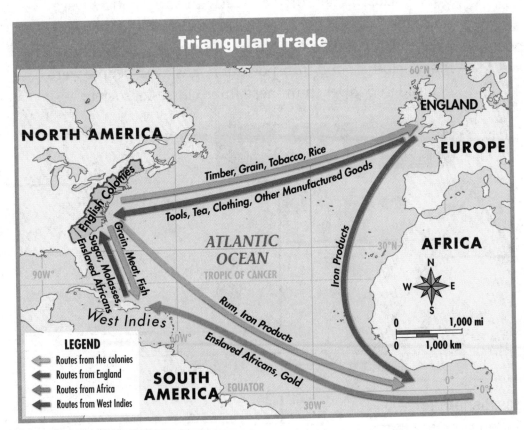

Triangular trade routes linked the colonies with Europe, Africa, the West Indies, and North America.

Classes of Society

Europeans in colonial society belonged to certain **classes**, or society groups, based on their wealth or importance. The gentry were the highest class in colonial society. They were large landowners, wealthy merchants, and bankers. The men in this class felt it was their right to control others, so they usually served in the government. Church leaders were also in the highest class.

The middle class had the largest number of colonists. These men and women worked in trades such as blacksmithing, silversmithing, and printing. They also worked as lawyers, doctors, or merchants who owned small stores. Most middle-class men were able to vote.

Regular workers and servants made up the lower class. This group did not own property or businesses. Members of the lower class were not allowed to vote. A farmer working on a small farm or a worker on a fishing boat belonged to this class. Indentured servants and apprentices were also members of the lower class of society. Indentured servants were those who worked without pay in return for food, clothes, and transportation. Enslaved people were considered lower than these three classes of society.

3. ☑ **Reading Check**
Main Idea and Details
Complete the diagram with information about the social classes in colonial society.

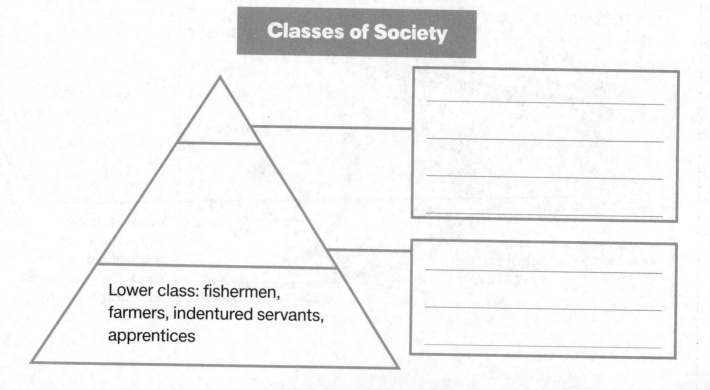

Classes of Society

Lower class: fishermen, farmers, indentured servants, apprentices

Daily Life

Working to survive was a big part of daily life. Every member of a family had tasks to do. Families worked and spent a lot of time together. Men worked on the farm. Women spun yarn, made clothes, prepared food for storage, and made soap and candles, along with caring for the children in the family. They filled in to take on their husbands jobs if they were away. They helped in the community and in church.

Starting at an early age, most children had chores to complete. As children grew older, the chores became more demanding. At about age 12, many children left their families to be trained in some type of trade, such as printing.

When their work was finished, colonial children made their toys out of things that were not needed. Girls made their dolls out of corn husks, rags, scraps, and sometimes used carved, dried apples as heads. The boys used sticks as imaginary horses.

Some children did go to school. Most New England towns were required to have schools. If parents were able to read and write, then their children were often given lessons at home. Wealthy people hired tutors for their children. Most children no longer received an education after about the age of 13 or 14 so that they could begin working full time to help support their families. Very few people went to college.

Artisans and Craftspeople

As Philadelphia, New York, Boston, and Charleston grew into large cities and trading centers, the need for people who had a special set of skills grew. These people, called **artisans**, specialized in one type of work or trade. They brought their handmade items to sell in the cities. Along with imports, merchants bought and sold these goods to others in the city. This brought wealth to merchants.

This modern girl shows how colonial children played with a hoop and stick toy.

Quest Connection

Underline details about the different jobs that people had in the cities and the country.

INTERACTIVITY

Learn about how life was different for children in the colonies as compared to today.

Artisans, such as blacksmiths, worked hard. They softened metal in hot coal-heated fire. Then, they hammered the heated metal into shapes.

In the country, workers had to perform many different types of tasks as part of their daily lives. Artisans, however, specialized in a variety of skills, such as blacksmithing, carpentry, wigmaking, and candlemaking. Artisans had skills that others didn't. These skills helped everyone else do what they needed to do. Artisans could make money for their families by producing the goods people in towns and farms wanted to buy but could not make on their own. Some colonial cities grew large enough to support artisans who made goods for the wealthy, such as watches and silver items.

Word Wise

Contractions
Contractions are the combination of two words to form a new word. For example, the word *didn't* is a contraction using the verb *did* and the adverb *not*. As you read, think about other verbs that could be made into contractions.

4. ✅ **Reading Check** **Infer** Discuss with a partner why colonists were able to specialize in different trades.

The Great Awakening

Religion was always important to colonial life. In the 1730s, a movement called the Great Awakening changed the way some people felt about religion. It began mainly in New England. Jonathan Edwards was an important figure during this movement. He felt that the colonists had lost their way with God and were not as committed to that relationship as they needed to be. Preachers, like Edwards, traveled from town to town, warning people against ignoring religion and its teachings.

Another preacher, George Whitefield, had different ideas. He inspired people to have stronger feelings towards God. In 1741, he wrote, "Venture [go out] daily upon Christ, go out in His strength, and He will enable you to do wonders."

During the time of the Great Awakening, different religious ideas were spread throughout the colonies. This movement weakened the power of church leaders. That is because the main message during this period was that people should be able to develop their connection to God. This helped some colonists realize that they did not have to depend upon church leaders to tell them how to live or worship.

George Whitefield

INTERACTIVITY

Check your understanding of the key ideas of this lesson.

☑ Lesson 2 Check

5. **Main Idea and Details** Provide two details to support the main idea that religion was important in the development of the colonies.

_____

_____

_____

6. **Describe** the route that traders used to bring enslaved people to North America.

_____

_____

7. **Understand the** *Quest* Connections What kinds of jobs did people have in the cities and the country in the colonies? Explain your answer with details from the text.

_____

_____

_____

Read Circle Graphs

Graphs are visuals that show information in a way that helps you compare and interpret information. One type of graph is a **circle graph**. Circle graphs are also sometimes called pie charts, as they are round and divided into sections, like slices of pie.

With a circle graph, the entire circle is the whole and the sections are the parts. Reading a circle graph can help you interpret numbers and facts.

To interpret a circle graph, first look at the title to understand what the graph is about. Next, read the legend to find out what each section shows. The title of the circle graph below is Colonial Diversity, 1700. This graph compares the percentage of different ethnic groups of people in the colonies in the year 1700.

What can you interpret about the ethnic makeup of the colonies by looking at this graph? You can understand that in 1700, English and Welsh colonists were the largest ethnic group in the 13 Colonies.

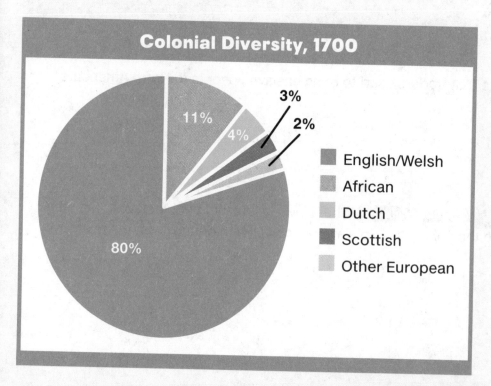

Colonial Diversity, 1700

- 80%
- 11%
- 4%
- 3%
- 2%

Legend:
- English/Welsh
- African
- Dutch
- Scottish
- Other European

On this page is another circle graph. The number of sections in the graph reflects the number of ethnic groups in the colonies in 1755.

 VIDEO

Watch a video about reading circle graphs.

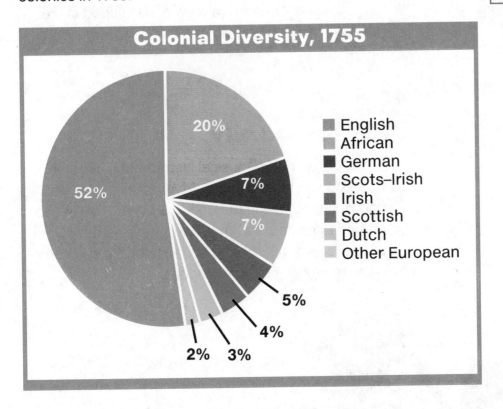

Colonial Diversity, 1755

- 20%
- 52%
- 7%
- 7%
- 5%
- 4%
- 3%
- 2%

Legend:
- English
- African
- German
- Scots–Irish
- Irish
- Scottish
- Dutch
- Other European

1. Which group had the most people in 1755? _____

2. How much did the percentage in the number of English people change between 1700 and 1755?

_____

3. **Infer** Why do you think the percentage of Africans increased?

_____

_____

_____

4. **Apply** Create a map based on the information in these graphs. Research to find out which colonial region was the most ethnically diverse.

Slavery in the Colonies

INTERACTIVITY

Participate in a class discussion to preview the content of this lesson.

Unlock The BIG Question

I will know how slavery developed in the United States.

Vocabulary

slavery
Middle Passage
uprisings

Academic Vocabulary

inspect
investigate

JumpStart Activity

What foods, music, musical instruments, or other items do you think came from Africa that have become part of our culture in the United States? Work in two groups to make a list. Then have one illustrator from each group draw pictures on the board to see if the other team can guess your ideas.

Enslaved Africans on a slave ship

In the summer of 1619, a Dutch ship carrying cargo that included a group of Africans landed at Jamestown. The local colonists paid for these Africans and forced them to work. The Africans were not paid and received only food and shelter for their work. In some areas, a few of them were given their freedom after working for some time. Within a few years, however, new laws were passed in Virginia and Massachusetts that took away all rights from African servants. They could be bought and sold as property. The practice, known as **slavery**, had begun in the English colonies.

INTERACTIVITY

Explore the key ideas of this lesson.

The Slave Trade

In the growing colonies, workers were needed. At first, indentured servants met this need. However, as the need for workers in the colonies grew, European colonists began to think that enslaved Africans could fill the need for workers. Many groups of people had been enslaved throughout history, usually as a result of war. This time it was different. Africans were captured, taken against their will without hope of freedom or return to their families in Africa.

At first, enslaved people came mostly from the western part of Africa, called the Gold Coast. Other Africans captured them and marched them to the coast where European traders waited in ships. Europeans traded guns and other goods for the slaves. Once the Africans were sold, they then had to make the long and horrific journey to the Americas. Known as the **Middle Passage**, this trip took a few weeks to several months. The ships were overcrowded, with the captives wedged below decks and chained to platforms stacked on top of one another. Unable to stand up or turn over, many of the enslaved died in this position. Olaudah Equiano, a young enslaved boy, suffered along with dying slaves. Later in his life, he described what he felt about the dead at the time:

Primary Source

I envied them the freedom they enjoyed, and as often wished I could change my condition for theirs.

–Olaudah Equiano, *The Interesting Narrative of the Life of Olaudah Equiano*, 1789

1. ☑ **Reading Check**
Analyze Underline the words in the text that explain why slavery grew in the colonies.

Slavery in the Northern Colonies

Not all enslaved Africans ended up in the English colonies of North America. Some continued on to the West Indies. There, they were sold in auctions. An auction is a public sale in which the highest bidder makes the purchase. Once purchased, enslaved Africans became the property of the winning bidder. They had few basic rights.

Every colony practiced slavery at some time during its history. In 1641, the Massachusetts Bay Colony was the first colony to pass a law that allowed slavery. Other colonies such as Maryland followed shortly after with their own laws. The Southern colonies, however, had the highest number of enslaved Africans. By the 1680s, slavery had been fully established in the colonies.

The types of work the enslaved Africans did varied. Some worked in shops, helping artisans with their work or learning how to do skilled work themselves, while others worked in inns or in the homes of wealthy residents.

In New York, an enslaved African welcomes a guest in his master's home.

In the Northern colonies, some enslaved Africans worked on farms helping farmers perform the daily chores. A farmer in the North might need only one or two slaves on his farm. Mostly, though, northern farmers did not grow crops that required large numbers of workers. For that reason, there were fewer enslaved farmworkers in the northern colonies.

A few African Americans in the northern colonies were free. Some were able to buy their freedom by saving money from working in the cities or selling produce they grew. Sometimes, a slaveholder would make the choice to set a person free. One such slave was Phillis Wheatley. Phillis was kidnapped and placed aboard a slave ship bound for Boston when she was seven or eight years old. In Boston, she was purchased directly from the ship by a local tailor. She became the personal servant of Wheatley's wife and was treated as a member of the family. She was sold to a Boston family in 1761 at an auction. She learned to write and became a noted poet. Her owners finally set her free.

Phillis Wheatley

Free African Americans often continued to live in the cities of the northern colonies. However, free African Americans had few rights and could be kidnapped and taken back into slavery at any time.

Slavery in the Southern Colonies

Slavery was very different in the southern colonies than in the northern colonies. In the southern colonies, farmers grew large crops, such as tobacco or rice. Later, they grew cotton. These crops required many workers to tend, pick, and prepare the plants for shipping. Many southern farmers relied on enslaved Africans to complete these tasks. Planters with large farms might purchase hundreds of enslaved people. In parts of the southern colonies, there were many more enslaved Africans than there were settlers.

Enslaved workers tend to cotton fields on a plantation.

Enslaved Africans did more than work in the fields on the large plantations. They brought special knowledge and skills from Africa. For example, some Africans had knowledge about growing rice. Because of this, rice became a key cash crop in the Carolinas. The success of rice had a bad result for many Africans, however. Rice plantations grew larger, and so their owners purchased many more enslaved Africans to work on them.

The way enslaved Africans lived in the South was different from in the North. In the South, enslaved Africans on large plantations lived in slave quarters, shacks that were clustered together. In many cases, they formed families that were a source of happiness and joy. Families, however, could also be a source of worry and fear. A family member could be sold at any time. It was common for slaveholders to separate family members from one another, such as husbands from wives, and children from their parents.

Although plantation life was hard on African American families, enslaved people developed their own unique and rich culture. On some plantations, people from different parts of Africa were together. Words, foods, and music with African origins blended with European languages and customs on the plantations. The result would have a long-lasting impact on American customs and music.

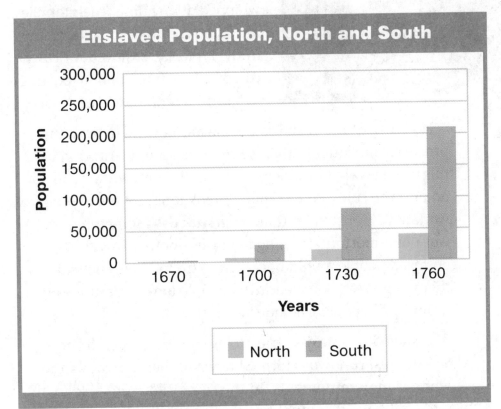

Enslaved Population, North and South

Population (y-axis): 0; 50,000; 100,000; 150,000; 200,000; 250,000; 300,000

Years (x-axis): 1670; 1700; 1730; 1760

Legend: North, South

Enslaved Africans played handmade banjos, such as this one.

2. ☑ **Reading Check** **Compare and contrast** slavery in the North and South between 1670 and 1760.

_____

_____

_____

_____

_____

Nat Turner talks with fellow enslaved African Americans as they prepare for a slave rebellion in Virginia in 1831.

Academic Vocabulary

inspect • *v.*, to look at something closely

Academic Vocabulary

investigate • *v.*, to study carefully

Fighting Back Against Slavery

Slavery was a brutal practice, whether the enslaved person lived in the Northern or Southern colonies. They basically had no rights, and they could be beaten or whipped at any time. Their families, including children, could be taken away. Typically, enslaved Africans could be kept from joining together or learning how to read and write.

However, many enslaved people found ways to resist this practice. Some taught themselves to read and write and used this new knowledge to help others find their own ways to go against the rules. Others might break tools, set fire to property, work slowly, or stall for time by **inspecting** something that was not important. Stealing food was another way that enslaved people fought back. The extra food also helped them to survive. Some enslaved people took or destroyed the property of people who had stolen their freedom.

Enslaved people also tried to escape from their owners. Sometimes, runaways formed new villages far away from white-owned settlements. In this way, they were able to hide and could avoid capture for longer periods of time. Often, runaways were relatively privileged slaves who had served as river boatmen or coachmen and they had **investigated** their surroundings before their escape.

In a few cases, enslaved Africans fought back in a more violent way. Slave **uprisings**, or rebellions, occurred in several colonies, including New York, Virginia, and South Carolina. Such rebellions were often bloody. In 1739, the Stono Rebellion in South Carolina left dozens of people, both white and black, dead.

3. ☑ **Reading Check** **Main Idea and Details** Discuss with a partner how enslaved Africans found ways to resist slavery.

These uprisings worried some slaveholders. They sometimes responded by being stricter on enslaved Africans. In 1741, for example, there was rumor of a slave rebellion in New York City that led to terrible violence against enslaved Africans. Whites who were thought to be helping enslaved people were also punished in the same cruel way.

Even after this, enslaved Africans did not back down. On plantations, they came up with ways of supporting one another and sharing important information. For example, they used songs to send secret messages among themselves. These songs helped enslaved Africans survive. With time, such songs became part of American culture.

INTERACTIVITY

Check your understanding of the key ideas of this lesson.

 **Lesson 3 Check**

4. **Describe** two characteristics of slavery in the Southern colonies.

_____

_____

_____

5. **Explain** how enslaved Africans were affected by the Middle Passage.

_____

_____

_____

6. **Compare and Contrast** Based on your investigation of the text, **describe** the differences between the large and small farms in the colonies and how this affected slavery.

_____

_____

_____

The Interesting Narrative of the Life of Olaudah Equiano

As you have read in the lesson, Olaudah Equiano was an enslaved African who was captured and forced on to a ship that sailed the Middle Passage from Africa to the Americas. He endured many injustices and horrible experiences. After Equiano won freedom, he wrote about his experiences so that others might know what it was really like to be an enslaved African on a slave ship. In this primary source excerpt, Equiano describes a slave auction.

Vocabulary Support

led

crammed

care

kept

item

faces

feeling

clamor, *n.*, a loud noise
apprehension, *n.*, fear
destruction, *n.*, causing a lot of damage

We were conducted immediately to the merchant's yard, where we were all pent up together, like so many sheep in a fold. . . . We were not many days in the merchant's custody, before we were sold after their usual manner, which is this: On a signal given (as the beat of a drum), the buyers rush at once into the yard where the slaves are confined, and make choice of that parcel they like best. The noise and clamor with which this is attended, and the eagerness visible in the countenances of the buyers, serve not a little to increase the apprehension of terrified Africans. . . . In this manner, without scruple, are relations and friends separated, most of them never to see each other again.

The Interesting Narrative of the Life of Olaudah Equiano, 1789

Close Reading

1. **Identify** and highlight words in the primary source excerpt that help the reader understand Equiano's point of view about the slave trade.
2. **Describe** the slave auction.

_____

_____

_____

_____

_____

_____

_____

Wrap It Up

Write two paragraphs telling what you think happened next to Olaudah Equiano. Draw an inference based on this primary source, as well as the lesson, which is a secondary source.

_____

_____

_____

_____

_____

_____

_____

_____

_____

_____

Cooperation and Conflict

INTERACTIVITY

Participate in a class discussion to preview the content of this lesson.

Unlock The BIG Question

I will know how conflicts between European settlers and American Indians broke out.

Vocabulary

boundary
King Philip's War

Academic Vocabulary

pollute
unify

JumpStart Activity

Choose an issue you feel strongly about, such as uniforms at school or no cell phone use during school hours. Try to convince others in your group to feel the same way you do about the topic.

In the beginning, the colonists and American Indians had peaceful encounters.

When the first English colonists arrived, the American Indians were generally helpful to them, especially with farming. Relations would soon change, though, as colonists began expanding farther into American Indian territory. Wars broke out, and with the introduction of gunpowder the wars became more violent.

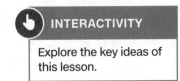

INTERACTIVITY

Explore the key ideas of this lesson.

Colonists and American Indians

Before the colonists arrived in the Americas, the American Indians used the land as needed. They used it for farming and some showed some of the colonists how to grow crops. They did not have a system of private land ownership. Instead, they believed that everyone could work together on the land.

The members of American Indian groups held that no individual owned land. When the European settlers and the American Indian leaders made agreements about a piece of land, the settlers thought they then owned the land. Indian groups thought they were agreeing only to share or rent the land. By American Indian custom, land could not be sold. This was just one of the many cultural differences that caused conflict.

Another source of conflict was that the Europeans did not consider themselves to be under any American Indian nation's rule. Instead, they claimed the land in the names of their home countries. The European settlers started creating **boundaries**, or lines that divide an area. The settlers also began to use force with weapons.

The 13 colonies were founded on American Indian lands.

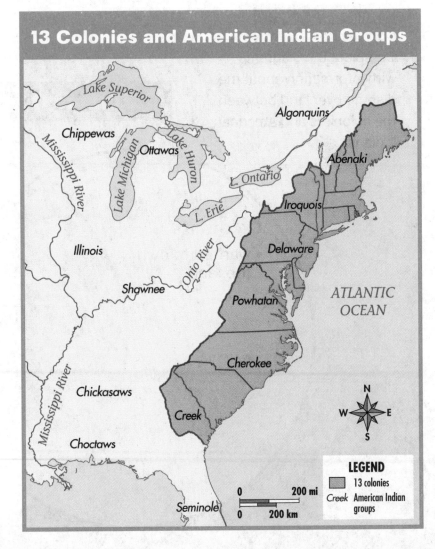

13 Colonies and American Indian Groups

Lake Superior

Algonquins

Chippewas

Ottawas

Lake Michigan

Lake Huron

Abenaki

Mississippi River

L. Ontario

L. Erie

Iroquois

Illinois

Ohio River

Delaware

Shawnee

Powhatan

ATLANTIC OCEAN

Cherokee

Mississippi River

Chickasaws

Creek

N
W · E
S

Choctaws

Seminole

LEGEND

13 colonies

Creek American Indian groups

0   200 mi
0   200 km

As the conflict between the colonists and the American Indians grew, distrust also began to grow. In the excerpt from the novel *Encounter,* by Jane Yolen below, the American Indian narrator tells of his experience when the colonists came to his Caribbean island.

So it was we lost our lands to the strangers from the sky. We gave our souls to their gods. We took their speech into our mouths, forgetting our own. Our sons and daughters became their sons and daughters, no longer true humans, no longer ours.

That is why I, an old man now, dream no more dreams. That is why I sit here wrapped in a stranger's cloak, counting the stranger's bells on a string, telling my story. May it be a warning to all the children and all the people in every land.

Jane Yolen, *Encounter*

1. ☑ **Reading Check**
Compare and Contrast
Complete the diagram with information about the dispute over land between the colonists and American Indians.

Dispute Over Land

Colonists
• wanted to own the land

American Indians
• did not own land

Conflicts Begin

Disagreement over land was not the only conflict between the colonists and the American Indians. In many instances, the English wanted to rule the Indian groups.

As you have read, the Jamestown, Virginia colony was within the territory of Chief Powhatan. He was the leader of the Tsenacommacah and led a confederacy, or several American Indian groups in the region. Often, American Indian groups formed alliances for political, economic, or military reasons. He had **unified** dozens of groups of American Indians before the settlers arrived. At first, Jamestown was not successful. It was located in a swampy area with **polluted** water and lots of insects that carried disease. The colony's leaders were not happy with their colony's location.

Conflict grew between the colonists and American Indians over land. As more settlers came, they wanted more land that was already occupied by American Indians. Captain John Smith, a colonial leader, imagined that American Indians would become subjects of England and also Christians. American Indians did not agree.

There were three wars between the colonists and Chief Powhatan's group. The first one started in 1610 and ended in 1614 when Pocahontas married English settler John Rolfe. This brought peace to the two groups for a period of time.

Chief Powhatan died in 1618 and his younger brother became the new leader. The English settlers continued to expand into the Powhatan's territory, and in 1622, the second Powhatan War began. The settlers and the American Indians continued their battle over land. Ten years later, in 1632, the second war came to an end.

Word Wise

Multiple-Meaning Words
Look at the word *rule* in the first paragraph under "Conflicts Begin." *Rule* has more than one meaning. It means "power or control over," and "a set of directions that must be followed." As you read, pay attention to words that might have more than one meaning. It is best to use context clues to help you decide which meaning of the word fits the text.

Academic Vocabulary

unify • *v.*, to come together
pollute • *v.*, to be impure

2. ✓ **Reading Check**
Identify Cause and Effect Fill in the chart with causes and effects of the wars between the American Indians and the English settlers.

The Puritans of Massachusetts also had conflicts with American Indian groups. As they spread further into Connecticut, they came into increasing conflict with the Pequots. Some colonists were killed. The governor of Massachusetts organized a large army to punish the Pequots. The Pequots attacked an English settlement, killing several colonists.

The attacks continued for several more months, with both sides winning battles. In May 1637, the Pequot War ended when the Puritans attacked and killed the people of a Pequot village. The colonists sold the survivors into slavery.

Powhatan and Pequot Wars

Causes

• English expanded into Powhatan territory.

→

Effects

• angered the Indian group

→

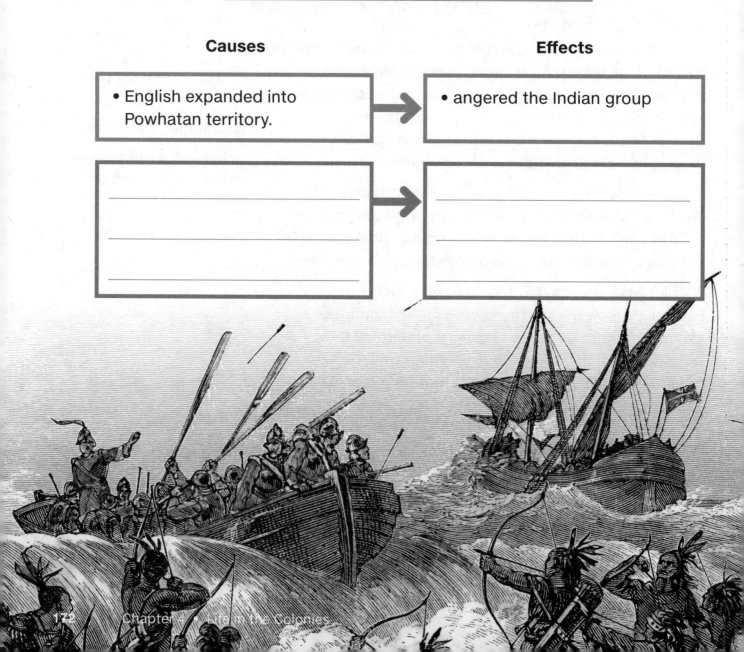

King Philip's War

In 1675, Metacom, a Wampanoag leader in New England, began a war against the New England colonists. Metacom was called King Philip by settlers. The conflict became known as **King Philip's War**. The result was a defeat for Metacom in which many of his people died. Not all American Indians supported Metacom. Some joined the colonists in the war.

Colonists accepted American Indian help. Yet what they really wanted was their land. As the American colonies grew, settlers pushed west, clearing woods for farms and building towns. By the mid-1700s, many had crossed the Appalachian Mountains to reach the Ohio River valley. This rich land was home to many powerful American Indian groups. The French also claimed the area. The stage was set for another bloody fight.

3. ☑ **Reading Check**
Main Idea and Details
Underline the motive that pushed settlers westward.

INTERACTIVITY

Check your understanding of the key ideas of this lesson.

☑ Lesson 4 Check

4. **Identify** What brought peace after the first Powhatan War?

_____

_____

5. **Analyze** How did American Indians cooperate with colonists and how did they come into conflict?

_____

_____

_____

6. **Explain** How did the Pequot War end?

_____

_____

The French and Indian War

Vocabulary

ally
treaty

Academic Vocabulary

reflect
persuade

Unlock The BIG Question

I will know Great Britain became the greatest colonial power in North America.

Jumpstart Activity

Think about a time you had a conflict with another student or a family member. What was the problem? How was it solved? Share your experience with a partner.

It was a war with two names fought on two continents. In Europe, it was called the Seven Years' War, one of many wars between France and Britain. In North America, it was called the French and Indian War. Here, a third party, the American Indians, took sides. They had been living on the land in dispute for a very long time. What side would they take?

The Road to War

French explorer Robert de La Salle claimed the Ohio River valley for France. The French built forts in the area to protect their claim from possible invaders.

The British also laid claim the huge region. Some British settlers established a trading post near the site of present-day Pittsburgh, Pennsylvania. They considered this area across the Appalachian Mountains to be part of the Virginia colony.

However, the French felt that they claimed the land first, so they would not give it up. French soldiers attacked the British trading post, destroying it. They built a fort nearby and called it Fort Duquesne (doo KAYN).

In 1753, the British sent a small army to the contested region. George Washington, a young soldier from Virginia, was the army's leader. Seeing that the fort was well guarded, Washington decided not to attack. Instead, his men fought and defeated a small group of French soldiers in the woods nearby. They then built their own fort called Fort Necessity.

American Indians joined the French soldiers in their attack on the fort. Working together, the large number of French and American Indians beat the smaller British force. The French army allowed Washington to take his surviving soldiers back to Virginia.

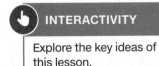

INTERACTIVITY

Explore the key ideas of this lesson.

1. ☑ **Reading Check** **Use Evidence From Text** Why were the French and American Indians able to capture Fort Necessity?

_____

_____

_____

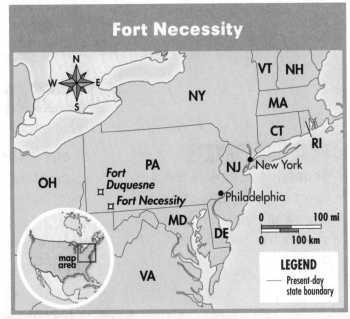

Fort Necessity

This is how Fort Necessity might have looked before it was attacked.

Academic Vocabulary

reflect • *v.*, to show

persuade • *v.*, to convince

The French and Indian War had begun. Its name **reflected** the fact that in North America, the British army fought both the French and their American Indian allies. An **ally** is a military partner. Many American Indians were **persuaded** to support the French because they feared that the British colonies were spreading into their territories. As a show of resistance, the British, sought the support of the powerful Iroquois as an ally. At first, the Iroquois resisted. One of their leaders said:

Primary Source

[The French and British] are both quarrelling about lands which belong to us, and such a quarrel as this may end in our destruction.

–Hendrick Peters, Iroquois leader, 1754

Later, the Iroquois decided to side with the British. They hoped this would help them keep control of their land.

2. ☑ **Reading Check**

Sequence Complete the chart by listing two other key events that led to the start of the French and Indian War.

Events Leading to War

The French and British both claim land in the Ohio River valley.

↓

↓

↓

The French defeat Washington at Fort Necessity with the help of American Indian allies.

A British Victory

In 1755, the British returned to the area in the hope of capturing Fort Duquesne. This time, they sent a leader with experience to try and defeat the enemy. Edward Braddock, a general, went to the area. Washington served as his advisor. However, the French and American Indian fighters defeated the British again, killing General Braddock. The effort to capture the fort failed.

The British lost many early battles. Then, in 1757, British leaders sent reinforcements from Europe. This made the British army stronger, and in 1758, they finally took control of Fort Duquesne.

The Iroquois decided to join forces with the British. This new alliance was unstoppable. In a key 1759 battle, the allies captured Quebec, the capital of New France. The next year, the British captured Montreal, another French settlement in present-day Canada. The French and their allies had been beaten. To end the war, France and England signed a **treaty**, which is a formal agreement between countries, in 1763. France agreed to surrender much of its territory in North America east of the Mississippi River.

The British now controlled the Ohio River valley. This upset many American Indians. They knew that more colonists from the east would soon arrive. Unlike the French, British settlers built towns and roads, changing the landscape. In 1763, an Ottawa leader named Pontiac took action to stop the British. He led an army that attacked British forts and villages in the Ohio River valley.

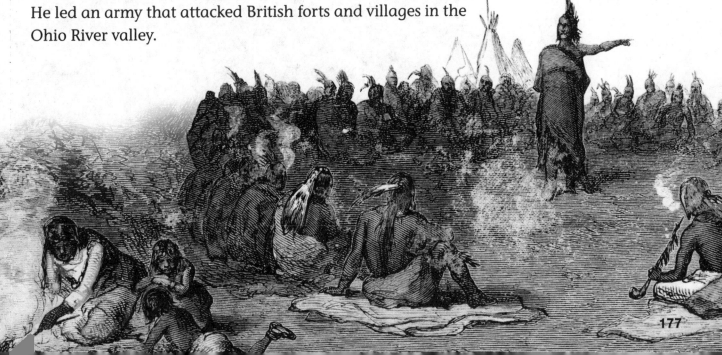

In 1763, Pontiac rallied American Indian groups to fight together to force the British to leave their lands.

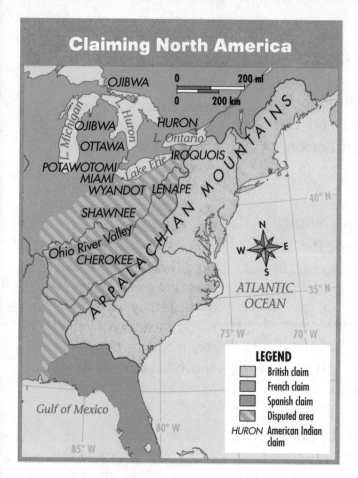

Claiming North America

OJIBWA

0 ——— 200 mi

0 ——— 200 km

L. Michigan

OJIBWA   HURON

L. Huron   L. Ontario

OTTAWA   IROQUOIS

POTAWOTOMI   Lake Erie

MIAMI

WYANDOT   LENAPE

APPALACHIAN MOUNTAINS

SHAWNEE

40° N

Ohio River Valley

CHEROKEE

N W E S

ATLANTIC
OCEAN   35° N

75° W   70° W

Gulf of Mexico

80° W

85° W

LEGEND
- British claim
- French claim
- Spanish claim
- Disputed area

HURON American Indian claim

3. ☑ **Reading Check**

Identify Draw a star and circle the area on the map where conflicts between the British and the French were most likely to occur in the 1750s.

After much fighting, the British destroyed Pontiac's men. Still, the clash alarmed many British leaders, because the fighting proved to be expensive. King George III issued an order called the Proclamation of 1763. It prohibited, or blocked, colonists from settling lands west of the Appalachian Mountains. The king hoped this order would help keep peace with American Indians and not cause further costs.

The proclamation upset colonists who were eager to settle in the Ohio River valley. Many of them pushed west despite the king's order. This added to the growing tensions between the colonies and Great Britain.

After the war, American Indians continued to try to stop settlers from taking their land. One Cayuga Indian leader, Logan, tried to keep the peace with white settlers. However, in what became known as Lord Dunmore's War, in 1774, Virginia settlers killed some of his family members and the Pennsylvania militia went into Ohio River valley to destroy several Indian villages. After these events, Chief Logan fought to keep white settlers out of the region. He did not want to make any treaties because he did not trust the colonists.

Chief Logan negotiates with a colony's leader.

☑ Lesson 5 Check

4. **Explain** What was the main difference between the French and British armies in the French and Indian War?

_____

_____

_____

5. **Identify** the effects of the French and Indian War.

_____

_____

6. **Causes and Effects** Complete the chart with the effects of the Proclamation of 1763 on colonization.

Proclamation of 1763

Causes

Britain passed the Proclamation of 1763 in the hope of keeping the peace with American Indians and cutting costs for defense.

Effects

_____

_____

_____

_____

_____

_____

_____

_____

Quality:
Individual Responsibility

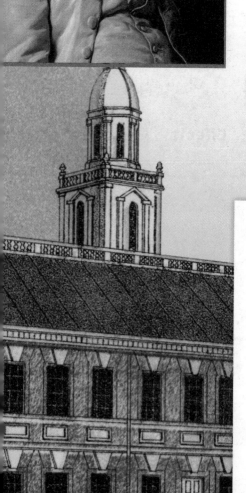

Benjamin Franklin (1706–1790)
A Life of Service

Benjamin Franklin was an intelligent man with many talents. He helped to shape the ideas of American colonists with his writings. Later, he was on the committee that wrote the Declaration of Independence, served his country as a diplomat, and helped shape the U.S. Constitution. He conducted scientific experiments and created useful tools, such as bifocals and the Franklin stove. Public libraries and fire departments were Franklin's ideas and were important civic contributions.

As a young man, Franklin became an apprentice to his brother, who owned a printing shop. There, he learned how to be a printer and helped run his brother's business. He also began writing articles for the newspaper. When he was 17, he decided to go to New York City to look for printing work but was unsuccessful. So, he decided to go to Philadelphia and later to England to learn more about the printing business.

He combined his love of writing and what he had learned as a printer when he published works such as *Poor Richard's Almanack*. In this best seller, he gave advice, weather data, and included many great sayings such as "early to bed and early to rise, makes a man healthy, wealthy, and wise." Franklin became a symbol for the spirit of individualism and hard work in the American colonies.

Find Out More

1. Benjamin Franklin started key civic institutions. Research to find out what other civic responsibilities he took on.

_____

_____

_____

2. Think of some ways that you take on individual responsibility at school.

_____

_____

Visual Review

Use these graphics to review some of the key terms, people, and ideas from this chapter.

Colonists and American Indians

Roger Williams	believed in freedom of religion; founded Rhode Island
Anne Hutchinson	offended Puritan leaders by speaking out on religious matters
Thomas Hooker	believed all men should be allowed to vote; started the Connecticut colony
William Penn	a Quaker who wanted to protect each person's freedoms; founded Pennsylvania colony
George Whitfield	a leader in the Great Awakening who inspired people to have stronger feelings towards God
Chief Powhatan	Powhatan leader who led wars against the Jamestown colonists
Metacom	a Wampanoag leader who led a war against New England colonists
George Washington	led the building of Fort Necessity at the start of the French and Indian War
Pontiac	an Ottawa leader who led an attack against British forts and villages

The 13 Colonies

New England	Middle	Southern
• Traded goods with England and other colonies • Timber was an important resource • Built ships, fished, or hunted whales • Meetinghouse was center of life	• Rich soil and warmer climate • Raised wheat to sell • More diverse than other colonial regions • Thriving trade center and port	• Very warm climate • Large plantations that grew cash crops • Relied heavily on enslaved Africans to work on plantations

🎮 GAMES

Play the vocabulary game.

Vocabulary and Ideas

1. Draw a line to match the definitions with the correct terms.

a society group   **proprietor**

someone who owns land or property   **treaty**

a product sold to another country   **export**

a formal agreement between countries   **class**

2. Define What is **mercantilism**?

_____

_____

_____

3. Interpreting a Map Analyze the map. How does this map support the positions that American Indian leaders like Pontiac and Logan took with settlers?

_____

_____

_____

_____

_____

_____

_____

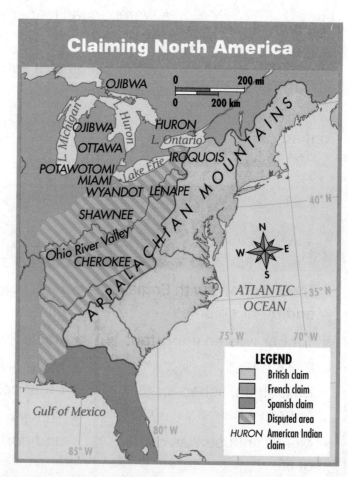

Claiming North America

LEGEND
- British claim
- French claim
- Spanish claim
- Disputed area
- *HURON* American Indian claim

Critical Thinking and Writing

4. **Analyze** In what way was the meetinghouse the center of town life?

_____

_____

_____

5. **Analyze** What was the significance of the triangular trade?

_____

_____

_____

_____

6. **Apply** What is the importance of a treaty in today's society? Has it changed over time?

_____

_____

_____

_____

7. **Revisit the Big Question** What does it take to build a new society?

_____

_____

_____

_____

_____

8. **Writing Workshop: Write Clearly** What would it be like to start a new society in a new place? Think about what you would need and the types of people who would most benefit the new society. Then write two paragraphs on another piece of paper describing your society and how it would be run and governed.

Analyze Primary Sources

"I inquired of these what was to be done with us. They gave me to understand we were to be carried to these white people's country to work for them. I then was a little revived, and thought if it were no worse than working, my situation was not so desperate. But still I feared that I should be put to death, the white people looked and acted in so savage [wild, animal-like] a manner. I have never seen among my people such instances of brutal cruelty . . ."

-Olaudah Equiano, *The Interesting Narrative of the Life of Olaudah Equiano*, 1789

9. What does Equiano mean by stating that he was "a little revived"? Do his feelings change? Cite evidence from the source in your response.

_____

_____

_____

_____

_____

Main Idea and Details

10. Write the details that support this main idea: The Great Awakening brought change to the colonies.

_____

_____

_____

_____

_____

11. What were the main reasons for founding the different colonies?

_____

_____

Quest Findings

You've Found Home!

Project-Based Learning

You've read the lessons in this chapter and now you're ready to create your infomercial. Remember that the goal of your infomercial is to try to convince other people to move to your colony. Include what makes your colony so great and why it is better than all the other colonies. Follow these steps:

INTERACTIVITY

Use this activity to determine the factors that are important about your colony.

1 Brainstorm Your Reasons

Think of the reasons your colony is the best one to live in. Write these ideas down in a list. Then write about why your colony is better than the others. Use these notes to help you create your infomercial.

3 Final Review of Script

Review your ideas with your group. Be honest, but polite with one another as you think of how to improve the infomercial. Make sure it's not too long and that it has a clear message.

2 Write Your Infomercial Script

Use your notes and the evidence from your Quest Connections to create the most convincing infomercial you can. Make sure your infomercial addresses the following questions:

- What is life like in your colony?
- Why is your colony the best?
- Why should people move to your area?

4 Film or Act Out Your Infomercial

Film or act out your infomercial using your script.

GO ONLINE FOR
DIGITAL RESOURCES

 VIDEO

 INTERACTIVITY

AUDIO

GAMES

ASSESSMENT

eTEXT

The **BIG** Question

VIDEO

What is worth fighting for?

Jumpstart Activity

 INTERACTIVITY

Divide into two teams—Team A and Team B. Play a round of a game such as charades. Team A will make up new rules as the game is played. Team A can also choose whether or not Team B is awarded points. Discuss what each team thinks of the rules and of playing a game this way.

Fighting for Freedom

Preview the chapter **vocabulary** as you sing the rap:

The colonists were upset that they were not represented
By British Parliament and what they did was resented.
Colonists banded together, to voice their frustration
And shouted, "No taxation without representation!"

There were those who didn't bend and refused to resist
And remained loyal to the throne who were called
   loyalists.
But the majority opposed Britain's policies and actions
These **patriots** wanted to put an end to these
   transactions.

George Washington supported boycotts, but there
   was no resolution
They went to war, it's called the American Revolution.
Many battles were fought, some were lost and some
   won.
But it all began with the battles of Concord and
   Lexington.

5 The American Revolution

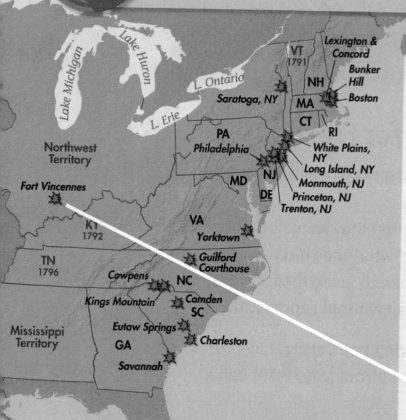

VT 1791
Lexington & Concord
Bunker Hill
NH
Saratoga, NY
MA
Boston
CT
RI
L. Ontario
L. Erie
PA
Philadelphia
White Plains, NY
Long Island, NY
Monmouth, NJ
Princeton, NJ
Trenton, NJ
NJ
Northwest Territory
MD
DE
Fort Vincennes
KY 1792
VA
Yorktown
TN 1796
Guilford Courthouse
Cowpens
NC
Kings Mountain
Camden
SC
Mississippi Territory
Eutaw Springs
Charleston
GA
Savannah

Where did the battles take place?

The 13 Colonies fought Britain in the American Revolution.

Where did the only battle fought outside the original 13 Colonies take place?

TODAY

Visitors can see this memorial to George Rogers Clark in Vincennes, Indiana. Inside the building, there are seven murals, three of Clark's quotations, and a statue of Clark.

What happened and When?

Read the timeline to find out about the events that led to the American Revolution.

1765

1765
The Stamp Act is passed.

1770

1770
The Boston Massacre takes place.

1774
The First Continental Congress meets.

1775

1775
The first shots of the American Revolution are fired.

Who will you meet?

Thomas Jefferson
Wrote the Declaration of Independence

George Washington
Served as commander in Chief of the Continental army

Deborah Sampson
Disguised herself as a man to serve in the Continental army during the American Revolution

James Armistead
Worked as a spy in the American Revolution and helped the Americans win a decisive battle

 INTERACTIVITY

Complete the interactive timeline.

1780

1785

1776
The Declaration of Independence is written.

TODAY
The ideas expressed in the Declaration of Independence are still the guiding principles of our government.

1781
Cornwallis surrenders at Yorktown.

1783
The Treaty of Paris is signed.

Read All About It!

The American Revolution was a war fought between Great Britain and the 13 American colonies. Colonists disagreed with Britain's King George III and Parliament before the battles began. Several events caused tensions to rise between 1765 and 1775. The written word was the best way to spread news throughout the colonies.

Quest Kick Off

Your mission is to create a class newspaper that provides stories of the events leading up to the revolution and the major battles that take place.

1 Ask Questions

What kinds of information do you think were most important for the people on the home front? Reporters use the questions *Who? What? Where? When? Why?* and *How?*

....

....

....

....

....

2 Investigate

Follow your teacher's instruction to learn about news stories online. Then use Media Center resources to read several newspaper stories about the same topic. How do they relate to each other? How does each story build on the last?

👆 INTERACTIVITY

Complete the interactivity to learn more about newspaper articles.

....

....

....

....

....

3 Look for *Quest* Connections

Turn to the next page to begin looking for Quest Connections that will help you create your news stories.

4 *Quest* Findings
Write Your News Stories

Use the Quest Findings page at the end of the chapter to help you write and design your newspaper.

INTERACTIVITY

Participate in a class discussion to preview the content of this lesson.

Vocabulary

congress
debt
Stamp Act
Sons of Liberty
boycott
Townshend Acts
tariff
custom

Academic Vocabulary

acknowledge
retain

Unlock
The BIG Question

I will know why the colonists rebelled against the British.

Jumpstart Activity

You and a small group will plan a fictional city. One member prepares small squares of paper. Half the squares have a dot; the other half have nothing. Each member picks one square. A dot means you can plan where the town will be, its layout, and how to pay for expenses. Is it fair that only half of the people have a say in planning the town? Explain your position.

The British and French, as well as the colonists and American Indians, all took part in the French and Indian War. Each group had its own reasons to go to war. France and Britain were European rivals who fought over land in North America. American Indians wanted to keep their lands. The British colonists felt loyal to Britain. Soon, however, tension between the colonies and Britain would rise. Then the idea of revolution began to grow, especially in the Middle Colonies. There colonists saw differences between themselves and the British.

Taxes Cause Trouble

The British became involved in the French and Indian War because they believed that the Ohio River Valley belonged to them. The king also believed that he was protecting the colonists who had settled on this land.

As you have read, the Proclamation of 1763 gave Britain large sections of North America, including French territories east of the Mississippi River. King George III of England kept colonists from expanding further westward. He hoped to keep the peace with American Indians who lived on those lands.

During the French and Indian War, the British ordered the colonies to organize so they could make treaties between the colonies and the Iroquois Confederacy. The result was the Albany Plan of Union. Proposed by Benjamin Franklin of Pennsylvania, the plan called for a **congress**, or a lawmaking body. The congress would represent all of the colonies. It would have the power to keep an army, levy taxes, and plan for westward expansion. The document said in part:

INTERACTIVITY

Explore the key ideas of this lesson.

Primary Source

That they make laws for regulating and governing such new settlements, till the crown shall think fit to form them into particular governments.

—Albany Plan of Union, 1754

George Washington, on horseback, was from the colony of Virginia. He fought for the British during the French and Indian War.

The plan was rejected by King George III who feared that it would make the colonies too powerful. In addition, leaders in Great Britain decided to tax American colonists to pay for the French and Indian War.

Great Britain had an enormous **debt**, which meant that it owed money. Britain then passed the **Stamp Act**, which taxed every piece of printed paper that colonists used. This included legal documents, newspapers, licenses, and even playing cards.

Colonists were not represented in Parliament (PAHR luh munt), Britain's assembly that makes laws. Many felt the British government should not tax them. "No taxation without representation!" became a common cry. Colonists believed only representatives they elected to their colonial assemblies could pass tax laws.

The Albany Plan caused colonists to begin thinking about forming a union. Some colonists, such as Patrick Henry from Virginia, became outspoken opponents of the Stamp Act. Soon the colonists were meeting to discuss the situation.

A one-penny stamp. Parliament required a stamp on every piece of printed paper in the colonies as part of the Stamp Act.

The Stamp Act Congress met in 1765 to discuss how to deal with Great Britain's unjust tax.

This political cartoon, published by Benjamin Franklin, shows the weakness of the colonies because they were divided. The pieces of the snake represent the colonies. The *N.E.* at the head of the snake stands for the four New England colonies.

JOIN, or DIE.

1. ☑ **Reading Check** **Cause and Effect** **Analyze** how the French and Indian War affected the relationship between Britain and the 13 Colonies. Discuss with a partner.

The Colonists Take Action

In response to what they believed to be unjust taxation, some colonies requested that Parliament repeal the Stamp Act. These requests were rejected. In 1765, representatives from nine colonies met in New York for a meeting that was called the Stamp Act Congress. The congress consisted of delegates, or representatives, from the colonies, including farmers, lawyers, and businessmen. As a group, they demanded that Parliament repeal the Stamp Act. Although the taxes were small, the colonists did not like the pattern they set.

At this time, most colonists were loyal to the crown. They took issue only with Parliament's taxation. The Stamp Act Resolves, the result of the Stamp Act Congress, **acknowledged** that the king still had the right to make laws in the colonies.

Other groups wanted to send a stronger message to the king. A group called the **Sons of Liberty** began to organize protests against the Stamp Act. They wrote literature encouraging **boycotts**, or refusals to buy British products. The Sons of Liberty was a secret group. It formed in 1765 to protect colonists' rights and protest British taxation.

Quest Connections

Identify and circle the most relevant facts about the Stamp Act. **Explain** how the act added to the tension between the colonies and Great Britain.

INTERACTIVITY

Learn how to use the causes and effects of the Stamp Act to organize a newspaper article.

Academic Vocabulary

acknowledge • *v.*, to recognize the authority of

Colonial protestors did not think Parliament had the right to tax them. Here colonists protest British taxes by confronting the Royal Governor of North Carolina.

Members also burned stamps and threatened stamp agents. The Daughters of Liberty, another part of the group, encouraged colonists to spin their own cloth instead of using British-made cloth.

In March 1766, Great Britain was losing money due to the boycotts. It was the boycotts, more than the congress, that led to the repeal of the Stamp Act. The repeal marked a milestone for the colonies. It was the first time that representatives from the colonies had come together. It was also the first time that the British government backed down when met with colonial resistance.

Along with the repeal, however, Parliament passed the Declaratory Act of 1766. The king feared that the colonies were becoming too strong. The Declaratory Act sent the message that the king **retained** the authority to make laws for the colonies.

Although many agreed with the king, some British lawmakers did not. William Pitt, the Elder, argued in front of Parliament that it was unconstitutional to tax the colonies.

Academic Vocabulary

retain • v., to keep

The Americans have not acted in all things with prudence [wisdom] and temper [calmness]. They have been wronged. They have been driven to madness by injustice. Will you punish them for the madness you have occasioned [caused]? Rather let prudence and temper come first from this side. I will undertake [take the side] for America, that she will follow the example.

—William Pitt's speech on the Stamp Act, January 14, 1766

2. ☑ **Reading Check** **Identify** the reasons for the colonists' anger about the Stamp Act.

_____

_____

_____

_____

The Townshend Acts

Repealing the Stamp Act meant that colonists were no longer taxed by the British government. But colonists were concerned that the Declaratory Act stated that Parliament could make laws in the colonies in "all cases whatsoever."

These concerns were confirmed in the summer of 1767, when the **Townshend Acts** were passed. Named after Charles Townshend, the member of Parliament who proposed them, these were a series of acts that placed **tariffs**, or taxes, on products coming into the colonies. Glass, tea, lead, and paper were all taxed. Tariffs are usually used to control trade, but in this case they were used to raise money for Great Britain. As part of the Townshend Acts, a strict system for **customs**, or tax collections, was established. The acts also lifted the British export tax on tea so that Great Britain could ship tea to the colonies for free.

Once again, colonists were taxed without representation. They reacted by boycotting British products, harassing tax collectors, and refusing to pay the taxes. British merchants began to lose money. To control the protests and scare colonists, King George III sent warships into Boston Harbor in 1768. This did not deter the colonists. Merchants continued to lose money. British merchants asked their government to repeal the acts. As a result of the turmoil they caused, the Townshend Acts were repealed in April of 1770. Only a tax on tea remained. Parliament wanted to send the message that they had the right to tax the colonies.

Although the repeal of the Stamp Act and the Townshend Acts were victories for colonists, tensions were still high. British troops were in Boston, and colonists were paying a tax on their tea.

3. ☑ **Reading Check** Use the chart to **describe** the Townshend Acts. Talk to a partner and **summarize** the acts and their effects.

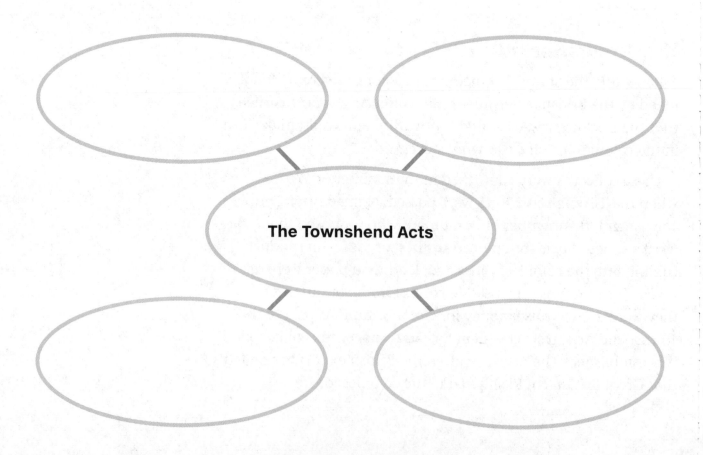

The Townshend Acts

☑ Lesson 1 Check

4. **Multiple Causes and Effects Analyze** how the French and Indian War affected the relationship between the British and the 13 Colonies. Then complete the chart to explain the effects of the war.

Causes

Effects

1. The British did not want to cause problems with the American Indians.

_____

_____

_____

2. The British passed the Stamp Act to pay for the war.

_____

_____

_____

5. In this lesson you have read about why people were against the Stamp Act and other taxes. However, some colonists were in favor of these actions. **Develop** and **present** a logical argument in support of the British taxes.

_____

_____

_____

6. **Understand the**  **Connections** How did King George III's actions contribute to anti-British feelings?

_____

_____

INTERACTIVITY

Participate in a class discussion to preview the content of this lesson.

Vocabulary

massacre
quarter
martial law
Patriot
Loyalist
neutral
militia

Academic Vocabulary

symbolic
significant

Unlock
The **BIG**
Question

I will know why the colonists decided to go to war with England.

JumpStart Activity

Divide into small groups. Each group will set up two teams. Team 1 will tell Team 2 what it will do at recess. How did Team 1 feel about telling Team 2 what to do? How did Team 2 feel about being told what to do?

The Townshend Acts were repealed in March 1770, but colonists were still angry. Unrest had spread through the colonies due to Great Britain's repeated attempts to collect taxes.

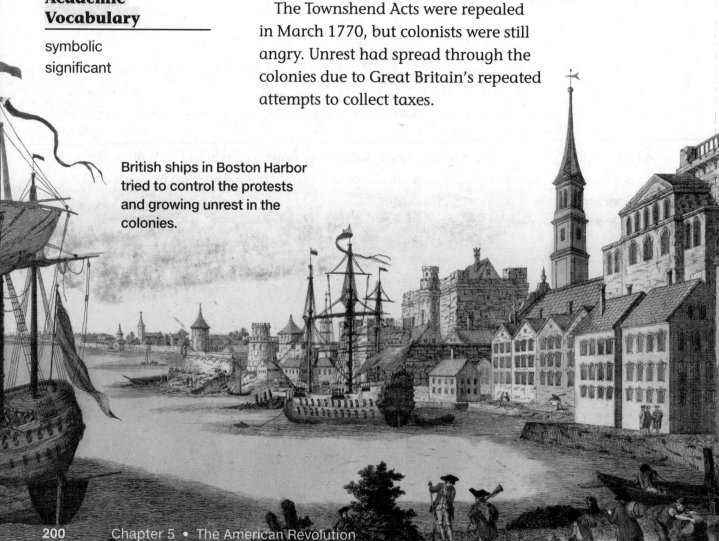

British ships in Boston Harbor tried to control the protests and growing unrest in the colonies.

Tensions Boil Over

In early 1770, people in Boston were angry at Great Britain. British warships had occupied Boston Harbor for more than a year trying to maintain peace.

On March 5, the same day that a member of Parliament proposed repealing the Townshend Acts, colonial anger boiled over in Boston.

A crowd began yelling insults and bothering a British guard near the Custom House. The Custom House was where taxes were collected. A British captain ordered soldiers to protect the guard and restore order. Someone hit a British soldier with a stick. The soldier shot into the crowd.

Other British soldiers began to shoot into the crowd. Five colonists died due to the skirmish, including Crispus Attucks. Attucks was an African American sailor who had escaped slavery. The incident is called the Boston Massacre. A **massacre** is the killing of many people. The event sent shockwaves through the colonies.

John Adams of Massachusetts was tasked with defending the British officers in court. Adams did not approve of the British being in Boston but believed that they deserved a fair trial. None of the soldiers was found guilty of murder.

Crispus Attucks was one of five colonists killed due to the Boston Massacre.

1. ☑ **Reading Check** **Identify** the cause of the Boston Massacre by underlining the appropriate text. **Explain** why Boston was at the center of the action.

_____

_____

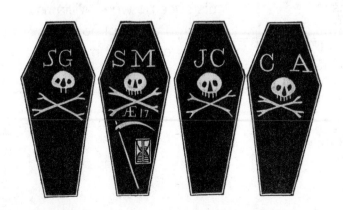

This illustration of the coffins of the victims of the Boston Massacre appeared in a colonial newspaper. The victims' initials can be seen on each coffin.

Committees of Correspondence

As tensions with Britain increased, colonists in Massachusetts felt the need to form a system of communication. Samuel Adams, cousin of John Adams, helped create a Committee of Correspondence in his colony so that even people in rural areas and other colonies had access to information. This committee, or group of people, had been active in urging colonies to send delegates to the Stamp Act Congress. Now, they were active in managing the "tea crisis."

Other colonies also formed committees. When colonists learned of the Boston Massacre, the importance of these committees became apparent. Members of the committees wrote letters and pamphlets about British policies and colonial protests. They spread the documents among the colonies. A man named Paul Revere was one of the express riders, who carried the letters and pamphlets throughout the colonies.

After the Boston Massacre, many colonists looked to religion to justify their opposition to British rule. They felt it was their Christian and moral duty to fight against a cruel tyrant. Many ministers preached this idea to the colonists. They felt it was morally correct to support political and military resistance to Britain.

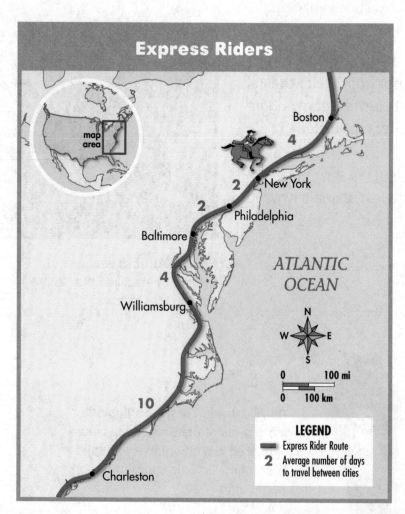

Express Riders

Boston

4

2 New York

2

Philadelphia

Baltimore

ATLANTIC
OCEAN

4

Williamsburg

N
W   E
S

0   100 mi
0   100 km

10

Charleston

LEGEND
— Express Rider Route
2 Average number of days to travel between cities

2. ☑ **Reading Check** Look at the map. **Describe** and **measure** the distance between Williamsburg and Baltimore. About how many miles did a rider cover in 4 days?

_____

_____

_____

The Boston Tea Party

In the spring of 1773, the "tea crisis" became worse. Great Britain passed the Tea Act, which stated that only the British East India Company could sell tea in the colonies. The company would not pay tax on tea sold in the colonies, but the colonists would continue to pay a tax on tea.

When the colonists heard about the Tea Act, they decided to take action. They believed the tea tax was unjust. They did not want to be forced to buy tea from one company. Groups such as the Daughters of Liberty organized boycotts, and the Sons of Liberty continued to protest in Boston. On the morning of December 16, 1773, led by Samuel Adams, the Sons of Liberty planned an open show of rebellion. That evening, more than 100 men from all walks of life met at Griffin's Wharf on Boston Harbor. Some members of the Sons of Liberty disguised themselves as Mohawk American Indians. The disguises were also **symbolic** of the fact that the colonists now considered themselves Americans and not British subjects. Three ships at the wharf carried British tea. The men climbed aboard the ships, broke open the chests of tea, and dumped it into Boston Harbor. Today, the tea that was destroyed would be worth more than one million dollars. The event became known as the Boston Tea Party.

The Sons of Liberty and other colonists destroyed tea at the Boston Tea Party to protest the tax on tea.

Academic Vocabulary

symbol • *n.*, an action or object that represents an idea or feeling

3. ☑ **Reading Check** **Use Evidence From Text** **Analyze** and highlight the causes and immediate effects of the Boston Tea Party.

The Coercive Acts

In response to the Boston Tea Party, the British government passed the Coercive Acts of 1774. *Coerce* means "to force someone to do something." The acts shut down Boston Harbor. The British wanted to force Boston to pay for the destroyed tea. The colonists called the acts the Intolerable Acts. *Intolerable* means "unbearable." The acts shut down Boston's economy and unified the colonists against Britain even more.

In addition to paying for the destroyed tea, the Intolerable Acts stated that colonists had to **quarter**, or shelter, British soldiers. Massachusetts was also placed under **martial law**, which meant that it would be controlled by the British military. Furthermore, any British officials accused of crimes while carrying out their duty as peacekeepers or tax collectors would not be tried in a colonial jury. They would be sent back to Britain for trial.

4. ☑ **Reading Check** **Analyze** how a Patriot and a Loyalist might have felt about the Intolerable Acts. Write their ideas in the speech bubbles.

Samuel Adams
Patriot

Thomas Hutchinson
Loyalist

The acts encouraged many colonists to join the cause of the **Patriots**. Patriots were colonists opposed to Britain's actions and policies. About one third of colonists were **Loyalists**, or people loyal to Great Britain. Some people remained **neutral** and did not take a side. The number of neutral colonists decreased as tensions between the countries rose.

The Boston Port Act, one of the Coercive Acts, also called the Intolerable Acts, closed Boston Harbor until the tea destroyed during the Boston Tea Party was paid for.

5. ✓ Reading Check **Analyze** how the Intolerable Acts could have affected the economy, and make inferences about the immediate effect on colonists. Turn and **talk with a partner** about your ideas.

_____

_____

_____

_____

The First Continental Congress

Colonists were furious over the Intolerable Acts. The Committees of Correspondence produced a great deal of writings about Britain's unjust policies so that all colonists would be informed. They planned protests and acts of coordinated resistance.

The most **significant** result of the acts was the meeting of the First Continental Congress. Because of increasing unrest in the Middle Colonies, Philadelphia became the meeting place. In September and October of 1774, the colonies met for the first time since the Stamp Act Congress in 1765. The 55 delegates included John Adams, George Washington, Samuel Adams, and Patrick Henry.

While some were ready to break away from Great Britain, more moderate delegates urged the Congress to appeal once more to the king. For example, John Dickinson of Pennsylvania argued against independence. He thought the colonists and Britain should work out their differences. He thought independence would lead to disaster.

Many merchants, too, urged peace. Many depended on British banks for credit. The British navy protected their trade. One Philadelphia merchant, Thomas Clifford, said that independence would "assuredly prove unprofitable." He feared that France and Spain would try to take advantage of the colonies without British protection.

Academic Vocabulary

significant • *adj.*, important

The First Continental Congress met in 1774 in Philadelphia. In the image below, the members walk out of Independence Hall.

The Continental Congress sent a Declaration of Rights to Parliament. The document asked the British government to repeal the Intolerable Acts. It also included a colonial bill of rights and a list of complaints. The delegates agreed before sending the petition that if the king rejected it, they would meet again to discuss their next actions.

Primary Source

That they are entitled to life, liberty and property: And they have never ceded [given] to any foreign power whatever, a right to dispose [decide] of either without their consent.

—The Declaration of Rights, 1774

Sending the Declaration of Rights to the king was a significant step. The delegates knew that they might have to decide to go to war at their next meeting.

6. **Reading Check** **Identify** three points that the Committees of Correspondence might have included in one of their pamphlets before the First Continental Congress. Discuss and **describe** your ideas with a partner.

The Shot Heard Round the World

In the spring of 1775, colonial **militias**, or volunteer armies of colonists, in Massachusetts began storing ammunition in a city named Concord. They wanted to prepare for a possible conflict with Great Britain. British General Thomas Gage learned about this. He set out to stop the colonists and arrest Patriots John Adams and John Hancock, who were in Lexington.

The colonists found out about Gage's plan. On the night of April 18, express riders Paul Revere and William Dawes set out to warn the minutemen that the British were coming. Minutemen were members of the local militias who would be ready to fight at a minute's notice. At about midnight, Revere reached Lexington to warn Adams and Hancock. Dawes arrived about 30 minutes later. Another rider, Samuel Prescott, joined the pair. The three continued on to Concord to warn that the British were coming to seize the ammunition.

When the British reached Lexington by dawn on April 19, 1775, they met a militia of 70 men. A shot, now referred to as the "shot heard round the world," was fired unexpectedly, causing both sides to shoot. Eight minutemen were killed. The British continued on to Concord, where they met more minutemen. The militia forced the British to retreat. The American Revolution had begun.

About two months later, the Patriots and British clashed again. The Patriots tried to keep British soldiers from taking Breed's Hill. On the morning of June 17, the Patriots forced the British down Breed's Hill twice. When the British came back a third time, the Patriots ran out of ammunition, and the British took the hill. The battle is known as the Battle of Bunker Hill. Although it was a British victory, the Patriots saw that they could defend themselves. These battles drove the wedge between Great Britain and America even deeper.

7. ☑ **Reading Check**
Identify and fill in the missing events for boxes 2 and 4. **Explain** to a partner how April 18 would have been different if not for Revere, Dawes, and Prescott.

The Revolution Begins

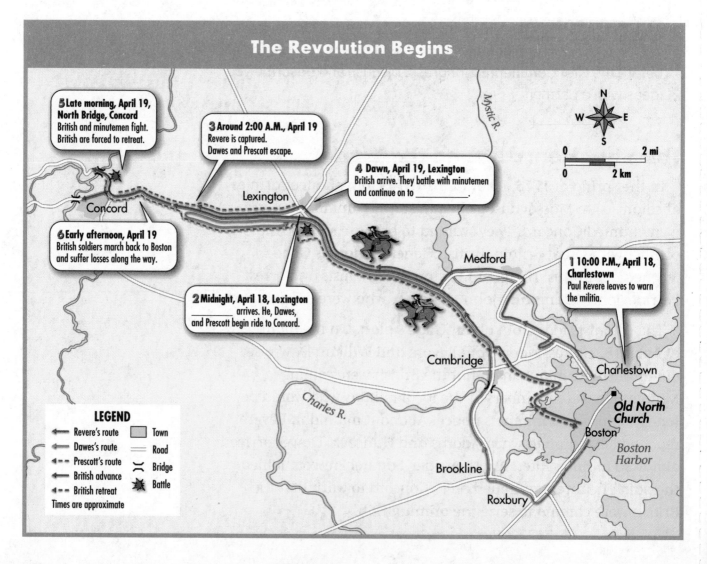

5 Late morning, April 19, North Bridge, Concord
British and minutemen fight. British are forced to retreat.

3 Around 2:00 A.M., April 19
Revere is captured. Dawes and Prescott escape.

4 Dawn, April 19, Lexington
British arrive. They battle with minutemen and continue on to _____.

6 Early afternoon, April 19
British soldiers march back to Boston and suffer losses along the way.

2 Midnight, April 18, Lexington
_____ arrives. He, Dawes, and Prescott begin ride to Concord.

1 10:00 P.M., April 18, Charlestown
Paul Revere leaves to warn the militia.

Mystic R.

Lexington

Concord

Medford

Cambridge

Charlestown

Old North Church

Boston

Boston Harbor

Charles R.

Brookline

Roxbury

N W E S

0   2 mi
0   2 km

LEGEND
⬅ Revere's route
⬅ Dawes's route
◄- - Prescott's route
⬅ British advance
◄- - British retreat
Times are approximate
▢ Town
═ Road
⌣ Bridge
✸ Battle

☑ Lesson 2 Check

8. **Cause and Effect** **Summarize** the reasons for the Boston Massacre, and **describe** what resulted from the event.

_____

_____

_____

_____

_____

9. **Identify** and **describe** why the American Revolution officially began.

_____

_____

_____

_____

10. **Explain** why the colonists referred to the Coercive Acts as the "Intolerable Acts."

_____

_____

_____

_____

Analyze Images

Today, we can view photographs and video of current events minutes after they happen. In the past, people had to draw illustrations of events. Examining these images gives us insight not only into the event, but also the mindset of the artist. The way in which events were shown could shape public opinion.

As you have read, the Boston Massacre occurred in 1770 as a result of rising tensions between the colonists and the British. The colonists were furious about the Townshend Acts and the British ships that occupied Boston Harbor. Below is an engraving made by Paul Revere. It shows the Boston Massacre. Although he was not at the event, Revere based his engraving on first-hand accounts and the work of another artist, Henry Pelham.

This engraving was created by Paul Revere and is called "The Bloody Massacre in King-Street" March 5, 1770.

1. **Identify** and circle in the picture the things described in the left-hand column of the chart. Then complete the chart by **describing** how each element of the engraving might have shaped the colonists' opinions.

VIDEO

Watch a video about analyzing images.

Elements in the Image	Effect of Each Element
1. The British soldiers are lined up and organized.	1. _____ _____ _____
2. The colonists do not have weapons.	2. _____ _____ _____
3. The British soldiers' faces are angular and harsh.	3. _____ _____ _____

2. **Analyze** the image and review your answers above. Use them to **describe** why viewing this image would lead colonists closer to war with Great Britain.

_____

_____

_____

_____

_____

_____

INTERACTIVITY

Participate in a class discussion to preview the content of this lesson.

Vocabulary

Continental army
independence
equality
treason

Academic Vocabulary

unite
foundation

Unlock The BIG Question

I will know why the colonies declared independence from Great Britain and were willing to fight for it.

Jumpstart Activity

With the flip of a coin, one group will represent the Patriots and the other the Loyalists. In about two minutes, create a quick 30-second skit that expresses your group's opinion about declaring independence from Great Britain. What are the opinions of each group?

Colonists became impatient with King George III. Here, they topple a statue of the king.

When delegates from the First Continental Congress sent the Declaration of Rights to King George III, they agreed that they would meet again if the king rejected it. In May 1775, not only had the king rejected the declaration, but a war had begun between the colonies and Great Britain. When the Second Continental Congress met, it had difficult decisions to make.

 **INTERACTIVITY**

Explore the key ideas of this lesson.

The Second Continental Congress

As British soldiers moved into Boston, the Second Continental Congress met in Philadelphia to decide what to do now that the colonies were at war with Great Britain. They decided to create a **Continental army**. George Washington would be commander in chief. The Congress also decided to print money to pay for the military and their supplies. The Congress had become a government.

Many delegates had not thought about declaring **independence**, or freedom, from Great Britain. Those who did, including John Adams, were considered extreme. Most colonists considered themselves British citizens even if they did not agree with all policies.

The Congress decided to try again to peacefully resolve the problems between the colonies and Great Britain. They wrote the Olive Branch Petition. This petition formally requested peace from the king and declared colonial loyalty. The king ignored the petition and declared the colonies rebellious. He banned all trade with the colonies. This drastic action made moderate delegates consider independence.

1. ☑ **Reading Check** **Use Evidence From Text** Highlight the text to **identify** decisions made by the Second Continental Congress. **Describe** why these decisions were significant.

_____

_____

_____

_____

Enlightenment and Independence

In 1776, Thomas Paine, born in Great Britain, shared his thoughts about the next steps for the colonies. He had come to America to support colonial freedom from Great Britain. In a pamphlet called *Common Sense*, Paine encouraged colonists to part with Great Britain and become an independent country.

Thomas Paine was influenced by Enlightenment philosophers, such as John Locke. The Enlightenment was a movement that had occurred in Europe a few decades before. The movement stressed that liberty and **equality**, or having the same rights as everyone else, are basic human rights.

John Locke's ideas about liberty and equality convinced many colonists that the time had come for independence.

Paine's persuasive argument convinced colonists and delegates alike that the time had come for independence. The idea that the king had denied colonists their basic rights was becoming popular.

Paine argued that America needed to break free from a government that violated the natural rights of its citizens. Paine declared, "We have it in our power, to begin the world over again. . . . The birthday of a new world is at hand." Paine also argued for the colonies to **unite** under a system of representative government. More than 200,000 copies of *Common Sense* sold within its first few months of publication.

Academic Vocabulary

unite • *v.*, to join together to achieve a common goal

2. ☑ **Reading Check** **Cause and Effect** **Analyze** and **explain** how the writings of John Locke affected colonists.

_____

_____

_____

_____

_____

Drafting the Declaration of Independence

By May 1776, eight of the colonies supported the decision to declare independence from Great Britain. Before making their plans known to Parliament, delegates wanted to have a written document formally declaring independence.

A "Committee of Five," which included Thomas Jefferson, John Adams, Benjamin Franklin, Roger Sherman, and Robert Livingston, set out to write the document. The committee asked Jefferson to write a draft of the Declaration of Independence. Like Paine, Jefferson was influenced by Locke. While writing the declaration, he used a phrase inspired by Locke: "life, liberty, and pursuit of happiness."

Once Jefferson completed his draft, Franklin and Adams suggested changes. Then they submitted the document to Congress for approval. Soon after, Congress voted on and officially declared independence on July 4, 1776. The delegates put themselves in danger by taking these actions. By declaring independence, they were vulnerable to accusations of **treason**, or attempting to overthrow one's government.

3. ☑ **Reading Check** **Describe** at least two points that you think were included in the Declaration of Independence.

_____

_____

_____

Benjamin Franklin, John Adams, and Thomas Jefferson work on the Declaration of Independence.

The Declaration of Independence

Academic Vocabulary

foundation • *n.*, the base or support of something

Written in the 1700s, the ideas of the Declaration of Independence became the **foundation** of American democracy. Its discussion of natural rights and the relationship between citizens and the government was new.

The Declaration of Independence outlined the ideas that many of the delegates to the convention would use to build a new nation. It stated that everyone is created equal and has certain natural rights. The government's job is to protect these rights using the authority given to it by its citizens.

The document can be divided into three parts—the Preamble, the charges against King George III, and the formal statement of separation from the British government.

1. The Preamble is an introduction. In it, Jefferson writes about the rights that all people have that cannot be taken away.

2. The second section lists ways the king violated the rights of the colonists.

3. The document concludes with a declaration that the 13 Colonies are now independent, united states.

Fifty-six delegates signed the Declaration of Independence. In doing so, they put their lives at risk. They could have been accused of treason by the British government and hanged.

From The Declaration of Independence

1. We hold these truths to be self-evident, that all men are created equal; that they are endowed by their Creator with certain unalienable rights [rights that cannot be removed]; that among these are Life, Liberty, and the pursuit of Happiness.

_____

_____

_____

_____

2. He has refused his Assent to Laws [refused to follow laws]. . . . He has combined with others to subject us to a jurisdiction [authority] foreign to our constitution [way of life]. . . . For cutting off our Trade with all parts of the world: For imposing Taxes on us without our Consent. . . . He has plundered [robbed] our seas, ravaged [destroyed] our Coasts, burnt our towns, and destroyed the lives of our people.

_____

_____

_____

_____

3. These United Colonies are, and of Right ought to be Free and Independent States; that they are Absolved [freed] from all Allegiance to the British Crown . . . they have full Power to levy [make] War, conclude Peace, contract Alliances, establish Commerce, and to do all other Acts and Things which Independent States may of right do.

_____

_____

_____

_____

_____

4. ☑ Reading Check In your own words, **analyze** and **explain** what each section of the Declaration of Independence means.

An Important First Step

"I desire you would remember the ladies…"

Abigail Adams

Jefferson's original version of the Declaration of Independence had included a section that condemned slavery. Congress removed this section before the document's approval. Although the Founders were divided over slavery, both northern and southern delegates opposed the clause referring to the practice.

In 1776, the phrase *all men are created equal* did not apply to African Americans, American Indians, or women. In a letter to her husband John, Abigail Adams famously asked him to "remember the ladies" as the new nation was formed. Abigail felt that it was not logical for the Patriots to fight and die for independence from the British if the rights of some Americans were ignored.

Although the rights of all people would not be recognized until many decades later, the Declaration of Independence was an important first step in the recognition of individual rights.

Today, Americans celebrate the Fourth of July as a day to reflect on our freedoms. Many also enjoy parades, food, and fireworks.

INTERACTIVITY

Check your understanding
of the key ideas of this
lesson.

☑ Lesson 3 Check

5. **Cause and Effect Identify** two effects, or reasons, for the cause provided.

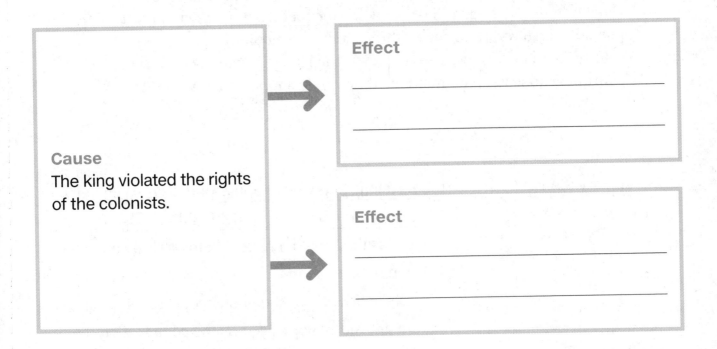

Cause
The king violated the rights of the colonists.

Effect
_____

_____

Effect
_____

_____

6. **Describe** how a colonist might have felt when reading the Declaration of Independence for the first time.

_____

_____

7. **Draw inferences** about how King George III might have reacted as he read the Declaration of Independence.

_____

_____

_____

Thomas Paine's *Common Sense*

In his pamphlet, *Common Sense*, Thomas Paine challenged British control over the colonies. Paine was an early supporter of independence from Great Britain and its king. He used plain language, so that his writing was popular with a variety of people throughout the colonies.

In 1776, many colonists were loyal to the king. *Common Sense* was an effort to change people's minds so they would support independence.

Vocabulary Support

A long period of mistreatment is a good reason to question how that mistreatment can be justified.

Colonists have the right to question both Parliament and the king's claims.

undertaken, *v.*, took on

grievously, *adv.*, seriously

oppressed, *adj.*, kept down by using harsh treatment

undoubted privilege, an absolute right

pretensions, *n.*, merits

usurpation, *n.*, taking by force

As a long and violent abuse of power, is generally the means of calling the right of it in question . . . and as the King of England hath undertaken in his own right, to support the Parliament in what he calls theirs, and as the good people of this country are grievously oppressed by the combination, they have an undoubted privilege to inquire into the pretensions of both, and equally to reject the usurpation of either.

–Thomas Paine, *Common Sense*, Philadelphia, February 14, 1776

Fun Fact

More than 200,000 copies of *Common Sense* sold in the first few months, making *Common Sense* the best-selling printed work ever at that time.

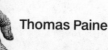

Thomas Paine

Close Reading

1. **Identify** and circle what Paine thinks the colonists should do in response to the king's abuse of power.

2. What does Paine mean? **Explain** in your own words. What other questions do you have about this quotation?

_____

_____

_____

_____

_____

_____

_____

Wrap It Up

Describe some reasons Paine had to write *Common Sense.* Support your answer with information from the chapter. Use one quotation from the selection shown here.

_____

_____

_____

_____

_____

_____

_____

_____

_____

On the Battlefield and at Home

 INTERACTIVITY

Participate in a class discussion to preview the content of this lesson.

Unlock The BIG Question

I will know that even when conditions were difficult, Patriots fought for independence.

Vocabulary

mercenary
retreat
alliance
scarcity
profiteering

Academic Vocabulary

confine
emerge

Jumpstart Activity

With a group, list items an army should be equipped with. What might happen if an army did not have all of the items on your list?

When the fighting began between British and Continental soldiers, many people thought the colonists could not win. The Continental army was an unlikely match for the fierce British army, but the Americans were fighting for their homeland.

The American Revolution was a war waged between the British army, or "Redcoats," and the Continental army.

American and British Military

The British army was one of the best in the world. Its soldiers were well trained, and had supplies. But they were fighting far from home, and supplies took a long time to reach them.

Britain had more money than the colonists. Early in the war, Britain hired 30,000 German soldiers, called Hessians, to help fight the war. These soldiers were **mercenaries**, or soldiers hired by a foreign country. The Patriots saw the Hessians as brutal. Their entry into the war convinced some neutral Americans to join the Patriot cause.

The Continental army was not well trained and had few resources. Financing the war was difficult. Generals sometimes could not agree on strategy, but they were fighting for a cause they believed in. The American forces included local militias. These were groups of armed men who stayed on their land and protected it from invasion.

Both the British and the Continental armies requested help from American Indians. The Cherokee and Mohawk fought with the British, hoping that they would stop westward expansion. The Oneida and Tuscarora fought with the Patriots. Some American Indians remained neutral. Most American Indians, however, sided with the British. If the colonists won, American Indians knew they could lose vast amounts of land. Approximately 1,500 Iroquois, for example, fought with British soldiers.

INTERACTIVITY

Explore the key ideas of this lesson.

1. ☑ **Reading Check** **Compare and Contrast** Use the chart to **identify** and **describe** differences and similarities between the British army and Continental army.

The British Redcoats and the Continentals

British Army	Continental Army	Both
plenty of supplies	few resources	_____
included hired soldiers	included local militias	_____
well trained	_____	_____
	_____	_____
	_____	_____

Major Battles of the Revolution

The Siege of Boston occurred as the Revolution broke out in Lexington and Concord. The conflict lasted until March 1776. During this time, the Continental army kept the British army **confined** within the city of Boston.

The British were still blocking all ships in the harbor, so the economy came to a halt. Supplies for the British military arrived slowly. On March 4, George Washington took control of Dorchester Heights, outside Boston. His troops opened cannon fire on the British ships in the harbor. Two weeks later, the British left the city.

A few months later, British General William Howe and his troops landed on Long Island. Their goal was to capture New York. On August 27, Howe marched toward George Washington and his soldiers at Brooklyn Heights. Howe forced the Americans out. Washington moved his men to Manhattan by boat to avoid capture.

During the fall and winter of 1776, more battles raged. After a loss in White Plains, New York, Washington and his men were pushed into New Jersey and then Pennsylvania. The British captured and sentenced to death a spy and 21-year-old teacher named Nathan Hale. Hale said, "I only regret that I have but one life to lose for my country."

Academic Vocabulary

confine • *v.*, to prevent from leaving; imprison

George Washington led his troops across the icy Delaware on the night of December 25, 1776. The next day, they defeated the British in a surprise attack on Trenton.

Washington needed a victory. So he planned a surprise attack in Trenton, New Jersey. On the night of December 25, Washington and his troops crossed the icy Delaware River toward New Jersey.

The next morning, they surprised and defeated the Hessians who controlled Trenton. Soon after, Washington was victorious in Princeton, New Jersey. These victories gave the Continental army a much-needed morale boost.

A Turning Point

In the fall of 1777, the Battle of Saratoga was a turning point in the war. Tadeusz Kościuszko (also spelled Thaddeus Kosciusko), an engineer from Poland, had helped the Patriots build a fort near the city.

On September 19, British General John Burgoyne won a small victory there against the Americans. The Americans were led by Horatio Gates and Benedict Arnold. Burgoyne attacked the Americans at Saratoga again on October 7. This time, he was defeated and forced to **retreat**, or withdraw. Ten days later, Burgoyne surrendered to the Americans.

Benedict Arnold later betrayed the Patriots. In 1780, he plotted to surrender to the British the fort at West Point, New York. The plan failed. He became one of the most famous traitors in American history.

In September 1777, Hessians descended on Philadelphia. This caused the delegates of the Second Continental Congress to flee to York, Pennsylvania, where they continued their work. The fight in Philadelphia lasted months. The Americans suffered many casualties. Washington withdrew his troops and spent the winter at Valley Forge. Eventually, King George III ordered British General Henry Clinton to leave the city, but many troops had died and the city was damaged.

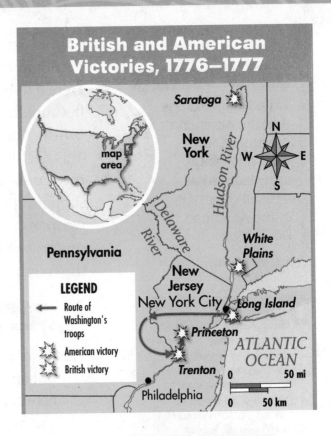

British and American Victories, 1776–1777

LEGEND
← Route of Washington's troops
✶ American victory
✶ British victory

2. ✓ **Reading Check**

Choose colors to represent the American and British victories on the legend. Use these colors to **identify** the victories on the map. **Analyze** and discuss with a partner where Washington's men stood at this point in the war.

Help From Other Countries

Quest Connections

Write three lessons that the American generals and the Continental army learned as a result of battles of the American Revolution.

INTERACTIVITY

Learn about the struggles of women and children on the home front as well as the battles fought on the field. Whose stories would you tell in your newspaper?

Benjamin Franklin tried several times to convince the French to help the Americans in the war. The French refused because they did not think the Americans could defeat the British. This changed after the American victory at Saratoga. This decisive Patriot victory convinced the French to recognize the American cause. They entered the war as an ally, or supporter, of the United States. They loaned money and sent weapons, ammunition, uniforms, and supplies. They also sent troops and ships. This support was important. It helped the colonists defeat the British at Yorktown in 1781.

Primary Source

If war should break out between France and Great Britain during the continuance of the present war between the United States and England, his Majesty and the said United States shall make it a common cause and aid each other mutually with their good offices, their counsels and their forces.

—Treaty of Alliance Between the United States of America and His Most Christian Majesty [France], February 6, 1778

Word Wise

Homonyms are words that are the same in sound and spelling but have different meanings. The word *class* is a homonym. One meaning of *class* is "a group of students in a room." Read this phrase from the lesson: *a harsh ruling class*. What do you think another meaning of *class* is?

Other countries joined the American cause as well. The Dutch people lived under a harsh ruling class at this time. They understood the plight of the Americans. They formed an **alliance** with America and sent ammunition. An alliance is a formal agreement of friendship between countries. Holland was also a trade partner with America. It angered Britain that Holland helped its enemy. As a result, Parliament declared war on Holland.

In 1779, Spain declared war on Britain over land west of the Mississippi. Spain was already allied with the Americans, but now it was involved in the war for its own reasons.

Catherine II of Russia refused Parliament's requests to send troops to America to help the British. The country remained neutral, continuing trade with the colonies and indirectly helping the Americans.

Women During the Revolution

The American Revolution was fought for freedom from an unjust government. But even if the colonists won the war, many people, women included, would not gain any liberties.

The revolution did bring about some change, however. Since women instructed children to be reasonable and responsible adults, a new idea **emerged** of wives and mothers as a "republican motherhood."

Women also worked as nurses, cooks, soldiers, and spies during the war. Many who joined the army did so to make money for their families. Deborah Sampson of Massachusetts fought in the Revolution disguised as a man. Molly Pitcher, a nickname for Mary Ludwig of New Jersey, became known for bringing men water during the Battle of Monmouth.

Well-known women were also involved in the war effort. Martha Washington spent most winters with George Washington, helping soldiers at the camps.

Mercy Otis Warren was a political writer and advocate of independence. She was critical of British rule and urged a fight for freedom. Phillis Wheatley was an enslaved African American. She was a poet and a strong supporter of independence.

Academic Vocabulary

emerge • v., to develop

3. ☑ **Reading Check**
Identify how each woman helped the revolutionary cause.

Women of the Revolution

Deborah Sampson

Molly Pitcher

Phillis Wheatley

African Americans During the War

The Declaration of Independence declared freedom for all, but it did not call for the end of slavery. Thousands of black men fought on both sides of the war. Free and enslaved African Americans fought with the Patriots at Lexington, Concord, and Bunker Hill. But the Continental Congress then stopped accepting African Americans into the army. When the states could not meet their quotas in 1778, they decided to make regiments of African American men. Many of the men who had been enslaved before the war were given their freedom when it ended.

Many African Americans fought with the Patriots.

James Armistead, an enslaved African American from Virginia, enlisted in the Revolutionary War. Armistead worked as a spy for the Marquis de Lafayette, a French officer fighting with the Patriots. Armistead provided information that allowed the Patriots to win a decisive battle in the war. He was given his freedom after the war.

In 1775, Lord Dunmore, the British governor of Virginia, promised freedom to slaves who escaped from Patriots and fought with the Loyalists. He kept his promise when the war was over.

The Home Front

As the British invaded cities, people fled to the country looking for food and work. In the country, many women ran family farms. They often stood in the way of advancing armies. Armies destroyed and robbed farms. The British punished families who housed Patriots.

The economy suffered. Anyone who worked in trade was unemployed because the British blocked ports so ships could not bring supplies. The blockades caused **scarcity**. This lack of supplies resulted in huge price increases.

Some people hoarded goods and hid them. They began **profiteering**, or charging very high prices for goods. This caused inflation, as the price of goods soared. Congress passed laws to stop both of these practices.

Although living on the home front was difficult, everyone hoped that the burden would be worth it. The war was fought for the ideals of liberty and independence. These ideals named in the Declaration of Independence were the foundation of the new nation. They were often included in state constitutions written after 1776.

4. ☑ **Reading Check** **Use Evidence From Text** **Identify** and highlight ways in which life was difficult for those on the home front.

Women on the home front took care of farms and protected their families from British invasion.

INTERACTIVITY

Check your understanding of the key ideas of this lesson.

☑ Lesson 4 Check

5. **Cause and Effect** **Analyze** and **explain** how the British blockade affected people in the countryside.

_____

_____

6. **Explain** how the Declaration of Independence did not extend freedoms to all Americans.

_____

_____

_____

7. **Quest** **Connections** Choose one of the first battles of the Revolution. On another sheet of paper, write a fictional eyewitness description of it for your newspaper.

Cause and Effect

A **cause** is a reason, an event, or a condition that makes something happen. An **effect** is the result of a cause. You can find causes and effects by asking yourself questions. To find a cause, ask "Why?" To find an effect, ask "What happened next?"

Historical events usually have multiple causes and effects. This means that more than one thing causes an event. The Siege of Boston, for example, was an event that had multiple causes and effects. Making note of what caused events and what happened as a result can give us a deeper understanding of history. Read the passage below and look for causes and effects of the Siege of Boston.

▶ VIDEO

Watch a video about cause and effect.

George Washington leads his troops.

The Siege of Boston occurred as the Revolution broke out. The conflict lasted until March 1776. During this time, the Continental army contained the British army within the city of Boston after the British had invaded.

The siege caused many Bostonians to flee. The British were still blocking all ships in the harbor, so the economy came to a halt. Supplies for the military were slow in coming. On March 4, George Washington took control of Dorchester Heights, outside Boston. His troops opened cannon fire on the British ships in the harbor. Two weeks later, on a day now called Evacuation Day, the British left the city.

Your Turn!

1. What are the causes and effects of the Siege of Boston as described in the passage? Fill in the graphic organizer showing causes and effects.

Causes and Effects of the Siege of Boston

Cause

The British occupied Boston.

→

Effect

_____

_____

_____

Cause

_____

_____

_____

→

Effect

_____

_____

_____

Cause

_____

_____

_____

→

Effect

_____

_____

_____

2. Read the fourth and fifth paragraphs in Lesson 4, under the head "Major Battles of the Revolution." Find causes and effects of the Battle of Trenton. Then write a statement that summarizes the causes and effects.

_____

_____

_____

_____

Lesson 5 Winning Independence

INTERACTIVITY

Participate in a class discussion to preview the content of this lesson.

Vocabulary

peninsula
negotiate
Treaty of Paris

Academic Vocabulary

recover
reinforcement

Unlock The BIG Question

I will know how the United States won its independence.

JumpStart Activity

With a partner, act out a meeting. One person is the leader, who wants to start the school day later in the morning. What can the leader do to convince the others to support this idea? Why would helping the leader be worth it?

As the year 1777 ended, America was still at war. Although the Patriot forces had won some important victories against the British, they still faced many obstacles. The path to independence looked uncertain.

A Turning Point in the War

When the British forced Washington and his troops out of Philadelphia, they retreated to Valley Forge outside of the city. Washington planned to prepare his troops for more battles in the spring, but they were discouraged, exhausted, and not properly trained. The Patriots had recently lost the Battle of Brandywine and the Battle of Germantown. The harsh winter would bring morale to a new low.

The conditions at Valley Forge that winter were terrible. There were not enough shelters. The troops did not have enough food or warm clothes. Many soldiers died of disease. Washington lost about 2,000 men that winter.

The tide slowly began to turn as Washington worked with Benjamin Franklin to provide adequate food, supplies, and troops. Then Franklin enlisted the help of Baron Friedrich von Steuben. Baron von Steuben had been a military officer in the Prussian army. He began training the Continental army and gave the troops a sense of pride and confidence. Morale was further boosted when Washington learned that the French had agreed to join the war on the side of the Americans. This was a crucial turning point. News of the revitalized unit at Valley Forge inspired Continental army troops throughout the states.

INTERACTIVITY

Explore the key ideas of this lesson.

1. ✓ **Reading Check** **Analyze** why the American troops regained their confidence by the spring of 1778. **Summarize** what led to this improvement.

_____

_____

Washington and his troops endured harsh conditions during their winter at Valley Forge.

Marching Toward Victory

Beginning in 1776, Spain began sending money and military supplies to America. Support from Spain during the American Revolution was due in part to its desire to see Great Britain lose its power. The Spanish wanted to **recover** some of the land that they had lost to the British.

In 1779 and 1780, the Spanish governor of Louisiana, Bernardo de Gálvez, attacked British forts at Baton Rouge, Mobile, Natchez, and Pensacola. Spain took these forts and stopped the British from reaching the Mississippi River.

Although southern Loyalists had helped the British win battles in Savannah, Georgia, and Charleston, South Carolina, in 1778 and 1780, the British overestimated their support. Many southerners were Patriots, including Francis Marion. Marion earned the name "Swamp Fox" for leading his small band in quick attacks on the British. After the attacks, the men retreated into the swamps.

In the South, General Nathanael Greene did not have enough troops. So he attacked and quickly retreated again and again until he wore out the British.

The Final Battles

In June 1778, British General Sir Henry Clinton and his men left Philadelphia. They marched toward New York City. Washington and his newly trained army left Valley Forge and met the British at Monmouth, New Jersey.

American General Charles Lee learned that British **reinforcements** were coming. He ordered a retreat. Washington was furious. He could not reorganize American ranks in time to take the British. Clinton continued toward New York, but Washington joined other American forces along the Hudson River.

Between 1780 and 1781, several battles were fought in North and South Carolina. The British had seized control of Savannah, Charleston, and Camden in 1778 and 1780. These battles were followed by two American victories at Kings Mountain and Cowpens.

Academic Vocabulary

recover • *v.*, to get back, regain

reinforcement • *n.*, more people, supplies, or weapons

Battles, 1778–1781

map area

Cahokia
Fort Vincennes
Ohio River
Kaskaskia
Yorktown
Guilford Courthouse
Cowpens
Kings Mountain
Camden
Eutaw Springs
Charleston
Savannah
Mississippi River
Natchez
Mobile
Pensacola
Baton Rouge
Gulf of Mexico

LEGEND
☐ United States
✹ British victory
✹ American victory
✹ Spanish victory

The news of these battles shook British General Charles Cornwallis, who waited for reinforcements. The battles of Guilford Courthouse and Eutaw Springs ended in victories for the British, but many British troops were killed. British General Charles Cornwallis abandoned the Carolinas and moved his troops back to Virginia to rest.

He then went to Yorktown, Virginia, which is on a **peninsula**, a piece of land almost surrounded by water but still attached to the mainland. Washington left New York with American and French soldiers. He planned to arrive in Yorktown at the same time as the French navy. Washington asked General Lafayette to lead an army of 4,500 soldiers to block Cornwallis's escape from Yorktown.

Washington's troops needed food, clothing, and supplies. He asked Haym Salomon, a Jewish immigrant from Poland, for money. Salomon was a Patriot who was arrested by the British twice but managed to escape. Salomon, now called "the Financial Hero of the American Revolution," provided vital supplies for Washington's troops before the Battle of Yorktown.

2. ☑ **Reading Check** Turn and **talk with a partner**. **Identify** and list the groups and people who fought on the side of the Americans and on the side of the British.

By late September, Washington arrived in Yorktown. While his army attacked the British on land, French navy ships sailed into Chesapeake Bay and blocked British ships from rescuing Cornwallis. He was trapped. After three weeks of battle, on October 17, 1781, Cornwallis surrendered to Washington in a field at Yorktown. This was the last major battle of the American Revolution.

The War Comes to an End

The United States won the American Revolution against the mighty British army. In 1782, Benjamin Franklin, John Adams, John Jay, and British officials **negotiated** the **Treaty of Paris**, a peace treaty.

Primary Source

His Brittanic Majesty acknowledges the said United States . . . to be free sovereign and independent states, that he treats with them as such, and for himself, his heirs [children], and successors, relinquishes [gives up] all claims to the government, propriety, and territorial rights of the same and every part thereof.

—The Treaty of Paris, 1783

The treaty stated that America was an independent nation. It allowed for westward expansion. The borders for the new nation were agreed upon. The United States now reached from Canada to Spanish Florida and as far west as the Mississippi River.

3. **Reading Check** **Make inferences** about why Franklin, Adams, and Jay included a mention of westward expansion in the Treaty of Paris.

_____

_____

Americans Benjamin Franklin, John Adams, and John Jay negotiated the Treaty of Paris with British officials after the American Revolution.

☑ Lesson 5 Check

4. **Cause and Effect** Write the causes that led to the effect in the chart. **Analyze** the outcome of the battles fought in the South between 1778 and 1780. **Explain** their effect on the outcome of the war.

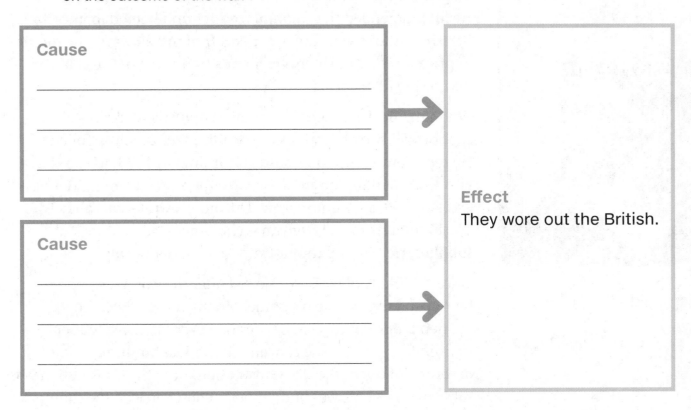

Cause

_____

_____

_____

Cause

_____

_____

_____

Effect
They wore out the British.

5. **Analyze** the events leading up to the surrender at Yorktown. **Describe** regrets that Cornwallis might have had.

_____

_____

_____

6. **Understand the** *Quest* **Connections** **Describe** how you think George Washington felt about the American Revolution and the outcome of the war.

_____

_____

_____

Quality:
Patriotism

George Washington (1732–1799)
Leader of a New Nation

George Washington dedicated his life to his country. When he was 21 years old, he was made a major in the British army. He fought against the French during the French and Indian War. He later defended the colonial frontier and helped to improve British relations with the American Indians. However, he did not approve of the British government's treatment of the colonies and resigned his post.

When the British taxed the colonists unjustly, Washington supported boycotts and disagreed with Parliament's policies. He represented his home state of Virginia in 1775 during the First Continental Congress. He was appointed commander in chief of the Continental army. During his winter at Valley Forge, Washington met and overcame challenges, such as lack of supplies. He built up a well-trained, confident army.

Once the Treaty of Paris was signed after the war, Washington retired and returned to his home, Mount Vernon. Encouraged by friends and colleagues, he presided over the Constitutional Convention in 1787. The convention produced a strong federal government under the U.S. Constitution. After the Constitution was ratified in 1788, he was unanimously chosen to lead the country as the first President of the United States. Washington became president in 1789 and led the country for two terms (8 years).

Find Out More

1. As he left office, George Washington advised against getting involved in foreign conflicts. Why might this advice have been considered patriotic?

_____

_____

_____

2. There are many ways to be patriotic. **Survey** your friends and family about what they think are good ways to show patriotism. **Report** your findings to your class.

Use the map to review some of the key terms and ideas from this chapter.

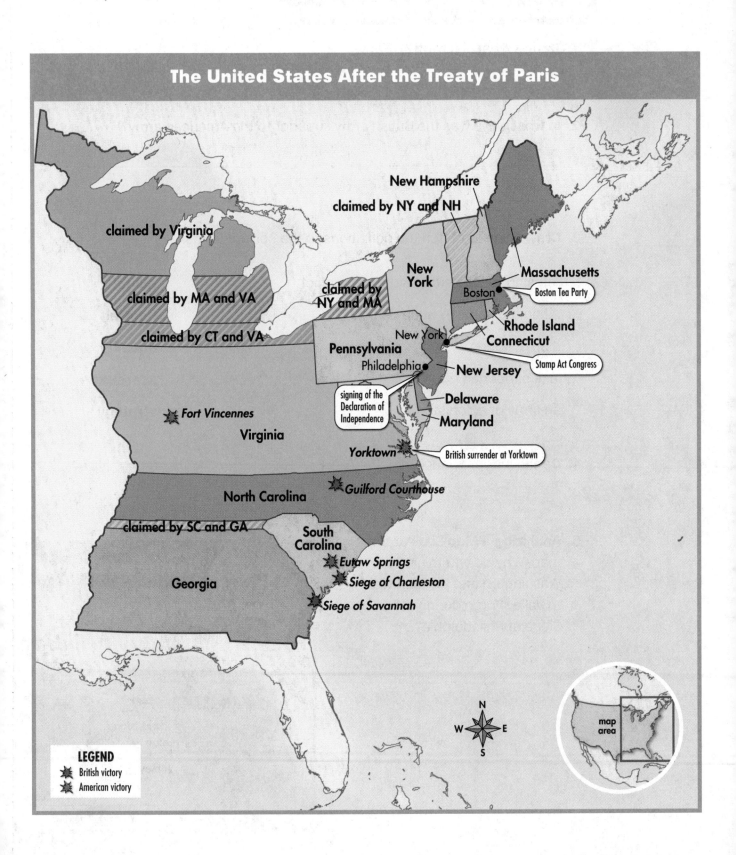

The United States After the Treaty of Paris

New Hampshire
claimed by NY and NH

claimed by Virginia

claimed by MA and VA

claimed by CT and VA

claimed by NY and MA

New York

Massachusetts

Boston ● — Boston Tea Party

Rhode Island
Connecticut

New York

Pennsylvania

Philadelphia ●

New Jersey — Stamp Act Congress

signing of the Declaration of Independence

Delaware

Fort Vincennes

Maryland

Virginia

Yorktown — British surrender at Yorktown

Guilford Courthouse

North Carolina

claimed by SC and GA

South Carolina

Georgia

Eutaw Springs

Siege of Charleston

Siege of Savannah

N
W   E
S

map area

LEGEND
✹ British victory
✸ American victory

Vocabulary and Key Ideas

1. Define What is a **tariff**?

_____

2. In what ways was the British army superior to the American army?

_____

_____

3. Draw a line to match the definitions to the correct terms.

refusing to take either side in a conflict   **militia**

being the same in value   **neutral**

plan of action   **equality**

lack of needed goods   **scarcity**

an army of colonists   **strategy**

4. Define independence.

_____

5. Analyzing a Map Look at the map. Why do you think General Washington and his men went to Valley Forge during the Siege of Philadelphia?

_____

_____

_____

Northeast Colonies

map area

ATLANTIC OCEAN

New York

Pennsylvania

Long Island

Valley Forge
Philadelphia • • Trenton
New Jersey

N
W ⊕ E
S

0   200 mi
0   200 km

Critical Thinking and Writing

6. **Analyze** reasons for the colonists' discontent after the Stamp Act was passed. **Explain** why "no taxation without representation" became a colonial motto.

_____

_____

_____

7. **Interpret** Fill in the circle next to the best answer. Which of the following actions was part of the Intolerable Acts?

Ⓐ The British military took control of Massachusetts.

Ⓑ Colonists would be punished for housing British soldiers.

Ⓒ British soldiers would be tried in the colonies.

Ⓓ The colonies did not have to replace tea destroyed during the Boston Tea Party.

8. **Analyze** How did the outcome of the American Revolution affect the world politically and economically?

_____

_____

_____

_____

9. **Revisit the Big Question** Why was the American Revolution worth fighting?

_____

_____

_____

_____

_____

10. **Writing Workshop Write an Opinion** Imagine you are a colonist. On separate paper, write a letter to the editor regarding the recent Declaration of Independence. Explain your opinion about how the rights of women and African Americans should be considered when building a new nation. Include details from the text to support your opinion.

Analyze Primary Sources

Vocabulary Support

shaft • *n.*, the stone column of the monument

Spirit, that made those heroes dare
To die, and leave their children free,
Bid Time and Nature gently spare
The **shaft** we raise to them and thee.

—The final stanza of Ralph Waldo Emerson's "Concord Hymn," 1836

11. Emerson's poem was published for the 1837 dedication of the Battle of Concord memorial. The monument remembers the Battles of Lexington and Concord. What do you think Emerson meant in this stanza? What questions do you have about the stanza?

_____

_____

_____

_____

_____

Cause and Effect

12. What were the reasons for and outcome of hoarding goods during the American Revolution?

_____

_____

_____

_____

_____

_____

_____

Quest Findings

Read All About It!

You've read the lessons in this chapter and now you're ready to organize your newspaper stories and editorials. Remember that the goal of the newspaper is to inform the colonists about the events before and during the American Revolution.

INTERACTIVITY

Complete this activity to learn about types of newspaper articles.

1 Prepare to Write

Organize your information. Decide what will be used for interviews, editorials, and letters to the editor. Discuss how to use each story or opinion piece to build on the last. Assign a written piece to each member of your group.

2 Write a Draft

Use your notes and the evidence from your Quest Connections to write your news stories and editorials. Make sure your stories answer the following questions:

- What is the story about?
- Who is involved?
- Where does it take place?
- When is it happening?
- Why is it happening?
- How does the outcome affect colonists?

3 Gather Your Images

As a group, choose which images, maps, and graphics will be paired with each story or editorial. Remember that visuals are an important way for a person to understand a news story.

4 Revise

Have a partner read your piece. Then revise as necessary. As a group, decide on the layout for your newspaper.

GO ONLINE FOR
DIGITAL RESOURCES

▶ VIDEO

👆 INTERACTIVITY

🔊 AUDIO

🎮 GAMES

☑ ASSESSMENT

📖 eTEXT

The **BIG** Question What is the purpose of government?

▶ VIDEO

JumPstart Activity

👆 INTERACTIVITY

With your class, create a rule for lining up in the front of the room. Then vote for two students to serve as leaders. Follow their instructions as you line up according to the rule you created.

Describe your activity. How did you choose a rule?

How did you elect your leaders?

_____

_____

_____

_____

_____

A More Perfect Union

Preview the chapter **vocabulary** as you sing the rap:

The Articles of Confederation

Outlined the plan of the new nation.

They needed central government to get by;

States voted yes to **ratify.**

With little power, central government was weak.

It was decided **delegates** needed to speak.

These representatives all met at a convention;

Some of the ideas were met with tension.

How would states have equal representation?

It couldn't come down to just population:

Each side gave up things to reach an agreement;

Compromises were made and this is how they went.

6 A New Nation

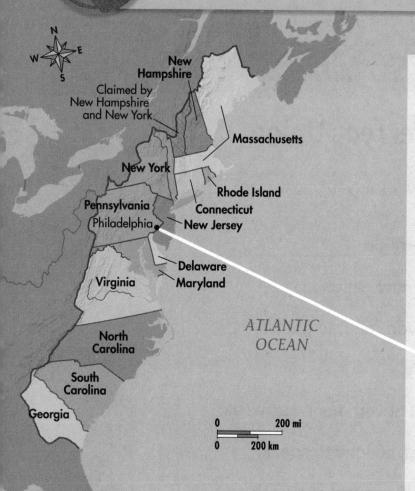

New Hampshire

Claimed by New Hampshire and New York

Massachusetts

New York

Rhode Island
Connecticut

Pennsylvania
Philadelphia
New Jersey

Delaware

Virginia
Maryland

North Carolina

ATLANTIC OCEAN

South Carolina

Georgia

0   200 mi
0   200 km

Where was the U.S. Constitution written?

In 1787, the nation's leaders met in Philadelphia to write a new constitution.

Locate Philadelphia on the map and identify the state it is in.

Independence Hall

TODAY
You can tour Independence Hall in Philadelphia.

What happened and When?

Read the timeline to find out about the events surrounding the creation of the Constitution.

1780

1785

1781
Articles of Confederation is ratified.

1786
Shays' Rebellion erupts over inflation and taxes.

Who will you meet?

Patrick Henry
An Anti-Federalist who was against a strong federal government

Alexander Hamilton
A Federalist who supported a strong federal government

Roger Sherman
Proposed the Great Compromise

Edmund Randolph
Presented the Virginia Plan

 INTERACTIVITY

Complete the interactive gallery.

1790

1788
U.S. Constitution is ratified.

TODAY
The Constitution has been amended 27 times.

1791
Bill of Rights wins state approval and is added to the Constitution.

TODAY
You can see the Bill of Rights in the Rotunda of the National Archives Building in Washington, D.C.

Yea or Nay, I Say!

Our Constitution, or plan of government, was written in 1787. Clearly, it was built to last! But when it was written, many Americans disagreed about it. Supporters had to work to persuade states to ratify, or approve, the Constitution. Those who were against the Constitution, tried hard to convince others to oppose it.

One way to persuade people is to write a letter to the editor. This is a short letter that is printed in a newspaper.

Quest Kick Off

Your mission is to take the role of a supporter or opponent of the Constitution in the year 1787. Write a letter to the editor to convince readers of your point of view.

1 Ask Questions

What do you think government should be allowed to do? What shouldn't it be allowed to do? Write two questions you have about the role of government.

....

....

....

....

Alexander
Hamilton

2 Research

Follow your teacher's instructions to find letters to the editor online or in your local newspaper. Read several. How do they try to persuade readers?

INTERACTIVITY

Analyze the parts of a letter to the editor and see some examples.

....

....

....

....

....

....

3 Look for Quest Connections

Turn to the next page to begin looking for Quest connections that will help you write your letter.

4 Quest Findings
Write Your Letter

Use the Quest Findings page at the end of the chapter to help you write your letter.

INTERACTIVITY

Participate in a class discussion to preview the content of this lesson.

Vocabulary

Articles of Confederation
ratified
legislative
executive
judicial
inflation
ordinances

Academic Vocabulary

currency
regulate

Unlock **The BIG Question**

I will know how the government was organized under the Articles of Confederation.

Jumpstart Activity

Divide into two groups. You will decide what to do at recess. The students in one group will call out their ideas aloud. The other group will discuss what to do and reach a group decision. This group will choose a spokesperson to announce the decision. Which group makes a decision more effectively? Discuss which group seems more organized.

As colonists were fighting the Revolutionary War, delegates from each state gathered once again. The delegates declared independence and worked together to form a new national government. After much debate, delegates created a government with limited power over its people. A government with limited power reflected the states' struggle against the power of the British king.

Forming a New Government

Just weeks after war erupted in Lexington and Concord, the Second Continental Congress met in Philadelphia. Although it had no legal authority, Congress took on the role of a national, or federal, government. It printed money and created a Continental Army.

The delegates outlined a plan for a new government. They called this plan the **Articles of Confederation**. In November 1777, Congress adopted the Articles. Congress sent the plan to individual states to be **ratified**. The 13 states ratified the Articles in March 1781.

INTERACTIVITY

Explore the key ideas of this lesson.

1. ☑ **Reading Check**
Identify how the Second Continental Congress acted as a national government. **Highlight** the actions in the text.

People go about their daily business outside Independence Hall in Philadelphia.

A Weak Government

Under the Articles of Confederation, the government had one branch—the **legislative** branch, which is the part of government that makes the laws. Each state had one vote for or against a law. For a law to be passed, at least nine states had to vote for it.

The Articles created a weak central government. There was no **executive** branch or **judicial** branch. The executive branch carries out the laws passed by the legislative branch. The judicial branch, made up of courts and judges, decides what laws mean. Under the Articles, the states controlled most of the laws. For example, Congress could not make laws about trade. Each state controlled trade with other states and with foreign governments.

2. ☑ Reading Check **Cause and Effect** Read about the problems caused by the Articles in the left column and write the effects of each cause in the right column.

Problems With the Articles

Causes	Effects
1. legislative branch only	_____
2. central government could not collect taxes	_____
3. central government had no control over trade	_____

The Articles had other economic weaknesses. One of the main reasons the Patriots fought for freedom was over unjust taxes. So the new central government had no power to tax. The only way the government could raise money to run the government was to ask the states for money, borrow money from another country, or sell land. To pay its war debts, Congress began printing a new national **currency** called "continentals." States printed their own currency too.

Congress asked the states to collect taxes to balance out the use of the new continentals. But as the war dragged on, states were unwilling to help fund the central government. The army could not be paid in full, causing the threat of an uprising. The continentals became worthless. This resulted in **inflation**, which meant that the price of goods increased while the value of money decreased. As a result of inflation, people could not buy as much as they had in the past.

As you read, the new nation was unable to **regulate** business between states and other countries. These weaknesses made it difficult for other countries to take the United States seriously.

Academic Vocabulary

currency • *n.*, money
regulate • *v.*, to control or adjust

3. ☑ **Reading Check**
Interpreting Graphs Due to inflation, the cost of goods increased. Between which two years did the cost of a bushel of potatoes increase the most?

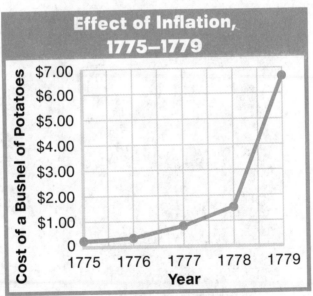

Source: *Massachusetts Bureau of Statistics of Labor, 1885*

Shays' Rebellion

While both the national and state governments were in debt from the war, only states had the power to collect taxes. In 1786, Massachusetts increased the taxes that people paid on their property. The tax would help pay the state's debts, or money it owed.

These new taxes put pressure on farmers. Many began losing their homes. Daniel Shays was one such farmer. He had been a Continental army captain during the American Revolution. He had not been paid in full for his service, but he was taken to court for not paying his debts. Shays became a vocal leader for those who believed the new taxes were unjust. These people organized protests to stop debt collectors.

Shays' militia met an army when they arrived at the federal weapons depot in Springfield, Massachusetts, in January 1787.

In January 1787, Shays and a militia of 1,500 men planned to steal guns and cannons from a federal weapons depot. The Massachusetts governor learned of this plan. He sent an army of 1,200 men. The army was waiting for Shays and his men when they arrived. The army fired shots, killing four men and wounding twenty. Shays' men quickly scattered. They retreated to Vermont.

Shays' Rebellion highlighted some of the weaknesses of the Articles of Confederation. People began to fear that citizens would take the law into their own hands. Leaders began to call for a stronger national government.

4. ☑ **Reading Check** **Analyze** How did Shays' Rebellion show the weaknesses of the government under the Articles of Confederation?

_____

_____

_____

_____

_____

New Land Policies

Under the Articles of Confederation, Congress needed to decide how to organize the territory the nation received under the Treaty of Paris. The first lands it organized were north of the Ohio River, called the Northwest Territory.

Congress issued several **ordinances**, or laws, to organize the territory. The first was the Land Ordinance of 1785. It explained how the land would be divided and called for public schools to be opened in the territory. The Northwest Ordinance of 1787 laid out a structure for the sale and settlement of the Northwest Territory, and three to five new states were to be created there. When a region reached 5,000 settlers, it would elect an assembly. When the population reached 60,000, residents could draft a constitution and apply to become a state.

Word Wise

Context Clues When you see an unfamiliar word, try to find a clue in the text to help you figure out the meaning. Find the word *assembly* in the second paragraph under "New Land Policies." What other words do you see in the description of the Northwest Ordinance that gives you a clue about its meaning? What do you think *assembly* means?

The ordinances had different effects on different people. Slavery was not permitted in the Northwest Territory and, therefore, slavery did not spread north of the Ohio River. However, this ordinance did not abolish slavery in the South, where nine out of ten enslaved African Americans lived. Religious freedom was guaranteed.

Many American Indians did not recognize the ordinance. Several groups came together and fought American soldiers in order to keep their lands. The United Indian Nations, which included the Shawnee and Miami nations, waged war on the United States to prevent settlers from pushing them off their land. In response, President Washington sent General Anthony Wayne into the territory with an army. The American Indians were defeated. The result was that settlers continued to move to western lands. Yet, the Northwest Ordinance of 1787 claimed that Indian lands would be protected.

Primary Source

The utmost good faith shall always be observed [given] towards the Indians; their lands and property shall never be taken from them without their consent; and, in their property, rights, and liberty, they shall never be invaded or disturbed, unless in just and lawful wars authorized by Congress; but laws founded in justice and humanity, shall from time to time be made for preventing wrongs being done to them, and for preserving peace and friendship with them.

—Northwest Ordinance, July 13, 1787

For a time in the nation's history, Indian nations and European settlers cooperated. Some Indians acted as traders and mediators. European settlers brought new foods and tools, including guns. Peaceful co-existence was short-lived, however. The Northwest Ordinance allowed for westward expansion of the United States, but it took its toll on American Indians.

5. ☑ Reading Check **Analyze a Primary Source** What did the Northwest Ordinance of 1787 state about American Indian groups that lived in the territories?

_____

_____

The Northwest Territory, 1781

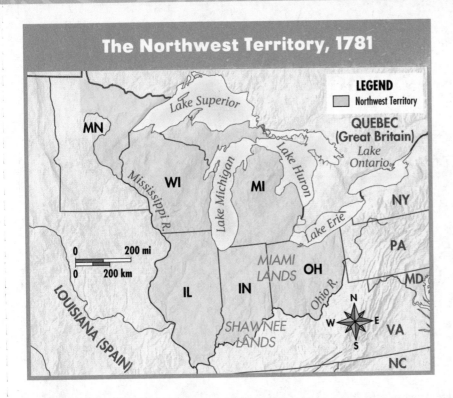

LEGEND
- Northwest Territory

6. **Reading Check**
Identify Circle on the map the names of the modern states where the Miami and Shawnee groups lived.

INTERACTIVITY

Check your understanding of the key ideas of this lesson.

Lesson 1 Check

7. **Summarize** the rights the states had under the Articles of Confederation.

8. **Describe** what happened because of the Northwest Ordinance.

9. **Analyze** and **explain** how inflation affected Americans after the Revolution.

Summarize

I liked hearing about the Articles of Confederation.

I liked it, too. What was your favorite part? Can you summarize it for me?

I'm not sure I know how to summarize. Can you help?

VIDEO

Watch a video about summarizing.

When you **summarize**, you retell the main idea and most important details in your own words. For example, you might summarize the Articles of Confederation by saying that the Articles were the first constitution, and that they formed a weak central government.

Writing a summary is a good way to analyze and remember information. Read the paragraph below. Look at the way it is divided into main idea and details.

There were economic problems created by the Articles. Unjust taxation had been one of the driving forces of the war. Therefore, the new central government had no taxation power.

The only way the government could raise money was to ask for money from the states, borrow money from another country, or sell land. In an effort to pay its war debts, Congress began printing a new national currency called "Continentals."

Use the organizer to list the main idea and details of this paragraph and write a summary.

Your Turn!

1. What is the main idea and what are the most important details of the paragraph you read? Fill in the organizer showing the main idea and details of the paragraph. Use the box labeled "Summary" to write one statement that summarizes the paragraph.

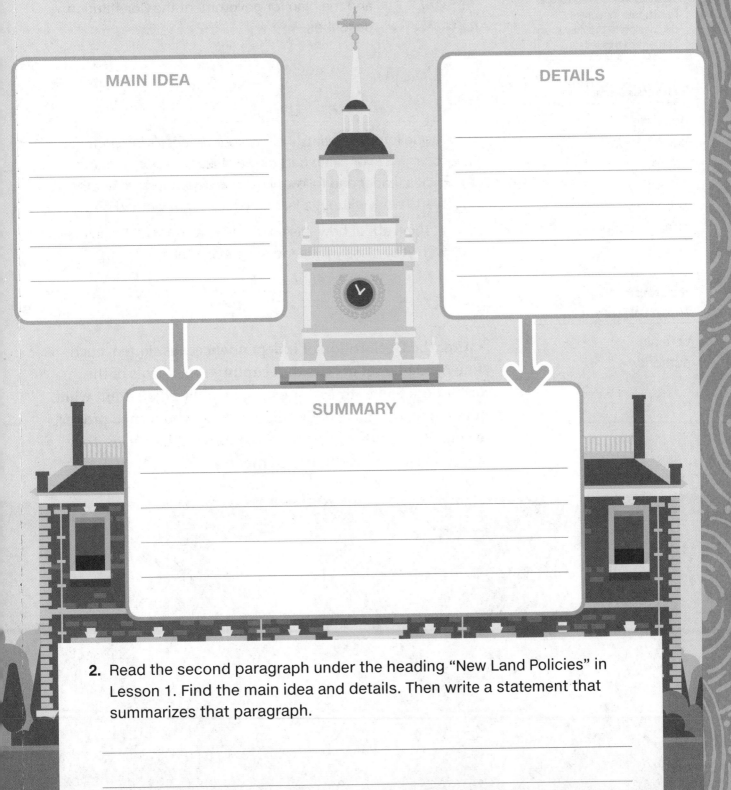

MAIN IDEA

DETAILS

SUMMARY

2. Read the second paragraph under the heading "New Land Policies" in Lesson 1. Find the main idea and details. Then write a statement that summarizes that paragraph.

Creating the Constitution

INTERACTIVITY

Participate in a class discussion to preview the content of this lesson.

Unlock The BIG Question

I will know how the Constitution was created and the plan for government the Constitution describes.

Vocabulary

delegate
constitution
compromise
Preamble
separation of powers
checks and balances
veto

Academic Vocabulary

consult
authority

JumpStart Activity

Divide into two teams. Follow your teacher's instructions to organize or clean part of the classroom. On one team, pick a leader and follow his or her directions. On another team, work without a leader. Which team worked better?

Think about how this relates to government. Discuss with your class why leaders are important.

After the Declaration of Independence was signed, each state needed a set of laws that captured the ideals of the Revolution. Some states, for example, allowed all adult white males to vote. Others allowed only those who owned property to vote. When the founders met to discuss the Articles, they looked to state constitutions as models.

In May 1787, many signers of the Declaration of Independence, called **delegates**, returned to Philadelphia. Their goal was to form a stronger government. Some came to strengthen the Articles of Confederation. Others came to craft a completely new **constitution**, or written plan for government. The Constitution created in 1787 has been changed over the years, but is still in use today.

INTERACTIVITY

Explore the key ideas of this lesson.

The Constitutional Convention

The meeting, known as the Constitutional Convention, included people who had steered the young nation toward independence. Benjamin Franklin, at age 81, was the oldest person to take part. He suffered from poor health but was present for most of the convention. Franklin supported a stronger national government.

James Madison, also a member of the Continental Congress, firmly believed in a strong national government. During the convention, he took detailed notes that historians still **consult** today.

Patrick Henry, who had argued fiercely for independence, refused to attend the convention. He defended the Articles of Confederation and opposed taking power from the states.

Academic Vocabulary

consult • v., to look for information in something

In 1787, American leaders met in Philadelphia at the Constitutional Convention. George Washington, standing on the right, was president of the convention.

George Washington, who had led the nation to victory during the Revolutionary War, also attended. Washington was elected president of the convention.

Alexander Hamilton had worked closely with George Washington during the Revolution. Later, he became a member of Congress and a lawyer. Hamilton agreed that the central government created by the Articles of Confederation was too weak.

There were 55 delegates who met between May and September in 1787. Although these delegates came from different states and held different ideas, they shared many characteristics. Most delegates were from the colonies and had fought in the American Revolution. Forty-one of the 55 had served in the Continental Congress. Although Benjamin Franklin was largely self-taught, most delegates were wealthy, well-educated slave owners.

1. ☑ **Reading Check**
Read and **analyze** the statements from each leader. Write *C* next to the quote if the person supported a strong central government and new Constitution, or *A* if the person supported the Articles of Confederation.

Benjamin Franklin

Opinions About the Articles of Confederation

"Thirteen [states] pulling against each other and all tugging at the . . . head [central government] will soon bring ruin on the whole." —**George Washington** ☐

"Thus I consent, Sir, to this Constitution because I expect no better, and because I am not sure, that it is not the best." —**Benjamin Franklin** ☐

"This power [described in the Constitution] is calculated to annihilate [destroy] totally the state governments." —**George Mason** ☐

"Our rights and privileges are endangered, and the sovereignty [power] of the states [will] be relinquished [given away]." —**Patrick Henry** ☐

Ideas for Debate

The Constitutional Convention began on May 25, 1787. Its original goal was to improve the Articles of Confederation, but some delegates clearly had other plans.

Edmund Randolph, from Virginia, argued for a whole new form of government. He presented the Virginia Plan at the start of the convention. It called for an executive branch to carry out laws and a judicial branch to decide their meaning. Congress, the legislative branch, had a great deal of power in this plan. It would decide who served in the other two branches and would be made up of representatives from each state. States with larger populations would have more representatives in Congress. Therefore, they would have more power in the government.

This plan was seen as a good starting point, except for one major issue. Delegates from the smaller states did not like the idea of having less power than those in the larger states.

William Paterson of New Jersey, one of the smaller states, proposed a new plan, the New Jersey Plan. It was similar to the Virginia Plan, except that it called for each state to have the same number of representatives. This would give all states equal power, no matter their size.

2. ☑ **Reading Check**
Delegates debated the Virginia and New Jersey plans. **Identify** and fill in the parts of the chart that tell how the two plans are different.

The Virginia and New Jersey Plans			
	Executive Branch	**Judicial Branch**	**Legislative Branch**
Virginia Population 747,819	Chosen by legislative branch	Chosen by legislative branch	
New Jersey Population 184,139	Chosen by legislative branch	Chosen by legislative branch	

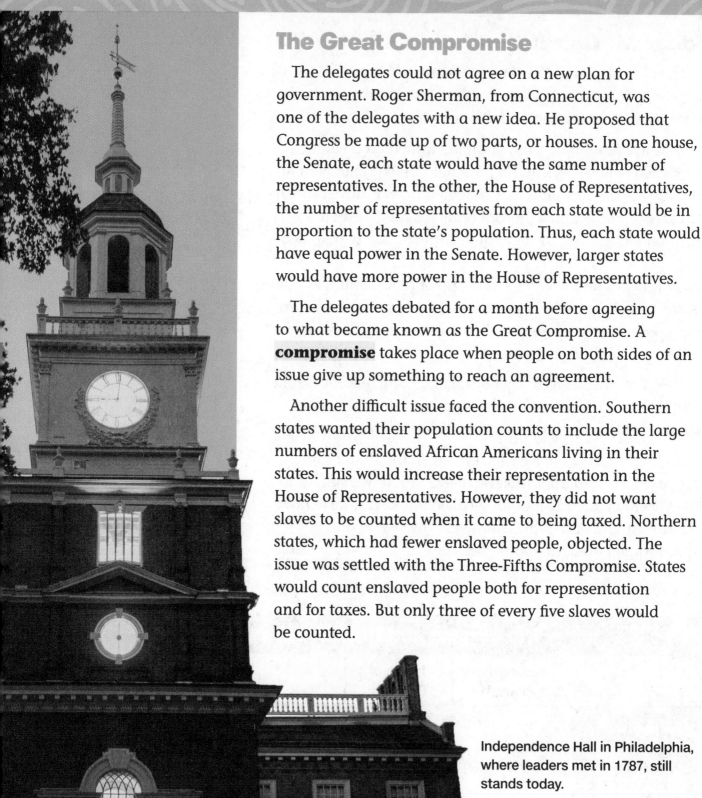

The Great Compromise

The delegates could not agree on a new plan for government. Roger Sherman, from Connecticut, was one of the delegates with a new idea. He proposed that Congress be made up of two parts, or houses. In one house, the Senate, each state would have the same number of representatives. In the other, the House of Representatives, the number of representatives from each state would be in proportion to the state's population. Thus, each state would have equal power in the Senate. However, larger states would have more power in the House of Representatives.

The delegates debated for a month before agreeing to what became known as the Great Compromise. A **compromise** takes place when people on both sides of an issue give up something to reach an agreement.

Another difficult issue faced the convention. Southern states wanted their population counts to include the large numbers of enslaved African Americans living in their states. This would increase their representation in the House of Representatives. However, they did not want slaves to be counted when it came to being taxed. Northern states, which had fewer enslaved people, objected. The issue was settled with the Three-Fifths Compromise. States would count enslaved people both for representation and for taxes. But only three of every five slaves would be counted.

Independence Hall in Philadelphia, where leaders met in 1787, still stands today.

A New Plan for Government

Delegates worked through the summer of 1787, writing the new plan for government. The **Preamble**, or introduction, expressed the main goals of the new constitution.

Primary Source

We the people of the United States, in order to form a more perfect Union, establish justice, insure domestic tranquility [peace], provide for the common defense [protection], promote the general welfare [well-being], and secure the blessings of liberty [freedom] to ourselves and our posterity [future], do ordain and establish this Constitution for the United States of America.

—Preamble to the United States Constitution

The new U.S. Constitution set up a government with three branches. In contrast, the Articles of Confederation had only one branch of government. Under the new U.S. Constitution, the legislative branch would make the laws. It would be called Congress. The executive branch, led by the president, would put the laws into effect and make sure they were obeyed. The judicial branch would interpret the laws and make sure they followed the Constitution. This **separation of powers** is the idea that the powers and duties of government are divided among separate branches.

3. ☑ Reading Check **Summarize** Read the Preamble.
Write its most important point in a sentence.
Talk with a partner about why you think it is important.

_____

_____

_____

_____

Quest Connection

Highlight some words from the Preamble that tell about the goals of the new constitution.

INTERACTIVITY

Take a closer look at the Preamble and answer the question.

The Supreme Court building in Washington, D.C.

The Constitution also set up a system of majority rule. This means that decisions are made by a majority of the people voting. For example, the majority of lawmakers must agree on a law before passing it.

The framers, or authors, of the Constitution wished to limit the power of government in other ways. They set up a system of **checks and balances**. In other words, each branch had ways of limiting the powers of the other branches. For example, Congress would pass laws, but the president would have to sign a law to make it official. In this way, no branch of the government could acquire too much power.

Limiting Government

The president can limit the power of Congress with a **veto**, or a refusal to sign a law. However, if two thirds of Congress wants a law, Congress can reject the veto. This is Congress's check on the power of the president.

The judicial branch can check the power of both Congress and the president. If the courts decide that the other branches are doing something against the Constitution, they can stop those actions. The president can check the power of the courts by choosing the justices and judges who serve in federal courts. Congress can check the power of the court by refusing to approve the choices of the president.

The Constitution gave the government power in many areas. Congress can make laws to stop people from mistreating others, for example. Courts can punish those who break these laws. Governments need enough power to protect people's rights.

Checks and balances limit the government's power. This also protects our rights. If one branch tries to misuse its power, the other branches can stop it.

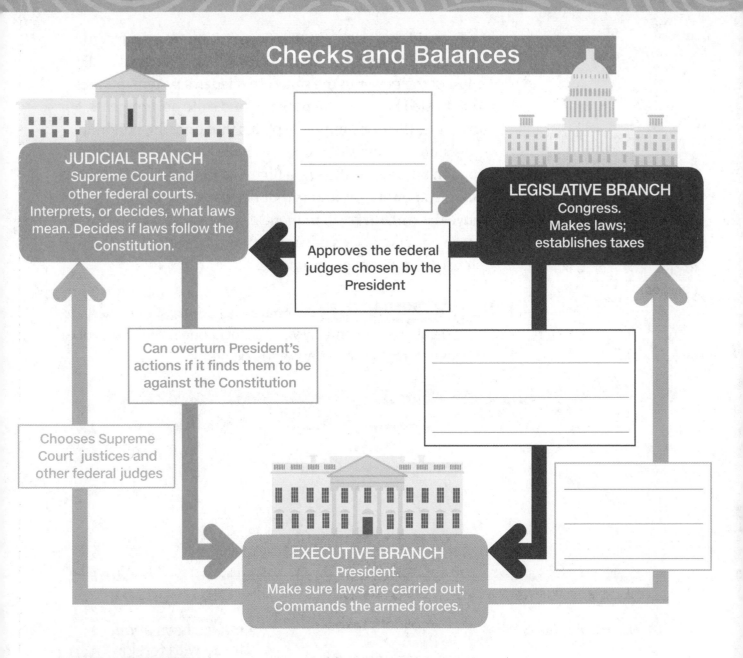

Checks and Balances

JUDICIAL BRANCH
Supreme Court and other federal courts. Interprets, or decides, what laws mean. Decides if laws follow the Constitution.

LEGISLATIVE BRANCH
Congress. Makes laws; establishes taxes

Approves the federal judges chosen by the President

Can overturn President's actions if it finds them to be against the Constitution

Chooses Supreme Court justices and other federal judges

EXECUTIVE BRANCH
President. Make sure laws are carried out; Commands the armed forces.

4. ☑ **Reading Check** **Identify** and fill in the chart with the missing checks and balances between branches of government.

Powers of Government

As the delegates debated the Constitution, they asked questions. Would the new government take away all the power of the states? Would it become the kind of government from which they had just freed themselves? Would the president gain too much power and become a kind of king?

To avoid these dangers, the Constitution set up a federal system of government. The Articles of Confederation had given most of the power to the states. In a federal system, powers are divided between the national and state governments. For example, the Constitution explains that only the national government can print money or make laws about trade with foreign nations. At the same time, the Constitution lists many reserved powers, or powers that belong to the states. The states have the **authority** to manage elections and issue licenses. Some powers, such as passing tax laws, are shared between the state and national governments.

Academic Vocabulary

authority • *n.*, the power to give orders or make decisions

5. ☑ Reading Check **Compare and contrast** state and federal governments by writing down one more power of government in each part of the diagram.

Powers of State and National Government

Powers of State Government

- manages elections
- organizes local government
- regulates trade within the states
- _____
- _____

Shared Powers

- collects taxes
- sets up courts
- _____
- _____

Powers of National Government

- makes laws about trade with foreign nations
- sets up military
- sets up postal service
- _____
- _____

For some delegates, the new Constitution was not enough. Many believed firmly that the Constitution should list the rights citizens have to protect their freedom. Others felt that the wording of the Preamble was enough. This debate would lead to one of the most important elements of the Constitution.

6. ☑ **Reading Check** This picture shows a federal worker at the U.S. Bureau of Printing and Engraving. **Identify** the power of government shown here.

_____

_____

INTERACTIVITY

Check your understanding of the key ideas of this lesson.

☑ Lesson 2 Check

7. **Compare and Contrast Analyze** the main differences between the Articles of Confederation and the U.S. Constitution. Include in your answer the duties of each of the branches of government.

_____

_____

_____

_____

_____

8. **Identify** Roger Sherman's contribution to the creation of the Constitution.

_____

_____

9. **Understand the** _Quest_ **Connections** Based on the Preamble, describe what you think was the framers' main goal in writing the Constitution.

_____

Benjamin Franklin's Final Speech

At the end of the Constitutional Convention, the framers were deeply divided. Some felt that the Constitution should list basic rights. Others believed this was unnecessary.

Benjamin Franklin, while admitting that the Constitution was not perfect, felt that it was as close to perfect as a group of men with varied opinions could create. In this excerpt, Franklin speaks about the strengths of the Constitution.

Vocabulary Support

a well-managed government will always benefit its people

when the people have become so willingly dishonest and unlawful that they require a broken government

sentiments, *n.*, feelings or attitude

despotism, *n.*, system of government where the ruler has unlimited power and the people do not have rights

incapable, *adj.*, unable to achieve something

Primary Source

"In these Sentiments, Sir, I agree to this Constitution, with all its Faults, if they are such; because I think a General Government necessary for us, and there is no Form of Government but what may be a Blessing to the People if well administered; and I believe farther that this is likely to be well administered for a Course of Years, and can only end in Despotism as other Forms have done before it, when the People shall become so corrupted as to need Despotic Government, being incapable of any other."

–Benjamin Franklin, final speech at the Constitutional Convention, September 17, 1787

Benjamin Franklin

Fun Fact

Benjamin Franklin invented a glass musical instrument called an armonica that was used by Beethoven and Mozart.

Close Reading

1. **Identify** and circle the words in the document that describe Benjamin Franklin's overall feelings about government.

2. **Describe** how Franklin feels about the plan for government outlined in the Constitution.

_____

_____

_____

_____

_____

Wrap It Up

Does the Constitution, as it was planned at the end of the Constitutional Convention, provide enough protection of citizens' individual rights? Support your answer with information from the chapter. Use one quotation from the primary source.

_____

_____

_____

_____

_____

_____

_____

_____

_____

INTERACTIVITY

Participate in a class discussion to preview the content of this lesson.

Vocabulary

Federalist
Anti-Federalist
Bill of Rights
proposal
anarchy
constitutional republic
popular sovereignty

Academic Vocabulary

sufficient
announce

Unlock
The **BIG**
Question

I will know why delegates disagreed over the Constitution and how they resolved their differences.

Jumpstart Activity

Work in small groups to list rights you think all Americans should have. Compare your lists with other groups. How are the lists similar? How are they different?

Once the Constitution was written, delegates as well as citizens were divided over striking the correct balance in government. Debates raged between both sides, resulting in a new compromise.

Debate Over the Constitution

The Constitution granted freedoms to American citizens unlike those granted in any other country. But there was still much to be debated. Delegates and citizens who supported the new Constitution were called **Federalists**. They were often wealthy merchants and plantation owners who wanted a strong central government. Those who supported the Articles of Confederation wanted more power to remain with the states. They were called **Anti-Federalists**. They were often farmers and tradesmen.

Federalists wanted the states to be united into one powerful nation. They believed the Constitution would be good for the economy. Anti-Federalists, including Thomas Jefferson, did not think that Congress could pass laws that worked for all states. They feared the president and Congress would have too much power under the Constitution.

Once Congress had adopted the Constitution, state conventions were held. These gave the public a place to learn about and discuss the new government. The Anti-Federalists were not able to oppose the Constitution in Congress. Therefore, they had to fight ratification, or official approval, of the Constitution state by state at the conventions. Patrick Henry was an outspoken opponent of the Constitution. In June of 1788, he delivered several speeches to Virginia delegates at their convention. He tried to convince them not to ratify the Constitution.

The debates between Federalists and Anti-Federalists occurred in meeting halls, on the streets, and in newspapers and pamphlets. The debates revolved around the best form of government, what rights should be protected, and what powers should be given to the nation and states.

INTERACTIVITY

Explore the key ideas of this lesson.

1. 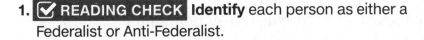 **READING CHECK** **Identify** each person as either a Federalist or Anti-Federalist.

I want a unified country and stronger federal government.

I want the power of the president and Congress to be limited and the states to make their own laws.

Alexander Hamilton

Patrick Henry

Here is a revolution as radical [extreme] as that which separated us from Great Britain. … our rights and privileges are endangered, and the sovereignty [independence] of the states will be relinquished [given up]: And cannot we plainly see that this is actually the case? The rights of … trial by jury, liberty [freedom] of the press, … all pretensions [claims] to human rights and privileges, are rendered [made] insecure, if not lost, by this change, so loudly talked of by some, and inconsiderately by others.

—Patrick Henry, speech, June 5, 1788

Ratifying the Constitution

Nine of the thirteen states had to ratify the Constitution for it to pass. At each state convention, Anti-Federalists gave speeches about the loss of individual freedoms under the Constitution. They argued that a **Bill of Rights**, which would guarantee basic rights for all citizens, should be added to the document. An initial **proposal** for a Bill of Rights had been rejected at the Constitutional Convention.

The Bill of Rights played a key role in the ratification of the U.S. Constitution.

The powers reserved [kept] to the several States will extend to all the objects which, . . . concern the lives, liberties, and properties of the people, and the internal order, improvement, and prosperity [success] of the State. The operations of the federal government will be most extensive [greatest] and important in times of war and danger; those of the State governments, in times of peace and security [safety].

—James Madison, "Federalist No. 45"

This became a critical issue for the Anti-Federalists. They felt that if the federal government was given more power, individual rights had to be guaranteed by law. They argued that if the Federalists had cared about individual rights, they would have spelled this out in the Constitution.

Federalists, such as James Madison, believed that the Constitution did a **sufficient** job of protecting liberty through the system of separation of powers. He worried that if the Constitution would not be ratified, there would be **anarchy**. Madison, Alexander Hamilton, and John Jay began writing essays. At first, the essays were published in New York newspapers. In 1788, they were published in a book called *The Federalist*. Eighty-five essays outlined why the framers of the Constitution made the decisions they did. They also responded to the Anti-Federalists. In "Federalist Number 45," James Madison argues that the states would keep their important role and power under the new government.

When it became clear that including a Bill of Rights would speed ratification, Federalists made a concession. They **announced** that the first task of the new government would be adopting a list of basic individual rights.

The U.S. Constitution was adopted by the Constitutional Convention in September 1787. New Hampshire became the ninth state to ratify it, ten months later in June 1788. It was ratified by all 13 states in May 1790.

James Madison

2. ✓ **READING CHECK** **Summarize** to a partner why a Bill of Rights was included in the U.S. Constitution. **Highlight** the appropriate text.

Members of the House of Representatives meet in this chamber in the U.S. Capitol building.

A Constitutional Republic

The Constitution outlined a plan for government called a **constitutional republic**. This form of government has a constitution and citizens elect representatives to Congress. In this way, the government gets its authority from the citizens and cannot do anything without the people's consent. This idea is called **popular sovereignty**.

Congress is based on the proposal that Roger Sherman made at the Constitutional Convention. It is made up of representatives and senators. Members of the House of Representatives serve for two years. States with larger populations elect a larger number of representatives. Members of the Senate serve for six years. Each state elects two senators. These members of Congress vote on and uphold the laws. The part they play in the separation of powers is important because many governmental tasks overlap causing unavoidable conflict.

The Constitution also explains how powers are shared between federal and state governments. The federal government can declare war, print money, levy taxes, make laws, and regulate trade between states and with other countries. States can ratify amendments to the Constitution, manage public safety, and regulate trade within the state.

3. ☑ READING CHECK
Identify Does the power to regulate trade with other nations reside with the federal or the state government?

The Founding Principles

The new Congress began to govern on March 4, 1789. Keeping its promise made during the ratification of the Constitution, Congress proposed ten amendments known as the Bill of Rights.

Because the framers had been focused on creating the federal government, the Constitution did not focus on individual rights. Many had feared that if these rights were not clearly stated, the government might become too powerful and endanger the rights of citizens.

Freedom of speech and the right to assemble are two of the basic rights guaranteed by the Bill of Rights.

Quest Connection

Highlight some of the founding principles of the Bill of Rights. Why do you think so many basic rights are in the Bill of Rights?

 INTERACTIVITY

Take a closer look at the Constitution.

Now the framers would list the rights each person was entitled to. The Bill of Rights, ratified in December 1791, protects freedoms including speech, religion, and the press; the right to assemble peacefully; and the right to bear arms. It also ensures a citizen's right to fair treatment within the judicial system. The rights outlined in this document are the founding principles of the country.

4. ☑ READING CHECK In the chart, **identify** and circle two of the rights guaranteed by the Bill of Rights that you think are very important. **Illustrate** one of the rights in the space provided.

The Bill of Rights

Amendments	Guaranteed Rights
First	Protects freedom of religion, speech, the press; the right to assemble peacefully; and the right to disagree with government decisions.
Second	Protects the right to own and bear firearms.
Third	Protects people's right not to house soldiers during peacetime.
Fourth	Protects people from having their property unfairly searched or taken.
Fifth	Guarantees that no one's life, liberty, or property can be taken unless decided by a court.
Sixth	In criminal cases, guarantees the right to a trial by a jury and to have a lawyer.
Seventh	In most civil cases, guarantees the right to a trial by a jury.
Eighth	Forbids very high bail, fines, and extraordinary punishment.
Ninth	Asserts that the people's rights are not limited to those stated in the Constitution.
Tenth	Asserts that all powers not stated as belonging to the federal government belong to the states or to the people.

INTERACTIVITY

Check your understanding
of the key ideas of this
lesson.

☑ Lesson 3 Check

5. Summarize the argument between the Federalists and Anti-Federalists.

_____

_____

_____

_____

_____

6. Describe the role state conventions played in the ratification of the Constitution.

_____

_____

_____

7. Understand the *Quest* Connections Describe why popular sovereignty is an important part of the Constitution.

_____

_____

_____

Compare Points of View

 VIDEO

Watch a video about comparing points of view.

The framers of the Constitution had different opinions about how power should be divided in the new government.

When you compare two points of view on the same topic, it means that you are taking a close look at two different opinions in order to find similarities and differences.

When comparing points of view, it is helpful to ask yourself questions, such as What is the purpose of these speakers? What is different about their messages to the audience? How are the speakers persuading their listeners? Read the following.

"Nothing is more certain than the indispensable [needed] necessity of government, and it is equally undeniable, that whenever and however it is instituted, the people must cede [yield] to it some of their natural rights in order to vest it with requisite [required, necessary] powers."

—John Jay, "Federalist No. 2"

John Jay

"This government will set out a moderate aristocracy [upper class; elite]: it is at present impossible to foresee whether it will, in its operation, produce a monarchy, or a corrupt, tyrannical [cruel, harsh] aristocracy;"

—George Mason, Objections to This Constitution of Government

George Mason

1. Fill in the diagram with the main point of each quote. Then **analyze** and write what is similar about both of the quotes.

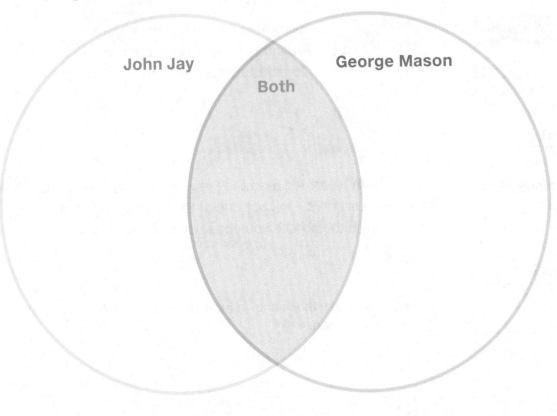

John Jay

George Mason

Both

2. Read the section in Lesson 3 called "Debate Over the Constitution." **Compare** the points of view of Federalists and Anti-Federalists.

_____

_____

_____

_____

_____

Key Concepts of the Constitution

Vocabulary

rule of law
domestic tranquility
suffrage

Academic Vocabulary

levy
commerce

Unlock The BIG Question

I will know the significance of the Preamble to the Constitution and how the Constitution can be changed.

JumpStart Activity

With a partner, read the Preamble of the Constitution in Lesson 2. Pick out one of the phrases, and act it out. Write the phrase you chose on a sheet of paper.

Navy sailors, like those shown here, protect the United States at home and abroad.

Introduction to the Constitution

The Preamble is the introduction to the Constitution. It describes the purpose of a government, which is to provide citizens with a fair, safe, and peaceful way of life. The government of the United States still has these goals today.

The Preamble uses the phrase "a more perfect union" to mean bringing the country together. Leaders hoped to strengthen and unify the country.

The framers wanted to make it clear that all citizens must obey the law, but are protected from misuse of power by the government. This idea, or principle is called **rule of law**. It is addressed in the phrase "establish justice." This phrase means that everyone will be treated fairly and equally in the judicial system and also reflects the personal safety promised in the Constitution. The phrases "**domestic tranquility**," "provide for the common defense," and "promote the general welfare" reflect the framers' desire to ensure safety from foreign threats, protection by armed forces, and the well-being of citizens.

The Preamble to the Constitution stands in stark contrast to the Preamble to the Articles of Confederation. The Articles stated an agreement between states; the Preamble to the Constitution states an agreement between the federal government and people of the United States.

Impact of the Constitution on the Economy

The framers carefully crafted certain parts of the Constitution to encourage a robust economy and to protect the country in lean times. The inability of the federal government to borrow money or **levy** taxes had been a major obstacle during the Revolution. As a result, the Spending Clause in Article 1 Section 8 states that Congress can levy taxes to pay the country's debts and to provide for the common defense. It also allows Congress to borrow money quickly when needed. These powers are limited, however. The power to borrow depends on the country's current credit.

INTERACTIVITY

Explore the key ideas of this lesson.

1. ☑ **Reading Check**
Identify The Preamble to the United States Constitution is an agreement between what two groups?

_____

_____

_____

Academic Vocabulary

levy • *v.*, to collect or impose

commerce • *n.*, business or trade between countries or states

Word Wise

Prefixes Sometimes prefixes can help you to understand the meaning of an unfamiliar word. You will see the words *interstate*, *import*, and *export* in this lesson. The prefix *inter-* means "between," *im-* means "into," and *ex-* means "out of." What do you think *interstate*, *import*, and *export* mean?

In the same Section, Congress is given the power to regulate **commerce**. Before the Constitution, there was a lack of interstate trade, or trade between the states, because the Articles had not given Congress the authority to regulate it or to resolve disputes. The Commerce Clause made trade and business between states worthwhile.

The Patent and Copyright Clause, also in Article 1 Section 8, states that artists' and scientists' writings and discoveries are protected for a specific time. The clause helps promote science and the arts.

The Appropriations [setting aside money for a purpose] Clause in Article 1 Section 9 allows Congress to decide how to use public funds, to limit money spent, and to keep a record of its spending.

Article 1 Section 10 is commonly referred to as the Contracts Clause. It seeks to prevent abuse of power by the states. It forbids states from coining money, levying taxes on imports and exports, or interfering with private contracts. This clause can be used to protect a wide range of business dealings.

The framers of the Constitution wanted to ensure that the economy of the United States would remain strong.

The Congress shall have Power
To lay and collect Taxes, Duties
[fees], Imposts [customs fee] and
Excises [taxes on goods], to pay
the Debts and provide for the
common Defence and general
Welfare of the United States; but
all Duties, Imposts and Excises
shall be uniform throughout the
United States.

—From the United States
Constitution, Article 1 Section 8

A cargo ship unloads
imports at a port.

2. ☑ **Reading Check** **Summarize** how today's economy
would be different if some sections of the Constitution did not
exist. Choose one section to focus on.

_____

_____

_____

_____

Quest Connection

Write three ways
in which the
Constitution keeps
the economy
strong.

👆 **INTERACTIVITY**

Play a matching game to
learn about the economy
and the Constitution.

Making Changes to the Constitution

At certain times, it is necessary to change or add to the
Constitution. The founding fathers allowed this to happen.

For an amendment to be added to the Constitution, a
two-thirds majority in both the House and Senate must vote
to propose the amendment. Following the proposal, three
fourths of the state legislatures must ratify the amendment.
There are now 27 amendments to the Constitution. They
reflect changing attitudes and changes in society.

African Americans Get the Right to Vote

Today, all Americans can vote in federal or local elections, but this was not always the case. Only free white men who owned land could vote for the first 100 years of the nation's history. African Americans and women struggled for many years for the right to vote.

African Americans were enslaved until after the Civil War in 1865. The Thirteenth Amendment ended slavery. The Fifteenth Amendment gave African Americans the right to vote. Although the amendment was ratified in 1870, there was a great deal of discrimination, or unfair treatment based on someone's race. To discourage them from voting in the South, African Americans had to pay taxes at the polls and pass literacy tests.

In 1965, the Voting Rights Act was passed due to the work of activists such as Dr. Martin Luther King, Jr. The winter before the Voting Rights Act became law, King had begun the Southern Christian Leadership Conference campaign in Selma, Alabama. Its goal was to get such laws passed. The passage of the Voting Rights Act was an important moment in the civil rights movement.

Martin Luther King, Jr., worked to get the Voting Rights Act passed.

Amendment	Year

Women's Suffrage

In 1920, the Nineteenth Amendment gave women the right to vote. This amendment was the result of a long struggle for equality. The **suffrage** movement spanned several generations and required a great deal of persistence.

Suffragists—advocates of women's voting rights—organized conferences, protests, and marches; drew up petitions; and even went on hunger strikes in the effort for their voices to be heard. Most who were involved in the movement at the beginning did not live to see the Nineteenth Amendment become law, but their work changed the United States.

3. ☑ **Reading Check** In the boxes next to the images, **identify** and write the amendment that affected voting rights for the group pictured and the year it was passed.

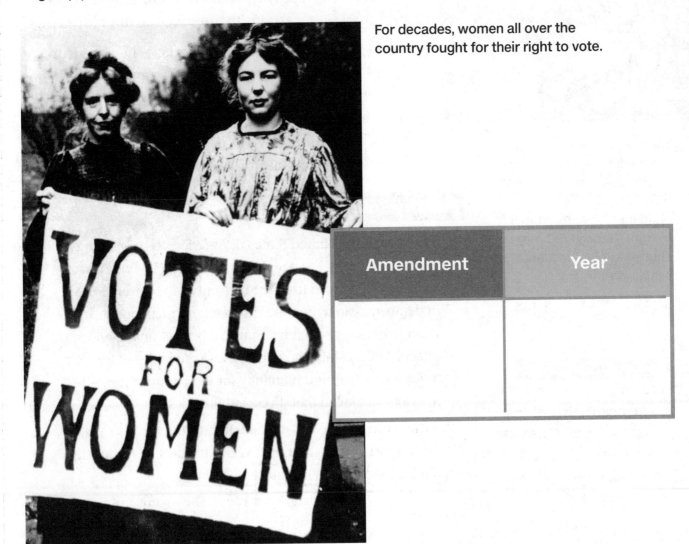

For decades, women all over the country fought for their right to vote.

Amendment	Year

Supreme Court Decisions

The Supreme Court is the highest court in the country. The Constitution established the jurisdiction, or official power, of this court.

The lawyers who argued the case of *Brown* v. *Board of Education* stand in front of the Supreme Court building. They are, from left to right, George E.C. Hayes, Thurgood Marshall, and James Nabrit, Jr.

There are nine Supreme Court justices. They hear cases that have to do with federal and state laws and how they affect the rights of citizens. In 1954, for example, the Supreme Court heard *Brown* v. *Board of Education*. The decision in this case stated that state laws allowing segregation (separating people based on race) were unconstitutional, or against the law.

By making decisions on these cases, the justices check the actions of Congress and the president. The power of the Supreme Court is limited by the other two branches as well. The president nominates a justice and then Congress has to approve the appointment.

In 1917, William Tyler Page wrote "The American's Creed" and entered it in a patriotic contest. He referenced many historical documents, including the Declaration of Independence and the Preamble to the Constitution. It was accepted by the House of Representatives on April 3, 1918.

Primary Source

I believe in the United States of America, as a government of the people, by the people, for the people; whose just powers are derived from the consent of the governed; a democracy in a republic; a sovereign independent Nation of many sovereign States; a perfect union, one and inseparable; established upon these principles of freedom, equality, justice, and humanity for which American patriots sacrificed their lives and fortunes.

I therefore believe it is my duty to my country to love it, to support its Constitution, to obey its laws, to respect its flag, and to defend it against all enemies.

—William Tyler Page, "The American's Creed"

4. ☑ **Reading Check**
Identify the parts of "The American's Creed" that you think most likely came from the Preamble to the Constitution. Underline those parts.

Lesson 4 Check

5. **Summarize** and list the founding principles that were addressed in the Preamble to the Constitution.

_____

_____

_____

_____

6. **Describe** the process by which an amendment to the Constitution is made.

_____

_____

_____

_____

7. **Understand the** *Quest* **Connections** Based on Article 1, Sections 8, 9, and 10 of the Constitution, **describe** what you think the founding fathers would consider a healthy, thriving economy.

_____

_____

_____

_____

Quality:
Speaking Out for Equal Rights

Abigail Adams (1744–1818)
Remember the Ladies

Abigail Adams lived a remarkable life. She lived through the American Revolution and the Constitutional era. In a way that was typical of the times Adams lived in, she did not receive a formal education. She read a lot and worked hard to teach herself. She was widely admired as an intelligent and capable woman. Abigail spoke up for the rights of women at a time when women had few rights.

When Abigail's husband, John Adams, served as a delegate to the Constitutional Congress in Philadelphia, she managed their family and farm. The couple wrote many letters to each other about politics and home life. As John and his fellow delegates worked to create a government, Abigail wrote in part, "in the new Code of Laws . . . I desire you would remember the ladies."

Although the framers of the Constitution did not follow Abigail's advice, she continued to speak and write for the rights of women.

Find Out More

1. Abigail Adams wrote these words in 1776. Review Lesson 4. When did women gain the right to vote? Which amendment to the Constitution gave voting rights to women?

   _____

   _____

2. Women fought for many years to amend, or change, the Constitution and win the right to vote. Create a series of questions with your classmates and survey students in your school to find out what amendment they would add to the Constitution today.

Visual Review

Use these graphics to review some of the key terms, people, and ideas from this chapter.

1788
United States Constitution ratified.

The Constitution creates the Senate and House of Representatives and includes a system of checks and balances between three branches of government.

1781
Articles of Confederation ratified.

1791
The Bill of Rights is added to the Constitution to protect individual rights.

| 1775 | 1780 | 1785 | 1790 | 1795 |

1777
Articles of Confederation adopted.

It creates a weak central government.

1787
Shays' Rebellion

Northwest Ordinance

United States Constitution adopted.

1789
Congress meets for the first time under a ratified Constitution.

In 1870 the fifteenth amendment was ratified. In 1920, the nineteenth amendment was ratified. These amendments granted voting rights to African Americans and women.

Debating the Constitution

Federalists	Anti-Federalists
• Supported the Constitution and a strong central government	• Critical of the Constitution and supported a weaker central government
• Wrote essays to explain why they supported a strong central government and pointed out weaknesses of the Articles of Confederation	• Believed states should have more power
• Alexander Hamilton	• Supported a Bill of Rights
• James Madison	• Thomas Jefferson
• John Jay	• Patrick Henry
	• George Mason

6 ☑ Assessment

 GAMES

Play the vocabulary game.

Vocabulary and Key Ideas

1. Draw a line to match the definitions with the correct terms.

the branch of government that makes laws   **veto**

to refuse to approve something   **legislative**

the principle that the law applies to everyone, equally   **ordinance**

a law   **rule of law**

the branch of government that interprets the laws   **judicial**

2. What is **inflation**? _____

_____

_____

3. **Define** concession. _____

_____

4. **Identify** Fill in the blanks to complete the sentence.

The United States _____ was ratified by the first _____

states in the year _____.

5. **Interpret a Line Graph**. If a colonist earned $35 per month, what fraction of this monthly income would be needed to buy a bushel of potatoes in 1779?

_____

What was the reason for the increase in the cost of goods?

_____

_____

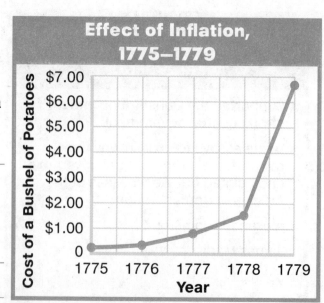

Effect of Inflation, 1775–1779

Cost of a Bushel of Potatoes

$7.00
$6.00
$5.00
$4.00
$3.00
$2.00
$1.00
0

1775   1776   1777   1778   1779
Year

Source: *Massachusetts Bureau of Statistics of Labor, 1885*

Critical Thinking and Writing

6. **Determine Effects** Fill in the circle next to the best answer.
   What was one effect of Shays' Rebellion?

   (A) More farmers were sent to prison.

   (B) More people called for a stronger national government.

   (C) New state courts opened.

   (D) The national government raised an army.

7. **Analyze** According to the American creed, what are some of the duties of American citizens?

   _____

   _____

   _____

8. **Analyze** What was the significance of the Northwest Ordinance?

   _____

   _____

9. **Apply** What are some of the ways the U.S. Constitution and Bill of Rights affect your life and life in your community? Explain.

   _____

   _____

   _____

10. **Revisit the Big Question** What is the purpose of government?

    _____

    _____

    _____

Analyze Primary Sources

The people are the only legitimate fountain of power, and it is from them that the constitutional charter, under which the several branches of government hold their power, is derived. —James Madison, Federalist No. 49

11. What do you think Madison meant by the phrase "people are the only legitimate fountain of power"?

_____

_____

_____

_____

_____

_____

12. **Writing Workshop: Write Informative Text** On separate paper, write two short paragraphs about delegates Edmund Randolph and Roger Sherman. Identify their home states, their contribution to the Constitutional Convention, and their contribution to the Constitution.

Compare Points of View

13. Compare and contrast how Federalists and Anti-Federalists felt about the power of the central government under the Constitution.

_____

_____

_____

_____

_____

_____

Quest Findings

Write Your Letter

You have read the lessons in this chapter and now you're ready to write a letter to the editor. Remember that the goal of your letter is to convince a reader to support or oppose the Constitution. Use facts to support your opinion and to show why you disagree with your opponents. Follow these steps:

INTERACTIVITY

Use this activity to help you prepare to write.

1 Prepare to Write

Write your three strongest arguments and add facts to support them. Then write three possible objections, and how you intend to argue against them. Use these notes to help you write your letter.

2 Write a Draft

Use your notes and the evidence from your Quest Connections to write the most persuasive letter you can. Make sure your letter answers the following questions:

- Was it necessary to write a new Constitution?

- Why is compromise needed?

- How will the Bill of Rights make the Constitution stronger?

- What do opponents of your point of view say? How do you respond?

3 Share With a Partner

Exchange your draft letter with a partner. Tell your partner what you like about the letter and what could be improved. Be polite when you provide suggestions.

4 Revise

Make changes to your letter after meeting with your partner. Correct any grammatical or spelling errors.

GO ONLINE FOR
DIGITAL RESOURCES

▶ VIDEO

👆 INTERACTIVITY

🔊 AUDIO

🎮 GAMES

☑ ASSESSMENT

📖 eTEXT

The **BIG** How do leaders
Question shape a nation?

▶ VIDEO

Lesson 1

JumpStart Activity

👆 INTERACTIVITY

Form small groups. Each member of your group should write down three ways that he or she thinks a leader can shape a country. Once everyone has written their ideas, compare your ideas with another student. Are many of the ideas the same? How are they different? Write down some of the similarities and differences.

_____

_____

_____

_____

_____

A Growing Nation

Preview the chapter **vocabulary** as you sing the rap:

At the very first **inauguration**

A ceremony of the occasion

Of getting sworn into the office of President,

George Washington was the first we'd present.

A **Cabinet** of four worked right by his side,

A wide range of views they came to provide

Trusted advisors to the President

Thoughts and opinions they would present.

A nation growing west with help from **pioneers**

They were people who moved to the **frontier**

The unexplored edge of the wilderness

What would await them they could only guess.

Life in the Young Republic

Louisiana Purchase

NH
VT
NY
MA
CT
RI
PA
NJ
DE
MD
Indiana Territory
OH
VA
KY
TN
NC
SC
GA
Mississippi Territory

ATLANTIC OCEAN

N
W E
S

0   500 mi
0   500 km

Gulf of Mexico

Where was the frontier in the 1800s?

Many explorers and settlers left from or near St. Louis, Missouri, to begin a journey west. Which states are shown on the map? Which territories are shown?

Gateway Arch

TODAY

You can visit St. Louis to see and ride to the top of the Gateway Arch.

What happened and When?

Read the timeline to find out how the nation grew and changed during the 1800s.

1780   1790   1800   1810

1789
George Washington is elected president.

TODAY
People can visit Washington's home in Mount Vernon.

1804—1806
Lewis and Clark explore the West.

1812
The War of 1812 begins.

Who will you meet?

Sacagawea
A guide and translator for explorers Lewis and Clark

James Monroe
The fifth president of the United States

John Marshall
Chief Justice who supported the Cherokee's argument that they had a right to their land

Frederick Douglass
A free African American and later an activist in the movement to end slavery

 INTERACTIVITY

Complete the interactive chart.

1820   **1830**   **1840**   **1850**

1828
Andrew Jackson is elected president.

1830
The Indian Removal Act is passed.

1848
The Seneca Falls Convention takes place.

Quest

Document-Based Writing

Finding Your Way

The early 1800s was a time of great change in the United States. The country was claiming more and more land in the West. At the same time, the United States fought a war to protect itself. There were also millions of newcomers coming into the country. In addition, African Americans and women struggled for freedom and equal rights.

Quest Kick Off

Your mission is to work with a group to write a short script to show a movie director. Choose one of the following topics: the Lewis and Clark expedition, the War of 1812, the surge of immigrants that came to the United States in the 1800s, or the activist movements of the 1800s.

1 Ask Questions

Once you have received your assignment, work with your group to answer these questions: Which qualities do you think your group showed? What were the circumstances that led to the expedition, the war, the need to immigrate, or protest?

2 Find Primary and Secondary Sources

Follow your teacher's instructions to find primary and secondary sources relating to your topic. As you research, think about what the sources tell you about the people involved. What are their motivations? What does this tell you about them?

INTERACTIVITY

Analyze the parts of a story to help you with writing your script.

3 Look for *Quest* Connections

Turn to the next page to begin looking for Quest Connections that will help you create your script.

4 *Quest* Findings Write Your Script

Use the Quest Findings page at the end of the chapter to help you write a script and create a video or skit for the class to show what you've learned from your sources.

The First Presidents

INTERACTIVITY

Participate in a class discussion to preview the content of this lesson.

Vocabulary

Electoral College
inauguration
Cabinet
political party

Academic Vocabulary

propose
accumulate

Unlock
The **BIG**
Question

I will know that George Washington's actions as the first President of the United States served as an example for all the presidents who followed him.

Jumpstart Activity

Work in small groups. Each member of your group should name a person they know who is a good leader and then explain their choice. Has this person led something that you were part of?

After the Constitutional Convention ended, George Washington returned to his home, Mount Vernon, in Virginia. Soon, he would be called upon to serve his country in another role.

Washington Takes Office

In 1789, many of his colleagues asked George Washington to become the first President of the United States. He was the only president to ever be *unanimously* elected to the position. This meant that all the electors voted for him. When U.S. citizens cast a vote for president, they are actually voting for electors who, in turn, vote for that presidential candidate. This system is called the **Electoral College** and is a group of people chosen by each state to choose the president and vice president. The number of electors is based on the number of representatives the state has in Congress. The popular vote is the number of votes a candidate receives based on U.S. citizens casting their votes.

At the time, John Adams was the person with the second most votes, so he became vice president. Today, two candidates, one for president and one for vice president, run on the same ticket. Washington was sworn in as president of the United States at his inauguration. An **inauguration** is an official ceremony to make someone president.

INTERACTIVITY

Explore the key ideas of this lesson.

George Washington was sworn into the office of president in New York City.

While in office, Washington started the tradition of a presidential **Cabinet** and decided how it would function. The Cabinet would be a group of trusted advisors who consult with the president on different issues while offering a wide range of views on those issues.

Today, there are 16 cabinet members: the vice president and 15 heads of the executive departments. The Constitution states that there would be executive departments under the president. Washington set a precedent by choosing four members for his Cabinet, one to lead four executive departments. Thomas Jefferson was the Secretary of State and handled relations with other countries. Alexander Hamilton was the Secretary of the Treasury and dealt with the nation's economy. Henry Knox was the Secretary of War. Edmond Randolph was the Attorney General and advised Washington on legal issues.

James Madison said that Washington's meetings were "the president's cabinet," which is how the term *Cabinet* was chosen.

Washington signed the Judiciary Act, which created the position of Attorney General as well as a six-member Supreme Court. In 1794, he created the United States Navy, ordering six ships to be built, including the USS *Constitution*.

During his time as president, Washington signed the first copyright law. The law was meant to encourage and protect the work of people who created maps and charts and who wrote books. It gave creators and authors the right to publish, print, and reprint their work.

The Constitution did not set term limits for the presidency. After serving two terms, however, Washington retired to Mount Vernon.

1. ☑ **Reading Check** **Identify** and circle the names of the men who were appointed to Cabinet positions. **Describe** their responsibilities and how they served President Washington.

_____

_____

_____

_____

The First Political Parties

Washington did not support **political parties**, or groups of people with the same general opinions about government. He believed that they would divide the country. Still, two parties existed by 1796. They were the Federalists and the Democratic-Republicans. The election for the second president of the United States would be the first time citizens would choose between two candidates from two distinct political parties. It was also the first time that candidates at the local, state, and federal levels ran for office as members of these two parties. They had previously been appointed.

The Federalists, the party led by Hamilton, were strongly in favor of the national bank, a strong federal government, and thriving trade and industry. Merchants were the strongest Federalists because they believed that Federalist policies would help their businesses grow.

In early presidential elections, citizens had to be property owners. Today, U.S. citizens who are at least 18 years old and are registered voters can vote for presidential candidates.

The Democratic-Republicans, led by Jefferson, supported a farming economy. They represented the common man and did not support a strong central government. They supported states' rights and did not want a national bank because they feared it would give the government too much power.

2. ☑ **Reading Check** **Compare and Contrast** the two political parties that existed in 1796 by completing the diagram.

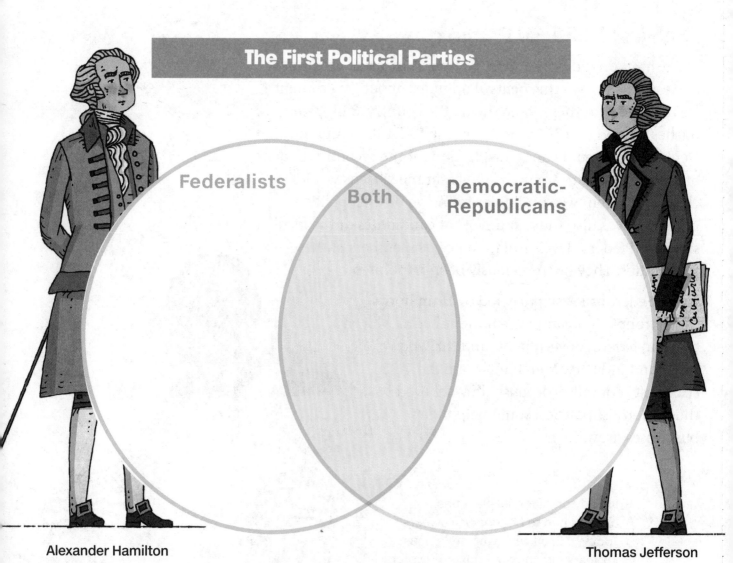

The First Political Parties

Federalists

Both

Democratic-Republicans

Alexander Hamilton

Thomas Jefferson

Building a Strong Economy

The Constitution states that Congress has the power to do what is "necessary and proper" for the country. Alexander Hamilton interpreted this to mean that Congress should do anything necessary to carry out its tasks. Hamilton also felt strongly that a national bank and a single national currency were necessary for the health of the new nation's economy. In 1791, he decided to **propose** this idea in order to deal with debt that had **accumulated** during the American Revolution.

Thomas Jefferson believed the Constitution stated that Congress should only act when absolutely necessary. Jefferson did not agree that creating a national bank was a necessary step. As a Democratic-Republican, he feared it would give the government too much power.

President Washington agreed with Hamilton. The First Bank of the United States was created in 1791. The United States began to pay its war debt, and using one currency made interstate trade much easier. Hamilton also supported tariffs, or taxes on imported goods. He believed that tariffs encouraged people to buy goods made in their own country and would help American businesses. Jefferson opposed tariffs because they raised prices for farmers. In the end, Congress voted against the tariffs. Hamilton thought tariffs would be good for business, but Congress did not agree.

Academic Vocabulary

propose • *v.*, to suggest

accumulate • *v.*, to gather an increasing amount of something

The First Bank of the United States opened in 1791.

3. ✓ **Reading Check** **Analyze** and **explain** how Hamilton's financial plan affected the United States economy.

_____

_____

_____

The New Capital

The Residence Act of 1790 stated that the capital city of the United States would be located along the Potomac River between Maryland and Virginia. It would be a city separate from any other existing city and not be a part of any of the states. As president, George Washington lived in the temporary capital, Philadelphia. Yet he chose the people who would design what would become the permanent capital, Washington, D.C.

A French engineer by the name of Pierre-Charles L'Enfant designed the capital city. Benjamin Banneker, a free African American, was a surveyor for the land. A surveyor measures land before something is built. Dr. William Thornton, a Scottish physician, designed the Capitol Building where Congress would meet. The Capitol would be the center of the city, situated on a hill.

Construction began on the Capitol Building in 1793, and progress was slow. The workers had to leave their homes and live in, what was at that time, wilderness. The building was not yet finished when Congress began working there in 1800.

Benjamin Banneker

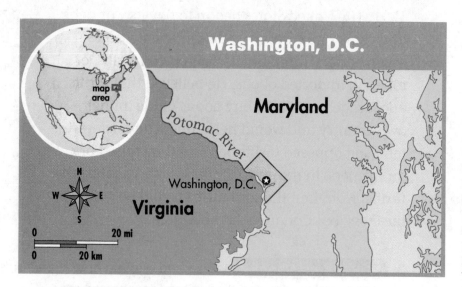

4. ☑ **Reading Check** **Use Evidence From Text** why you think the nation's capital was not located in any particular state.

_____

_____

_____

John Adams Becomes President

The 1796 presidential election was the first election with competing parties and a contested election. The Federalist Party nominated John Adams and Thomas Pinckney. The Democratic-Republican Party nominated Thomas Jefferson and Aaron Burr.

Each Electoral College member cast two votes for President. The person with the most votes became the president, and the one with the next highest number of votes became vice president.

On Election Day, Adams won the presidency by just three electoral votes. Jefferson won the vice presidency. The country would have a president from one party and a vice president from another. Look at the map. Most of Adams's votes had come from northern electors, and most of Jefferson's had come from southern electors.

After the election, John Adams and his wife Abigail moved to Washington, D.C. They were the first family to live in the President's House, which was later named the White House. Although the house was unfinished when they moved in, John and Abigail Adams made this new building the official home of the president of the United States.

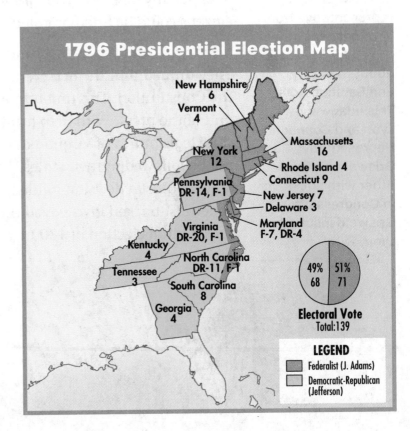

1796 Presidential Election Map

New Hampshire 6
Vermont 4
New York 12
Massachusetts 16
Rhode Island 4
Connecticut 9
Pennsylvania DR-14, F-1
New Jersey 7
Delaware 3
Virginia DR-20, F-1
Maryland F-7, DR-4
Kentucky 4
North Carolina DR-11, F-1
Tennessee 3
South Carolina 8
Georgia 4

49% 68 | 51% 71

Electoral Vote
Total:139

LEGEND
Federalist (J. Adams)
Democratic-Republican (Jefferson)

5. ☑ **Reading Check** **Draw inferences** Why do you think electors in the North voted for Adams, while electors in the South voted for Jefferson?

_____

_____

_____

_____

Alien and Sedition Acts

Soon after John Adams became president, a crisis erupted. French ships began to take over American ships in the West Indies. In response, Adams cut off trade with France. Soon after, Congress passed laws known as the Alien and Sedition Acts in 1798. The word *alien* was used to refer to foreigners or immigrants. Sedition means stirring up a rebellion against a government. These acts made it harder for immigrants to become citizens and allowed the president to expel any foreigner thought to be dangerous. In addition, U.S. citizens could be fined or jailed if they criticized the government.

Jefferson and the Democratic-Republicans opposed these acts. They argued that the acts went against the First Amendment to the Constitution. This amendment guarantees freedom of speech and of the press. With help from Jefferson and James Madison, the state legislatures of Virginia and Kentucky declared the laws would not be followed in their states. This was the first time the states had gone against a decision made by the federal government. These Federalist-backed laws paved the way for a change in power in the presidential election of 1800.

Matthew Lyon, a representative from Vermont, was put in prison for his opinion about the Alien and Sedition Acts. This image shows Lyon and Connecticut Representative Roger Griswold hitting each other with sticks in Congress after Griswold insulted Lyon.

6. ☑ **Reading Check** **Describe** why the Alien and Sedition Acts did not support American ideals.

_____

_____

_____

_____

INTERACTIVITY

Check your understanding of the key ideas of this lesson.

☑ **Lesson 1 Check**

7. **Draw Inferences** **Analyze** the political environment at the end of Washington's presidency. Why do you think separate political parties emerged by this time?

_____

_____

_____

_____

8. **Describe** the outcome of the election of 1796. **Explain** whether you think this outcome was a positive or negative circumstance for the nation.

_____

_____

_____

_____

9. **Explain** the significance of having a new capital city built.

_____

_____

Jefferson and the Louisiana Purchase

Unlock The BIG Question

I will know that Jefferson's actions changed where and how people in the United States lived.

Vocabulary

pioneer
frontier
caravan
interpreter

Academic Vocabulary

crucial
capable

Jumpstart Activity

With a partner, act out a camping trip in the middle of the wilderness. Discuss the dangers that you might encounter and what you have brought with you to protect yourselves.

Before the United States gained its independence, people began moving into the western territories. There was fertile land between the Appalachian Mountains and the Mississippi River. Yet the land was not empty; many American Indian groups lived on these lands.

Pioneers came to the frontier to build a new life on fertile land.

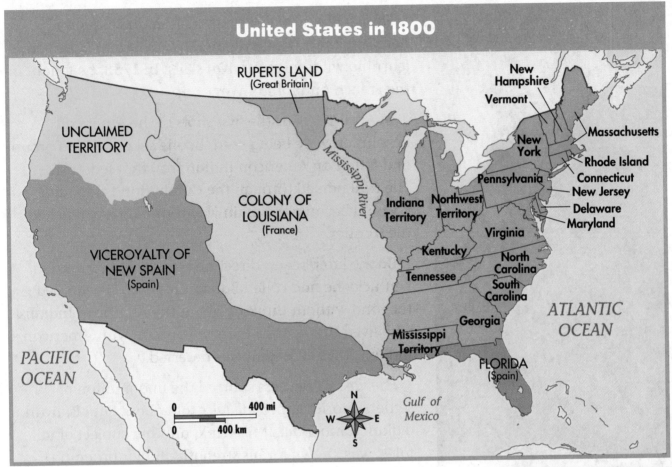

United States in 1800

RUPERTS LAND
(Great Britain)

UNCLAIMED TERRITORY

COLONY OF LOUISIANA
(France)

Mississippi River

VICEROYALTY OF NEW SPAIN
(Spain)

New Hampshire
Vermont
New York
Massachusetts
Rhode Island
Pennsylvania
Connecticut
New Jersey
Delaware
Maryland
Indiana Territory
Northwest Territory
Virginia
Kentucky
North Carolina
Tennessee
South Carolina
Georgia
Mississippi Territory
FLORIDA
(Spain)

ATLANTIC OCEAN

PACIFIC OCEAN

0   400 mi
0   400 km

Gulf of Mexico

N
W   E
S

Moving West

Great Britain had tried to stop westward expansion. It wanted peace with the American Indians. Yet many colonists moved west anyway. After the American Revolution, westward movement continued.

Much of the area between the Appalachian Mountains and the Mississippi River was wilderness in the early 1800s. Between 1789 and the mid-1800s, not only Americans but continuous waves of European immigrants moved into the Ohio Valley. These were **pioneers**, or people who moved to the **frontier**, the edge of the wilderness. They built homes and began farming. However, groups of American Indians had been living on the land for centuries.

The decision to move west was a difficult one to make. Packing everything they could fit into a covered wagon, pioneers would start the journey west. Sometimes families traveled alone and sometimes more than one family would move together in what is called a **caravan**. They farmed, hunted, and raised livestock. Eventually, towns and cities began sprouting up around the pioneer settlements.

INTERACTIVITY

Explore the key ideas of this lesson.

1. ☑ **Reading Check**
Turn and talk to describe how you think the American Indians felt when the pioneers began settling in the west in large numbers.

Daniel Boone

Daniel Boone was a frontiersman and explorer. Born in 1734 in Pennsylvania, he spent his childhood learning wilderness survival skills. In 1755, he fought in the French and Indian War.

In April 1775, as the first shots of the American Revolution were being fired, Boone set out with a group and found an American Indian trail that led west. The trail passed through the Cumberland Gap, and it would become the main way that pioneers reached the frontier.

Boone later began directing colonists to an area in Kentucky he had called Boonesborough. He claimed the land without thinking about the American Indians who lived there. After years of conflicts with American Indians, the settlement was deserted.

The vast wilderness spurred the imagination of settlers. Stories called *tall tales* told about Paul Bunyan, a giant lumberjack. Mike Fink, another subject of tall tales, was known for his strength and for bragging. The tall tales were symbols of hard work and might, qualities those moving west needed.

Jefferson Becomes President

By 1800, the country was divided. John Adams's Alien and Sedition Acts were viewed by many as unconstitutional. Thomas Jefferson did not like these acts. His point of view helped him to be elected as the third president of the United States.

Daniel Boone was an American frontiersman and explorer.

The Cumberland Gap

TENNESSEE

CUMBERLAND RIVER

Cumberland Gap

Blockhouse

VIRGINIA

Two years later, France took control of the land west of the Mississippi from Spain. Jefferson worried the French would refuse to allow Americans access to the port of New Orleans. This port was **crucial** to U.S. commerce, so Jefferson sent James Monroe to France to convince the French to sell the port and some nearby land to the United States. He was told that he could spend $10 million.

The French leader Napoleon Bonaparte needed money to pay for the war he was fighting in Europe. He also could not afford to send military forces to protect the entire area, so the French offered all of the Louisiana Territory to the United States. Monroe agreed to buy the land for about $15 million.

Jefferson struggled with whether the Constitution gave a U.S. president the power to buy new land. He believed in a strict interpretation of the Constitution, and it did not mention buying territory. However, the Constitution allows the president to make treaties, or agreements, with other countries. Jefferson decided to apply that idea to the Louisiana Purchase. In 1803, the United States completed the purchase with France.

With the Louisiana Territory, the United States stretched from the Atlantic Ocean to the Rocky Mountains and from the border of Canada in the north to New Orleans in the south.

2. ☑ **Reading Check** **Turn and talk** with a partner about why Jefferson felt so strongly about the United States purchasing New Orleans.

KENTUCKY

KENTUCKY RIVER

Boonesborough

The Lewis and Clark Expedition

Soon after the Louisiana Purchase, Jefferson finalized plans for an expedition to explore the new lands. He asked Meriwether Lewis to lead the expedition. Lewis had worked as Jefferson's secretary. He was also an explorer and frontiersman.

Lewis asked fellow frontiersman William Clark to go with him. Together, they put together the Corps of Discovery, a group of **capable** men who would take the nearly two-year journey to the Pacific Ocean. Jefferson was hoping that they would find a water route that would link the Mississippi with the Pacific Ocean. Such a route would provide access to the western part of North America. Jefferson also wanted Lewis and Clark to learn about the American Indians who lived in the West, as well as bring back information about the land itself.

The expedition began in St. Louis, Missouri, in May 1804. Both men kept detailed journals of the expedition, including their contact with American Indians and descriptions of the plants and animals they found. Clark also drew accurate maps that featured the mountains and plains of the West. He named rivers and creeks and identified important parts of the landscape. These maps were valuable resources for future explorers and settlers.

Academic Vocabulary

capable • *adj.*, having the necessary ability

This diary was kept by Meriwether Lewis during the expedition. Ask a partner a question about this diary and about Lewis's quote.

Primary Source

This scenery, already rich, pleasing, and beautiful, was still further heightened [improved] by immense [big] herds of buffalo, deer, elk, and antelopes, which we saw in every direction, feeding on the hills and plains. I do not think I exaggerate when I estimate the number of buffalo which could be comprehended [understood] at one view to the amount of 3,000.

-from the *Journal of Meriwether Lewis*, September 17, 1804

Along the way, Charbonneau, a French trapper, and his wife, Sacagawea, joined the Corps of Discovery as **interpreters**. This means that they translated what American Indians were saying into English or French for the explorers. Sacagawea helped the Corps of Discovery have good relations with American Indians.

The journey to the Pacific Ocean and back to Missouri took two and a half years. During this time, the members of the expedition had to face extreme elements and dangerous animals such as bears and mountain lions. The group reached the Pacific in November 1805. They had not found the water route they had been looking for, but they had learned a great deal about the geography of this region of the United States. The expedition returned to St. Louis in September 1806.

Quest Connections

Make a list of the hardships and successes that the Lewis and Clark expedition encountered. What kind of men do you think were involved in the Corps of Discovery?

INTERACTIVITY

Take a closer look at the Lewis and Clark expedition.

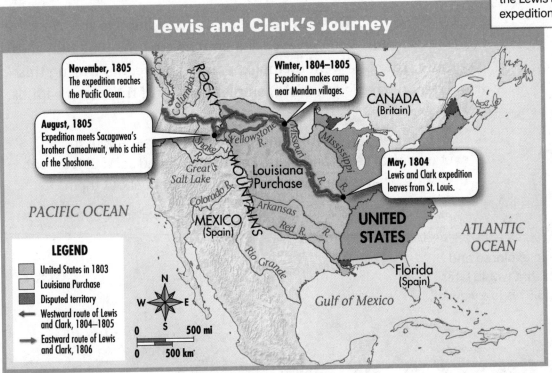

Lewis and Clark's Journey

November, 1805
The expedition reaches the Pacific Ocean.

Winter, 1804–1805
Expedition makes camp near Mandan villages.

CANADA
(Britain)

August, 1805
Expedition meets Sacagawea's brother Cameahwait, who is chief of the Shoshone.

May, 1804
Lewis and Clark expedition leaves from St. Louis.

Columbia R.
ROCKY
Snake
Yellowstone R.
Missouri R.
Mississippi
MOUNTAINS
Great Salt Lake
Louisiana Purchase
Colorado R.
Arkansas R.
Red R.
PACIFIC OCEAN
MEXICO
(Spain)
UNITED STATES
ATLANTIC OCEAN
Rio Grande
Florida
(Spain)
Gulf of Mexico

LEGEND
United States in 1803
Louisiana Purchase
Disputed territory
Westward route of Lewis and Clark, 1804–1805
Eastward route of Lewis and Clark, 1806

N W E S

0   500 mi
0   500 km

3. ☑ **Reading Check** On the map, circle the natural western boundary where the Louisiana Purchase ended. **Explain** why Jefferson wanted to find a route to the Pacific Ocean.

_____

_____

_____

Other Explorers

Following in the footsteps of Lewis and Clark, Zebulon Pike and a small group of men were sent by President Jefferson to explore the southern and western regions of the Louisiana Purchase. Pike was asked to find where the Arkansas River began.

In November 1806, Pike came upon a large mountain, today called Pikes Peak in Colorado. A few months later, the group found the source of the Arkansas River and began their trip home.

On the way, because of a series of navigational mistakes, they ended up in Spanish territory and were captured. The Spanish took Pike and his men into Mexico. After being held for five months, the men were released and returned home. The ordeal allowed Pike to learn more about the Southwest.

In 1842, John C. Frémont set out on an expedition to the West. He left from St. Louis and surveyed the land around the Platte River in Nebraska. Later, he went on an expedition to Oregon. During this trip, Frémont created the first complete survey of the western lands.

4. ☑ **Reading Check** **Turn and talk** with a partner about the expeditions of Lewis and Clark, Zebulon Pike, and John C. Frémont. **Describe** what is the same and what is different about them.

Pike and his group explored and mapped the land that would later become Colorado. This is a view of Pikes Peak.

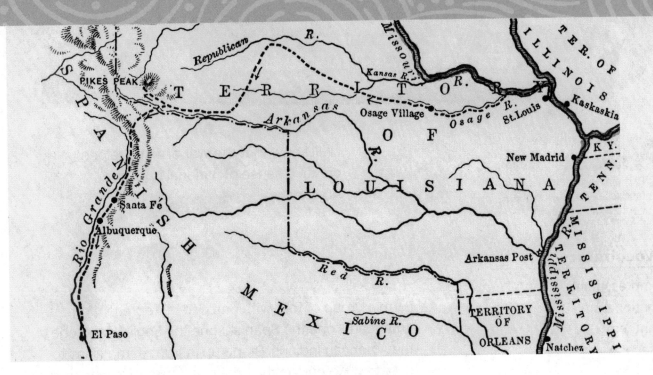

This map shows Pikes Peak. Zebulon Pike was not successful in climbing the mountain.

 **Lesson 2 Check**

5. **Draw Inferences** Why were people moving west during this time in history, given the danger of living on the frontier?

_____

_____

_____

6. **Sequence** List the three significant events that led to the Louisiana Purchase.

_____

_____

_____

7. **Understand the** *Quest* **Connections** Why did President Jefferson ask Lewis to explore the newly purchased land to the west?

_____

_____

3 The War of 1812

 INTERACTIVITY

Participate in a class discussion to preview the content of this lesson.

Vocabulary

impressment
nationalism
anthem
secede

Academic Vocabulary

eliminate
construct

The French and the British were fighting wars in Europe in the late 1700s and early 1800s. These French and British ships are battling each other.

Unlock The BIG Question

I will know that the War of 1812 helped create a sense of national pride for Americans.

Jumpstart Activity

Form a group of four with one person representing Americans, one the Spanish, one the English, and one the American Indians. Stand up in front of the class to debate why yours is the best claim to land in what is today the eastern United States.

As Americans were moving west, France under the leadership of Napoleon Bonaparte was going to war with other European countries. Although the United States tried to remain neutral, the country would become involved in a war for the second time in its short history.

Another War Nears

James Madison was elected the fourth president of the United States in 1808. France and Great Britain had begun seizing, or taking, American ships and interfering with trade. When Madison was Secretary of State under Thomas Jefferson, he had warned the two countries that this practice went against international law. The countries paid little attention to Madison's warnings.

When he was elected president in 1808, Madison tried to remain neutral and stopped trade with both countries. In May 1810, Congress decided to resume trading with both countries. It declared that if one of the countries formally acknowledged America as neutral, Madison would cut off trade with the other country. Napoleon agreed, and the United States stopped trading with Great Britain.

In the American West, Great Britain was giving American Indians weapons and encouraging hostility against Americans who were moving west. A Shawnee leader named Tecumseh asked the American governor of the Indiana Territory, William Henry Harrison, to stop taking lands from American Indian groups. He wanted Harrison to restore lands that had already been taken.

 INTERACTIVITY

Explore the key ideas of this lesson.

James Madison

Primary Source

The white people have no right to take the land from the Indians, because they had it first; it is theirs. They may sell, but all must join. Any sale not made by all is not valid.

—from Tecumseh's speech to Governor Harrison, August 12, 1810

Tecumseh

Tecumseh had worked to unite different groups of American Indians to beat the Americans. He thought that if different American Indian groups worked together, they could win. Tecumseh's hopes were not met. Americans and the American Indians fought in the Battle of Tippecanoe in November 1811. The battle was over the Northwest Territory. Harrison and his men defeated the American Indians who then allied themselves with the British.

At the same time, Britain began capturing American sailors. The **impressment** of American sailors meant that Americans were being captured and forced to work on British ships. British interference with trade, British impressment, and the desire for expansion westward into British Canada soon led Madison to agree with people who supported going to war against Great Britain. These supporters, who had a strong sense of **nationalism**, or national pride, were called War Hawks. They were led by Henry Clay and John C. Calhoun. The President asked Congress to declare war in June of 1812.

1. ☑ Reading Check **Analyze** the conflict between Great Britain and the United States and the role of American Indians like the Shawnee. **Turn and talk** with a partner about how each of the reasons for declaring war affected the United States.

_____

_____

Battles at Sea

The United States was not ready to fight another war. The U.S. Navy had only about a dozen ships while Great Britain had hundreds. American soldiers were also outnumbered.

Despite the obstacles, the United States won a decisive sea victory in August 1812. The battle lasted only 35 minutes, during which the British onboard the HMS *Guerriere* watched their cannonballs bouncing off the oak hull of the American USS *Constitution*. This battle earned the American ship the nickname "Old Ironsides."

The British ship was so damaged that its men set fire to it once everyone had gotten off of the ship. The battle marked the first time an American ship had captured a British one. The victory had taken the British by surprise.

The USS *Constitution* defeated the HMS *Guerriere*.

In September of 1813, U.S. Captain Oliver Perry led nine ships to victory against six British warships during the Battle of Lake Erie. Perry's ship was destroyed. Perry moved to another ship and sailed directly into the British line of fire, forcing the British to surrender. The American victory **eliminated** the British from the Northwest Territory.

Near the end of the war, the British entered New York from Canada and moved toward Plattsburgh. The British were soon exchanging fire with American troops on the ground. A few days later, a group of British warships battled a smaller American force at Plattsburgh Bay on Lake Champlain. Soon after the battle began, the British leader was killed, and then the British surrendered. The battle on land was called off, and the British retreated into Canada.

The naval victories during the War of 1812 showed other countries that though the United States Navy was new and still small, Americans knew how to **construct** strong ships and how to sail them.

Academic Vocabulary

eliminate • *v.*, to remove

construct • *v.*, to build

2. ☑ **Reading Check** **Turn and talk** with a partner about the significance of the United States being able to defeat the British at sea during the War of 1812.

Battles on Land

When the war began, most of the battles were taking place near Canada's border. Soon, the war moved to the Chesapeake Bay area. A British admiral set his sights on Washington, D.C., in August 1814. The British slowly closed in on the capital city. The Americans, including President Madison himself, tried to fend off the British. Madison's wife Dolley had made sure that a full-length portrait of George Washington was safe before agreeing to leave the White House.

The British then set fire to the White House, the Treasury building, and the Capitol Building, which housed the Supreme Court and the Library of Congress. Then the city fell.

Also in the late summer of 1814, the British decided to take Baltimore by way of Fort McHenry. On the morning of September 13, British ships began attacking Fort McHenry thinking they would quickly scare the Americans away. For twenty-five hours, the Americans fired back and drove the British away.

After the battle, the American flag still waved above the fort. A man named Francis Scott Key had witnessed the battle and was inspired to write a poem. The poem was later set to music and became our national **anthem**, or song, "The Star-Spangled Banner."

The British burned several government buildings in Washington, D.C., during the War of 1812.

Primary Source

O say can you see, by the dawn's early light,
What so proudly we hail'd at the twilight's last gleaming,
Whose broad stripes and bright stars through the perilous fight
O'er the ramparts we watch'd were so gallantly streaming?
And the rocket's red glare, the bomb bursting in air,
Gave proof through the night that our flag was still there,
O say does that star-spangled banner yet wave
O'er the land of the free and the home of the brave?

—"The Star-Spangled Banner"

The battles that took place in the South were mostly against groups of American Indians that were rising up in rebellion to protect their land. General Andrew Jackson, who had also fought in the American Revolution, led troops to victory against the Creek Indians in the Battle at Horseshoe Bend.

The American naval victory at Lake Champlain, which had driven the British back into Canada, led to peace negotiations and the Treaty of Ghent. Finally, the treaty was signed in Belgium and ended the war in December 1814. However, word did not reach parts of the United States for weeks. Two weeks after the treaty was signed, Jackson achieved the most famous victory of the war.

On January 8, 1815, the British marched into New Orleans. The Americans troops led by Jackson had been warned about the British approach. The British were unable to break American lines. After a half hour, 2,000 British soldiers had been killed or wounded and the rest of the army retreated. Jackson had only lost about 70 men.

3. ☑ **Reading Check** **Turn and talk** with a partner about the strategic outcome of the major conflicts in the War of 1812, as well as how each must have affected American morale.

General Andrew Jackson led American forces to victory at the Battle of New Orleans.

Word Wise

Context Clues You will see the word *diplomatic* in this lesson. What other words do you see that give you a clue about its meaning? Circle these words. What do you think *diplomatic* means?

Quest Connections

Highlight the effects of the War of 1812 on Americans. What qualities are reflected in Americans' desire to keep expanding westward?

INTERACTIVITY

Take a closer look at a battle of the War of 1812.

The Treaty of Ghent ended the War of 1812.

The Effects of the War

The War of 1812 is sometimes called the "second War of Independence," because it showed the strength of the United States. Americans had not only been willing to come together in the name of liberty, but they would continue to defend it.

Although the Battle of New Orleans did not affect the outcome of the war, Jackson's victory created a strong sense of nationalism, or national pride. The battle also marked the last time that the United States and Great Britain would engage in battle. Although the Treaty of Ghent did not address two major reasons for the war—impressment and the rights of a neutral United States—it guaranteed peace and declared that all territory conquered during the war would be returned. It also allowed for U.S. expansion in the Great Lakes area and was considered a diplomatic victory for the United States.

Other effects of the war were that the relationship between Americans and American Indian nations were further strained, and the Federalist Party came to an end. The party had been against becoming involved in the war, some even talking about **seceding**, or breaking away, from the union. This position was considered unpatriotic and the party quickly dissolved.

4. **☑ Reading Check** **Draw Inferences** Why was an unwillingness to go to war thought to be unpatriotic?

_____

_____

_____

_____

_____

INTERACTIVITY

Check your understanding of the key ideas of this lesson.

☑ Lesson 3 Check

5. **Draw Inferences Explain** why you think that the port of New Orleans was so important to both the Americans and the British.

_____

_____

_____

6. **Explain** the importance of "The Star-Spangled Banner" during the War of 1812. Cite a phrase from the anthem that shows American ideals.

_____

_____

_____

7. **Quest Connections** What were the causes and effects of the War of 1812?

_____

_____

_____

_____

_____

Draw Inferences

▶ VIDEO

Watch a video about drawing inferences.

An inference is a conclusion or guess that you make when you put new information together with what you already know about a topic. Authors do not always include all of the information in their work, so being able to make inferences is an important skill that will help you to better understand what you read. You can draw an inference from artwork in the same way. Follow these steps to draw an inference:

1. After reading a text or looking at an image, ask yourself, "What is my inference?"

2. Once you have made an educated guess about the text or image, think about what clues you used to make the inference.

3. Put those clues together with what you already know about the topic and make sure there is enough evidence to support your inference.

4. If there is text in the image, use it to help you make an inference.

Study the image. It is a political cartoon that shows, from left to right, King George III, Thomas Jefferson, and Napoleon Bonaparte. Use the visual clues that you see and what you already know about these people to draw an inference.

Your Turn!

1. Complete each sentence in the graphic organizer to help you draw an inference about the political cartoon. Write down the clues that you see in the image, based on what you learned in this lesson and other lessons in the chapter. Think about how these people or the countries they represent dealt with each other.

What I See	What I Know	Inference/Conclusion
I see King George III and Napoleon	Great Britain and France	The artist is saying that
	Napoleon	

2. Use evidence from the text to support the inference you drew about the political cartoon. Why did the artist draw a cartoon to make this point?

Lesson 4
American Indians and the Trail of Tears

INTERACTIVITY

Participate in a class discussion to preview the content of this lesson.

Vocabulary

Monroe Doctrine
foreign policy
Trail of Tears

Academic Vocabulary

violate
adapt

Unlock The **BIG** Question

I will know that Andrew Jackson's policies shaped the United States and forced thousands of American Indians to leave their homes.

Jumpstart Activity

Imagine that you live on the border of Florida and Georgia and you were told to move with your family to Oklahoma. With a partner, look at a map and figure out how many miles the journey would be. Discuss with your partner how hard the journey would be on foot and what other challenges you would face.

After the War of 1812, the United States had a renewed sense of pride and hope for the future. The focus of government and citizens alike returned to expanding the borders of the United States. Some people called the time after the war an "Era of Good Feelings."

Many Seminole lived in thatched homes like these in the marshy Florida Everglades. This environment provided a good shelter and hiding place.

Acquiring Florida

After the American Revolution, the Florida territory had returned to Spanish control. For years, enslaved African Americans had been running away from farms and plantations in the South to find refuge in Florida. There, Seminole American Indians gave them shelter. The Seminole people also led raids against settlers on the Florida border to protect their land.

In 1817, James Monroe became the fifth president of the United States. The next year, Monroe sent General Andrew Jackson to put an end to the raids on American settlers. Jackson invaded Florida and took control of several forts and cities.

At this time, Spanish leaders were worried about their territories in Latin America and they realized it was not possible for them to be able to defend Florida. Thus, John Quincy Adams persuaded Spain to sell Florida to the United States in return for the United States dropping its claim to Texas. This agreement was called the Adams-Onís Treaty of 1819.

INTERACTIVITY

Explore the key ideas of this lesson.

1. ☑ **Reading Check**

   On the map, **identify** and circle the land that the United States gained in 1819. **Turn and talk** with a partner about why this new land was important.

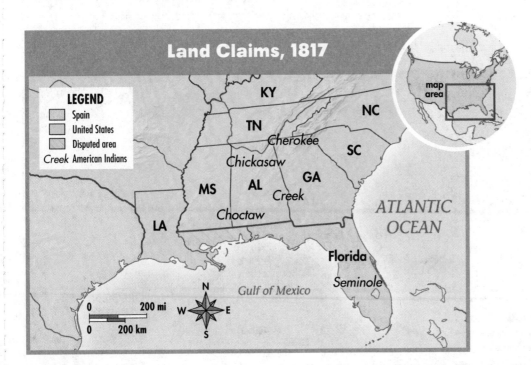

Land Claims, 1817

LEGEND
- Spain
- United States
- Disputed area

Creek American Indians

KY
NC
TN
Cherokee
SC
Chickasaw
GA
MS   AL   Creek
Choctaw
LA
ATLANTIC OCEAN
Florida
Seminole
Gulf of Mexico

0   200 mi
0   200 km

N W E S

map area

The Monroe Doctrine

During the 1700s, Russia established fur trading posts in parts of Alaska. In the early 1800s, Russia began colonizing the coastal areas of this territory. Monroe did not want Russia claiming land near the United States. He felt that it set a bad precedent, because the American Revolution had been fought to keep a foreign country out of the colonies. There was also concern that Spain might try to recolonize in the United States.

So, the president issued the **Monroe Doctrine** warning European leaders that they were not to colonize or recolonize in the Western Hemisphere. Monroe also repeated the United States policy of neutrality regarding European conflicts. The policy was part of Monroe's annual message to Congress in 1823. The doctrine became a key part of U.S. **foreign policy**, or official rules and ideas one nation's government uses to define its relationship with with another nation's government.

2. ☑ Reading Check **Draw Inferences** Circle the area on the map that Russia claimed. Why did President Monroe want to discourage Russia from setting up colonies in Alaska? Think about the advantages and disadvantages that it had.

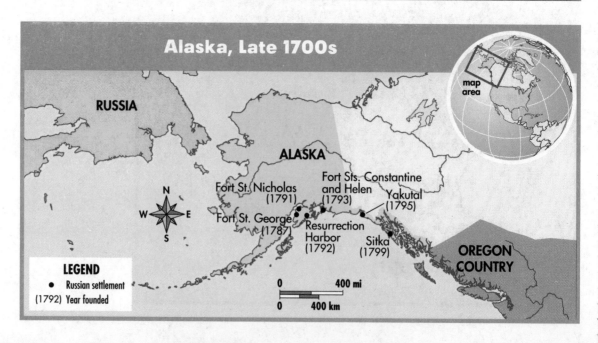

Alaska, Late 1700s

RUSSIA

ALASKA

map area

Fort St. Nicholas (1791)

Fort Sts. Constantine and Helen (1793)

Yakutal (1795)

Fort St. George (1787)

Resurrection Harbor (1792)

Sitka (1799)

OREGON COUNTRY

LEGEND
- Russian settlement
(1792) Year founded

0   400 mi

0   400 km

This 1836 cartoon makes fun of Andrew Jackson's plan to get rid of the Second Bank of the United States. Jackson (left) is shown with Vice President Martin Van Buren (center) and Jack Downing (a made-up character) struggling against a many-headed snake. Each snake head stood for a state in the country.

Andrew Jackson Becomes President

When the U.S. Constitution was first written, only white men who owned land could vote. By the 1820s many states allowed all white men to vote. African Americans and women were not permitted to vote.

When the Federalist Party fell apart after the War of 1812, there was only the Republican Party left. The Republican Party was mostly supported by businessmen, plantation owners, and those looking for social reform. In 1828, the Democratic Party formed. This party represented mostly farmers, factory workers, and new immigrants.

Having more male voters helped presidential nominee Andrew Jackson win the presidency in 1828. Jackson's goal was to represent the common man, and he was the first president to represent the Democratic Party. He became known as "the People's President."

One of Jackson's ideas was to get rid of the Second Bank of the United States because he thought it only helped wealthy people. It also put all of the country's financial interests in one institution. He also believed it had too much control over Congress. Republican leaders and attorneys for the bank, Henry Clay and Daniel Webster, fought with Jackson over it. In the end, Jackson vetoed a bill that would have kept the bank open. Partly because of these policies, he won the approval of enough Americans to be elected to a second term.

John C. Calhoun

In 1832, some southern states tried to get rid of tariffs because they felt the taxes only benefitted the North. Jackson wanted the tariffs to remain in place because they would increase the price of imported products and keep the prices of American products low. In this way, Jackson would again be helping the common man. The president told John C. Calhoun, one of the southern leaders behind the movement, that he would not sign a bill nullifying the tariffs. Calhoun and Clay came up with a compromise to lower the tariffs as opposed to getting rid of them.

Indian Removal Act

In the 1830s, there were five groups of American Indians living in the Southeast: the Cherokees, Choctaws, Chickasaws, Creeks, and Seminoles. The Cherokees had farms, traded, and built towns much like the white settlers who lived near them. Sequoyah, a Cherokee American Indian, had created a system for reading and writing in the Cherokee language.

White settlers were also trying to settle in the Southeast where American Indians lived at this time. Conflicts arose between the two groups as settlers moved onto the land of the American Indians. Jackson took the side of the settlers, agreeing that they had a right to the land.

In response, the Cherokees created a government, wrote a constitution, and had a two-house legislature similar to the American government. They sent delegates to the Supreme Court to argue their case. The Cherokees declared that they were a sovereign nation and could not be forced off the land.

In May 1830, Congress passed the Indian Removal Act. The act stated that American Indians had to leave their homes and move west of the Mississippi River to what was called Indian Territory. This land in present-day Oklahoma.

That it shall and may be lawful for the President of the United States to cause so much of any territory belonging to the United States, west of the river Mississippi, not included in any state or organized territory . . . to be divided into a suitable number of districts, for the reception of such tribes or nations of Indians as may choose to exchange the lands where they now reside, and remove there.

—The Indian Removal Act, 1830

The move was supposed to be voluntary, but American Indians faced pressure. Some American Indians, including the Seminoles, fought settlers for years. Competing claims for land would continue into much of the 1800s. Some American Indian groups made alliances among each other to fight against the United States, with little success. By 1871 the United States would pass a law that ended all treaty-making with American Indians.

4. ☑ **Reading Check** Study the map of American Indian removal. **Identify** the groups that moved west. **Turn and talk** to a partner about some of the challenges they would have faced in Indian Territory.

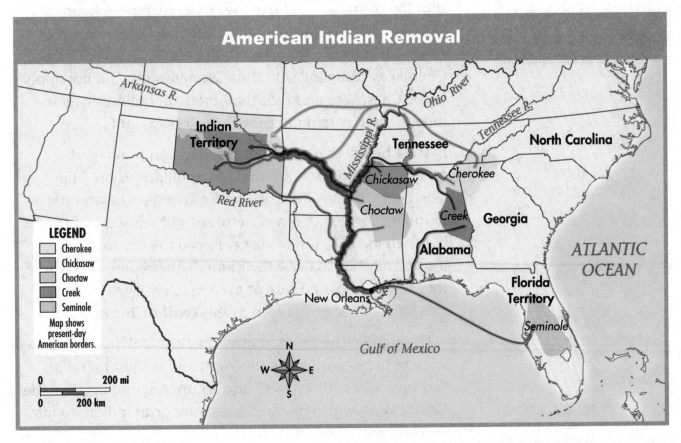

American Indian Removal

LEGEND
- Cherokee
- Chickasaw
- Choctaw
- Creek
- Seminole

Map shows present-day American borders.

0   200 mi
0   200 km

This painting of the Trail of Tears shows the suffering that the Cherokees endured during the forced march to Indian Territory.

Academic Vocabulary

violate • *v.*, to do something that is against the law

adapt • *v.*, to become adjusted to new conditions

The Trail of Tears

When the Indian Removal Act was passed, leaders in Georgia said that their state laws applied to the Cherokees who lived there. The Cherokees responded by taking legal action to keep their land and rights. Cherokee Chief John Ross filed a case with the Supreme Court stating that the Indian Removal Act did **violate** a treaty the Cherokees had with the United States. In this case, the justices decided that the court did not have the power to oppose Georgia's state laws. The decision was appealed, and Supreme Court Chief Justice John Marshall decided in favor of the Cherokees. Marshall said that Georgia's laws did not apply to the Cherokees and that the American Indians lived in independent communities with their own rights.

The Cherokees hoped that this decision would end removal, but Jackson ignored Marshall's decision. The Cherokees had to either live under Georgia's laws or move to Indian Territory. Some Cherokees still refused to move, but then in 1838, the U.S army forced the Cherokees to move. They had to leave their homes, unprepared for where they were going, and **adapt** to completely new elements. This journey became known as the **Trail of Tears**.

Throughout the 1800s, many American Indians were forced to move to reservations in the West, and not just to Indian Territory. Reservations were also set up west and north of the Great Plains, which required some American Indians to move east and south from their tribal lands.

5. ☑ **Reading Check** **Compare and contrast** the viewpoints of John Marshall and Andrew Jackson.

_____

_____

_____

_____

_____

Chief Justice John Marshall agreed with the Cherokees that the land was theirs.

INTERACTIVITY

Check your understanding of the key ideas of this lesson.

☑ Lesson 4 Check

6. **Summarize** the events that led to the acquisition of Florida.

_____

_____

_____

_____

7. **Describe** the key ideas in the Monroe Doctrine.

_____

_____

_____

_____

8. **Analyze** the Cherokees' reaction and response to the conflicts with American settlers.

_____

_____

_____

_____

Use and Interpret Evidence

When you make a claim or take a position on a topic, you need evidence to support your ideas. When looking for evidence, you should ask yourself questions. Once you find a piece of evidence, ask yourself, "How does this evidence support my position or ideas?"

Then ask yourself, "What else does this evidence tell me? Can this evidence be used to support another point of view or idea?" These questions help you interpret your evidence. Sometimes information can be read in two different ways.

Look at the example. Evidence to support a claim has been highlighted.

> ▶ **VIDEO**
>
> Watch a video about using and interpreting evidence.

Jackson's goal was to represent the common man, and he was the first president from the Democratic Party. He became known as "the People's President."

In a controversial move early in his presidency, Jackson decided to eliminate the Second Bank of the United States because he thought it only helped the wealthy, it put all of the country's financial interests in one institution, and it had too much control over Congress. Republican leaders and attorneys for the bank, Henry Clay and Daniel Webster, fought with Jackson over it. Ultimately, Jackson vetoed a bill that would have kept the bank open and won the approval of enough Americans to be elected to a second presidential term.

In 1832, some southern states tried to get rid of tariffs because they felt the taxes only benefitted the north. Jackson wanted the tariffs to remain in place because they would increase the price of imported products and keep the prices of American products low.

Andrew Jackson

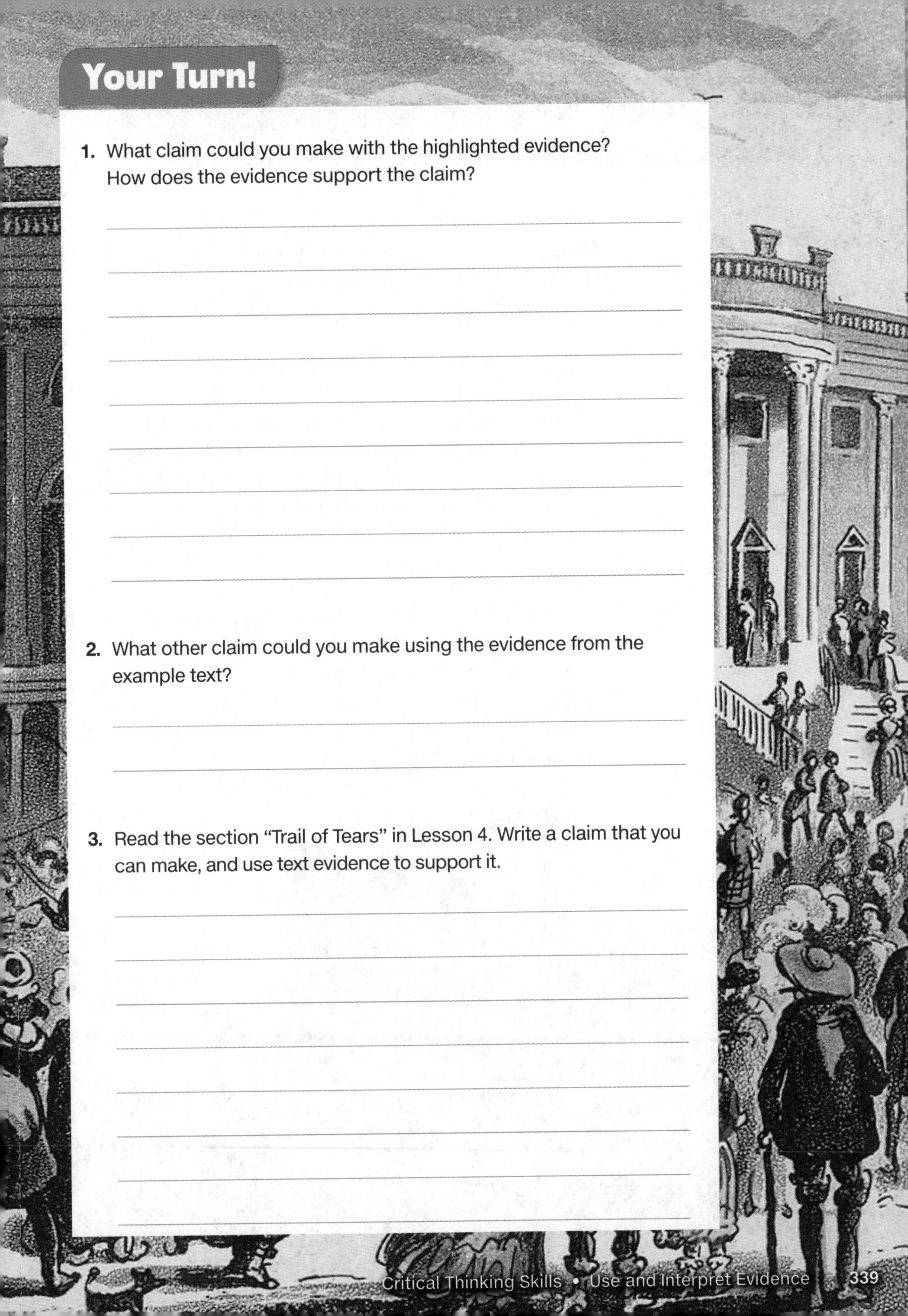

Your Turn!

1. What claim could you make with the highlighted evidence? How does the evidence support the claim?

_____

_____

_____

_____

_____

_____

_____

_____

_____

2. What other claim could you make using the evidence from the example text?

_____

_____

3. Read the section "Trail of Tears" in Lesson 4. Write a claim that you can make, and use text evidence to support it.

_____

_____

_____

_____

_____

_____

_____

Lesson 5 New Arrivals and the Fight for Freedom

INTERACTIVITY

Participate in a class discussion to preview the content of this lesson.

Vocabulary

reform
famine
abolition

Academic Vocabulary

advocate
academy

New immigrants board a ship to come to America.

Unlock The BIG Question

I will know that women and African Americans worked to improve American society in the mid-1800s.

JumpStart Activity

Form small groups. Talk about different customs and traditions that you have seen practiced in your school, town, or city. Present the information that you discussed with your group to the class.

The population of the United States grew at a high rate in the early and mid-1800s. Immigrants were coming to the United States from all over the world. The largest groups of immigrants came from Europe. Also during this time, different groups of Americans were trying to bring about social **reform**, or change.

New Immigrants

There were many factors that made the United States an appealing place to live in the early to mid-1800s. A push factor is a problem that forces someone to leave their home. A pull factor is something positive that attracts people to come to a new place. There were many pull factors that attracted people to the United States. After the War of 1812, people around the world believed that the young country would endure. Immigrants could find jobs, land, and higher wages. Many Europeans were also looking for a way to escape the turmoil in their home countries, a push factor.

European immigration gradually increased throughout the early 1800s with about 100,000 arriving in the 1820s, almost 600,000 in the 1830s, and 1.7 million in the 1840s. This was the largest wave of immigration in American history. German, Irish, and English people made up the biggest immigrant groups during this time.

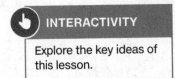

INTERACTIVITY

Explore the key ideas of this lesson.

1. ☑ **Reading Check**
   Analyze the graph.
   Discuss with a partner how immigration from 1789–1820 was different from immigration from 1821–1850. Use details from the graph to support your discussion.

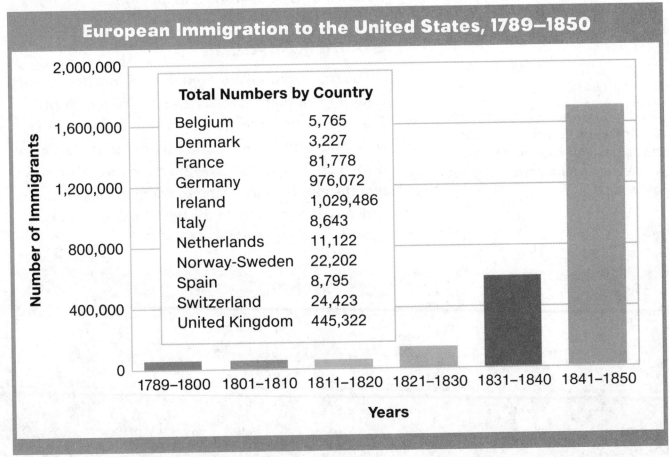

European Immigration to the United States, 1789–1850

Number of Immigrants (y-axis): 0, 400,000, 800,000, 1,200,000, 1,600,000, 2,000,000

Years (x-axis): 1789–1800, 1801–1810, 1811–1820, 1821–1830, 1831–1840, 1841–1850

Total Numbers by Country

Country	Total
Belgium	5,765
Denmark	3,227
France	81,778
Germany	976,072
Ireland	1,029,486
Italy	8,643
Netherlands	11,122
Norway-Sweden	22,202
Spain	8,795
Switzerland	24,423
United Kingdom	445,322

Source: U.S. Department of Homeland Security

The Great Irish Famine forced many people in Ireland to come to America.

In the 1840s, the numbers of Irish immigrants more than tripled from the 1830s due to a potato famine in Ireland. A **famine** is an extreme shortage of food. It was caused by a disease that attacked the potato plants. Potatoes were an important food source in Ireland. Over a million people died in Ireland because of hunger and disease. During the Great Irish Famine, people who could pay for the journey came to America. Most settled in the large coastal cities such as New York and Boston because they often could not afford to buy land in the West.

Between 1830 and 1860, more than 1.5 million Germans came to the United States. Many German immigrants were educated and wealthy and were fleeing a failed revolution in their country. Most of them could afford land and so they settled in the Midwest in large numbers. German immigrants often traveled west via the Cumberland Gap. Many settled in Cincinnati and St. Louis, and they usually became farmers or worked in factories.

Slavery Spreads

The cotton gin saved time but with a sharp rise in cotton production, the demand for more enslaved African Americans increased greatly in the South.

The cotton gin was created in 1793, making it much faster to separate the seeds from the cotton plant. The cotton gin made growing cotton very profitable. So, plantations across the South grew more cotton to meet a growing need. Growing more cotton, however, had the effect of increasing the demand for enslaved African Americans to do the back-breaking work of growing and picking the cotton.

When the Louisiana Territory was purchased in 1803, plantation owners in the South wanted to spread the practice of slavery to the new states. People living in the states in the north did not want slavery in the new states. The first state from this territory to be organized and join the Union was Missouri. Its state leaders wanted Missouri to become a slave state in 1820. This decision would disrupt the balance of the free and slave states. At the time, there were 11 free states and 11 slave states. Both the north and the south wanted to maintain this balance so that there would be equal representation in Congress. Neither side wanted the other group to have an advantage when passing laws.

The Missouri Compromise was a temporary solution. It was decided that Maine would be admitted to the Union as a free state. This would keep the balance. The compromise also set a line north of which slavery would not be permitted. Although the states remained in balance, the population of enslaved African Americans in Missouri grew from 10,000 to 45,000 between 1810 and 1830.

Quest Connection

Why were immigrants willing to make the journey to the western parts of the United States? Was this journey easy in the mid-1800s? Why or why not?

👆 INTERACTIVITY

Read and analyze a letter from a Polish immigrant to help you write a script about immigration to America.

2. ✅ Reading Check **Analyze** the map. **Turn and talk** with a partner about what you think will happen between the states in the north that oppose slavery and the states in the south where slavery is allowed.

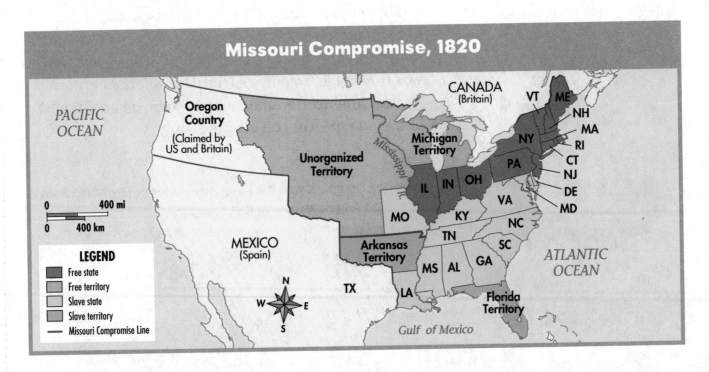

Missouri Compromise, 1820

Abolition

Beginning in the 1830s, people worked for the **abolition**, or end, of slavery. Abolitionists called for the immediate freedom of all enslaved African Americans. There were also other more moderate groups who favored a gradual end to slavery and still others who wanted the practice to be confined to existing areas.

The abolition movement met with a hostile response in both the north and the south. Mobs of angry people would protest the movement, and mailbags of abolitionist literature were burned.

William Lloyd Garrison was a journalist and abolitionist who started an anti-slavery newspaper called *The Liberator*. The newspaper was largely supported and distributed by free African Americans. Garrison joined about sixty other white and African American activists to found the American Anti-Slavery Society in 1833. The organization called slavery a sin and encouraged nonviolent participation in the movement. The group produced large amounts of abolitionist literature.

In the 1840s, Frederick Douglass became a well-known speaker, writer, and **advocate** in the abolitionist movement. Douglass had been born into slavery and his description of life as an enslaved person was true to life. Sojourner Truth was a former enslaved African American woman who became an abolitionist and made speeches all over the country.

In addition to being an abolitionist, William Lloyd Garrison also supported women's rights.

Academic Vocabulary

advocate • *n.*, person who supports a particular cause

Frederick Douglass was the long-time editor of *The North Star*, an African American newspaper.

THE NORTH STAR.

I am above eighty years old; it is about time for me to be going. I have been forty years a slave and forty years free, and would be here forty years more to have equal rights for all. I suppose I am kept here because something remains for me to do; I suppose I am yet to help to break the chain.

—Sojourner Truth, "Address to the First Annual Meeting of the American Equal Rights Association", May 9, 1867

Sojourner Truth

Abolitionists commonly cited phrases from the Declaration of Independence and the Constitution as anti-slavery documents that promised freedom for all. The movement continued as tensions rose after the Kansas-Nebraska Act, which was passed in 1854. This act allowed people living in the Kansas and Nebraska territories to decide for themselves whether the practice of slavery would be allowed. It repealed, or cancelled, the Missouri Compromise line that had been north of Arkansas.

Some African Americans found more opportunities and freedoms in the western territories. Some enslaved African American women like Biddy Mason gained their freedom in the West. Mason gained her freedom in California, started a business, and became the first female African American land owner. Unlike the East, the West opened up new possibilities for African Americans, as well as for women.

3. ☑ **Reading Check** Sojourner Truth and Frederick Douglass spoke out against slavery. **Draw an inference** about why African Americans were convincing speakers for abolition.

_____

_____

_____

_____

_____

Seneca Falls Convention

Women had few rights in the 1800s. They could not vote and rarely received a full education. Married women could not hold property.

Academic Vocabulary

academy • *n.*, a place for study or training

Susan. B. Anthony

After the Revolutionary War, in 1787, the Young Ladies **Academy** was co-founded by Benjamin Rush in Philadelphia. Rush was a doctor and writer and had been one of the signers of the Declaration of Independence. Some people at this time, including Rush, thought that if women were to be responsible for raising sons who were active and responsible citizens, they would need to have more education. The Young Ladies Academy offered classes in reading, writing, grammar, math, and chemistry.

Susan B. Anthony, Elizabeth Cady Stanton, and Lucretia Mott had all been active in the abolition movement. This work made them more aware of their own lack of rights, and they began to work toward reform. Like the founders of the Young Ladies Academy, they believed that all girls should have a good education. Anthony later became president of the National American Woman Suffrage Association.

Primary Source

And it is downright mockery to talk to women of their enjoyment of the blessings of liberty while they are denied the use of the only means of securing them provided by this democratic-republican government-the ballot.

—Susan B. Anthony, "Is It a Crime for a U.S. Citizen To Vote?", 1873

In 1848, Stanton and Mott set up a convention in Seneca Falls to discuss equality for women. At the convention, Stanton read a statement that was based on the Declaration of Independence. The convention was the start of the women's rights movement.

In 1869, Wyoming led the way in the western territories and in the nation for granting women the right to vote. Later, Utah, Colorado, and Idaho also granted women the right to vote.

4. **✓ Reading Check** **Explain** why women's education became important in the late 1700s and 1800s.

_____

_____

_____

_____

Both women and men attended the Seneca Falls Convention.

 INTERACTIVITY

Check your understanding of the key ideas of this lesson.

✓ Lesson 5 Check

5. **Cause and Effect** Explain how the invention of the cotton gin caused the spread of slavery.

_____

_____

_____

6. **Explain** why the abolitionist movement considered the Declaration of Independence and the Constitution to be anti-slavery documents.

_____

_____

_____

7. **_Quest_ Connections** **Compare and contrast** the journey of Lewis and Clark, the War of 1812, and the plight of immigrants. Consider why these efforts were made and whether the effort was worth it for each group or event.

_____

_____

_____

_____

"The Declaration of Sentiments"

Elizabeth Cady Stanton

In 1848, Elizabeth Cady Stanton and Lucretia Mott organized the Seneca Falls Convention to bring attention to women's rights. Half of the U.S. population was made up of women, but they were not allowed to vote.

A document called "The Declaration of Sentiments" was read at the convention. It was modeled after the Declaration of Independence. It said that the rights promised to all men should also be recognized for women.

"The Declaration of Sentiments" also listed things that were unfair to women, much like the Declaration of Independence listed reasons why the colonies were angry with Britain. One of these demands was that women should be allowed to vote.

Vocabulary Support

The signers of the document, sixty-eight women and thirty-two men, believe the following

some of these basic individual rights that everyone has are

self-evident, *adj.*, not requiring an explanation
endowed, *v.*, given
inalienable, *adj.*, unable to be taken away

"We hold these truths to be self-evident: that all men and women are created equal; that they are endowed by their Creator with certain inalienable rights; that among these are life, liberty, and the pursuit of happiness; that to secure these rights governments are instituted, deriving their just powers from the consent of the governed."

–from *"The Declaration of Sentiments"*

1848

Close Reading

1. **Identify** and circle the one difference in the excerpt between the "Declaration of Sentiments" and the Declaration of Independence. (See reference center.) Highlight the rights that the signers of the "Declaration of Sentiments" believed should be recognized for women.

2. **Describe** what the signers of the "Declaration of Sentiments" were hoping would happen as a result of the convention. Why did people who created the document use the Declaration of Independence as a model?

_____

_____

_____

_____

_____

_____

Wrap It Up

What other kinds of reforms were being made at this time? How were the efforts to make changes alike and different? Support your answer with information from the chapter.

_____

_____

_____

_____

_____

_____

Quality:
Courage

Frederick Douglass (1818–1895)
Writing and Speaking Out for Change

Frederick Douglass was born in February 1818 in Maryland. He was born into slavery. When he was eight years old, he was sent to Baltimore to live with a ship carpenter.

At the age of 15, Douglass was sent back to the country, where he worked on a farm run by a man who was known to be cruel. In 1838, after two failed attempts, Douglass escaped slavery with the help of Anna Murray, a free African American woman. They later married and moved to Massachusetts.

Douglass began attending abolitionist meetings. He had a subscription to William Lloyd Garrison's newspaper, the *Liberator*, and went to listen to Garrison's speeches.

Douglass took a big risk when he published his autobiography in 1845. He could have endangered his freedom. His book was widely read in the United States and translated into many European languages. He later began publishing *The North Star*. Douglass wrote in 1851 that the Constitution should be used as a document that promoted freedom for all.

Explore More

1. **Identify** three times in his life when Frederick Douglass exhibited courage. **Explain** why his actions were courageous.

   _____

   _____

   _____

   _____

2. Conduct research about another well-known abolitionist. Compare and contrast his or her story with that of Douglass. How did this person also show courage? Report your findings to your class.

Visual Review

Use these graphics to review some of the key terms, people, and ideas from this chapter.

1796
John Adams is elected president.

1800
Thomas Jefferson is elected president.

1816
James Monroe is elected president.

1788　　　　　**1808**　　　　　**1828**

1789
George Washington is elected president.

1808
James Madison is elected president.

1828
Andrew Jackson is elected president.

Key Events and People

In 1775, **Daniel Boone** discovered an American Indian trail through the Cumberland Gap.

The United States paid $15 million for the Louisiana Purchase in 1803.

William Henry Harrison fought **Tecumseh**, a Shawnee leader, over western land in 1811.

The United States fought a second war with Great Britain in the War of 1812.

The Indian Removal Act of 1830 forced many American Indians to relocate to the Indian Territory in modern-day Oklahoma.

William Lloyd Garrison became a leading activist in the abolition movement.

☑ Assessment

Vocabulary and Key Terms

1. Draw a line to match the definitions to the correct terms.

the edge of the wilderness   **interpreter**

a person who lived on the edge of the wilderness   **caravan**

a group of people who move together   **pioneer**

a person who understands several languages   **frontier**

2. What is **suffrage** and why did those who did not have it, want it?

_____

3. What is a **Cabinet**?

_____

4. What is a **famine**?

_____

5. **Analyze a Graph** Identify and circle the two ten-year periods when immigration more than doubled. **Compare and contrast** the push and pull factors on a separate piece of paper.

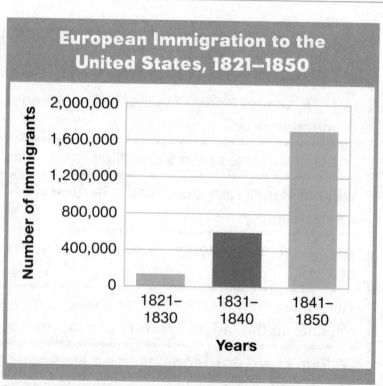

European Immigration to the United States, 1821–1850

Source: U.S. Department of Homeland Security

Critical Thinking and Writing

6. **Analyze** the events leading up to the Indian Removal Act. **Explain** how the American Indians tried to defend their land against encroachment of the settlers. Cite three specific examples from the text.

_____

_____

_____

_____

_____

_____

_____

_____

7. **Identifying Points of View** Fill in the circle next to the best answer. Which person ruled that the Cherokee were a sovereign nation and had a right to their land?

(A) Andrew Jackson

(B) John Marshall

(C) William Clark

(D) James Monroe

8. **Revisit the Big Question** Choose one President that you learned about in this chapter and summarize how he shaped the young nation. What were his most prominent policies? Did these policies affect the nation in a positive or negative way? Use evidence from the text to support your answer.

_____

_____

_____

_____

_____

Analyze Primary Sources

At the proposal of the Russian Imperial Government ... a full power and instructions have been transmitted ... to arrange by amicable [friendly] negotiation the respective rights and interests of the two nations on the northwest coast of this continent.
—Monroe Doctrine, December 2, 1823

9. **Explain** what Monroe was referring to when he said "to arrange by amicable negotiation the respective rights and interests of the two nations".

_____

_____

_____

_____

_____

_____

_____

10. **Writing Workshop: Write a Narrative** On a separate sheet of paper, write a short story describing the life of a young man living in Baltimore in the days leading up to the War of 1812. Describe why the man is willing to fight in the war and what he hopes the outcome will be. The story can be written in the first or third person.

Draw Inferences

11. **Analyze** the social, economic, and political impact of the large waves of European immigrants who came to the United States in the early and mid-1800s.

_____

_____

_____

_____

_____

Quest Findings

Finding Your Way

You've read the lessons in this chapter, and now you're ready to gather your research and write your script. Remember that the goal of the video or skit is to inform your audience about the qualities that the people involved in a specific historic event showed. Use your sources to support your claims. Follow these steps:

INTERACTIVITY

Use this activity to help you prepare your assignment.

1 Prepare to Write

Organize your information and decide which sources tell the best and most accurate stories about your group. Discuss how the triumphs and struggles of your group show their qualities.

2 Write a Draft

Use your notes and the evidence from your Quest Connections to write a draft for your script. Make sure you answer the following questions:

- What did the group accomplish?
- Why did the group set out to do this?
- Who was responsible for the decision?
- What triumphs and struggles resulted from the decision?
- What conclusions can you draw about this group?

3 Discuss

As a group, read the draft of the script. Make sure that you have enough evidence to support the claims you made about your group.

4 Present Your Script

Present your finished script to the class. Decide as a group which proposal a movie director most likely would select, and explain your choice.

GO ONLINE FOR
DIGITAL RESOURCES

▶ VIDEO

👆 INTERACTIVITY

🔊 AUDIO

🎮 GAMES

☑ ASSESSMENT

📖 eTEXT

The BIG Question What are the costs and benefits of growth?

▶ VIDEO

Lesson 1

Inventions, Roads, and Railroads

Lesson 2

Independence for Texas and California

Lesson 3

Trails to the West

Lesson 4

The California Gold Rush

JumpStart Activity

👆 INTERACTIVITY

Think about moving to a new place that is far away. With a partner, create a list of the positives and negatives about the move and share them with another pair of students.

_____

_____

_____

_____

_____

♪ Rap About It! ♪

 🔊 AUDIO

From Sea to Shining Sea

Preview the chapter **vocabulary** as you sing the rap:

Throughout that whole time people moved west

Traveling together proved to be best

Trails were made by these **wagon trains**

Across the mountains and the Great Plains

The reason for leaving was different for each

Some people **persecuted** for the religions they teach

This poor and cruel treatment led them to leave

In search of a place where they could believe

California's **gold rush** was at a full rate

Many people quickly flocked to the state

Some found gold and some settled down

These settlers were the start of cities and towns

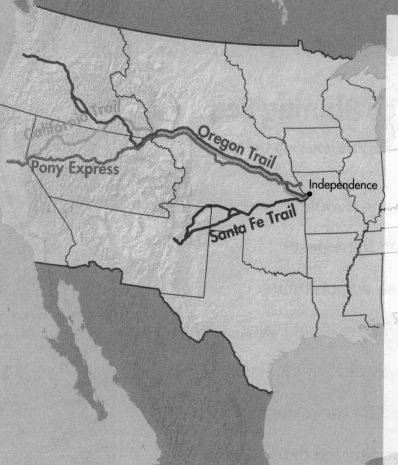

Where did the trails heading west begin and end?

The westward trails began in Independence, Missouri. The trails ended in the Oregon Territory, California, and Santa Fe.

Locate where the Santa Fe Trail goes after leaving Missouri and identify the state this area is now in.

TODAY
Wagon ruts from the Oregon Trail days are still visible in many places.

What happened and When?

Read the timeline to find out about the events that helped spark westward expansion.

1830

1831
Cyrus McCormick invents the mechanical reaper.

TODAY
Many features of McCormick's reaper are still used in crop harvesting machines.

1835

1836
Texas declares independence from Mexico.

Who will you meet?

Samuel Morse
Invented Morse code, an early way of communicating across long distances

Narcissa Whitman
Missionary who taught American Indians about Christianity

Antonio Lopez de Santa Anna
President of Mexico who led an army into Texas

Levi Strauss
Jewish German immigrant entrepreneur who started a clothing company

 INTERACTIVITY

Complete the Interactive gallery to preview content.

1845

1850

1844
First telegraph message is sent.

1848
Mexican War ends; California gold rush begins.

1850
California becomes a state.

TODAY
We communicate using cell phones, e-mail, and social media.

Quest
Collaborative Discussion

Is the West the Best?

Westward expansion is an important part of American history. Traveling into unknown areas took determination and strength. There were sometimes dangers. There was also a chance for a new kind of life at the end of the trail.

One way to think about an issue such as westward expansion is through a collaborative discussion. This helps people exchange and build on new ideas.

Quest Kick Off

Your mission is to prepare for a collaborative discussion about the costs and benefits of moving from east to west in the mid-1800s. You should be able to discuss whether a family should leave home to become pioneers.

1 Ask Questions

What did people have to sacrifice when they moved west? What kind of life awaited them in the Oregon or California territories? Write two questions of your own.

....

....

....

....

2 Plan Your Evidence

What type of information will you need to gather to help you think about the costs and benefits of moving west? What facts do you need to gather?

INTERACTIVITY

Get help thinking about how to evaluate costs and benefits of moving west.

....

....

....

....

....

....

3 Look for Quest Connections

Turn to the next page to begin looking for Quest Connections that will help you prepare for your discussion.

4 Quest Findings
Discuss It

Use the Quest Findings page at the end of the chapter to help you prepare for your discussion and present your opinion.

Lesson 1

Inventions, Roads, and Railroads

INTERACTIVITY

Participate in a class discussion to preview the content of this lesson.

Unlock The BIG Question

I will know that new inventions and forms of transportation had costs and benefits.

Vocabulary

profit
mass production
canal

Academic Vocabulary

process
determine

JumPstart Activity

Where would you like to visit in the United States or the world? On a map or globe, show a partner where this place is. How do you think it feels to visit a new place? Share your ideas with your partner.

The invention of the McCormick reaper made farm work easier and more profitable.

The main reason that most people work in business is to make a profit. A **profit** is the money a business earns after its debts have been paid. A way to increase profits is to reduce, or shorten, the amount of time it takes to produce goods to be sold. Another way to make a profit is to lower the costs of materials or make workers more efficient. In the early 1800s, new inventions in science and technology helped businesses make a profit and changed the way people lived and worked.

INTERACTIVITY

Explore the key ideas of this lesson.

Inventions Bring Changes

In the late 1700s, cotton was a profitable crop. To make money selling it, however, required many hours of work by enslaved African Americans. In 1793, Eli Whitney built an improved version of the cotton gin. This new machine greatly reduced the time it took to separate seeds from the cotton plant. This made cotton a very profitable crop. However, it led to an increase in the use of enslaved African Americans to pick cotton. As cotton plantations spread from east to west across the South, slavery spread too.

In 1831, Cyrus McCormick invented the mechanical reaper. This machine was pulled by horses and made cutting grain easier. Before this invention, farmers had to cut their wheat or barley by hand with a scythe. A scythe is a tool with a long, curved blade. The reaper helped farmers plant more seeds and grow more grain to sell.

In colonial times, women sewed nearly all of their family's clothes by hand. In 1846, Elias Howe invented the sewing machine. The sewing machine reduced the amount of time it took to sew an item of clothing. In that same year, a substance called ether began to be used as an anesthetic. An anesthetic keeps people from feeling pain. This was an important medical discovery to help patients during surgery.

The discovery of electricity helped scientists, such as Samuel F.B. Morse, create machines that improved communication between people. In 1844, Morse sent the first electric telegraph message. He also developed Morse code, a system of dots and dashes used to send messages over wires. Before this invention, letters traveled by horse or boat. These new technologies benefited many individuals and society in the United States.

1. ☑ **Reading Check**
Main Idea and Details
Discuss with a partner how each of these inventions made life easier for people.

New Ways to Work

New inventions changed the way people worked. Eli Whitney, the inventor of the cotton gin, was hired by the U.S. government to produce thousands of muskets for its armies. Before this request, guns were made one at a time. All of the parts of the gun fit nicely together, but they only fit that one gun. Whitney wanted to find a way to make the **process** easier. He **determined** that using interchangeable parts, or parts that are the exact shape and size, to make many of the same item at the same time was the best process. This process is called **mass production**.

In this new system, any part of one gun could be exchanged for that same part in another gun. A worker could use a single set of tools to make the same part over and over again. Each part would be exactly the same as the next.

The idea of mass production helped bring about the Industrial Revolution. This period saw a shift from making goods by hand to making them in a factory. Before this time, most goods were made in home workshops, where workers could set their own hours. They could work at their own pace. In a factory, however, the process was different.

Academic Vocabulary

process • *n.*, system by which something is done

determine • *v.*, to decide

In the 1830s, textile mills lined the Merrimack and Concord rivers in Lowell, Massachusetts.

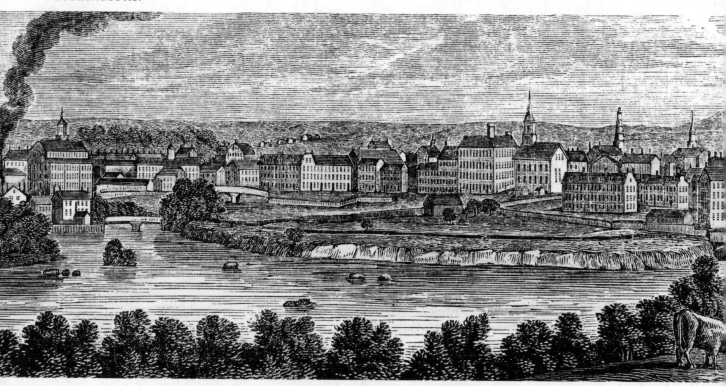

Workers in factories were expected to work during the same hours as other workers. The pace to create the goods was usually faster than most workers were used to. Most factories were built in cities or new factory towns. These factory towns grew as workers migrated from the countryside to work in the factories. Factory towns also saw an increase in immigrants who would come to towns or cities looking for work.

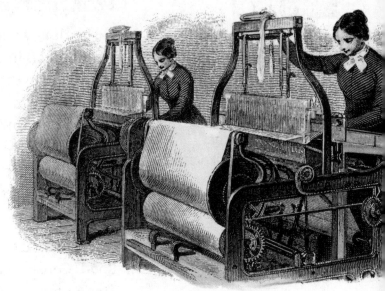

"Mill girls" weaving in a Massachusetts textile mill in the 1850s

Inside a Textile Factory

Cotton textiles, or cloth, were produced in some of the earliest American factories. Samuel Slater, a skilled mechanic from Britain, helped make this possible. The Industrial Revolution started in Britain in the late 1700s. The British had invented machines to spin yarn and weave it into cloth. The process was kept a secret. Slater learned how to build a spinning machine. Although he was British, he brought this secret knowledge with him when he moved to the United States.

In 1793, Slater helped build a factory in Rhode Island. His design involved using flowing river water to power the machines. These machines spun cotton fibers into yarn. Francis Cabot Lowell of Massachusetts learned how to make weaving machines. He opened a factory in 1813 that used both the spinning and weaving machines in one place.

Lowell's factory relied mainly on young women, from all over New England, to run the machines. Known as "mill girls," they worked ten or more hours a day, with a half-hour break for breakfast and for dinner. Most of them lived away from their families in rented rooms near the factory. The rise of factories in cities attracted many people from small country towns. Throughout the 1840s, the population of cities and large towns near mills grew.

2. ☑ Reading Check
Analyze the image of the interior of a textile factory with a partner. **Explain** what you see using one fact and one opinion.

Transportation Improves

The United States had many natural resources. Its land, water, and minerals allowed the population to grow and businesses to thrive. As the population in the East increased, available farmland decreased. Some people decided to move west. People and goods traveled by road, but the roads were rough. Travel was difficult across the mountains, forests, and prairies into the Ohio and Mississippi River valleys. Loaded wagons moved slowly. New roads were expensive to build and maintain.

The federal government decided to build the National Road. Construction started in 1811 and was finished in 1837. This 66-foot-wide highway ran from Cumberland, Maryland, to Vandalia, Illinois. It became a main route for settlers, including many new immigrants from Europe, heading across the Appalachian Mountains into the Ohio Valley.

Context Clues As you read, use context clues to help you identify the meaning of an unknown word or phrase. Context clues are words that appear near an unknown word that help you to define it. Near the word *thrive* are the words *many natural resources* and *allowed the population to grow.* These words help you understand how businesses can be successful, or thrive.

3. ☑ **Reading Check Analyze** the map and circle the names of the states through which the National Road ran.

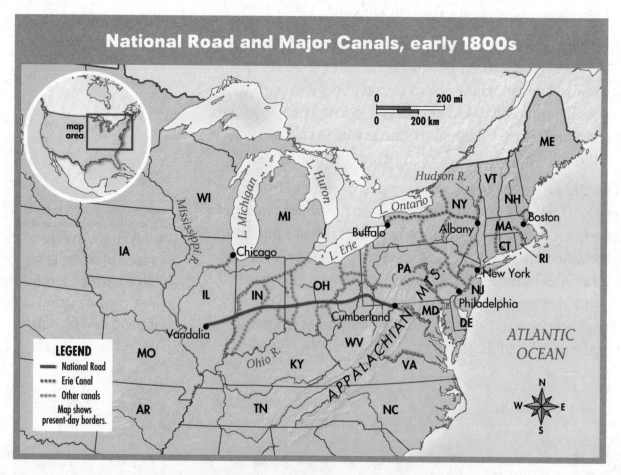

National Road and Major Canals, early 1800s

LEGEND
— National Road
···· Erie Canal
···· Other canals
Map shows present-day borders.

In the West, farmers grew cotton, tobacco, corn, and wheat. They also raised cattle and hogs. Cities in the East shipped tools and other manufactured goods to the West. These goods were shipped on flatboats, or cargo boats with flat bottoms. The flatboats floated on rivers that drained into the Mississippi River. These boats ended up in New Orleans, Louisiana, on the Gulf of Mexico. Sailing ships then carried western goods from New Orleans, around the tip of Florida, and then up the East Coast. These were long and expensive journeys.

Flatboats could easily travel downstream with the river's current. Traveling upstream, however, was more difficult. Robert Fulton, an American engineer, invented a way to solve this problem. He designed and built the *Clermont*, a boat powered by a steam engine. In August 1807, the *Clermont* traveled up the Hudson River from New York City to Albany in 32 hours. The same 150-mile trip took other ships four days. Steamboats could now carry goods more quickly.

The Erie Canal

In the early 1800s, a trip from New York City to Chicago took around six weeks by horse and wagon. By 1830, the creation of the Erie Canal cut the travel time in half. A **canal** is a human-made waterway.

Workers began digging the Erie Canal in 1817. It was ready for travelers by 1825. The canal ran from Albany to Buffalo, New York, about 363 miles. Travelers and products could move west from New York City, up the Hudson River, along the Erie Canal, and across one or more of the Great Lakes completely by water. The Erie Canal carried many settlers west.

Business owners could now send freight faster and cheaper than ever before. It took 8 days instead of 20 to get from New York City to Buffalo. Shipping a ton of freight used to cost $100 but now cost $10. Farmers in the West also took advantage of the canal by shipping grain and other bulk goods east. The success of the Erie Canal led to more canal building. For a while, the country had "canal fever."

A steam-powered boat tows a barge on the Erie Canal.

Invention of Railroads

Transportation continued to improve. Travel speed increased and costs went down. When the invention of the railroads first came along, they were expensive to build and maintain, but they would change the way people and goods were moved.

The earliest railroads were similar to a horse-drawn buggy. They were horse-drawn carts that ran on rails. Although useful, they could not compete with the Erie Canal. So, the horse was replaced with a steam engine.

The Baltimore & Ohio, or B&O, was the first true railroad in the United States. Its first section of track was 13 miles long over a steep and twisting route. The Tom Thumb, a small steam engine, made the first run in the summer of 1830. Forty passengers made the first trip on the Tom Thumb with no trouble. This mighty engine proved that a steam engine could operate over hilly and difficult land.

4. ☑ **Reading Check**
Identify and fill in the chart with the advantages and disadvantages of transportation in the early 1800s.

Types of Transportation in the Early 1800s		
Form of Transportation	**Advantages**	**Disadvantages**
Road		• travel was slow • building new roads was expensive
Canal	• made travel faster • goods and people could travel all the way by water	
Railroad		

Railroad Settlements

One advantage of railroads is that the tracks could be put down nearly anywhere. Rivers or canals no longer controlled where travelers and freight were able to travel. Goods produced from farms could travel directly to their end location. Investors understood the value of the new railroads. They poured money into railroad companies, expecting to make a big profit. Their investments would continue to grow and their profits increased tremendously.

As with factory towns, new railroad tracks attracted more migrants and businesses to the West. By the mid-1800s, rail companies had laid more than 9,000 miles of track. Tracks were laid across the Mississippi River. Linking the Atlantic and Pacific oceans by rail would soon become a reality.

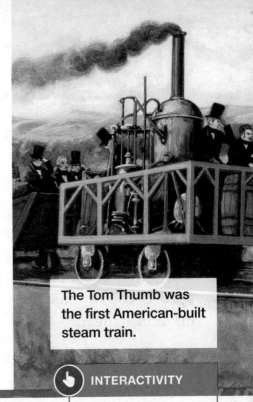

The Tom Thumb was the first American-built steam train.

INTERACTIVITY

Check your understanding of the key ideas of this lesson.

✓ Lesson 1 Check

5. **Cause and Effect Explain** why the federal government built the National Road.

_____

_____

6. **Explain** how the invention of the mechanical reaper improved life for farmers.

_____

_____

_____

7. **Describe** how improvements in technology and transportation changed American businesses.

_____

_____

_____

Analyze Costs and Benefits

Suppose you lived in a rural area in America during the 1830s. You heard that there were jobs available in a new factory town. Should you move from the family farm to a busy, new industrial town? What will you have to sacrifice? What might you gain?

Analyzing costs and benefits is a process that can help you make a decision. Costs can be the amount of money paid, time spent, or the work needed. Benefits include the money or valuable experience earned. Follow these steps to decide if something is worth the cost to gain the benefit.

1. Gather information about both costs and benefits.

2. Think about the lists. Are there more costs or more benefits? Are certain costs or benefits more important to you than others?

3. Identify a solution to your question based on its costs and benefits.

Read the text. Then use the graphic organizer to determine the costs and benefits of life in a new factory town.

The change from hand-made to machine-made products created change for workers in the eastern United States. Increased productivity created a higher standard of living for many people. Modern inventions helped create factory towns with booming economies. They were also booming centers of social activity. A factory town offered regular employment at good wages. Working in a factory also meant long hours and often tedious work. A sense of freedom may have come with a move to a factory town. But the confined, indoor factory work did not always charge the spirit. Some workers grew homesick.

Your Turn!

1. Would you have moved to a new factory town? Fill in the organizer to identify costs and benefits of factory life based on the paragraph. Then add other costs and benefits from your own perspective.

 VIDEO

Watch a video about analyzing costs and benefits.

Should I Move to a Factory Town?

Costs	Benefits

2. Write a short paragraph describing why you would or would not move to a factory town. Use the costs and benefits you listed as evidence to support your position.

INTERACTIVITY

Participate in a class discussion to preview the content of this lesson.

Vocabulary

vaquero
annex
Manifest Destiny

Academic Vocabulary

defend
declare

Unlock The **BIG** Question

I will know that achieving independence and statehood had costs and benefits for Texas and California.

JumpStart Activity

On a separate sheet of paper, draw a picture that describes the phrase "from sea to shining sea" from the lyrics of the song "America the Beautiful." Use your imagination and your own interpretation of the lyrics.

Seeing the opportunity for growth and land, American pioneers kept moving west throughout the early 1800s. Despite the stories and tales of the hardships of life on the frontier, people could not resist the rich, cheap farmland available on the frontier. These people had the "frontier spirit," and many brought this spirit of adventure and determination to Texas and California. Their feelings were captured in the song "America the Beautiful" by Samuel A. Ward and Katharine Lee Bates.

Primary Source

O beautiful for spacious skies,
For amber waves of grain,
For purple mountain majesties
Above the fruited plain!
America! America!
God shed His grace on thee,
And crown thy good with brotherhood
From sea to shining sea!

—"America the Beautiful," 1913

Americans Move to Mexico

In the 1820s, The Mexican government granted Stephen F. Austin the right to bring American families into Texas. At that time, Texas was a part of Mexico. However, few Mexicans lived there. Most of the people living in this vast area were Apache and Comanche American Indians. The government of Mexico wanted people to settle in Texas, work the land, and become Mexican citizens.

It was not hard for Austin and other land agents to find people to settle in Texas. The cost of land was less than in parts of the United States. By 1832, some 20,000 American settlers had moved to Texas, far more than the number of Mexicans and American Indians living there. Spanish-speaking people living in Texas were called Tejanos (teh HAH nohz).

The settlers used the land in different ways. Farming was more limited in this region than in the East, due to the drier climate and rocky soil. Some grew cotton, while many started ranches. Prairie grasses on the plains provided excellent feed for cattle. **Vaqueros** (vah KER ohz), or Mexican cowboys, were known for their skills at riding horses and handling cattle. They taught the settlers their ranching techniques.

INTERACTIVITY

Explore the key ideas of this lesson.

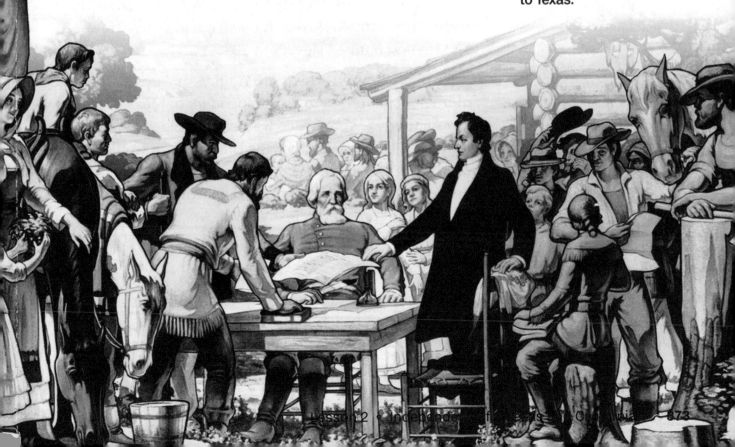

Stephen F. Austin (standing) brought American settlers to Texas.

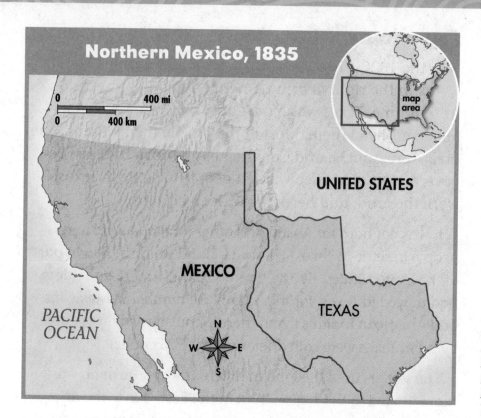

Northern Mexico, 1835

0 — 400 mi
0 — 400 km

UNITED STATES

MEXICO

PACIFIC OCEAN

TEXAS

N W E S

map area

In 1835, Texas was part of Mexico. It shared a border with the United States.

The Texas settlers found that they missed the freedoms they had left behind in the United States. They did not like the strict control the Mexican government had on its citizens. They wanted more open trade with the United States. The settlers came mainly from the South and had brought thousands of enslaved African Americans with them. They wanted slavery made legal in Texas. However, Mexico had banned slavery in 1829.

By 1835, many Texans, both Anglos, or American settlers, and Tejanos, wanted to be independent of Mexico and to govern themselves. Mexico wanted to protect its northern territory. They worried that the United States would take over Texas and make it a state. In the fall of 1835, clashes between Mexican government troops and armed Texans marked the start of the Texas Revolution.

The Texas Revolution

The first shots of the revolution were fired when fighting broke out at Gonzales between Mexican soldiers and Texas settlers and soldiers. The Mexicans retreated and the Texans, who suffered no losses, considered it a victory.

Word Wise

Suffixes When added to the end of a word, suffixes change the meaning of the original word. The word *govern* is a verb that means "to exercise authority over," usually by making rules and decisions. When the suffix *–ment* is added to *govern*, it changes the word to a noun. It also changes the word's meaning to "a system for making rules and decisions."

On October 10, 1835, Texas soldiers attacked Mexican soldiers **defending** a fort near Goliad. About 120 Texans surprised the 27 Mexicans there and defeated them.

There were more battles in Texas's fight for independence. The Battle of the Alamo, however, stood out as the turning point for Texas. Antonio Lopez de Santa Anna was a general and the president of Mexico. In early 1836, he led an army of several thousand men toward San Antonio. Some 180 Texans were there to defend the area at a walled mission called the Alamo.

The Texas forces were small, but they held off Santa Anna's army for nearly two weeks. On March 6, the Mexican forces stormed the walls. Bloody fighting followed. By the end of the battle, all of the Texas soldiers were killed, including Davy Crockett and James Bowie, two famous men of the frontier. Around 600 of Santa Anna's men were either killed or wounded.

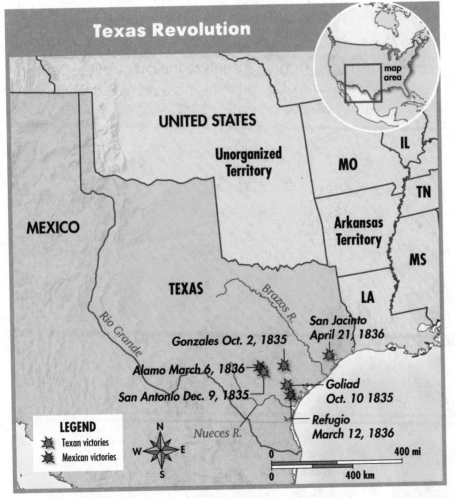

Texas Revolution

UNITED STATES

Unorganized Territory

MO

IL

TN

MEXICO

Arkansas Territory

MS

TEXAS

Brazos R.

LA

Rio Grande

San Jacinto April 21, 1836

Gonzales Oct. 2, 1835

Alamo March 6, 1836

San Antonio Dec. 9, 1835

Goliad Oct. 10 1835

Refugio March 12, 1836

Nueces R.

LEGEND
Texan victories
Mexican victories

N W E S

0   400 mi
0   400 km

1. ☑ **Reading Check**
Both the Texan and Mexican armies had victories during the Texas Revolution. **Identify** and circle the battle that started the Texas Revolution.

The Texas flag has a single star. It represents the independent Republic of Texas, before it became a state. Today, Texas is still known as the Lone Star State.

On March 2, 1836, Texan leaders **declared** independence. They created a constitution and formed a government. Sam Houston was chosen to take command of the Texas army, which included a unit of Tejano soldiers led by Juan Seguin (hwahn suh GEEN). Houston would soon lead the army into a major battle.

Santa Anna's army was winning battles, and by April, his army had Houston's men retreating. Santa Anna thought that the Texas Revolution would soon end. The Texans had a surprise for him, though, when they stopped their retreat at the San Jacinto (juh SIN toh) River, near Galveston Bay. Here, Houston's army launched a surprise attack on Santa Anna.

The Mexican army was defeated. Santa Anna was forced to sign a treaty giving Texas its independence. Sam Houston was voted president of the Republic of Texas in September 1836. Stephen F. Austin became the secretary of state. Texas had won its independence.

2. ☑ **Reading Check** **Analyze** the image of the Battle of San Jacinto. Do you think it is a primary or secondary source? Why?

_____

_____

_____

Independence Leads to Tensions

After Texas won its independence, many Texans thought the United States would **annex** Texas, or take it over and make it a state. Many Americans worried that if this happened slavery would spread.

As you read in Chapter 7, Congress passed the Missouri Compromise in 1820. It brought two states, Maine and Missouri, into the Union. Maine would be a free state, where slavery would not be allowed. Missouri would be a slave state. This law also banned slavery in the rest of the Louisiana Purchase. Issues of slavery caused great disagreements in the states. The South did not want slavery to end. Many relied on enslaved African Americans to work on their large plantations and farms. States in the North wanted slavery to end.

Tensions also flared over **Manifest Destiny**, or the idea that the United States had a right to add territory until it reached the Pacific Ocean. In 1845, Congress voted to annex Texas and make it a state. To many Americans, event was a step toward the idea of Manifest Destiny. Even though Santa Anna signed a treaty giving Texas its independence, the Mexican government protested Texas becoming a state. Texans claimed that their border with Mexico ended at the Rio Grande. Mexico disputed this too, claiming it was further north.

3. ☑ **Reading Check**
Analyze the timeline. **Identify** how many years passed between when Texas declared independence and when it was made into a state.

The Texas Revolution

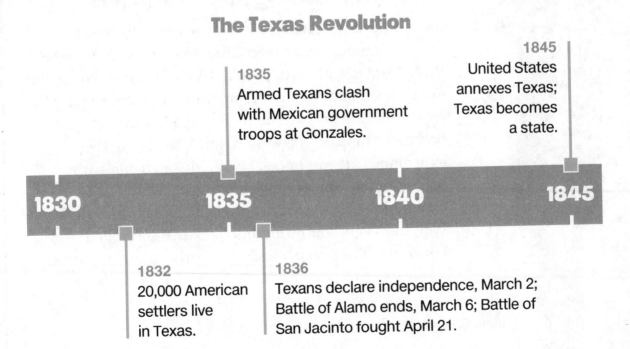

1835
Armed Texans clash with Mexican government troops at Gonzales.

1845
United States annexes Texas; Texas becomes a state.

1830   1835   1840   1845

1832
20,000 American settlers live in Texas.

1836
Texans declare independence, March 2; Battle of Alamo ends, March 6; Battle of San Jacinto fought April 21.

Conflict With Mexico

To defend what he considered a U.S. border, U.S. President James Polk sent an army into the border region of southern Texas in January 1846. General Zachary Taylor led this army. In April of that same year, Mexican troops crossed the Rio Grande and attacked the Americans. The Mexican War had begun.

Primary Source

Mexico has passed the boundary of the United States, has invaded our territory and shed American blood upon the American soil.

—James Polk, Address to Congress, May 11, 1846

The war only lasted a few months. American soldiers crossed into Mexico's northern territory and captured Santa Fe, New Mexico. By 1847, all of northern Mexico was under American control. However, most of the battles took place in the south. Another general, Winfield Scott, was sent to invade Mexico by sea. On September 14, Scott's forces captured Mexico City. This ended the war's main fighting. The borders between the United States and Mexico were forever changed

California During the Mexican War

After the annexation of Texas, the desire to explore and settle more western territories was at the front of the United States's interests. John C. Frémont, whom you read about in Chapter 7, was an important figure in helping this expansion. He was sent on many expeditions to explore and make maps of the western land. On one of these expeditions, he was joined by Kit Carson, a guide who helped him travel over difficult areas. Frémont and Carson explored the Pacific Northwest. Just before the Mexican War, they went southward into Mexican-controlled territory in California, crossing over the disputed border.

John C. Frémont

At this time, most settlers in California wished to be free of Mexican control. In the spring of 1846, a small group of them started their own revolt. Supported by Frémont, the settlers attacked Mexican troops and declared California to be an independent republic. This became known as the Bear Flag Revolt because of the grizzly bear on their flag. Shortly after this event, American naval forces landed on the coast of California and declared the entire territory part of the United States. The independent republic of California lasted only three weeks, but settlers achieved their goal of independence from Mexico.

The California state flag

4. ☑ **Reading Check** **Cause and Effect** Fill in the chart to **identify** causes and effects of western expansion.

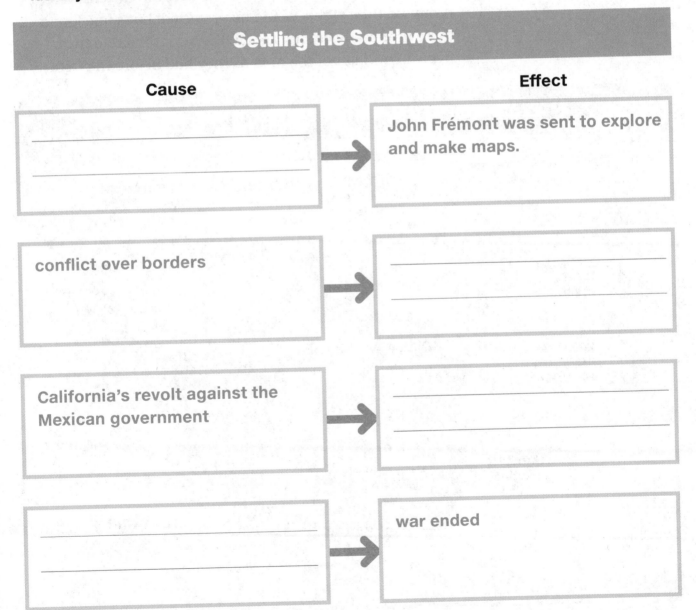

Settling the Southwest

Cause	Effect
_____ _____	John Frémont was sent to explore and make maps.
conflict over borders	_____ _____
California's revolt against the Mexican government	_____ _____
_____ _____	war ended

A Peaceful Ending

The Treaty of Guadalupe Hidalgo (gwah duh LOOP ay ee DAHL goh) officially ended the Mexican War in 1848. Mexico turned over its claims to Texas. It also turned over most of its other northern territory to the United States.

This new territory was large. It included present-day California, Nevada, and Utah. It also included most of New Mexico and Arizona, and smaller parts of Wyoming and Colorado. The United States paid Mexico $15 million for more than 525,000 square miles.

There were about 75,000 Mexicans living in this territory. They were given a choice to move to Mexico or to become U.S. citizens. Those who stayed and became citizens were promised their rights would be protected, but some found these promises were not kept. Others continued to travel freely in and out of the area as they had before the treaty.

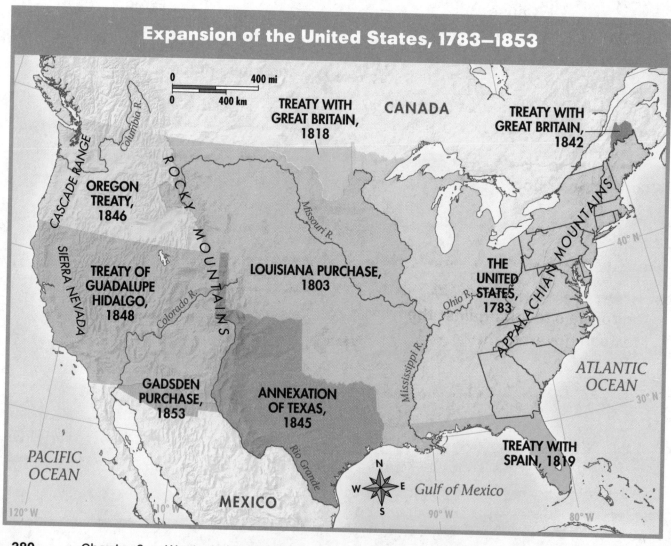

Expansion of the United States, 1783–1853

In 1853, the United States paid $10 million to Mexico for another piece of land. Called the Gadsden Purchase, this completed the southern boundaries of New Mexico and Arizona. The lands gained as a result of the Mexican War completed the American Southwest. Manifest Destiny was achieved for the United States. With lands stretching from the Atlantic Ocean to the Pacific Ocean, the United States could now claim to reach "from sea to shining sea."

5. ☑ **Reading Check** Study the map. **Identify** which treaty first gave the United States access to the Pacific Ocean. Which river forms the border between Texas and Mexico?

_____

_____

INTERACTIVITY

Check your understanding of the key ideas of this lesson.

☑ Lesson 2 Check

6. **Distinguish Fact From Opinion** Identify one fact about Manifest Destiny. Then write an opinion statement about that fact.

_____

_____

_____

7. **Explain** how the Treaty of Guadalupe Hidalgo affected territorial expansion in the United States.

_____

_____

_____

8. **Describe** John C. Frémont's role in the Mexican War.

_____

_____

_____

Lesson 3 Trails to the West

INTERACTIVITY

Participate in a class discussion to preview the content of this lesson.

Vocabulary

wagon train
prairie schooner
persecution

Academic Vocabulary

challenge
enable

Unlock The BIG Question

I will know that traveling on the westward trails had costs and benefits.

Jumpstart Activity

List ways people travel today. Then discuss with a partner which ways are the most efficient.

Between 1840 and 1860, hundreds of thousands of American settlers followed trails west. These trails had been used by fur traders, sometimes called mountain men, for years. In addition to the mountain men, many groups of American Indians, some British, Russians, Chileans, Mexicans, and Asians from a number of nations lived out west. Most of those who came from the East left from the town of Independence, Missouri. There they joined wagon trains. A **wagon train** is a line of wagons traveling as a group. Most of the wagon trains were headed to places such as California and Oregon, where the land was rich with ancient forests and fertile valleys. The journey, 2,000 miles across the Great Plains and through the Rocky Mountains, was a test of strength and courage.

The Trail West

Horses, oxen, and mules were valuable animals on the trail. Some pioneers rode horses, but many walked because their wagons were heavy with supplies. The oxen and mules pulling the wagons were already strained and the migrants did not want to add any more weight to the loads.

Other animals were also valuable on the journey. Cows were brought for milk, and chickens for eggs. Settlers hunted wild animals for meat. The wagons were packed with barrels of water, butter churns, shovels, axes, and other necessary supplies.

There were different types of wagons on the trail. The most common wagon was the **prairie schooner**. It was named after a type of sailing ship and was designed for the trip west. The dangerous journey often included rough ground. The schooner was built for this type of terrain, or land. Its cover kept out the sun, wind, and rain. It had large wheels, which kept the wooden bed of the wagon out of the mud. The bed itself, like a ship, was watertight. This helped it float across slow-flowing rivers.

Some pioneers did not survive the journey west. Disease, accidents, and nature itself claimed lives. Raging rivers, parched deserts, sandstorms and snowstorms, and lack of water or medicine were just some of the hardships along the way.

The Oregon Trail

The Oregon Trail was the westward route for settlers to the Oregon Territory. This region contained the present-day states of Oregon, Washington, and Idaho, as well as lands to the north. In 1846, the United States and Great Britain split the region. The southern part, where most Americans had settled, went to the United States. "Oregon or bust!" was a common attitude among pioneers. It meant they would make it to the Oregon Territory or die trying.

INTERACTIVITY

Explore the key ideas of this lesson.

1. ☑ **Reading Check**
The images show a wagon train along the Oregon Trail and a close-up of a prairie schooner. Circle some features of the prairie schooner in the text and on the image. With a partner, **discuss** how these features made the wagon a useful vehicle on the westward trail.

Transportation: Then and Now

	Prairie Schooner	Sport Utility Vehicle (SUV)
Length	10 feet	16 feet
Width	4 feet	6 feet
Height	10 feet	6 feet
Weight	1,300 pounds	4,455 pounds
Power	4–6 oxen or 6–10 mules	210 horsepower gasoline engine

Source: Historic Oregon City

2. ☑ **Reading Check**
Compare and Contrast
Analyze the chart about transportation in the past and compare it with today. Circle the vehicle that could climb a mountain more easily. Explain your answer to a partner.

Pioneers began their journeys in the spring. Usually, wagons headed west in a caravan, or group. A train of wagons was often several miles long. Captains, guides, and other officers helped keep order during the trip. Each individual or family was responsible for bringing any supplies they needed, including their own prairie schooners. Most migrants heading west took only what they needed for the trip.

Once the new grass on the prairie was high enough to feed their animals, the pioneers left. They followed the Platte River westward across the Great Plains, which was a flat and dry region. In areas without grasses, the animals would have to eat shrubs, such as sagebrush. The pioneers then came to the Rocky Mountains, which were steep and rough. The closer they came to Oregon, the harder and more dangerous the trail became. Wagons were forced to inch slowly along cliff ledges and up mountain tracks. An early snowfall could trap pioneers in the mountains.

An average wagon train traveled about 12 to 15 miles per day. If the train moved fast, it could make the trip in about four months. However, most settlers spent six months on the trail to Oregon.

Settling the Oregon Country

Most settlers moved west for several reasons. Married couples could claim 640 acres of farmland free of charge. Rivers, mountains, and forests dotted the land. Filled with wilderness, the area attracted those with a spirit of adventure and the hope of a good life on the frontier.

Marcus and Narcissa Whitman were some of the earliest settlers to head west from the United States. They were Christian missionaries who settled in what is present-day Washington in 1836. The Whitmans taught American Indians about Christianity. In 1843, after returning to the East, Marcus Whitman led about 1,000 migrants to Oregon. This was the first large wagon train migration to Oregon. The success of the journey along the Oregon Trail led to the use of the route for thousands more.

Once settled, life on the frontier was a **challenge**. Often, there were forests to clear for farmland. Homes and shelters for animals had to be built. Women often worked side by side with men. They helped with the harvest and drove teams of horses. Women also made clothing, tended to gardens, and cooked the food.

Quest Connection

On an archaeological dig, you help dig up an abandoned wagon from a section of the Oregon Trail. It is about 10 feet long, smaller than you thought it would be. How does knowing the size of the wagon help you imagine the pioneers' journey?

 INTERACTIVITY

Find out more about the costs and benefits of moving west.

Academic Vocabulary

challenge • *n.*, something difficult

Marcus Whitman and other Christian missionaries first traveled west in 1836, led by fur traders.

The Mormon Trail

One group moved west to seek religious freedom. They were known as Mormons. Joseph Smith founded the church in 1830 in New York State. Smith and his followers soon moved to Ohio. Some Mormons established homes in Missouri and Illinois.

The Mormons, and their religious beliefs, were not accepted by many people. They faced **persecution**, or unfair treatment because of their beliefs. In 1844, a mob killed Joseph Smith. His followers decided it was time to find a place where they could practice their beliefs freely.

In 1846, the church's new leader, Brigham Young, led 150 Mormons west from Illinois. As with the Oregon Trail, the Mormons followed the Platte River across the Great Plains. They stopped near the Great Salt Lake in what is now Utah. The 1,300-mile route they followed is known as the Mormon Trail.

They founded Salt Lake City in Utah. Thousands of people migrated to the area. The region was too dry to farm, so the Mormons built canals to bring water from streams in the Rocky Mountains. Their farms thrived, which **enabled** more people to settle and live there. By 1860, about 40,000 settlers were living in more than 150 communities.

Academic Vocabulary

enable • to let happen

Mormon settlers approach the Great Salt Lake.

Southwest Trails

From Independence, Missouri, it took about two months to travel to what was then Mexico on the Santa Fe Trail. This trail stretched almost 900 miles through a landscape of prairies, deserts, and mountains. Few settlers took this route. It was mainly used by traders traveling to Santa Fe with their cargo. It was also used as a major military route during the Mexican War.

Traders used Conestoga wagons to transport manufactured goods. These wagons were larger and more rugged than the prairie schooners. They could haul up to five tons of cargo.

covered wagons with trade goods on the Plaza in Santa Fe, New Mexico

In Santa Fe, traders sold cloth, tools, jewelry, religious objects, and other items. When the traders returned to Missouri, they brought mules, silver, furs, and other goods with them. These early traders could make high profits because Mexicans in Santa Fe paid well for American goods. The furs and silver brought to Missouri from Mexico also sold well. When the Mexican War ended, big freight-hauling companies pushed many of the smaller traders out of business. At this time, American Indians increased their attacks on traders along the route. They resented the loss of their territory, which the Santa Fe Trail crossed.

3. ☑ **Reading Check** **Use Evidence From Text** What goods did traders sell in Santa Fe, and what did they bring back to Missouri?

_____

_____

_____

_____

Trails to California

In 1829, trade with California became a possibility. A Mexican trader explored a new trail from Santa Fe to the west coast. Traders sold woolen goods from New Mexico and brought horses and mules from California back with them. The trail, called the Old Spanish Trail, crossed the deserts and mountains of Mexico's northern territory and ended in the small frontier town of Los Angeles.

Settlers did not take the same route to California as traders. They traveled to California from Missouri on the California Trail. This trail followed the same route as the Oregon Trail through the eastern Rocky Mountains. The trail split near the Snake River. The California Trail went southwest and crossed over the high mountains of the Sierra Nevada. It ended in Sacramento, today the capital of California.

4. ☑ **Reading Check**
Analyze the map of the western trails. Circle the trails that fulfill the concept of Manifest Destiny. **Discuss with a partner** the similarities and differences among the Oregon, California, and Mormon Trails.

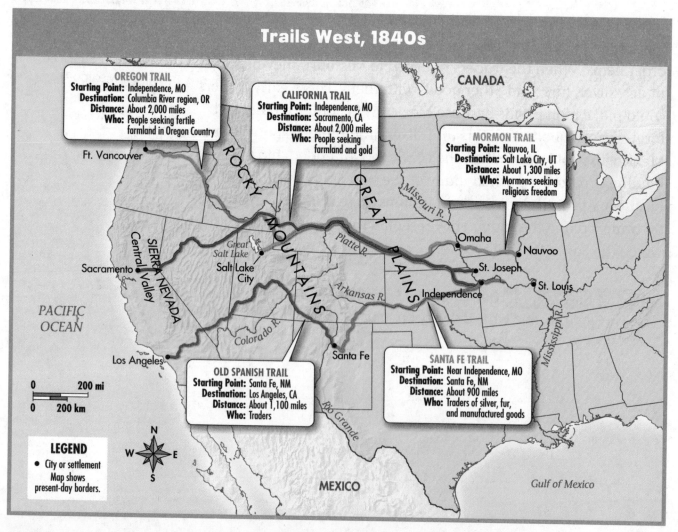

Trails West, 1840s

OREGON TRAIL
Starting Point: Independence, MO
Destination: Columbia River region, OR
Distance: About 2,000 miles
Who: People seeking fertile farmland in Oregon Country

CALIFORNIA TRAIL
Starting Point: Independence, MO
Destination: Sacramento, CA
Distance: About 2,000 miles
Who: People seeking farmland and gold

MORMON TRAIL
Starting Point: Nauvoo, IL
Destination: Salt Lake City, UT
Distance: About 1,300 miles
Who: Mormons seeking religious freedom

OLD SPANISH TRAIL
Starting Point: Santa Fe, NM
Destination: Los Angeles, CA
Distance: About 1,100 miles
Who: Traders

SANTA FE TRAIL
Starting Point: Near Independence, MO
Destination: Santa Fe, NM
Distance: About 900 miles
Who: Traders of silver, fur, and manufactured goods

CANADA

Ft. Vancouver
ROCKY MOUNTAINS
SIERRA NEVADA
Central Valley
Great Salt Lake
Salt Lake City
Sacramento
PACIFIC OCEAN
Colorado R.
Los Angeles
Arkansas R.
GREAT PLAINS
Platte R.
Missouri R.
Omaha
Nauvoo
St. Joseph
Independence
St. Louis
Mississippi R.
Santa Fe
Rio Grande
MEXICO
Gulf of Mexico

0   200 mi
0   200 km

LEGEND
• City or settlement
Map shows present-day borders.

N W E S

American Indians and Settlers in the West

Portions of various trails west crossed land occupied by American Indians. Along the trails, Americans sometimes traded with American Indians. At other times, Indian groups attacked American settlers and traders who entered their territory. Some Indian groups made agreements with the U.S. government to leave the area near trails. The movement of settlers west, however, eventually led to conflict as American Indian groups were pushed off their homelands.

INTERACTIVITY

Check your understanding of the key ideas of this lesson.

☑ Lesson 3 Check

5. **Compare and Contrast Identify** the reasons for people moving west on the Oregon Trail and people moving west on the Mormon Trail.

_____

_____

_____

6. **Identify** some costs and benefits of travel along the Santa Fe Trail.

_____

_____

_____

_____

7. **Understand the** *Quest* Connections Based on your investigation of the text, describe some costs and benefits of a pioneer's journey west.

_____

_____

_____

_____

Distinguish Fact From Fiction

I'm going to write about a family that traveled west with Marcus Whitman in 1843.

Is that a fact?

VIDEO

Watch a video about distinguishing fact from fiction.

Distinguishing fact from fiction will help you to better understand and interpret what you read. Each chapter in this book is nonfiction, or informational text. Informational texts are full of *facts*. A fact can be proved true. In Lesson 3, you read that in 1843, Marcus Whitman led the first large wagon train migration to Oregon. You can check this information in reference sources or primary sources.

Fiction texts are stories that tell about imaginary people and events. Fictional stories can be based on real events and include facts, but they include made-up details.

Read the two paragraphs about children who traveled west with their families. As you read, notice how similar ideas are presented as facts and fiction. To distinguish fact from fiction, look for details that can be checked and others that are made up.

Many children moved west with their families on horse-drawn wagons to settle on the frontier. Along the trail, they often worked to help the family. Some of their chores included getting drinking water from nearby streams. Children might also care for the animals traveling with them.

As his family crossed the Great Plains, Thomas stayed under the wagon cover during the long, hot days. When they reached a camping site each evening, Pa had him lead the team of horses to a nearby water source. Thomas enjoyed this time away from the wagon train. He was in a new place every day and was alert to the different sights and sounds at dusk.

1. What factual and fictional statements appear in the paragraphs about children who settled the American West with their families? Fill in the organizer.

Children on the Frontier	
Facts	**Fiction**

2. Reread the section "Settling the Oregon Country" in Lesson 3.

Write a fact about settling in the Oregon Territory.

_____

_____

_____

Make up a character or event related to the Oregon Territory and write a fictional sentence.

_____

_____

_____

The California Gold Rush

👆 **INTERACTIVITY**

Participate in a class discussion to preview the content of this lesson.

Unlock The BIG Question

I will know that the California gold rush had costs and benefits.

Vocabulary

gold rush
entrepreneur
discrimination
Pony Express

Academic Vocabulary

method
innovation

JUMPstart Activity

To make coins, gold was melted, shaped, and stamped with a design. Design and draw a $5 gold coin.

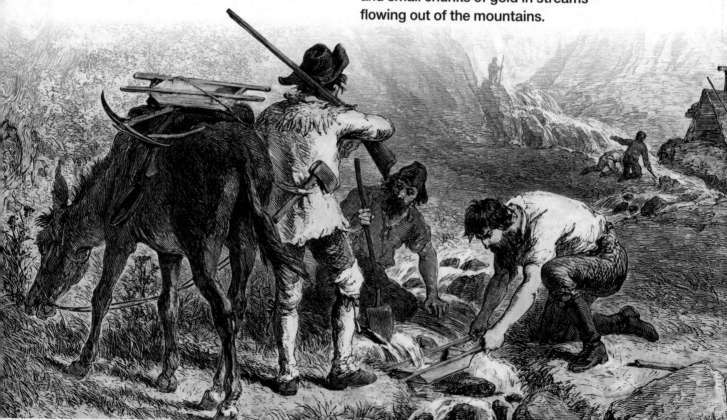

California gold miners found gold dust and small chunks of gold in streams flowing out of the mountains.

In the 1840s, land in California was abundant. Farmers worked the rich land and had little competition. The American Indian population was about 150,000 and declining. Not including American Indians, only about 14,000 people lived in the area. Then someone found gold and everything changed.

INTERACTIVITY

Explore the key ideas of this lesson.

Gold!

Gold is a unique mineral and has great worth. It will not discolor or become dull. It is also hard to find. Finding lots of it can and did excite people. The California gold rush was a time of great possibilities. A **gold rush** is a rapid flood of people into an area where gold has been discovered.

James Marshall first discovered gold in California in January 1848. He was building a sawmill when he found shiny flakes of gold in the river. Soon, the discovery became big news and prospectors, or people who searched for minerals, rushed to California to find gold.

Before the gold rush, most of the people living in California, besides American Indians, were Mexicans and British, with small numbers of Russians and Chinese. On the coast, there were whalers. New England sailors sailed their ships around South America and up the Pacific Coast to trade sea otter and seal skins for cattle. After the discovery of gold, around 90,000 people arrived between 1848 and 1849. Called "forty-niners," the gold miners came from all over the world. Chileans, Chinese, Japanese, Koreans, Indians, Filipinos, Australians, African Americans, white Americans, and others were drawn to California.

Posters such as this one offered to get people to San Francisco from the eastern United States, by ship.

Whenever gold was discovered in a new place, miners would move in and make a mining camp. Sometimes these camps would rapidly grow into towns called boomtowns. The city of San Francisco is an example of a boomtown during the gold rush. When gold was first discovered, San Francisco was a small town of around 1,000 people. A few years later it had over 30,000 residents. By 1853, the gold rush had drawn more than 250,000 people to California with "gold fever."

The Search for Gold

Academic Vocabulary

method • n., way of doing something

Quest Connection

Your archaeological team has found the remains of a gold-rush town. What does this town tell you about the costs and benefits of looking for gold?

INTERACTIVITY

Learn more about the gold rush and the costs and benefits of being a "forty-niner."

At first, a fairly simple **method** was used to mine for gold. Water rushed down from mountainsides. This washed a lot of gold out of the rock. The gold had settled to the bottom of streams farther down the slopes. The original miners panned for gold. When "panning" for gold, miners put gravel and water into a pan and then shook the pan back and forth. Because gold is heavy, it will eventually work its way to the bottom of the pan. Other miners used a sluice. They ran water through a long, sloping wooden box. Lighter material ran through bars, but the heavier gold stayed at the bottom of the box. Then the miners extracted the gold and set it aside.

Miners often found themselves in dangerous situations. They faced freezing streams, disease, poor diet, and accidents. Some miners struck it rich, but many more did not.

Between 1848 and 1849, California miners produced over 50 tons of gold. By 1850, less gold was found in streambeds. Soon, mining companies brought in rock-cutting mills to find gold on a large scale. Miners who did not strike it rich on their own often decided to work for these large companies.

California gold prospectors using a sluice, in 1852

1. ☑ **Reading Check** **Analyze** the image and **describe** the process shown for finding gold.

_____

_____

_____

_____

_____

_____

_____

New Goods and Services Meet the Needs of the Forty-Niners

Gold miners were after one thing: making a profit. People who never lifted a pan or a pick, however, made some of the largest gold-rush fortunes by meeting the needs of the "forty-niners." Miners needed supplies such as pans, picks, shovels, kettles, tents, blankets, clothing, and food. Merchants were happy to sell these necessary items to miners who were seeking their own fortunes. Supplies were hard to find in mining country. As a result, merchants were able to charge high prices for their products. A gold-mining pan that cost around 20 cents in the East might cost $8 or more in California.

Others made money through **innovation**, by creatively offering new goods and services to meet the needs of the miners. An **entrepreneur** (ahn truh pruh NUR) is someone who takes risks to start a business. Levi Strauss, a Jewish entrepreneur, opened a store in San Francisco in 1853. Strauss sold cloth, linens, and clothing to miners and others. He saw the need for a durable, longer-lasting work pant for the miners. He produced a pair made out of blue denim held together with copper rivets, or tiny bolts. He called them Levi's jeans.

The original Levi Strauss building in San Francisco

Another entrepreneur provided the miners with a different kind of service. Luzena Stanley Wilson opened a hotel in which miners could also get a meal. She used the money she earned to start a successful store.

2. ✓ **Reading Check** **Summarize** **Analyze** the chart. Discuss with a partner what it shows.

Cost of Goods in 1850

	Wisconsin	California
cheese	$.62 per pound	$25 per pound
flour	$.10 per bag	$13 per bag
beef	$.14 per pound	$10 per pound

Source: California Dept. of Parks and Recreation

The State of California

Many gold seekers chose to remain in California after their first few months of mining. California's population rose dramatically. In 1850, California had enough people to become the nation's thirty-first state.

Chinese immigrants working in the California gold fields

Many of California's new residents were immigrants. This upset some Americans who did not like the competition for gold. Mexican and Chinese miners worked hard and some found a lot of gold. Both of these groups experienced **discrimination**, or unfair treatment, based on where they came from.

The foreign miners faced further unfair treatment. In 1850, the California government passed a law taxing all noncitizens $20 per month. If the tax was not paid, they were forced out of the gold fields. Many of the miners forced out were Mexican Americans. Since the treaty settling the Mexican War had made them citizens, the tax on foreign miners should not have applied to them. Later, the state passed a new foreign miner's tax that targeted the new large population of Chinese immigrant miners.

With so many new residents, a fast way to get mail into and out of California was necessary. The **Pony Express** was a system of carrying mail by horse. Riders left St. Joseph, Missouri, at full speed. Then they raced on to their next goal, a station that was 70 to 100 miles west. Upon arrival, they passed the mailbag to the next rider, who raced the mail to yet another station.

It took about 10 days for the mail to reach the state of California. After telegraph lines reached California, the Pony Express service ended in 1861.

The gold rush left a lasting impact on California. Lumber companies, ranches, and huge farms were developed to meet the needs of new residents. This created new jobs. By 1869, businesses in California could deliver their products east by train. The state's economy continued to grow.

3. ☑ **Reading Check** **Explain** how the Pony Express contributed to westward expansion. Why did the telegraph replace it?

_____

_____

_____

_____

☑ Lesson 4 Check

INTERACTIVITY

Check your understanding of the key ideas of this lesson.

4. **Explain** the reason why some Americans did not like the Mexican and Chinese miners.

_____

_____

_____

5. **Analyze** the effects the gold rush had on the economic development of California.

_____

_____

_____

6. **Understand the** *Quest* **Connections** Based on what you have learned, what were the costs and benefits of moving to California during the gold rush?

_____

_____

_____

Manifest Destiny

As you have read, Manifest Destiny was the idea that the United States had a right to add territory until it reached the Pacific Ocean. When Congress annexed Texas, it was a step toward Manifest Destiny. Mexicans and American Indians lived in these lands and opposed U.S. expansion west.

John Gast was an American painter who lived in the late 1800s. In 1872, he painted a portrait called *American Progress*. In the image, a woman represents America's expansion to the West.

American
Indians

settlers
heading
west

fur trappers
and gold
prospectors

telegraph
line

farmers

Close Reading

1. **Identify** parts of the painting that show American technology.

_____

_____

2. **Identify** parts of the painting that show America's westward expansion.

_____

_____

3. **Describe** how the female image represents the idea of American progress.

_____

_____

_____

4. **Infer** why the painting is light on the right side and darker on the left side.

_____

_____

_____

Wrap It Up

What do you think about the painting? Write a paragraph of your interpretation of its meaning. Include your interpretation of the American Indians in the painting. Support your response with information from the chapter.

_____

_____

_____

_____

_____

Quality:
Determination

Narcissa Whitman (1808–1847)
Pioneer

What does it take to be a pioneer to a new land? When Narcissa Prentiss Whitman traveled to Oregon Country she was one of the first white women to travel there. Born in Prattsburg, New York, she married Dr. Marcus Whitman in 1836. They left for Oregon Country that same year. They built a mission at Fort Walla Walla in what is now Walla Walla, Washington.

Life in Oregon Country was lonely for the Whitman family. Narcissa, however, stuck to her goals. She worked to convert the local Cayuse Indians to Christianity and to open a school for them. She did not learn much about the Cayuse, but she was frustrated when they were not as eager to adopt the religion as she had hoped.

When more settlers arrived, measles spread among the Cayuse. They had no natural immunity, or resistance, to the disease. Despite Narcissa's care, many Cayuse died. Angry about the deaths, Cayuse attacked the mission, resulting in the death of Narcissa, Marcus, and others.

Find Out More

1. In what ways did Narcissa demonstrate determination?

_____

_____

_____

_____

2. What does determination mean to you and your classmates? Work with a partner and share a time when you set goals and were determined to meet them.

Visual Review

Use these graphics to review some of the key terms, people, and ideas from this chapter.

Westward Expansion

1825
Erie Canal is
finished.

1845
Texas becomes
a state.

1848
California gold
rush begins.

1810

1830

1850

1811
National Road
construction begins.

1835
Texas Revolution
begins.

1846
Oregon Territory
is created.

1850
California
becomes a state.

Technological Advances

1793 first factory in America opened	1831 mechanical crop harvester
1807 *Clermont* is the first steam-powered boat	1837 National Road completed
1825 Erie Canal completed	1844 electric telegraph
1830 first railroad traveled	1846 sewing machine

☑ **Assessment**

🎮 **GAMES**

Play the vocabulary game.

Vocabulary and Key Ideas

1. Complete the sentences below. Choose from these words: Industrial Revolution, Stephen F. Austin, Missouri Compromise, wagon train.

   The _____ changed the way goods were manufactured.

   People traveled in a _____ as they journeyed west.

   _____ was responsible for bringing American settlers into Mexican territory.

   The _____ allowed slavery in some states but not in others.

2. **Describe** the idea of **Manifest Destiny**. _____

   _____

   _____

3. **Explain** what **mass production** is. _____

   _____

4. **Analyzing a Chart** What happened to the population of San Francisco between 1847 and 1850?

   _____

   _____

   Why did the population increase so much after 1848?

   _____

   _____

Population of San Francisco, 1847–1852

Year	Population
1847	460
1848	850
1849	5,000
1850	25,000
1852	36,000

Source: *San Francisco Genealogy*

Critical Thinking and Writing

5. **Infer** How did Texas's fight for independence affect other parts of the United States?

_____

_____

_____

6. **Analyze** What were the advantages of the prairie schooner?

_____

_____

_____

_____

7. **Apply** In what way did the inventions of the cotton gin, the telegraph machine, and the mechanical reaper change life in the 1800s? How do these inventions affect American life today?

_____

_____

_____

8. **Revisit the Big Question** What are the costs and benefits of growth?

_____

_____

_____

_____

_____

_____

9. **Writing Workshop: Informative Text** On a separate sheet of paper, write two short paragraphs about the conflict over land between American settlers and Mexicans in Texas and California.

Analyze Primary Sources

Pa said there were too many people in the Big Woods now. Quite often Laura heard the ringing thud of an ax which was not Pa's ax, or the echo of a shot that did not come from his gun. The path that went by the little house had become a road. Almost every day Laura and Mary stopped their playing and stared in surprise at a wagon slowly creaking by on that road.

Wild animals would not stay in a country where there were so many people. Pa did not like to stay, either. He liked a country where the wild animals lived without being afraid. —*Little House on the Prairie,* by Laura Ingalls Wilder

10. Laura Ingalls Wilder traveled west with her family in the late 1800s. She wrote books about her adventures. How do her words help you to understand the reasons why some people chose to move west?

_____

_____

_____

_____

Distinguish Fact From Fiction

11. Suppose you were writing a short story about a "forty-niner" during the gold rush in California. What kind of a character would you write about? What events might happen to your character?

_____

_____

_____

_____

_____

_____

_____

Quest Findings

Is the West the Best?

You've read the lessons in this chapter and now you are ready for your discussion. Remember to use facts to support your opinion. Follow these steps:

👆 INTERACTIVITY

Learn more about evaluating costs and benefits with an online activity.

1 Form Your Opinion

Think of the reasons why settlers wanted to move west. Also think of the reasons why people would not want to make the journey west. Write these ideas in a list. Then write down your opinions of these ideas. Use these notes to help you prepare for your discussion.

2 Gather Evidence

Use your notes and the evidence from your Quest Connections to form ideas to share during the discussion. Answer the following questions to help you prepare:

- Why did settlers want to move west?
- What kinds of sacrifices did the pioneers have to make?
- What kinds of risks did they face?
- What benefits were there to life in the East during the 1800s?

3 Hold the Discussion

Share what you have learned about the costs and benefits of moving west with your classmates. State your opinion and your reasons. Listen to their opinions and reasons. Be open to new ideas.

4 Revise

Make changes to your ideas after the discussion. Did some of your classmates have ideas that were different from yours? Did you agree about some things?

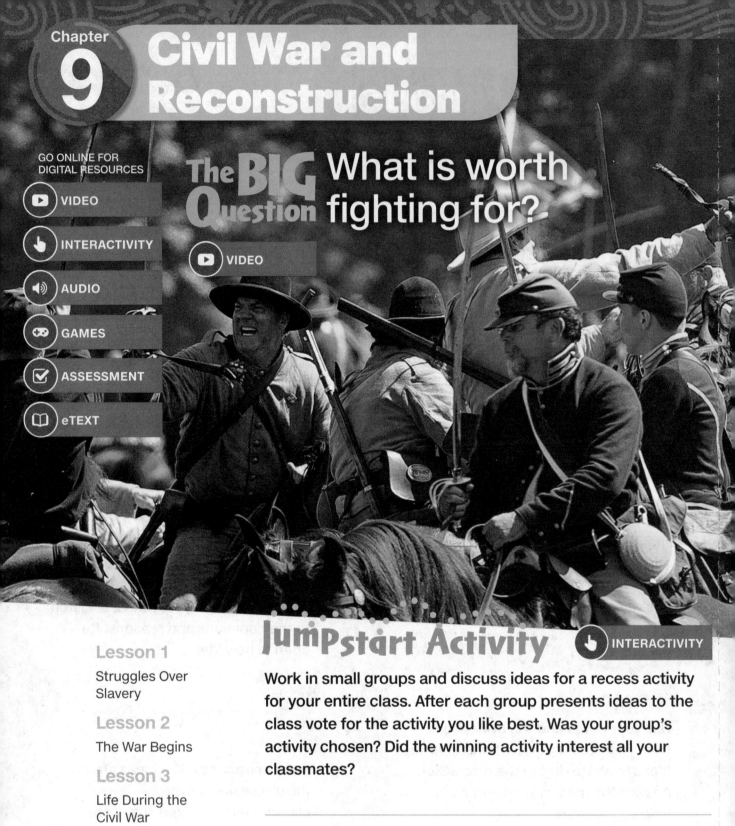

Chapter 9
Civil War and Reconstruction

GO ONLINE FOR
DIGITAL RESOURCES

- ▶ VIDEO
- 👆 INTERACTIVITY
- 🔊 AUDIO
- 🎮 GAMES
- ☑ ASSESSMENT
- 📖 eTEXT

The BIG Question

What is worth fighting for?

▶ VIDEO

Jumpstart Activity

👆 INTERACTIVITY

Work in small groups and discuss ideas for a recess activity for your entire class. After each group presents ideas to the class vote for the activity you like best. Was your group's activity chosen? Did the winning activity interest all your classmates?

_____

_____

_____

_____

_____

Rap About It!

Fighting for Freedom and Union

Preview the chapter **vocabulary** as you sing the rap:

Division between the North and South grew when
New free and slave states joined the **Union**.
After Lincoln's election, Southern states would secede
And leave the Union to form the **Confederacy**.

At Ft. Sumter shots fired in the early morning mist,
The Civil War had begun, both sides ran to **enlist**.
No one guessed at the time, that the war would last long;
Battles at Bull Run, Gettysburg, Antietam, and more.

During the war, Lincoln issued a **proclamation**,
It set some enslaved free, that's called **emancipation**.
It didn't end slavery but it changed the war,
African Americans joined and gave the Union their all.

Civil War and Reconstruction

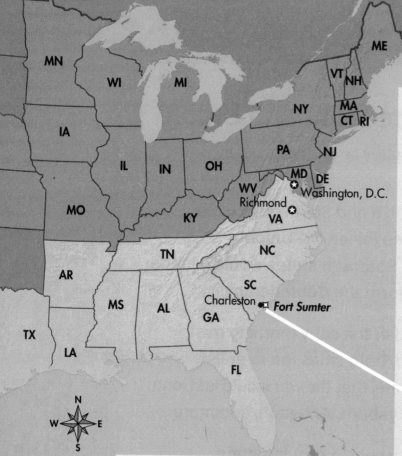

Washington, D.C.

Richmond

Charleston • Fort Sumter

N W E S

Where did the Civil War start?

The Civil War began on April 21, 1861, when the South's Confederate Army fired on Fort Sumter. Locate Fort Sumter on the map.

Fort Sumter

TODAY
You can tour Fort Sumter National Monument in South Carolina.

What happened and When?

Read the timeline to find out about the events that took place before and after the Civil War.

1850

1855

1860

1850
Congress passed the Compromise of 1850.

1854
The Kansas-Nebraska Act splits the Nebraska Territory.

Who will you meet?

Abraham Lincoln
The sixteenth president of the United States led the nation during the Civil War

Sojourner Truth
A former enslaved African American activist who collected supplies for African American regiments during the Civil War

Jefferson Davis
The president of the Confederate States during the Civil War

Clara Barton
A hospital nurse during the Civil War and founder of the American Red Cross

 INTERACTIVITY

Complete the interactive digital activity.

1865　　　　　　　　　　**1870**

1861
The Civil War begins.

1863
The Battle of Gettysburg is fought.

1865
The Civil War ends.

1868
Fourteenth Amendment passed.

TODAY
You can visit the Civil War battle sites in many states.

Sing Along!

Music during the Civil War played an important role for both the soldiers and their families. While in camp and the hospital, soldiers would sing ballads, funny songs, patriotic songs, and sentimental songs that inspired feelings of pride, home, or loved ones.

One way to inspire or entertain people is to write a song. A song is a group of words or a poem that is set to music.

Quest Kick Off

As a new soldier in the army, your mission is to write a song for soldiers that provides comfort, entertainment, or shows patriotism.

1 Ask Questions

How do you want the words and music of your song to make the soldiers feel? What kind of song do you think soldiers would like? Write three ideas for a song.

....

....

....

2 Research

INTERACTIVITY

Complete the interactivity to learn more about music during the Civil War.

Follow your teacher's instructions to find songs that were popular among soldiers during the Civil War. Read the lyrics of several songs. How do the songs make you feel?

....

....

....

....

....

3 Look for Quest Connections

Begin looking for Quest Connections that will help you write your song.

4 Quest Findings
Write Your Song

Use the Quest Findings page at the end of the chapter to help you write your song.

INTERACTIVITY

Participate in a class discussion to preview the content of this lesson.

Vocabulary

plantation
Union
states' rights
compromise
Underground Railroad
abolitionist
secession
Confederacy

Academic Vocabulary

obtain
according

Unlock The BIG Question

I will know the causes of the Civil War.

JumpStart Activity

You want to go to the movies and your friend wants to go on a hike. How do you decide what to do? Share your ideas of how to compromise. With a classmate, act out one idea.

Proud Union soldiers march by the White House as President Lincoln looks looks on.

The song "The Battle Cry of Freedom" was popular during the U.S. Civil War.

Primary Source

"Yes, we'll rally round the flag, boys, we'll rally once again,
Shouting the battle cry of Freedom."

—George F. Root, 1862

Both sides were fighting for freedom but disagreed about what *freedom* meant. Their fight was the bloodiest in U.S. history. What divided our nation so deeply? Read on to find out.

The North and South Grow Apart

Much of the South is low and level with rich soil. The climate is warm and sunny for much of the year. Many people lived on big farms called **plantations**. The economy was primarily based on agriculture, supplying raw goods to the North. Many of the farmworkers were enslaved African Americans and the Southern economy depended upon their work.

The geography of the North is very different. It has hills, mountains, and lakes. The climate is cold and snowy in the winter. Northeastern resources include coal for making steel and fueling factory machines. In the 1800s, the Industrial Revolution changed life in the North. Many people moved to urban areas to work in factories. Factories used raw materials from the South, such as cotton, to produce finished products.

The Southern port of New Orleans was important to both regions. To meet the demand for manufactured products, goods were shipped from the North down the Mississippi River to New Orleans. Differences in geography and industrialization shaped the culture and economy of the North and South and divided the two regions. This was called sectionalism, and many feared it would lead to a civil war.

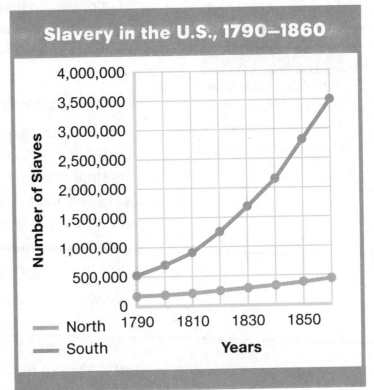

Slavery in the U.S., 1790–1860

Number of Slaves — Years

— North
— South

Source: University of Virginia Library

Tough Compromises

Academic Vocabulary

obtain • *v.*, to get or acquire
according • *prep.*, in agreement

After the American Revolution, the United States **obtained** the region called the Northwest Territory. This was the area we call the Midwest, and it doubled the country. Congress passed a law called the Northwest Ordinance of 1787. It outlined how new states could be formed. Once admitted to the **Union**, or the United States, a new state would have the same rights as other states.

Slavery was prohibited in this territory, and this ban sparked arguments. Many wanted the same number of slave states, where slavery was allowed, and free states, where it was illegal. They feared that if there were more representatives in Congress for either side, it might threaten **states' rights**, the rights of states to make their own local laws.

In 1819, Missouri asked to join the Union as a slave state. That would upset the balance in Congress. A compromise was worked out. A **compromise** occurs when each side gives in a little to reach an agreement. A law known as the Missouri Compromise was passed in 1820.

According to the Missouri Compromise, Missouri could be a slave state and Maine would join the Union as a free state. In addition, an imaginary line, called the Mason-Dixon line, was used. States north of the line would be free states. States south of the line could allow slavery if they wished.

More New States

In 1845, the Republic of Texas was annexed (united or joined) to the United States. Part of the republic became the state of Texas, a slave state. The rest of the territory was to be divided into four new states. Of the other four new states, those north of the line set by the Missouri Compromise would be free. But those south of the line could vote on whether to allow slavery.

Tensions flared again in 1849 when California applied to join the Union as a free state. The solution was the Compromise of 1850. To satisfy the North, California was admitted as a free state. To satisfy the South, the North agreed to the Fugitive Slave Law.

1. ☑ **Reading Check**
Turn and talk with a partner. Discuss the three parts of the Missouri Compromise.

A fugitive is someone who escapes and runs away. The Fugitive Slave Law said that escaped enslaved African Americans must be returned to their owners, even if they had reached a free state. Congress hoped that this law would keep the country united.

In 1854, Nebraska was split into the Nebraska Territory and Kansas Territory. Under the Kansas-Nebraska Act, the people of each territory could vote to decide if they would allow slavery.

"Bleeding Kansas"

A majority vote would decide whether Kansas would be free or allow slavery. Both sides rushed to Kansas to vote. When the votes were counted, the proslavery side had won. The Kansas Territory would allow slavery.

Northerners demanded that the vote be thrown out. Southerners argued that the vote should stand. Most people who lived in Kansas wanted peace. People clashed all over the Kansas Territory. By 1856, this violence had earned the territory the sad name "Bleeding Kansas."

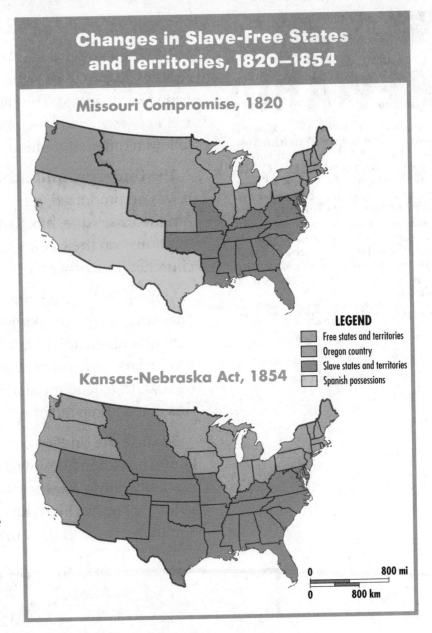

Changes in Slave-Free States and Territories, 1820–1854

Missouri Compromise, 1820

Kansas-Nebraska Act, 1854

LEGEND
- Free states and territories
- Oregon country
- Slave states and territories
- Spanish possessions

0   800 mi
0   800 km

2. ☑ Reading Check Study the maps. **Describe** how the Kansas-Nebrask Act affected the spread of slavery.

_____

_____

_____

Escape to Freedom

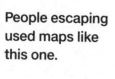

$100 REWARD.

Ranaway from the subscriber's farm, near Washington, on the 11th of October, negro woman **SOPHIA GORDON**, about 24 years of age, rather small in size, of copper color, is tolerably good looking, has a low and soft manner of speech. She is believed to be among associates formed in Washington where she has been often hired.

I will give the above reward, no matter where taken and secured in jail so that I get her again.
GEORGE W. YOUNG.

November 16th, 1858.

B. Polkinhorn's Steam Job Printing Office, D street, bet. 6th & 7th sts., Washington, D.C.

reward flyer for escaped enslaved African American woman

The Fugitive Slave Law said the escaped enslaved African Americans had to be returned to their owners, even if they were in a free state. This did not stop thousands of slaves from trying to escape to freedom, however. The fugitives usually followed different routes on the Underground Railroad.

The **Underground Railroad** was not an actual train. It was an organized, secret system to help enslaved African Americans escape, mostly to the North or to Canada. The "stations" on the Underground Railroad were the houses, churches, and other places the fugitives hid and rested.

Many people helped the escaping African Americans. These people became known as "conductors." Harriet Tubman, an escaped slave, was one of the most famous conductors. At great personal risk, Tubman made many trips south to lead more people to freedom. Tubman's route was one of three major routes that went through New Jersey.

Because the Underground Railroad was secret, no one knows how many enslaved African Americans escaped—probably only a few thousand each year between 1840 and 1860. This seems like a lot of people, but in the 1860s, nearly 4 million people in the United States were enslaved.

People escaping used maps like this one.

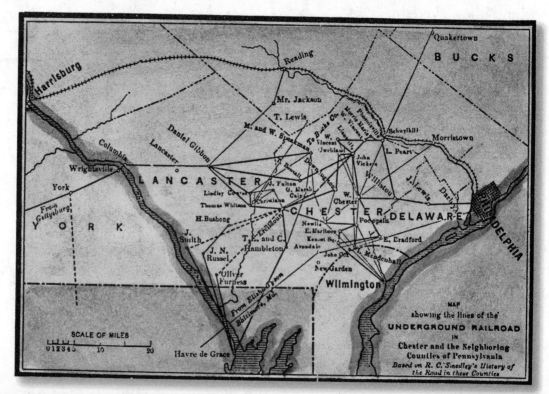

Starting Down the Road to War

The North and South became further divided. In Boston, William Lloyd Garrison published a newspaper called *The Liberator*. Frederick Douglass, an African American who had escaped from slavery, published an antislavery newspaper called *The North Star*. Garrison and Douglass were **abolitionists**, people who wanted to abolish, or get rid of, slavery. In the South, writers and speakers argued for states' rights and the freedom to keep their way of life.

Women played a big role in fighting slavery. Sojourner Truth was an African American woman who had been enslaved in New York, but she was freed when New York outlawed slavery. In 1843, she joined the abolition movement. Harriet Beecher Stowe published a novel called *Uncle Tom's Cabin*. This book described the cruelties of slavery and convinced many people to oppose it.

Anger Grows

One event that made people angry was the case of an enslaved man named Dred Scott from Missouri. Scott's owner had taken him to two free states, Illinois and Wisconsin, before returning to Missouri. When Scott's owner died, Scott claimed he was free because he had lived in free states. In 1857, the Supreme Court ruled that Scott had no rights because African Americans were not citizens.

Then, in 1859, abolitionist John Brown attacked Harper's Ferry, Virginia. Brown had fought in Bleeding Kansas. Now he wanted to attack slavery supporters in Virginia, but he needed weapons. He decided to steal weapons the army had stored at Harper's Ferry. Brown and 21 other men raided Harper's Ferry on October 16, but soldiers stopped them. Brown was caught, tried, and hanged. John Brown's raid did not succeed, but it showed that the fight over slavery was getting fiercer.

3. ☑ **Reading Check**
Sequence Fill in the missing items to **show the sequence** of events leading to the Civil War.

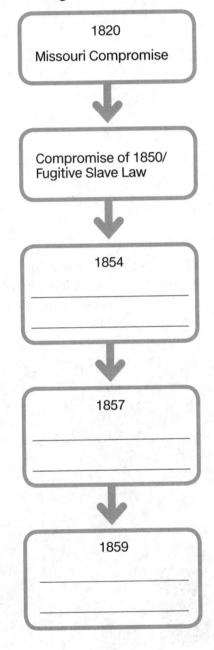

1820
Missouri Compromise

Compromise of 1850/ Fugitive Slave Law

1854
_____
_____

1857
_____
_____

1859
_____
_____

4. ☑ **Reading Check** **Explain** how John Brown's raid might have been a sign that war was unavoidable.

_____

_____

The Election of 1860

Abraham Lincoln wanted to keep slavery from spreading to new territories and states. "I hate it because of the monstrous injustice," he said in 1854. The Republican Party in Illinois chose Lincoln to run for the U.S. Senate in 1858. Lincoln's opponent, Democratic senator Stephen Douglas disagreed. He believed that each state had the right to decide whether or not to allow slavery. Douglas won that election, but Lincoln's arguments in a series of famous debates with Douglas made him a leader of the new Republican Party.

The 1860 presidential election had four major candidates. The Democratic Party had split in two. The Northern Democrats chose Stephen Douglas. The Southern Democrats chose John Breckenridge. The Republicans chose Abraham Lincoln. The Constitutional Union Party chose John Bell.

The election reflected the sharp divide between the North and South. Lincoln won, but he did not win any electoral votes in the Southern states because voters there worried that he would end slavery if elected.

While running for the U.S. Senate in 1858, Lincoln had said:

Abraham Lincoln, standing, argued for stopping the spread of slavery during the Lincoln-Douglas debates.

Primary Source

"'A house divided against itself cannot stand.' I believe this government cannot endure permanently half slave and half free. I do not expect the Union to be dissolved . . . but I do expect it will cease to be divided. It will become all one thing, or all the other."

—Abraham Lincoln's acceptance speech to Illinois Republican Party, June 16, 1858

This was a frightening prediction. Soon, Lincoln and his fellow Americans would find out if the Union could survive.

5. ☑ **Reading Check** **Analyze** what the 1860 election showed about what was going on in the country.

_____

_____

The South Breaks Away

Even before the election, some Southern leaders had talked about **secession**, or separating, from the Union. Many Southerners wanted their own country. After Lincoln's election, South Carolina became the first to secede.

By March 1861, Alabama, Florida, Mississippi, Georgia, Louisiana, and Texas had also seceded. These states formed their own government, called the Confederate States of America, also known as the **Confederacy**. *Confederacy*, like *Union*, means "joined together."

The Confederate leaders wrote a constitution and elected Jefferson Davis as president. They seized forts across the South.

States that remained loyal to the U.S. government were still called the Union. A civil war now seemed certain. The word *civil* refers to citizens, so a civil war is a war among citizens of the same country.

Confederate president Jefferson Davis

 INTERACTIVITY

Check your understanding of the key ideas of this lesson.

☑ Lesson 1 Check

6. **Describe** one of the differences that made the Missouri Compromise necessary.

_____

_____

7. Write a sentence from the viewpoint of presidential candidate Abraham Lincoln **describing** what he would be willing to fight for.

_____

_____

8. **Quest Connections** **Identify** the words in the song "Battle Cry of Freedom" that would serve to excite people and strengthen their feelings of patriotism.

_____

_____

Make Decisions

VIDEO

Watch a video about making decisions

Suppose you lived in the United States in the 1860s. Think about the decisions the president had to make as Northern and Southern states grew more divided. How did Congress create the compromises that kept the free and slave states balanced? How did people go about making these life-changing decisions?

Making decisions is a process. By following these steps in order, you can increase your chances of making the right decision.

1. **Identify the situation that requires a decision.** To make a good decision, you must first recognize the problem or question you face. Identify your goal and the outcome you want.

2. **Think of options.** Gather information about how to solve the problem or answer the questions. These are your options.

3. **Predict outcomes.** Focus on each of your options. Ask yourself: What might happen if I choose this option? What are the possible good and bad outcomes?

4. **Take action.** Choose the option that has the greatest chance of meeting your goals. By choosing the option you think is best, you have made your decision.

Once you have made a decision, you can act on it. Develop a plan to carry out the option you chose. Keep your mind open, however. You should be willing to change your decision if the action you take does not work out as well as you hoped.

You make a decision each time you choose which food to buy.

Read the sections in your book titled "Tough Compromises," "More New States," and "'Bleeding Kansas'" in Lesson 1. The country faces a lot of very hard decisions that had to be made to keep the country together. What were the issues? How would you have made a decision? Use the decision-making process to help you decide what you might do.

1. What is the issue or situation that requires a decision?

_____

_____

_____

2. What are the options?

_____

_____

_____

_____

3. What are consequences of each option?

_____

_____

_____

_____

_____

4. What option is best?

_____

_____

_____

Vocabulary

enlist
blockade

Academic Vocabulary

overwhelm
horrific

Unlock The BIG Question

I will know the strategies and key battles in the first years of the Civil War.

JumpStart Activity

Move into small groups. Each group suggests an activity for the class to do. One group decides what to do. How do the other groups feel about not having a choice?

Most leaders of the Confederacy expected the secession to be peaceful. They believed deciding to secede was one of a state's rights. They didn't think their actions would lead to a long, bloody war. They were very wrong.

Confederate forces fired on Fort Sumter on April 12, 1861. This event touched off the Civil War.

The First Shots

A Union force controlled Fort Sumter in South Carolina. It was in a Confederate state, so Confederate president Jefferson Davis thought the Union force should surrender the fort. He sent South Carolina's governor to ask the Union soldiers to leave the fort, but they refused.

On April 8, 1861, the governor learned that Lincoln was sending a ship to resupply the fort. Jefferson Davis sent soldiers to help the governor.

On April 11, the Confederates again asked the Union soldiers to leave. Again, they refused. At 4:30 A.M. on April 12, Confederate forces began to fire on the fort. The next day, with no supplies left, the Union force surrendered the fort to the Confederates. No one had been killed, but the Civil War had begun.

The Civil War Begins

Lincoln responded to the attack on Fort Sumter by raising an army. Virginia, Arkansas, Tennessee, and North Carolina joined the Confederacy. The Confederacy now had 11 states; the Union consisted of 23. Men on both sides eagerly enlisted. To **enlist** is to join the military. After all, it was an important cause. The North wanted to preserve the unity of the United States as a whole. The North also didn't want to lose access to the Mississippi River. The South was fighting for states' rights and a way of life.

The First Battle of Bull Run

At first, it seemed that the war *would* be over soon—and the Confederates would win. Lincoln sent 35,000 troops against the Confederate capital in Richmond, Virginia. On July 21, 1861, they met Confederate troops at a stream called Bull Run. The Union soldiers did well at first. But the Confederates stood their ground, inspired by a general named Thomas Jackson. "There stands Jackson like a stone wall," declared another Confederate general. His actions earned the general the nickname "Stonewall" Jackson. When Southern reinforcements arrived, the **overwhelmed** Union soldiers fled.

INTERACTIVITY

Explore the key ideas of this lesson.

Quest Connection

Music was often used to stir up patriotic feelings. Underline words and phrases that you might use to write a song.

INTERACTIVITY

Learn more about music during the Civil War by going online.

Academic Vocabulary

overwhelm • *adj.*, beat; vanquish

Lincoln Versus Davis

Abraham Lincoln, the president of the Union, and Jefferson Davis, the president of the Confederacy, were both skilled leaders. Both were born in Kentucky, but Davis had moved to Mississippi and Lincoln had moved to Illinois. Lincoln was trained as a lawyer. Davis, a West Point graduate, became an army officer. Both served in Washington, D.C.

Lincoln and Davis faced different challenges as the war began. The South had fewer resources than the North, but it had better military leaders and stronger reasons to fight.

The two men were different in their wartime strategies, too. Lincoln sought advice from General Winfield Scott, a Mexican War veteran.

1. ☑ **Reading Check** **Compare and Contrast** Complete the chart to **compare** the Union and the Confederacy.

This painting of Abraham Lincoln is based on a photograph taken by Matthew Brady just before Lincoln became president.

The Union and the Confederacy

	United States of America	Confederate States of America
President		
Strategy		
Strengths	• Produced 90% of the country's weapons, cloth, shoes, and iron • Produced most of the country's food • Had more railroads and roads • Had more people	• Had more experienced hunters and soldiers • Had a history of producing great military leaders • Believed they were fighting for freedom • Were fighting for—and on—their own land
Challenges	• Didn't have many war veterans • Didn't have as many talented military leaders	• Lacked big manufacturing centers • Had fewer railroads

Scott planned a three-part strategy. First, the Union would form a naval blockade of the coasts. A **blockade** is a barrier of troops or ships to keep people and supplies from moving in and out of an area. Under a blockade, the South would not be able to ship cotton to European countries and wouldn't have money to pay for the war.

Second, Scott planned to take control of the Mississippi River, which would cut the Confederacy in half. Third, Scott planned to attack the Confederacy from the east and west. He called his strategy the Anaconda Plan because it would squeeze the Confederacy like an anaconda, a huge snake.

Davis had his own strategy. First, he planned to defend Confederate land until the North gave up. Southerners believed that Union troops would quit fighting because they weren't defending their own land. Second, Davis believed the British would help because they needed Southern cotton. Davis was wrong. Britain offered no help to either side.

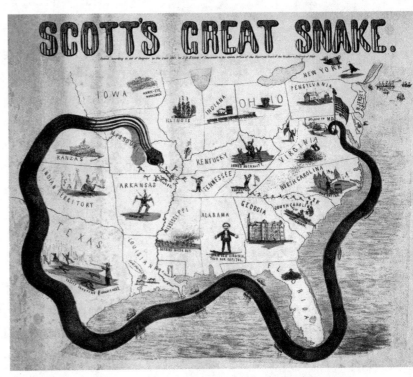

General Scott's plan was to wrap around the South and "squeeze" it, like a giant snake.

New Tools of War

Wars often result in the invention of new tools and technologies. During the Civil War, guns were improved. The new guns could shoot farther and more accurately. Both Union and Confederate soldiers used early versions of the hand grenade. The Confederacy built a submarine, a ship that could travel underwater.

The Confederates created another new weapon: the ironclad. It was a ship covered, or clad, in iron, so cannonballs simply bounced off it. To make the ironclad, the Confederates covered an old Union ship, the *Merrimack*, with iron plates. They named it the *Virginia*. The *Virginia* successfully sank several Union ships. The Union built its own ironclad, the *Monitor*, which fought the *Virginia*. Since both ships were ironclads, they were unable to cause serious damage to each other.

2. ☑ **Reading Check**
Turn and talk with a partner about what made the *Monitor* and the *Virginia* special.

Brilliant Confederate Generals

While the Union had far greater resources than the Confederacy, the South had brilliant generals, especially Thomas "Stonewall" Jackson and Robert E. Lee. These generals often outsmarted Union forces many times larger than their own.

In 1862, Union general George McClellan hoped to capture the Confederate capital of Richmond, Virginia. McClellan planned to sail his troops to a place on the coast of Virginia, to avoid the Confederate army in northern Virginia. At first, it seemed as though McClellan's plan would work. However, Stonewall Jackson was fighting so successfully in Virginia's Shenandoah Valley that extra Union troops had to be sent there. There was no help for McClellan. Robert E. Lee then badly defeated McClellan's forces at Richmond. Some people feared that the Confederates would now move on Washington, D.C.

With each Confederate success, there was more pressure on Lincoln. Northerners had expected a swift, easy victory. It was beginning to look like the war might be long, and people began to question Lincoln's decision to fight.

General Robert E. Lee commanded the Confederate army of northern Virginia.

The Battle of Fredericksburg in Virginia, in December 1862, was a huge Confederate victory.

The Battle of Antietam

The Union needed a victory. It got one on September 17, 1862, at the Battle of Antietam (an TEET um). This battle was the single bloodiest day in the war. In the end, about 23,000 men lay dead or wounded, evenly divided between North and South. This **horrific** battle led Lincoln to make a decision that would change the war and the country.

Academic Vocabulary

horrific • *adj.*, having the power to horrify; frightening or shocking

3. ☑ **Reading Check** **Turn** and **talk** with a partner. Discuss the reasons why a Northern victory was so important.

☑Lesson 2 Check

INTERACTIVITY

Check your understanding of the key ideas of this lesson.

4. **Main Idea and Details** Fill in this chart. **Identify** the purpose, or main idea, of the Anaconda Plan. Then fill in details to show how the plan would work.

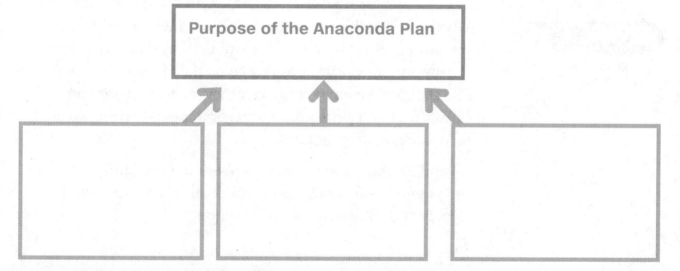

Purpose of the Anaconda Plan

5. **Describe** why Davis was willing to fight.

_____

_____

6. **Understand the** *Quest* **Connections** Why did many Civil War songs appeal to people's feelings of patriotism?

_____

_____

_____

Classify and Categorize

I liked reading about the strengths of the Union and Confederate states.

I liked it too. What was your favorite part? Can you classify and categorize the information for me?

VIDEO

Watch a video about classify and categorize.

When you **classify** and **categorize** information or things, you arrange them based on the features they share. We might classify and categorize books based on their subject. We might also classify them on how difficult they are to read. We can classify and categorize information or things based on two or more categories, or groups.

Read the following paragraph about the strengths of the Union and Confederate states. Think about how you could classify and categorize the information.

There are lots of different factors that can influence the outcome of battles and a war. The Union and Confederacy had different strengths during the Civil War. The Union states had a large population and lots of railroads and roads. They produced most of the country's food, weapons, cloth, shoes, and iron. In contrast, the Confederate states had experienced hunters and soldiers and a history of producing great military leaders. Also, they were fighting on their own land and believed they were fighting for freedom.

1. What are the strengths of the Union states? What are the strengths of the Confederate states? Fill in the graphic organizer to classify and categorize the strengths of each country.

Strengths of the Union and the Confederacy

United States of America	Confederate States of America
_____	_____
_____	_____
_____	_____
_____	_____
_____	_____

2. Read the section titled "Lincoln Versus Davis" in Lesson 2. Write several facts about President Lincoln and President Davis that would help you classify and categorize the two different presidents. On a separate piece of paper, write a paragraph summarizing the facts about the two leaders.

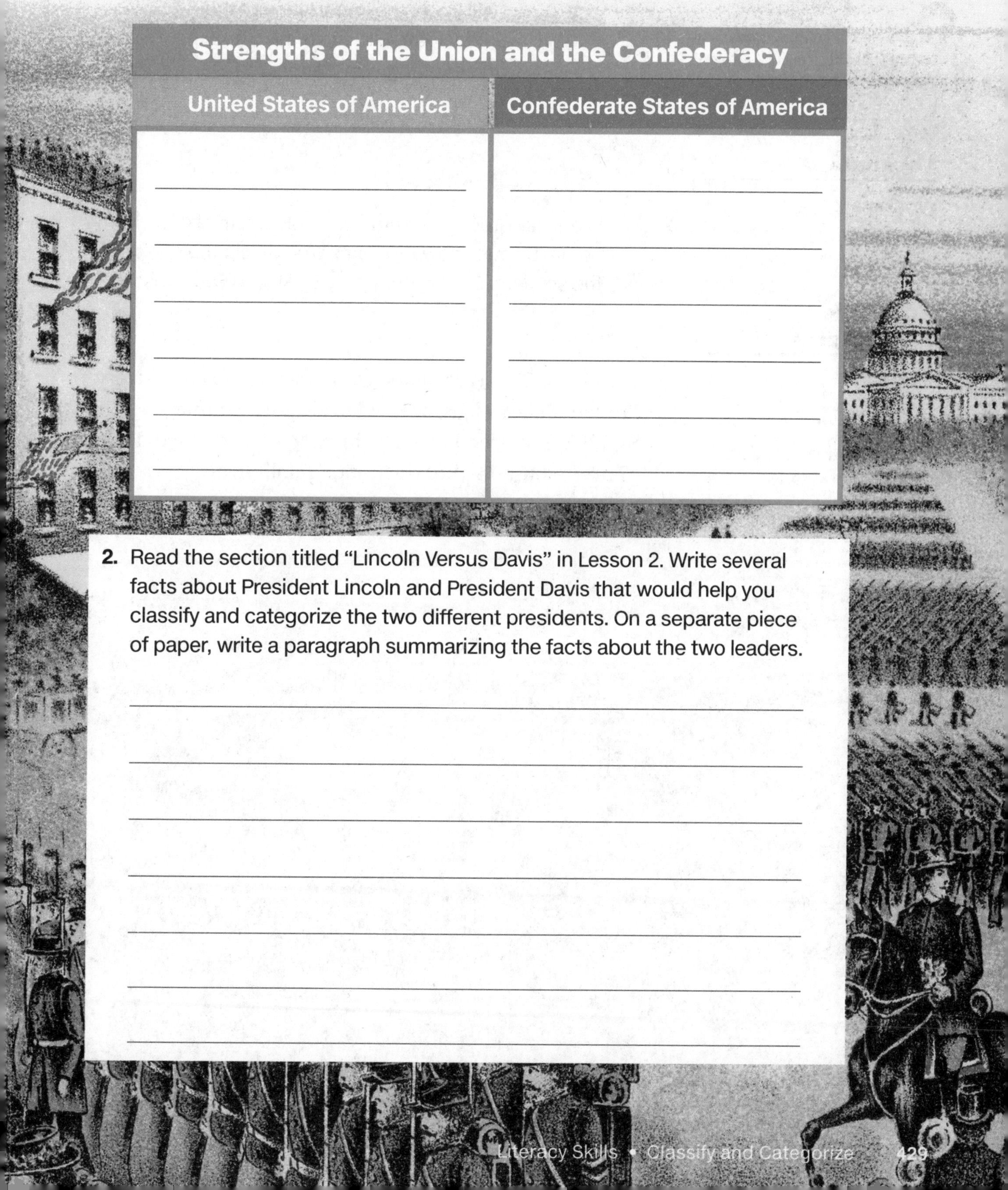

_____

_____

_____

_____

_____

_____

Life During the Civil War

 INTERACTIVITY

Participate in a class discussion to preview the content of this lesson.

Vocabulary

proclamation
emancipation
Juneteenth

Academic Vocabulary

prove
exhibit

African American soldiers of the 107th United States Colored Troops

 Unlock **The BIG Question**

I will know the importance of the Emancipation Proclamation and the roles of different groups in the Civil War.

JumPstart Activity

In a small group, list items that soldiers might like from home. Discuss how the items would help the spirits of the soldiers. Share your group's list with your class.

The U.S. Civil War did not start as a war to end slavery. President Lincoln just wanted to keep the country together. By 1862, however, Lincoln's thinking had changed. He said, "Slavery must die that the nation might live."

The Emancipation Proclamation

Some of Lincoln's advisors said ending slavery would divide the North and unite the South. They were right. But Lincoln was determined. On January 1, 1863, he issued a **proclamation**, or official announcement. It called for the **emancipation**, or setting free, of enslaved African Americans. Lincoln's Emancipation Proclamation freed enslaved African Americans in states at war with the Union.

The proclamation did not end slavery in the border states, slave states that stayed loyal to the Union. These were Delaware, Kentucky, Maryland, Missouri, and West Virginia. It freed enslaved African Americans in the Confederacy, but only those areas controlled by the Union benefited. As a result, most African Americans remained enslaved.

When the Civil War ended, General Gordon Granger was sent to the state of Texas. On June 19, 1865, he read to the people of Galveston, "The people of Texas are informed that . . . all slaves are free." African Americans in Texas celebrated this day as their day of freedom. The tradition of celebrating on this day is now known as **Juneteenth**.

INTERACTIVITY

Explore the key ideas of this lesson.

A Diverse Army

African American abolitionist Frederick Douglass supported Lincoln and encouraged other African Americans to help the Union. Large numbers of them responded by joining the Union army. By the end of the war, about 179,000 African American men had served as soldiers in the Union army.

Many recent immigrants also enlisted. Many German, Irish, British, and Canadian soldiers joined in the fight.

About 20,000 American Indians served in either the Confederate or Union armies. General Ely S. Parker, a Seneca, wrote the surrender document that General Robert E. Lee signed at the end of the war. Parker later told how, during the surrender, Lee said to him, "I am glad to see a real American here." Parker replied to the general, "We are all Americans."

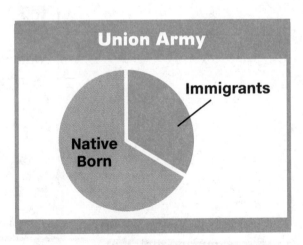

Circle graph showing the breakdown of the Union Army

Quest Connection

There were songs written about boredom, marching, and even food. Circle two or three words or phrases that you might use in your song.

Academic Vocabulary

prove • *v.*, find out something is difficult, a problem

INTERACTIVITY

Find out more about how to use the soldiers' experiences to compose your song.

A Soldier's Life

The average age of a Civil War soldier was 25. However, boys as young as 12 went into battle as drummer boys. For young soldiers and old, life on the Civil War battlefields was dirty, dangerous, and difficult.

Battles were horrible, but long, boring waits between battles were hard, too. Most battles were in the South, where summers were very hot. Soldiers almost always traveled on foot and might march up to 25 miles a day. The supplies in their backpacks weighed as much as 50 pounds. Marching **proved** even more difficult for Confederate soldiers. The Union blockade kept supplies from reaching the Southerners, so soldiers could not replace worn-out shoes. They often marched and fought in bare feet.

Food was a problem, too. It was rarely fresh. The armies supplied beef and pork. Both were preserved so they did not spoil. Fresh pork had been salted to become "salt pork." Beef was pickled, or preserved in water and spices. In addition, the troops had beans and biscuits. These biscuits were tough flour-and-water biscuits called "hardtack." To survive, troops raided local farms to steal fresh fruits and vegetables.

1. ☑ **Reading Check** For most soldiers, life was very different in the army. **Turn and talk** with a partner to discuss what you would have found to be the most difficult part of being a soldier during the Civil War.

Union soldiers sitting outside their tent

Sick and Wounded

In the mid-1800s, the idea that germs caused disease was a new and untested theory. Most doctors had not heard of it. Many doctors never washed their hands or medical instruments.

A wounded soldier who made it to a hospital might be put in a bed in which someone had just died of fever—without the sheets being changed. Infections were common, and disease spread quickly. There were few medicines and no antibiotics. Twice as many soldiers died of disease as died of gunshot wounds.

Caring for the Soldiers

At this time, there were almost no nursing schools in the United States. Most nurses learned as they worked. One nurse described a field hospital this way:

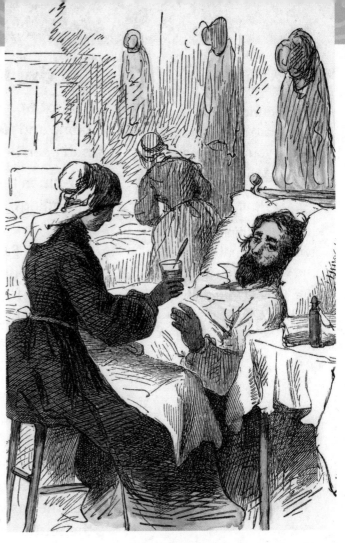

Civil War nurse cares for a wounded soldier

Primary Source

". . . just across the lawn there are some of the worst cases & the sight & sounds we have to encounter daily are most distressing. I am mightily afraid we shall have some sort of infectious fever here for it is impossible to keep the place clean & there is a bad smell everywhere."

Clara Barton was the most famous of the volunteer nurses. She went out to where the soldiers were. Barton said her place was "anywhere between the bullet and the battlefield." At the Battle of Antietam, as the cannons boomed, she held the operating table steady for the surgeon. She became known as "the Angel of the Battlefield." After the war, in 1881, she founded the American Red Cross.

Hundreds of women helped on both sides. Juliet Opie Hopkins from Alabama cared for Confederate soldiers. In 1861 she sold all her property and gave the money to the Confederacy to establish hospitals. Hopkins was shot twice while rescuing wounded men on the battlefield.

2. ☑ **Reading Check**
Identify two things you might do to help nurse soldiers.

_____

_____

_____

_____

On the Home Front

Most women did not work on the battlefield, they stayed home and took care of their families. They filled the jobs that had been held by men. They ran stores and planted crops.

Women in the South often had to move their families and belongings, as homes and towns were destroyed. They also had to deal with shortages of supplies caused by the North's blockade. Prices increased sharply. The average Southern family's monthly food bill rose from $6.65 just before the war to $68 by 1863. Almost no one could afford food. In April of that year, hundreds of women in Richmond, Virginia, rioted to protest the rise in prices. Women in other Southern cities rioted over the price of bread, too.

When they could, women hid their livestock as the armies came through. Hungry soldiers would kill and eat all the chickens and pigs. Of course, the army would take any other food they could find, too. Often, after an army had passed through, the civilians were left starving. This was the case when the Union army marched through the South.

Women also hid possessions from the enemy soldiers. These included items that had been in their families for generations.

People in the North read about the war. Many sent husbands or sons to fight. In the South, families struggled with the direct effects of the war's destruction.

A family prepares to flee the approaching army

3. ☑ **Reading Check**
Identify three things you would take with you if you had to escape before an enemy army came.

_____

_____

Women in Wartime

Women on both sides contributed to the war effort. In addition to being nurses on the battlefield or keeping farms and family businesses running, they sewed clothing and made bandages. They sold personal possessions to raise money and sent food to the armies.

Some women traveled with their soldier husbands and sons, cooking for them, nursing them, and helping them. A few women even became soldiers. Frances Clalin, for example, disguised herself as a man so that she could fight in the Union army.

Sojourner Truth, a former enslaved African American, had worked for abolition before the war and would work for women's rights after the war. During the war, she gathered supplies for African American regiments. A popular speaker, she often told stories of her life as an enslaved African American.

Sojourner Truth told of her own life as she worked to end slavery.

Primary Source

I have borne thirteen children, and seen most all sold off to slavery, and when I cried out with my mother's grief, none but Jesus heard me!

—Sojourner Truth

Some women became spies. Documents and even weapons could be hidden under the large hoop skirts they wore.

Belle Boyd, nicknamed "La Belle Rebelle," was one of the most famous female Confederate spies. Union soldiers arrested her six times, but she kept spying for the Confederates. After one arrest, Boyd communicated to a Confederate by hiding messages inside rubber balls and throwing them between the bars of her cell windows!

Bringing the War Home

New technology changed the way the war was fought, but it also changed the way people at home experienced the war. People still got news from the battlefield through the "old" technology of soldiers' letters and newspapers.

For the first time, people back home also got to see something of what these soldiers were living through. A new technology, photography, made this possible. The Civil War was the first war to be "taken home" in images. Mathew Brady thought it was important to photograph the war.

People still learn from Brady's photographs showing the details of war. He took pictures of soldiers posing, resting, and cooking. Brady and other photographers also took photos of field hospitals, weapons, and dead bodies on the battlefield. Their photos appeared in newspapers and special **exhibits**.

Academic Vocabulary

exhibit • *n.*, collection of items put out so that people can see them

4. ☑ Reading Check **Describe** what caption you would write if you were the photographer of this photograph.

_____

_____

This photograph by Mathew Brady shows wounded soldiers resting between battles beneath a tree.

Camera technology was not well developed at the time. Cameras were large and heavy. All the preparation and developing had to be done in the dark, so the photographers used a "darkroom" wagon. Photographs at that time were taken on specially treated glass plates. The glass plates had to be handled carefully as the wagon bumped through the countryside and across battlefields. Some people claim that as a result of all the letters home and all the photographs, civilians knew more about the Civil War than about any war before.

Mathew Brady spent his own money, buying equipment and hiring assistants, to capture the war in photographs.

INTERACTIVITY

Check your understanding of the key ideas of this lesson.

☑ Lesson 3 Check

5. **Sequence Organize** these events in the correct sequence: Emancipation Proclamation, Juneteenth holiday created, First Battle of Bull Run, Clara Barton starts the Red Cross, Battle of Antietam.

_____

_____

_____

6. Write a letter from the point of view of a Confederate or Union soldier **describing** his experiences to his family. Use an additional sheet of paper if needed.

_____

_____

_____

_____

_____

7. **Understand the Quest Connections** Why would soldiers like songs for marching?

_____

_____

_____

The Emancipation Proclamation

President Lincoln reading the Emancipation Proclamation to his Cabinet.

When the Civil War began, President Lincoln was careful to make the war about preserving the Union. He did not support slavery and would have liked to abolish it but Lincoln feared that by ending slavery, he would lose support for the war.

As African Americans joined the Union Army, Lincoln decided to take action. He told a member of his cabinet, that "emancipation had become a military necessity.... The Administration must set an example."

President Lincoln issued the Emancipation Proclamation on January 1, 1863. It did not free all enslaved African Americans. It freed enslaved African Americans in the areas controlled by the Confederacy and anyone who escaped to a free state. The war was now about freeing enslaved African Americans.

Vocabulary Support

The Confederate states rebelling against the United States

will not stop or interfere

thenceforward, *adv.*, going forward from that time or place

thereof, *adv.*, of the thing that is said or mentioned

"...all persons held as slaves within any State or designated part of a State, the people whereof shall then be in rebellion against the United States, shall be then, thenceforward, and forever free; and the Executive Government of the United States, including the military and naval authority thereof, will recognize and maintain the freedom of such persons, and will do no act or acts to repress such persons, or any of them, in any efforts they may make for their actual freedom."

—Emancipation Proclamation

Close Reading

1. **Identify** and circle the organizations or groups that will not interfere with the freedom of enslaved African Americans and their efforts to gain freedom.
2. **Explain** what the Emancipation Proclamation states about the people who are enslaved African Americans and what it means in relationship to the Fugitive Slave Act. In your own words, explain how you think enslaved African Americans would feel when they heard this.

_____

_____

_____

_____

_____

_____

_____

Wrap It Up

Describe how the Emancipation Proclamation is different from other compromises and laws that had been created up to this point. What does it say about a different belief in the Union?

_____

_____

_____

_____

_____

_____

INTERACTIVITY

Participate in a class discussion to preview the content of this lesson.

Vocabulary

siege
total war
assassinate

Academic Vocabulary

style
strategy

Unlock
The **BIG**
Question

I will know the people, battles, and events that led to the end of the Civil War.

JumpStart Activity

In a small group, list several actions you can take to help restore peace between two friends who have been arguing.

People were eager to see the Civil War end, and both sides became more aggressive. In July 1863, for the first time, Lee led his forces north of the Mason-Dixon line. This line had come to represent the division between free and slave states. The Confederates marched toward Gettysburg, Pennsylvania.

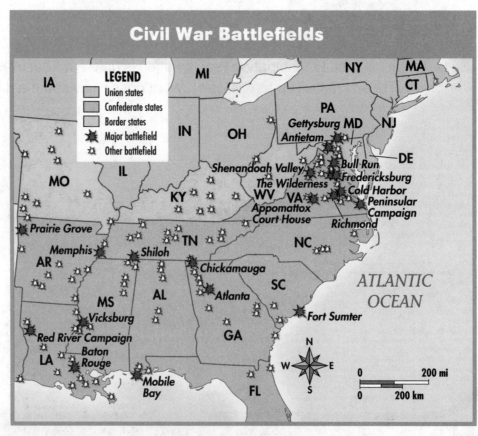

Civil War Battlefields

LEGEND
- Union states
- Confederate states
- Border states
- Major battlefield
- Other battlefield

IA
MI
NY
MA
CT
IN
OH
PA
Gettysburg MD
NJ
Antietam
DE
Shenandoah Valley
Bull Run
Fredericksburg
MO
IL
The Wilderness
Cold Harbor
KY
WV
VA
Peninsular
Appomattox
Campaign
Court House
Richmond
Prairie Grove
TN
NC
Memphis
Shiloh
Chickamauga
AR
ATLANTIC
MS
AL
Atlanta
SC
OCEAN
Vicksburg
Fort Sumter
Red River Campaign
GA
Baton
Rouge
LA
Mobile
FL
Bay

0   200 mi

0   200 km

Union Victory at Gettysburg

INTERACTIVITY

Explore the key ideas of this lesson.

The Battle of Gettysburg was one of the most important battles of the war. It lasted three brutal days and was a turning point in the war.

General George Meade led the Union troops. On July 1, 1863, after a successful Confederate attack, Union soldiers retreated. However, the weary Confederates were unable to follow and gain the victory.

On July 2, fresh Union troops arrived. The Confederates attacked again, but this time the Union troops held their ground. The fighting was fierce.

On July 3, the Confederate forces fired more than 150 cannons. Northern cannons roared back. Commanded by General George Pickett, thousands of Confederate troops attacked. But "Pickett's Charge," as it was called, was a disaster. By the time it ended, more than 5,000 Confederate soldiers lay dead or wounded. The Union had won.

The Battle of Gettysburg was a key victory for the Union, but it came at a steep cost. More than 23,000 Union soldiers and 28,000 Confederate soldiers were dead or wounded.

Union Victory at Vicksburg

The Confederates had turned back all previous Union attacks at Vicksburg, Mississippi. But controlling Vicksburg meant controlling the Mississippi River, so the Union wanted to take Vicksburg.

Union general Ulysses S. Grant attacked Vicksburg again and again, from the east and then, crossing the river, from the south. But direct attack continued to fail. So Grant laid siege.

A **siege** is a military blockade designed to make a city surrender. The siege lasted 48 days. People in Vicksburg dug caves into the hillside to escape fire from Union cannons. Confederate soldiers and civilians faced starvation. Vicksburg surrendered on July 4, 1863. The tide had finally turned in favor of the Union.

President Lincoln visits Union Army soldiers and officers in Antietam, Maryland battlefield, October 1862.

Grant and Lee		
	Ulysses S. Grant	**Robert E. Lee**
Birthplace	Ohio	Virginia
Education	U.S. Military Academy at West Point	U.S. Military Academy at West Point
Prior military service	Mexican-American War	Mexican-American War
Military rank	General	General
Side	North	South

Ulysses S. Grant

Robert E. Lee

Grant Versus Lee

President Lincoln once said of Ulysses S. Grant, "I can't spare this man. He fights." In March of 1864, Lincoln promoted Grant and gave him control over the entire Union army. Grant was famous for his aggressive fighting **style** and for being relentless.

Robert E. Lee, the chief commander of the Confederate troops, faced a terrible decision when the Civil War broke out. Lee loved the United States and was an officer in the U.S. Army. However, he felt tied to Virginia. He resigned from the Union army and sided with the South.

As a general, Lee was famous for his brilliant military tactics. He was skilled, smart, and daring on the battlefield. He was also known as a gentleman. He was a soldier with refined manners. He used **strategy** rather than brute force. He inspired his troops, because they respected him so much.

Grant and Lee were alike in many ways. Both had received their military training at the U.S. Military Academy at West Point. Both had served in the Mexican-American War. Both were brilliant military leaders.

Academic Vocabulary

style • *n.*, a distinctive, particular, or characteristic of acting or way of moving

strategy • *n.*, a thought-out plan to accomplish a goal over a long time

1. ☑ **Reading Check** **Turn** and **talk** with a partner about how Lee and Grant's military approaches were similar and different.

Sherman in Georgia

Union general William Tecumseh Sherman played a major role in ending the war. Sherman's idea was that war should be as horrible as possible, so the enemy would stop fighting. He didn't just attack military targets; he worked to destroy the South economically, so it could no longer support an army. Sherman's approach came to be known as **total war**.

Leading 100,000 Union troops, Sherman began his invasion of Georgia in May 1864. He headed first for Atlanta. Confederate troops tried to stop Sherman's advance but were driven back by the huge number of Union soldiers.

Sherman began a siege of the city of Atlanta. By September 2, Sherman's forces controlled the city. They destroyed Atlanta's railroad center to disrupt the South's transportation system.

Sherman ordered everyone to leave and then burned much of the city. Union soldiers also took all the food and supplies they could find. Atlanta could no longer offer help to the Confederate army.

From Atlanta, Sherman headed for Savannah on the coast. With 62,000 soldiers, he cut a path of destruction across Georgia. This campaign came to be called "Sherman's March to the Sea." Union troops destroyed everything that might help the South keep fighting. Sherman gave his soldiers only bread to force them to raid villages for food.

Confederate soldiers continued to follow and fight Sherman's forces. They couldn't win, but they reduced the amount of damage done by the Union forces.

On December 21, 1864, Savannah fell without a fight. Union soldiers had caused $100 million worth of damage in their march across Georgia. They then turned north, marching into South Carolina, causing even more destruction in the state where the war began.

Sherman's army left a path of destruction across Georgia as they marched to the sea.

The Road to Appomattox

Union forces were closing in on Lee's army in Virginia. On April 2, 1865, General Lee sent a message to Jefferson Davis that the Confederates should leave Richmond, Virginia. The next day, Union troops entered the city. The Union had captured the capital of the Confederacy! When President Lincoln arrived to tour Richmond, the city's former enslaved African Americans cheered him.

Exhausted and starving, Lee's army of 55,000 men tried to escape west. Grant's force of about 113,000 soldiers trapped them. Grant met Lee in one last battle near the village of Appomattox Court House, Virginia, and once again defeated the weary Confederates. The end had come. The Civil War was over.

On April 9, 1865, General Grant and General Lee met at a farmhouse at Appomattox to discuss the terms of surrender. Among the many Union officers who witnessed the surrender was Ely S. Parker. A Seneca lawyer and Union officer, he had helped write up the terms of surrender.

2. ☑ **Reading Check**
Identify Generals Lee and Grant in the painting by labeling them.
Turn and talk with a partner about what the posture of each general suggests.

Grant wanted the healing of the nation to start right away. He didn't take Confederate soldiers prisoner. Instead, he allowed Lee's soldiers to go free. In addition, the Union allowed the Southerners to keep their personal weapons and any horses they had. Grant also offered to give Lee's men food from Union supplies. Lee accepted. As Lee returned to his men, the Union soldiers cheered and fired their rifles, to celebrate their victory over the South. Grant silenced them, saying, "The war is over; the rebels are our countrymen again."

The Cost of the Civil War

The Civil War was the most destructive war in our history. The human costs were very high. About 620,000 people died. Families were torn apart, as some members sided with the Union and others with the Confederacy. The governments of both sides spent billions to fight the war. After the Civil War, many people were in mourning. Eventually a national holiday called Memorial Day was created. It honors all of our nation's fallen soldiers.

Other economic costs were shattering as well. Towns, farms, and industries in the South were ruined. Factories in the North that had relied on Southern cotton were in trouble. However, the economy of the South suffered far greater losses, particularly because the slaves on whom the economy depended were now freed.

Children sitting near ruined buildings in Charleston, South Carolina.

In spite of the destruction, Lincoln still hoped for the healing of the nation. After news of the Confederate surrender reached Washington, D.C., Lincoln appeared before a crowd and asked a band to play "Dixie," one of the battle songs of the Confederacy. "I have always thought 'Dixie' one of the best tunes I ever heard," he told the crowd.

President Lincoln delivering the Gettysburg Address.

The Gettysburg Address

In 1863, thousands of Americans had been killed at Gettysburg, so the battlefield was made into a national cemetery to honor them. On November 19, 1863, about 15,000 people gathered for the ceremony to establish the cemetery. At this event, President Lincoln gave what has become one of America's most famous speeches.

Lincoln's speech, now known as the Gettysburg Address, began with the words "Four score and seven years ago our fathers brought forth upon this continent a new nation." (A score is 20.) Lincoln was reminding people that it had been 87 years since the Declaration of Independence. The fight was about preserving the nation and about self-government.

In the address, Lincoln also praised the soldiers who had given their lives to keep the dream of America alive. It reminded Americans that there was still more work to be done, but also why the work was important.

Primary Source

3. ☑ **Reading Check** Underline the words in this excerpt that **describe** democracy.

"We here highly resolve that these dead shall not have died in vain, that this nation under God shall have a new birth of freedom, and that government of the people, by the people, for the people shall not perish from the earth."

—Abraham Lincoln, from the Gettysburg Address

A Terrible Loss for the Nation

Friday evening, April 14, 1865, President Lincoln and his wife, Mary, attended a play at Ford's Theater. During the play, President Lincoln was shot! He died a few hours later, on the morning of April 15.

Lincoln was **assassinated**, or murdered for political reasons, by John Wilkes Booth, a 26-year-old actor who supported the Confederacy. Booth escaped from the theater. But federal troops found him later in a Virginia barn. He refused to surrender. The soldiers shot and killed him. Booth had not worked alone, and Lincoln was not the only target. The whole group of plotters was captured, tried, and hanged.

A funeral train took Lincoln's body to his hometown of Springfield, Illinois, to be buried. It was a tragic loss for the nation. But, before he died, Lincoln had achieved his goal. He had saved the Union.

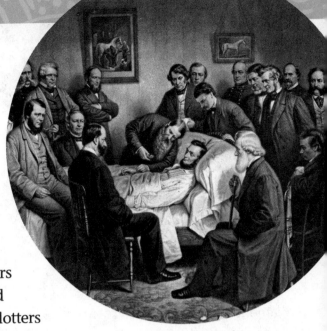

Doctors surround President Lincoln after he is shot.

☑ Lesson 4 Check

INTERACTIVITY

Check your understanding of the key ideas of this lesson.

4. **Main Idea and Details** List three supporting details for the Main Idea: The war turned in the Union's favor. Then explain to a partner how the details support the main idea.

_____

_____

5. **Explain** why Union leaders like General Grant and President Lincoln did not want to punish the South.

_____

_____

_____

6. List at least three major actions that Lincoln is remembered for.

_____

_____

Lesson 5 Reconstruction

INTERACTIVITY

Participate in a class discussion to preview the content of this lesson.

Vocabulary

Reconstruction
amendment
impeachment
carpetbaggers
segregation
black codes
sharecropping

Academic Vocabulary

enforce
create

Unlock The BIG Question

I will know the different plans for Reconstruction and the effects of new amendments to the Constitution.

JumpStart Activity

In a group of two to three classmates, act out how people on different sides of an argument might react when they meet on the street or playground. Can one person help to make you friends again?

After President Lincoln's assassination, Vice President Andrew Johnson became president. Johnson wanted to carry out Lincoln's plan for **Reconstruction**, the rebuilding and healing of the country. However, Johnson lacked Lincoln's skill at dealing with people. He and Congress fought fiercely.

Like much of the South, Richmond, Virginia, had been destroyed during the Civil War.

Lincoln's plan was to pardon Southerners who swore loyalty to the United States and promised to obey the country's laws. They would also welcome states back into the Union if they outlawed slavery and asked to be let back in. Congress thought these plans were too gentle and felt that the South should be punished for having seceded. However, Congress did want to help newly freed African Americans, called freedmen.

INTERACTIVITY

Explore the key ideas of this lesson.

Congress and Reconstruction

The Republicans who controlled Congress did not trust Johnson. He was a Southerner and had been a Democrat before becoming Lincoln's vice president. Members of Congress began developing a new plan of Reconstruction. They passed the Civil Rights Act of 1866 to grant freedmen full legal equality. Congress then passed several Reconstruction Acts between 1867 and 1868.

The Acts divided the former Confederate states into military districts. The president sent federal troops to the South to keep order and **enforce** emancipation of enslaved African Americans. The Acts required Southern states to write new state constitutions giving African American men the right to vote. The Acts prevented former Confederate leaders from voting or holding elected office. Congress also passed three new amendments to the Constitution. An **amendment** is a change or addition. You will read about these amendments later in this lesson.

Academic Vocabulary

enforce • *v.*, to make people obey a law or rule

Johnson argued that the Reconstruction Acts were against the law because they had been passed without the Southern states being represented in Congress. He said passing laws with half the country unrepresented was unconstitutional. Johnson used his veto power to try to stop Congress. However, Congress was able to override Johnson's vetoes.

Angry about Johnson's attempts to block their laws, the Republicans in Congress tried to impeach Johnson. **Impeachment** is the bringing of charges of wrongdoing against an elected official by the House of Representatives. If an impeached president is found guilty in a Senate trial, he can be removed from office. In May 1868, the Senate found Johnson not guilty. However, Johnson's ability to lead the nation had been seriously weakened.

Academic Vocabulary

create • *v.*, to design or invent something

1. ☑ **Reading Check**
Turn and talk with a partner. **Explain** why education is important for freedom.

Reconstruction had many successes. The Freedmen's Bureau had been **created** by President Lincoln to help freed slaves and refugees of the war. The Freedmen's Bureau built schools and hospitals. It hired African American and white teachers from the South and North. New leaders raised taxes to help rebuild roads and railroads and to establish a free education system. Many industries were expanded to provide more jobs.

For the first time, African Americans became elected officials. In Mississippi, two African Americans were elected to the U.S. Senate. In 1870, Hiram R. Revels won the Senate seat that Jefferson Davis once held. In 1874, Blanche K. Bruce was also elected to the Senate. Twenty other African Americans were elected to the House of Representatives.

Some Southerners resented the new state governments that had been forced on them. Others disliked the Northerners who moved South to start businesses. Because they often carried their possessions in cloth suitcases called carpetbags, these newcomers were called "**carpetbaggers**." Some carpetbaggers came to help, but many came to take advantage of the South's ruined condition. Southerners who supported Reconstruction were given the insulting nickname "scalawags."

People also disliked the new taxes. Many Southerners had a hard time paying these taxes because they were trying to rebuild their farms and homes.

Reconstruction also had some failures and segregation was one of these. **Segregation** is the separation of people, usually by race. Schools, hospitals, theaters, railroad cars, even whole towns were segregated.

Right after the war, some Southern states passed **black codes**. These laws denied African American men the right to vote. It kept them from owning guns or taking certain types of jobs. The Civil Rights Act was designed to protect African Americans from these codes.

Schools were opened to teach young African Americans to read and write.

New Amendments

Ending slavery was one of the first steps in Reconstruction—and the most important. The Emancipation Proclamation had not ended all slavery. The Republicans in Congress now wanted slavery to be illegal everywhere in the United States.

Congress passed the Thirteenth Amendment on January 31, 1865. It abolished slavery. The Fourteenth Amendment was approved in July 1868. It guaranteed equality under the law for all citizens—and it gave Congress the power to enforce this guarantee. It also ruled that important Confederate leaders could not be elected to political office.

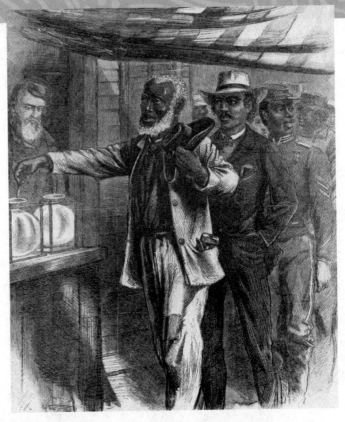

African American men voting

The Fifteenth Amendment, passed by Congress in 1869 and approved by the states in February 1870, gave all male citizens the right to vote without regard to race. It was a big step forward for formerly enslaved African Americans.

Before being allowed back into the Union, former Confederate states had to accept all three amendments. Eventually, all did. By July 15, 1870, all the former Confederate states had been allowed back into the Union.

2. 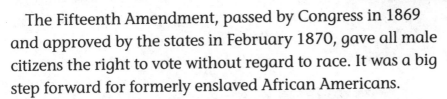 **Reading Check** **Summarize** Use your own words to **describe** how each of these amendments extended rights for U.S. citizens.

13th Amendment	14th Amendment	15th Amendment
ended slavery		

After Reconstruction

After Reconstruction, the South remained poor. Rebuilding was slow. Poverty was widespread. African Americans lost much of the political power they had gained.

Sharecroppers picking cotton after the Civil War.

Many African Americans and poor whites in the South became trapped in a system called sharecropping. **Sharecropping** is a system in which someone who owns land lets someone else "rent" the land to farm it. The renter, or tenant farmer, pays rent with a share of the crops he or she raises. The renter then uses the rest of the crops to feed the family or sell for income.

Sharecropping often kept people in debt. Landowners would charge high interest on money tenant farmers borrowed for seeds and tools. It was often impossible to pay off the debt.

3. ☑ **Reading Check** **Analyze** the picture. What can you infer about the life of a sharecropper?

_____

_____

Negative Reaction

During Reconstruction, some white Southerners objected to rights for African Americans. A few formed a group called the Ku Klux Klan. This group used terror to restore white control. They burned African American schools and homes. They attacked African Americans who tried to vote. They also lynched, or killed, many African Americans. Lynching is when someone is put to death by a mob who has no legal authority.

In 1877, the federal government withdrew the last federal troops from the South. White Southern Democrats regained power in state governments. They passed new laws known as Jim Crow laws that reinforced segregation. Other laws kept African Americans from voting. Some states charged a poll tax, or payment, to vote.

Some states required African Americans to take a reading test before they could vote. Under slavery, many had not been allowed to learn to read or write, and so they failed the test.

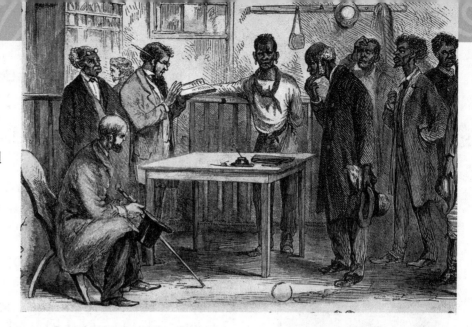

A "grandfather clause" was added to some state constitutions. It said that men could vote only if their father or grandfather had voted before 1867. This "grandfather clause" kept most African Americans from voting, because they had not gained the right to vote until 1870. It would be a long time before most African Americans enjoyed the civil rights they should have as citizens.

In some areas, tests or other means were created to prevent African Americans from voting.

 **Lesson 5 Check**

INTERACTIVITY

Check your understanding of the key ideas of this lesson.

4. **Explain** how the struggles of freed African Americans changed after the end of the Civil War and how the amendments that were added to the Constitution helped them.

_____

_____

_____

_____

5. As a result of the war, you are now freed from slavery. In a letter to a friend, **describe** how things have changed for you because of the war.

_____

_____

6. **Identify** three effects the Civil War had on the Constitution.

_____

_____

Quality:
Courage

Harriet Tubman (about 1820–1913)
Fighting for Freedom

Around 1820, Harriet Tubman (born Araminta Ross) was born into slavery in Maryland. Harriet served others and endured harsh living conditions and frequent physical beatings. In her early teens, Harriet courageously stood up for a fieldworker and was forcefully struck on the head; she never fully recovered from this injury.

In 1844 Harriet married John Tubman, a free African American. Fearing she would be sold away, Tubman began her escape to Canada in 1849. She changed her name to Harriet so that her identity would be kept a secret. On her way, she settled in Pennsylvania and met members of the Philadelphia Anti-Slavery Society. She learned all about the Underground Railroad.

After her escape, Tubman worked hard to save money so she could lead rescue missions. In 1851 she returned to Maryland. Over the next six years Tubman put her life at risk and successfully conducted about 300 African Americans to freedom in the North including members of her family. John Brown, a leading abolitionist, described Tubman as, "one of the bravest persons on this continent."

During the Civil War, Tubman served the Union as a scout, a nurse, and even a spy. She was unfairly paid for her wartime service and had to support herself by selling homemade baked goods. After the war, Tubman made a living giving antislavery speeches.

Find Out More

1. Why do you think Harriet Tubman risked her life and freedom to help others?

_____

_____

_____

2. Harriet Tubman was a courageous woman who took great risks to bring people to freedom. Work with a partner to find out about other African Americans who helped the enslaved, such as Harriet Jacobs, Nat Turner, Denmark Vesey, and Gabriel Prosser.

Visual Review

Use these graphics to review some of the key terms and ideas from this chapter.

Union and Confederate Forces and Casualties

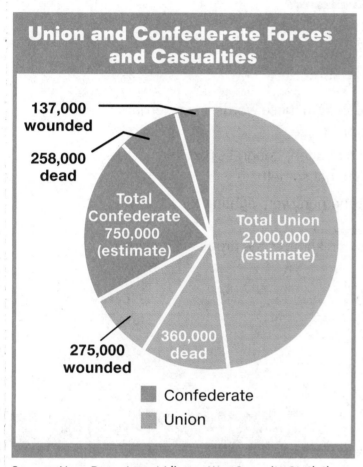

137,000 wounded

258,000 dead

Total Confederate 750,000 (estimate)

Total Union 2,000,000 (estimate)

275,000 wounded

360,000 dead

■ Confederate
■ Union

Source: Navy Department Library War Casualty Statistics

States with 15 or More Civil War Battles

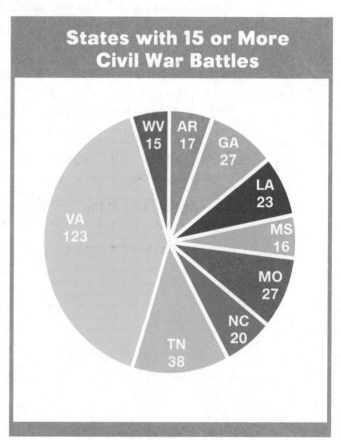

WV 15

AR 17

GA 27

LA 23

MS 16

MO 27

NC 20

TN 38

VA 123

Source: National Park Service

Laws and Amendments

1820 – Missouri Compromise	1866 – Civil Rights Act
1850 – Compromise of 1850	1867 – First Reconstruction Act
1854 – Kansas–Nebraska Act	1868 – Fourteenth Amendment
1863 – Emancipation Proclamation	1870 – Fifteenth Amendment
1865 – Thirteenth Amendment	

☑ **Assessment**

🎮 **GAMES**

Play the vocabulary game.

Vocabulary and Key Ideas

1. What is **segregation**?

_____

2. Complete the sentences. Choose from these words: siege, enlist, amendment, states' rights, compromise.

In an attempt to keep the country united, Congress had to _____ and each side gave something to get something.

At the start of the Civil War Southerners were fighting for _____.

3. **Explain** what sharecropping is and some of the problems it caused.

_____

_____

_____

_____

4. **Analyzing a Map** Look at the map. Why did the Confederate government want to capture Fort Sumter? Why did the Union government want to keep it?

_____

_____

_____

_____

_____

_____

_____

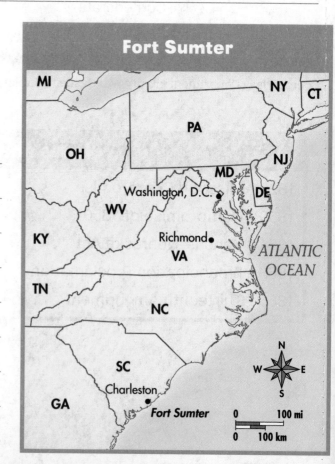

Fort Sumter

Critical Thinking and Writing

5. **Analyze** the economic and geographic differences between the North and the South that helped lead to the feelings of sectionalism.

_____

_____

_____

_____

_____

_____

_____

6. **Interpret** Fill in the circle next to the best answer. Which of the following was part of the Compromise of 1850?

Ⓐ Maine joined the Union as a free state.

Ⓑ The Fugitive Slave Law became a law.

Ⓒ African American men were allowed to vote.

Ⓓ The U.S. Supreme Court declared that African Americans were not citizens.

7. **Analyze** What did the Emancipation Proclamation accomplish? How was it limited?

_____

_____

_____

_____

8. **Revisit the Big Question** Why might many people say the Civil War was worth fighting?

_____

_____

_____

_____

9. **Writing Workshop: Write an Opinion** Imagine you heard President Lincoln deliver the Gettysburg Address. On a separate paper, write a letter to a friend and explain how you felt about the speech and how the audience reacted. Include details from the text to support your opinion.

Analyze Primary Sources

"Times are very hard here every thing is scarce and high ... corn is selling for 10 dollars, bacon 45 cents per pound .... We cannot get a yard of calico for less than one dollar."

—In a letter dated August 23, 1862,
a Virginia woman complaining to her sister about hard times and high prices

10. This letter was written by a woman living in Virginia during the Civil War. During the war the armies often took food from farmers as they passed by. How does this letter help you to understand the hardships that people living in the Southern states experienced?

_____

_____

_____

_____

Make Decisions

11. You are a doctor during the Civil War and the Union army needs doctors. You want to support your country and the soldiers. However, you have patients in your town who need a doctor also. What can you consider as you try to make a good decision?

_____

_____

_____

_____

_____

_____

Quest Findings

Sing Along!

You have read the lessons in this chapter and now you are ready to plan and write your song. Remember that the goals of the song are to offer comfort, to entertain, or to inspire others.

 INTERACTIVITY

Learn more about Civil War music with an online activity.

1 Prepare to Write

Organize the information you have learned about the Civil War. Decide what type of song you want to write. Should it be a marching song, a ballad, or a funny song? Choose the type you want to write.

3 Write Your Song

Put the words and music together to create your song. Share your song with a partner or another group. Listen to what others say. Is your message getting through?

2 Write a Draft

Use your notes and the music you have collected from your Quest Connections to write a draft. Some ideas to consider while you are writing include:

- What is the song about?
- How do you want your audience to feel when they listen to it?
- Is there a chorus in your song? How often should it be used?

4 Revise

Make changes to the words and music to improve your song. Did other classmates use different musical styles? How does each style make you feel?

The Declaration of Independence

In Congress, July 4, 1776
The Unanimous Declaration of the Thirteen
United States of America

The first part of the Declaration of Independence is called the Preamble. A preamble is an introduction, or the part that comes before the main message. The Preamble states why the Declaration was written.

When in the Course of human events it becomes necessary for one people to dissolve the political bands which have connected them with another, and to assume among the powers of the earth, the separate and equal station to which the Laws of nature and of nature's God entitle them, a decent respect to the opinions of mankind requires that they should declare the causes which impel them to the separation.

The second paragraph lists the basic rights that all people should have. The founders called these **unalienable** rights, meaning that these rights cannot be taken or given away. If a government cannot protect these rights, the people must change the government or create a new one.

We hold these truths to be self-evident, that all men are created equal, that they are endowed by their Creator with certain unalienable Rights, that among these are Life, Liberty and the Pursuit of Happiness. That to secure these rights, Governments are instituted among Men, deriving their just powers from the consent of the governed; That whenever any Form of Government becomes destructive of these ends it is the Right of the People to alter or to abolish it, and to institute new Government, laying its foundation on such principles and organizing its powers in such form, as to them shall seem most likely to effect their Safety and Happiness. Prudence, indeed, will dictate that Governments long established should not be changed for light and transient causes; and accordingly all experience hath shown, that mankind are more disposed to suffer, while evils are sufferable, than to right themselves by abolishing the forms to which they are accustomed. But when a long train of abuses and usurpations, pursuing invariably the same Object evinces a design to reduce them under absolute Despotism, it is their right, it is their duty, to throw off such Government, and to provide new Guards for their future security.

1. According to the Declaration, what are three "unalienable rights"? Circle these words in the text.

The third paragraph introduces the List of Grievances. Each part of this list begins with the words, "He has…." These words refer to King George III's actions in the colonies. To prove that the king had abused his power over the colonies, this list of 27 complaints described how the British government and the king had treated the colonists.

Such has been the patient sufferance of these Colonies; and such is now the necessity which constrains them to alter their former Systems of Government. The history of the present King of Great Britain is a history of repeated injuries and usurpations, all having in direct object the establishment of an absolute Tyranny over these States. To prove this, let Facts be submitted to a candid world.

He has refused his Assent to Laws, the most wholesome and necessary for the public good.

He has forbidden his Governors to pass Laws of immediate and pressing importance, unless suspended in their operation till his

Assent should be obtained; and when so suspended, he has utterly neglected to attend to them.

He has refused to pass other Laws for the accommodation of large districts of people, unless those people would relinquish the right of Representation in the Legislature, a right inestimable to them and formidable to tyrants only.

He has called together legislative bodies at places unusual, uncomfortable, and distant from the depository of their Public Records, for the sole purpose of fatiguing them into compliance with his measures.

He has dissolved Representative Houses repeatedly, for opposing with manly firmness his invasions on the rights of the people.

He has refused for a long time, after such dissolutions, to cause others to be elected; whereby the Legislative powers, incapable of Annihilation, have returned to the People at large for their exercise; the State remaining in the mean time exposed to all the dangers of invasions from without, and convulsions within.

He has endeavored to prevent the population of these States; for that purpose obstructing the Laws for Naturalization of Foreigners; refusing to pass others to encourage their migration hither, and raising the conditions of new Appropriations of Lands.

He has obstructed the Administration of Justice, by refusing his Assent to Laws for establishing Judiciary powers.

He has made Judges dependent on his Will alone for the tenure of their offices, and the amount and payment of their salaries.

He has erected a multitude of New Offices, and sent hither swarms of Officers to harass our people and eat out their substance.

He has kept among us in time of peace, Standing Armies, without the Consent of our legislatures.

He has affected to render the Military independent of, and superior to, the Civil Power.

He has combined with others to subject us to a jurisdiction foreign to our constitutions, and unacknowledged by our laws; giving his Assent to their Acts of pretended Legislation:

For quartering large bodies of armed troops among us;

For protecting them, by a mock Trial, from punishment for any Murders which they should commit on the Inhabitants of these States;

In the List of Grievances, the colonists complain that they have no say in choosing the laws that govern them. They say that King George III is not concerned about their safety and happiness. They list the times when the king denied them the right to representation. The colonists also state that the king has interfered with judges, with the court system, and with foreigners who want to become citizens.

2. There are many words in the Declaration that may be unfamiliar to you. Circle three words you do not know. Look the words up in the dictionary. Write one word and its meaning on the lines below.

_____

_____

_____

_____

_____

_____

_____

This page continues the colonists' long List of Grievances.

3. In your own words, briefly sum up three grievances.

_____

_____

_____

4. Match each word from the Declaration with its meaning. Use a dictionary if you need help with a word.

abolishing	tried to achieve
plundered	changing
suspending	doing away with
altering	stopping for a time
endeavored	robbed

Statement of Independence
After listing their many grievances, the signers begin their statement of independence. Because the king has refused to correct the problems, he is an unfair ruler. Therefore, he is not fit to rule the free people of America.

For cutting off our Trade with all parts of the world;

For imposing Taxes on us without our Consent;

For depriving us, in many cases, of the benefits of Trial by Jury;

For transporting us beyond Seas to be tried for pretended offenses;

For abolishing the free System of English Laws in a neighboring Province, establishing therein an Arbitrary government, and enlarging its Boundaries so as to render it at once an example and fit instrument for introducing the same absolute rule into these Colonies;

For taking away our Charters, abolishing our most valuable Laws, and altering fundamentally the Forms of our Governments;

For suspending our own Legislatures, and declaring themselves invested with Power to legislate for us in all cases whatsoever.

He has abdicated Government here, by declaring us out of his Protection, and waging War against us.

He has plundered our seas, ravaged our Coasts, burned our towns, and destroyed the lives of our people.

He is at this time transporting large Armies of foreign mercenaries to complete the works of death, desolation and tyranny, already begun with circumstances of Cruelty and perfidy scarcely paralleled in the most barbarous ages, and totally unworthy the Head of a civilized nation.

He has constrained our fellow Citizens taken Captive on the high Seas to bear Arms against their Country, to become the executioners of their friends and Brethren, or to fall themselves by their Hands.

He has excited domestic insurrections amongst us, and has endeavored to bring on the inhabitants of our frontiers the merciless Indian Savages whose known rule of warfare, is an undistinguished destruction of all ages, sexes, and conditions.

In every stage of these Oppressions We have Petitioned for Redress in the most humble terms. Our repeated Petitions have been answered only by repeated injury. A Prince, whose character is thus marked by every act which may define a Tyrant, is unfit to be the ruler of a free People.

Nor have We been wanting in attentions to our British brethren. We have warned them from time to time of attempts by their legislature to extend an unwarrantable jurisdiction over us. We have reminded them of the circumstances of our emigration and settlement here. We have appealed to their native justice and magnanimity, and we have conjured them by the ties of our common kindred to disavow these usurpations, which, would inevitably interrupt our connections and correspondence. They too have been deaf to the voice of justice and of consanguinity. We must, therefore, acquiesce in the necessity, which denounces our Separation, and hold them, as we hold the rest of mankind, Enemies in War, in Peace Friends.

We, therefore, the Representatives of the United States of America, in General Congress, Assembled, appealing to the Supreme Judge of the world for the rectitude of our intentions, do, in the Name, and by the Authority of the good People of these Colonies, solemnly publish and declare, That these United Colonies are, and of right ought to be Free and Independent States; that they are Absolved from all Allegiance to the British Crown, and that all political connection between them and the State of Great Britain, is and ought to be totally dissolved, and that as Free and Independent States, they have full Power to levy War, conclude Peace, contract Alliances, establish Commerce, and to do all other Acts and Things which Independent States may of right do. And for the support of this Declaration, with a firm reliance on the protection of Divine Providence, we mutually pledge to each other our Lives, our Fortunes, and our sacred Honor.

New Hampshire:
Josiah Bartlett
William Whipple
Matthew Thornton

Massachusetts Bay:
John Hancock
Samuel Adams
John Adams
Robert Treat Paine
Elbridge Gerry

Rhode Island:
Stephan Hopkins
William Ellery

Connecticut:
Roger Sherman
Samuel Huntington
William Williams
Oliver Wolcott

New York:
William Floyd
Philip Livingston
Francis Lewis
Lewis Morris

New Jersey:
Richard Stockton
John Witherspoon
Francis Hopkinson
John Hart
Abraham Clark

Delaware:
Caesar Rodney
George Read
Thomas M'Kean

Maryland:
Samuel Chase
William Paca
Thomas Stone
Charles Carroll of
  Carrollton

Virginia:
George Wythe
Richard Henry Lee
Thomas Jefferson
Benjamin Harrison
Thomas Nelson, Jr.
Francis Lightfoot Lee
Carter Braxton

Pennsylvania:
Robert Morris
Benjamin Rush
Benjamin Franklin
John Morton
George Clymer
James Smith
George Taylor
James Wilson
George Ross

North Carolina:
William Hooper
Joseph Hewes
John Penn

South Carolina:
Edward Rutledge
Thomas Heyward, Jr.
Thomas Lynch, Jr.
Arthur Middleton

Georgia:
Button Gwinnett
Lyman Hall
George Walton

In this paragraph, the signers point out that they have asked the British people for help many times. The colonists hoped the British would listen to them because they have so much in common. The British people, however, paid no attention to their demand for justice. This is another reason for why the colonies must break away from Great Britain.

In the last paragraph, the members of the Continental Congress declare that the thirteen colonies are no longer colonies. They are now a free nation with no ties to Great Britain. The United States now has all the powers of other independent countries.

5. List three powers that the signers claim the new nation now has.

_____

_____

_____

_____

_____

6. The signers promised to support the Declaration of Independence and each other with their lives, their fortunes, and their honor. On a separate sheet of paper, tell what you think this means. Then explain why it was a brave thing to do.

United States Constitution

PREAMBLE

This **Preamble** gives the reasons for writing and having a Constitution. The Constitution will form a stronger and more united nation. It will lead to peace, justice, and liberty and will defend American citizens. Finally, it will improve the lives of people.

We the People of the United States, in Order to form a more perfect Union, establish Justice, insure domestic Tranquility, provide for the common defense, promote the general Welfare, and secure the Blessings of Liberty to ourselves and our Posterity, do ordain and establish this Constitution for the United States of America.

ARTICLE I

Section 1. Congress

The legislative branch of government makes the country's laws. Called the Congress, it has two parts, or houses: the House of Representatives and the Senate.

Section 1.

All legislative Powers herein granted shall be vested in a Congress of the United States, which shall consist of a Senate and House of Representatives.

Section 2. The House of Representatives

Members of the House of Representatives are elected every two years. Representatives must be 25 years old and United States citizens. They must also live in the states that elect them.

The number of Representatives for each state is based on the population, or number of people who live there.

Section 2.

1. The House of Representatives shall be composed of Members chosen every second Year by the People of the several States, and the Electors in each State shall have the Qualifications requisite for Electors of the most numerous Branch of the State Legislature.
2. No Person shall be a Representative who shall not have attained to the age of twenty-five Years, and been seven Years a Citizen of the United States, and who shall not, when elected, be an Inhabitant of that State in which he shall be chosen.
3. Representatives and direct Taxes shall be apportioned among the several States which may be included within this Union, according to their respective Numbers, which shall be determined by adding to the whole Number of free Persons, including those bound to Service for a Term of Years and excluding Indians not taxed, three fifths of all other Persons. The actual Enumeration shall be made within three Years after the first Meeting of the Congress of the United States, and within every subsequent Term of ten Years, in such Manner as they shall by Law direct. The Number of Representatives shall not exceed one for every thirty Thousand, but each State shall have at Least one Representative; and, until such enumeration shall be made, the State of New Hampshire shall be entitled to choose three, Massachusetts eight, Rhode Island and Providence Plantations one, Connecticut five, New York six, New Jersey four, Pennsylvania eight, Delaware one, Maryland six, Virginia ten, North Carolina five, South Carolina five, and Georgia three.

1. Why do some states have more Representatives in Congress than other states?

_____

_____

_____

_____

Over the years, the Constitution has been altered, or changed. These altered parts are shown here in gray type.

4. When vacancies happen in the Representation from any State, the Executive Authority thereof shall issue Writs of Election to fill such Vacancies.

5. The House of Representatives shall choose their Speaker and other Officers; and shall have the sole Power of Impeachment.

Section 3.

1. The Senate of the United States shall be composed of two Senators from each State chosen by the Legislature thereof for six Years; and each Senator shall have one Vote.

2. Immediately after they shall be assembled in Consequences of the first Election, they shall be divided, as equally as may be, into three Classes. The Seats of the Senators of the first Class shall be vacated at the Expiration of the second Year; of the second Class, at the Expiration of the fourth Year; and of the third Class, at the Expiration of the sixth Year; so that one-third may be chosen every second Year; and if Vacancies happen by Resignation, or otherwise, during the Recess of the Legislature of any State, the Executive thereof may make temporary Appointments until the next Meeting of the Legislature, which shall then fill such Vacancies.

3. No Person shall be a Senator who shall not have attained to the Age of thirty Years, and been nine Years a Citizen of the United States, and who shall not, when elected, be an Inhabitant of that State for which he shall be chosen.

4. The Vice President of the United States shall be President of the Senate but shall have no Vote, unless they be equally divided.

5. The Senate shall choose their other Officers, and also a President pro tempore, in the Absence of the Vice President, or when he shall exercise the Office of President of the United States.

6. The Senate shall have the sole Power to try all Impeachments. When sitting for that Purpose, they shall be on Oath or Affirmation. When the President of the United States is tried, the Chief Justice shall preside: And no Person shall be convicted without the Concurrence of two thirds of the Members present.

7. Judgment in Cases of Impeachment shall not extend further than to removal from Office, and disqualification to hold and enjoy any Office of honor, Trust, or Profit under the United States: but the Party convicted shall nevertheless be liable and subject to Indictment, Trial, Judgment and Punishment, according to Law.

A state governor calls a special election to fill an empty seat in the House of Representatives.

Members of the House of Representatives choose their own leaders. They also have the power to impeach, or accuse, government officials of crimes.

Section 3. Senate

Each state has two Senators. A Senator serves a six-year term.

At first, each state legislature elected its two Senators. The Seventeenth Amendment changed that. Today, the voters of each state elect their Senators.

Senators must be 30 years old and United States citizens. They must also live in the states they represent.

2. How is the length of a Senator's term different from a Representative's term?

_____

_____

The Vice President is the officer in charge of the Senate but only votes to break a tie. When the Vice President is absent, a temporary leader (President Pro Tempore) leads the Senate.

The Senate holds impeachment trials. When the President is impeached, the Chief Justice of the Supreme Court is the judge. A two-thirds vote is needed to convict. Once convicted, an official can be removed from office. Other courts of law can impose other punishments.

Section 4. Elections and Meetings of Congress

The state legislatures determine the times, places, and method of holding elections for senators and representatives.

Section 5. Rules for Congress

The Senate and House of Representatives judge the fairness of the elections and the qualifications of its own members. At least half of the members must be present to do business. Each house may determine the rules of its proceedings and punish its member for disorderly behavior. Each house of Congress shall keep a record of its proceedings and from time to time publish the record.

3. Why is it important for Congress to publish a record of what they do?

_____

_____

_____

_____

Section 6. Rights and Restrictions of Members of Congress

The Senators and Representatives shall receive payment for their services to be paid out of the Treasury of the United States. Members of Congress cannot be arrested during their attendance at the session of Congress, except for a very serious crime, and they cannot be arrested for anything they say in Congress. No person can have a government job while serving as a member of Congress.

Section 4.

1. The Times, Places and Manner of holding Elections for Senators and Representatives, shall be prescribed in each State by the Legislature thereof; but the Congress may at any time by law make or alter such Regulations, except as to the Places of choosing Senators.
2. The Congress shall assemble at least once in every Year, and such Meeting shall be on the first Monday in December, unless they shall by Law appoint a different Day.

Section 5.

1. Each House shall be the Judge of the Elections, Returns and Qualifications of its own Members, and a Majority of each shall constitute a Quorum to do Business; but a smaller Number may adjourn from day to day, and may be authorized to compel the Attendance of absent Members, in such Manner, and under such Penalties, as each House may provide.
2. Each House may determine the Rules of its Proceedings, punish its Members for disorderly Behavior, and, with the Concurrence of two thirds, expel a Member.
3. Each House shall keep a Journal of its Proceedings, and from time to time publish the same, excepting such Parts as may in their Judgment require Secrecy; and the Yeas and Nays of the Members of either House on any question shall, at the Desire of one fifth of those Present, be entered on the Journal.
4. Neither House, during the Session of Congress, shall, without the Consent of the other, adjourn for more than three days, nor to any other Place than that in which the two Houses shall be sitting.

Section 6.

1. The Senators and Representatives shall receive a Compensation for their Services, to be ascertained by Law, and paid out of the Treasury of the United States. They shall in all Cases, except Treason, Felony, and Breach of the Peace, be privileged from Arrest during their Attendance at the Session of their respective Houses, and in going to and returning from the same; and for any Speech or Debate in either House, they shall not be questioned in any other Place.
2. No Senator or Representative shall, during the Time for which he was elected, be appointed to any civil Office under the Authority of the United States, which shall have been created, or the Emoluments whereof shall have been increased during such time; and no Person holding any Office under the United States, shall be a Member of either House during his Continuance in Office.

Section 7.

1. All Bills for raising Revenue shall originate in the House of Representatives; but the Senate may propose or concur with amendments as on other Bills.

2. Every Bill which shall have passed the House of Representatives and the Senate, shall, before it become a law, be presented to the President of the United States: If he approve, he shall sign it, but if not he shall return it, with his Objections to that House in which it shall have originated, who shall enter the Objections at large on their Journal, and proceed to reconsider it. If after such Reconsideration two thirds of the House shall agree to pass the Bill, it shall be sent, together with the Objections, to the other House, by which it shall likewise be reconsidered, and if approved by two thirds of that House, it shall become a Law. But in all such Cases the Votes of both Houses shall be determined by Yeas and Nays, and the Names of the Persons voting for and against the Bill shall be entered on the Journal of each House respectively. If any Bill shall not be returned by the President within ten Days (Sunday excepted) after it shall have been presented to him, the Same shall be a law, in like Manner as if he had signed it, unless the Congress by their Adjournment, prevent its Return, in which Case it shall not be a Law.

3. Every Order, Resolution, or Vote to which the Concurrence of the Senate and House of Representatives may be necessary (except on a question of adjournment) shall be presented to the President of the United States; and before the Same shall take Effect, shall be approved by him, or, being disapproved by him, shall be repassed by two thirds of the Senate and House of Representatives, according to the Rules and Limitations prescribed in the Case of a Bill.

Section 8.

The Congress shall have Power

1. To lay and collect Taxes, Duties, Imposts and Excises to pay the Debts and provide for the common Defense and general Welfare of the United States; but all Duties, Imposts and Excises, shall be uniform throughout the United States;

2. To borrow Money on the credit of the United States;

3. To regulate Commerce with foreign Nations, and among the several States, and with the Indian Tribes;

4. To establish an uniform Rule of Naturalization, and uniform Laws on the subject of Bankruptcies throughout the United States;

Section 7. How Laws are Made

All bills for raising money shall begin in the House of Representatives. The Senate may suggest or agree with amendments to these tax bills, as with other bills.

Every bill which has passed the House of Representatives and the Senate must be presented to the President of the United States before it becomes a law. If the President approves of the bill, the President shall sign it. If the President does not approve, then the bill may be vetoed. The President then sends it back to the house in which it began, with an explanation of the objections. That house writes the objections on their record and begins to reconsider it. If two thirds of each house agrees to pass the bill, it shall become a law. If any bill is neither signed nor vetoed by the President within ten days, (except for Sundays) after it has been sent to the President, the bill shall be a law. If Congress adjourns before ten days have passed, the bill does not become a law.

Section 8. Powers of Congress

Among the powers of Congress listed in Section 8 are:

- establish and collect taxes on imported and exported goods and on goods sold within the country. Congress also shall pay the debts and provide for the defense and general welfare of the United States. All federal taxes shall be the same throughout the United States.
- borrow money on the credit of the United States;
- make laws about trade with other countries, among the states, and with the American Indian tribes;
- establish one procedure by which a person from another country can become a legal citizen of the United States;
- protect the works of scientists, artists, authors, and inventors;
- create federal courts lower than the Supreme Court;

- declare war;
- establish and support an army and navy;
- organize and train a National Guard and call them up in times of emergency;
- govern the capital and military sites of the United States; and
- make all laws necessary to carry out the powers of Congress.

4. The last clause of Section 8 is called "the elastic clause" because it stretches the power of Congress. Why do you think it was added to the Constitution?

_____

_____

_____

_____

_____

_____

_____

5. To coin Money, regulate the Value thereof, and of foreign Coin, and fix the Standard of Weights and Measures;

6. To provide for the Punishment of counterfeiting the Securities and current Coin of the United States;

7. To establish Post Offices and post Roads;

8. To promote the Progress of Science and useful Arts, by securing, for limited Times to Authors and Inventors the exclusive Right to their respective Writings and Discoveries;

9. To constitute Tribunals inferior to the supreme Court;

10. To define and punish Piracies and Felonies committed on the high Seas, and Offences against the Law of nations;

11. To declare War, grant Letters of Marque and Reprisal, and make Rules concerning Captures on Land and Water;

12. To raise and support Armies; but no Appropriation of Money to that Use shall be for a longer Term than two Years;

13. To provide and maintain a Navy;

14. To make Rules for the Government and Regulation of the land and naval Forces;

15. To provide for calling forth the Militia to execute the Laws of the Union, suppress Insurrections and repel Invasions;

16. To provide for organizing, arming, and disciplining the Militia, and for governing such Part of them as may be employed in the Service of the United States, reserving to the States respectively the Appointment of the Officers, and the Authority of training the Militia according to the discipline prescribed by Congress;

17. To exercise exclusive Legislation in all Cases whatsoever, over such District (not exceeding ten Miles square) as may, by Cession of Particular States, and the Acceptance of Congress, become the Seat of the Government of the United States, and to exercise like Authority over all Places purchased by the Consent of the Legislature of the State in which the Same shall be, for the Erection of Forts, Magazines, Arsenals, Dockyards and other needful Buildings;—And

18. To make all Laws which shall be necessary and proper for carrying into Execution the foregoing Powers and all other Powers vested by this Constitution in the Government of the United States, or in any Department or Officer thereof.

Section 9.

1. The Migration or Importation of such Persons as any of the States now existing shall think proper to admit, shall not be prohibited by the Congress prior to the Year one thousand eight hundred and eight, but a Tax or duty may be imposed on such Importation, not exceeding ten dollars for each Person.
2. The Privilege of the Writ of Habeas Corpus shall not be suspended, unless when in Cases of Rebellion or Invasion the public safety may require it.
3. No Bill of Attainder or ex post facto Law shall be passed.
4. No Capitation, or other direct, Tax shall be laid, unless in Proportion to the Census of Enumeration herein before directed to be taken.
5. No Tax or Duty shall be laid on Articles exported from any State.
6. No Preference shall be given by any Regulation of Commerce or Revenue to the Ports of one State over those of another: nor shall Vessels bound to, or from, one State, be obliged to enter, clear or pay Duties in another.
7. No Money shall be drawn from the Treasury, but in Consequence of Appropriations made by Law; and a regular Statement and Account of the Receipts and Expenditures of all public Money shall be published from time to time.
8. No Title of Nobility shall be granted by the United States: And no Person holding any Office of Profit or Trust under them, shall, without the Consent of the Congress, accept of any present, Emolument, Office, or Title, of any kind whatever, from any King, Prince, or foreign State.

Section 10.

1. No State shall enter into any Treaty, Alliance, or Confederation; grant Letters of Marque and Reprisal; coin Money; emit Bills of Credit; make any Thing but gold and silver Coin a Tender in Payment of Debts; pass any Bill of Attainder, ex post facto Law, or Law impairing the Obligation of Contracts, or grant any Title of Nobility.
2. No State shall, without the Consent of the Congress, lay any Imposts or Duties on Imports or Exports, except what may be absolutely necessary for executing its inspection Laws; and the net Produce of all Duties and Imposts, laid by any State on Imports or Exports, shall be for the Use of the Treasury of the United States; and all such Laws shall be subject to the Revision and Control of the Congress.

Section 9: Powers Denied to Congress

Congress cannot
- stop slaves from being brought into the United States until 1808;
- arrest and jail people without charging them with a crime, except during an emergency;
- punish a person without a trial; punish a person for something that was not a crime when he or she did it;
- pass a direct tax, such as an income tax, unless it is in proportion to the population;
- tax goods sent out of a state;
- give the seaports of one state an advantage over another state's ports; let one state tax the ships of another state;
- spend money without passing a law to make it legal; spend money without keeping good records;
- give titles, such as king and queen, to anyone; allow federal workers to accept gifts or titles from foreign governments.

5. Why do you think the writers included the last clause of Section 9?

_____

_____

_____

_____

_____

Section 10: Powers Denied to the States

After listing what Congress is not allowed to do, the Constitution tells what powers are denied to the states.

State governments do not have the power to
- make treaties with foreign countries; print money; do anything that Section 9 of the Constitution says the federal government cannot;
- tax goods sent into or out of a state unless Congress agrees;
- keep armed forces or go to war; make agreements with other states or foreign governments unless Congress agrees.

6. What problems might arise if one state went to war with a foreign country?

_____

_____

_____

_____

_____

Article 2 describes the executive branch.

Section 1. Office of President and Vice President

The President has power to execute, or carry out, the laws of the United States.

Electors from each state choose the President. Today, these electors are called the Electoral College and are chosen by the voters.

Before 1804, the person with the most electoral votes became President. The person with the next-highest number became Vice President. The Twelfth Amendment changed this way of electing Presidents.

3. No State shall, without the Consent of Congress, lay any Duty of Tonnage, keep Troops, or Ships of War in time of Peace, enter into any Agreement or Compact with another State, or with a foreign Power, or engage in War, unless actually invaded, or in such imminent Danger as will not admit of delay.

ARTICLE II

Section 1.

1. The executive Power shall be vested in a President of the United States of America. He shall hold his Office during the Term of four Years, and, together with the Vice President, chosen for the same Term, be elected as follows:

2. Each State shall appoint, in such Manner as the Legislature thereof may direct, a Number of Electors, equal to the whole Number of Senators and Representatives to which the State may be entitled in the Congress: but no Senator or Representative, or Person holding an Office of Trust or Profit, under the United States, shall be appointed an Elector.

3. The Electors shall meet in their respective States, and vote by Ballot for two Persons, of whom one at least shall not be an Inhabitant of the same State with themselves. And they shall make a List of all the Persons voted for, and of the Number of Votes for each; which List they shall sign and certify, and transmit sealed to the Seat of the Government of the United States, directed to the President of the Senate. The President of the Senate shall, in the Presence of the Senate and House of Representatives, open all the Certificates, and the Votes shall then be counted. The Person having the greatest Number of Votes shall be the President, if such Number be a majority of the whole Number of Electors appointed; and if there be more than one who have such Majority, and have an equal Number of Votes, then, the House of Representatives shall immediately choose by Ballot one of them for President; and if no Person have a Majority, then from the five highest on the List the said House shall in like Manner choose the President. But in choosing the President, the Votes shall be taken by States, the Representatives from each State having one Vote; a quorum for this Purpose shall consist of a Member or Members from two thirds of the States, and a Majority of all the States shall be necessary to a Choice. In every Case, after the Choice of the President, the Person having the greatest Number of Votes of the Electors shall be the Vice President. But if there should remain two or more who have equal Votes, the Senate shall choose from them by Ballot the Vice President.

4. The Congress may determine the Time of choosing the Electors, and the Day on which they shall give their Votes; which Day shall be the same throughout the United States.

5. No Person except a natural born Citizen, or a Citizen of the United States, at the time of the Adoption of this Constitution, shall be eligible to the Office of President; neither shall any person be eligible to that Office who shall not have attained to the Age of thirty-five Years, and been fourteen Years a Resident within the United States.

6. In Case of the Removal of the President from Office, or of his Death, Resignation, or Inability to discharge the Powers and Duties of the said Office, the Same shall devolve on the Vice President, and the Congress may by Law provide for the Case of Removal, Death, Resignation or Inability, both of the President and Vice President, declaring what Officer shall then act as President, and such Officer shall act accordingly, until the Disability be removed, or a President shall be elected.

7. The President shall, at stated Times, receive for his Services, a Compensation, which shall neither be increased nor diminished during the Period for which he shall have been elected, and he shall not receive within that Period any other Emolument from the United States, or any of them.

8. Before he enter on the Execution of his Office, he shall take the following Oath or Affirmation: "I do solemnly swear (or affirm) that I will faithfully execute the Office of President of the United States, and will to the best of my Ability, preserve, protect and defend the Constitution of the United States."

Section 2.

1. The President shall be Commander in Chief of the Army and Navy of the United States, and of the Militia of the several States, when called into the actual Service of the United States; he may require the Opinion, in writing, of the principal Officer in each of the executive Departments, upon any Subject relating to the Duties of their respective Offices, and he shall have Power to Grant Reprieves and Pardons for Offences against the United States, except in Cases of Impeachment.

Congress decides when electors are chosen and when they vote for President. Americans now vote for the electors on Election Day, the Tuesday after the first Monday in November.

To become President, a person must be born in the United States and be a citizen. Presidents also have to be at least 35 years old and have lived in the United States for at least 14 years.

If a President dies or leaves office for any reason, the Vice President becomes President. If there is no Vice President, Congress decides on the next President. (In 1967, the Twenty-fifth Amendment changed how these offices are filled.)

7. Why is it important to agree on how to replace the President or Vice President if one should die or leave office?

_____

_____

_____

_____

The President's salary cannot be raised or lowered while he is in office. The President cannot accept other money or gifts while in office. Before taking office, the President must swear to preserve, protect, and defend the Constitution.

Section 2. Powers of the President
The President controls the armed forces and National Guard, and can ask for advice of those who run government departments. (These advisers to the President are members of the Cabinet.) The President can pardon, or free, people convicted of federal crimes.

The President can make treaties, but two thirds of the Senate must approve them. The President, with Senate approval, can name Supreme Court judges, ambassadors, and other important officials.

8. What is the Senate's ability to approve or reject treaties an example of?

_____

_____

Section 3. Duties of the President

From time to time, the President must talk to Congress about the condition of the nation. (Today, we call this speech the State of the Union address. It is given once a year in late January.) In an emergency, the President can call on Congress to meet. The President also meets with foreign leaders, makes sure the nation's laws are carried out, and signs the orders of military officers.

Section 4. Removal From Office

The President, Vice President, and other high officials can be impeached. If proved guilty, they are removed from office.

2. He shall have Power, by and with the Advice and Consent of the Senate, to make Treaties, provided two thirds of the Senators present concur; and he shall nominate, and by and with the Advice and Consent of the Senate, shall appoint Ambassadors, other public Ministers and Consuls, Judges of the supreme Court, and all other Officers of the United States, whose Appointments are not herein otherwise provided for, and which shall be established by Law: but the Congress may by Law vest the Appointment of such inferior Officers, as they think proper, in the President alone, in the Courts of Law, or in the Heads of Departments.

3. The President shall have Power to fill up all Vacancies that may happen during the Recess of the Senate, by granting Commissions which shall expire at the End of their next Session.

Section 3.

He shall from time to time give to the Congress Information of the State of the Union, and recommend to their Consideration such Measures as he shall judge necessary and expedient; he may, on extraordinary Occasions, convene both Houses, or either of them, and in Case of Disagreement between them, with Respect to the Time of Adjournment, he may adjourn them to such Time as he shall think proper; he shall receive Ambassadors and other public Ministers; he shall take Care that the Laws be faithfully executed, and shall Commission all the Officers of the United States.

Section 4.

The President, Vice President and all Civil Officers of the United States, shall be removed from Office on Impeachment for and Conviction of, Treason, Bribery, or other high Crimes and Misdemeanors.

ARTICLE III

Section 1.

The judicial Power of the United States, shall be vested in one supreme Court, and in such inferior Courts as the Congress may from time to time ordain and establish. The Judges, both of the supreme and inferior Courts, shall hold their Offices during good Behavior, and shall, at stated Times, receive for their Services, a Compensation, which shall not be diminished during their Continuance in Office.

Section 2.

1. The judicial Power shall extend to all Cases, in Law and Equity, arising under this Constitution, the Laws of the United States, and Treaties made, or which shall be made, under their Authority;— to all Cases affecting Ambassadors, other public ministers, and Consuls;— to all Cases of Admiralty and maritime Jurisdiction;— to Controversies to which the United States shall be a Party;— to Controversies between two or more States;— between a State and Citizens of another State;— between Citizens of different States;— between Citizens of the same State claiming Lands under Grants of different States, and between a State, or the Citizens thereof, and foreign States, Citizens, or Subjects.

2. In all Cases affecting Ambassadors, other public Ministers and Consuls, and those in which a State shall be a Party, the supreme Court shall have original Jurisdiction. In all the other Cases before mentioned, the supreme Court shall have appellate Jurisdiction, both as to Law and Fact, with such Exceptions, and under such Regulations as the Congress shall make.

3. The trial of all Crimes, except in Cases of Impeachment, shall be by Jury; and such Trial shall be held in the State where the said Crimes shall have been committed; but when not committed within any State, the Trial shall be at such Place or Places as the Congress may by Law have directed.

Article 3 deals with the judicial branch.

Section 1. Federal Courts
The judges of the Supreme Court and other federal courts have the power to make decisions in courts of law. If they act properly, federal judges hold their offices for life.

9. Do you think it's a good idea that federal judges hold their offices for life? Why?

_____

_____

_____

_____

_____

_____

_____

Section 2. Powers of Federal Courts
Federal Courts have legal power over
- laws made under the Constitution
- treaties made with foreign nations
- cases occurring at sea
- cases involving the federal government
- cases involving states or citizens of different states
- cases involving foreign citizens or governments

Only the Supreme Court can judge cases involving ambassadors, government officials, or states. Other cases begin in lower courts, but they can be appealed, or reviewed, by the Supreme Court. In criminal cases other than impeachment, trials are held in the state in which the crime took place. A jury decides the case.

Section 3. Treason

Treason is waging war against the United States or helping its enemies. To be found guilty of treason, a person must confess to the crime; or, two people must have seen the crime committed.

10. Name the three branches of federal government described in Articles 1-3.

_____

_____

_____

Congress decides the punishment for a traitor. The traitor's family cannot be punished if innocent.

Article 4 deals with relationships between the states.

Section 1. Recognition by Each State

Each state must respect the laws and court decisions of the other states.

Section 2. Rights of Citizens in Other States

Citizens keep all their rights when visiting other states.

A person charged with a crime who flees to another state must be returned to the state in which the crime took place.

A slave who escapes to another state must be returned to his or her owner. (The Thirteenth Amendment outlawed slavery.)

Section 3. New States

Congress may let new states join the United States. New states cannot be formed from the land of existing states unless Congress approves.

Congress has the power to make laws to govern territories of the United States.

Section 3.

1. Treason against the United States shall consist only in levying War against them, or in adhering to their Enemies, giving them Aid and Comfort. No Person shall be convicted of Treason unless on the Testimony of two Witnesses to the same overt Act, or on Confession in open Court.
2. The Congress shall have Power to declare the Punishment of Treason, but no Attainder of Treason shall work Corruption of Blood, or Forfeiture except during the Life of the Person attainted.

ARTICLE IV

Section 1.

Full Faith and Credit shall be given in each State to the public Acts, Records, and judicial Proceedings of every other State. And the Congress may by general Laws prescribe the Manner in which such Acts, Records and Proceedings shall be proved, and the Effect thereof.

Section 2.

1. The Citizens of each State shall be entitled to all Privileges and Immunities of Citizens in the several States.
2. A Person charged in any State with Treason, Felony, or other Crime, who shall flee from justice, and be found in another State, shall on Demand of the executive Authority of the State from which he fled, be delivered up, to be removed to the State having Jurisdiction of the Crime.
3. No Person held to Service or Labor in one State, under the Laws thereof, escaping into another, shall, in Consequence of any Law or Regulation therein, be discharged from Service or Labor, but shall be delivered up on Claim of the Party to whom such Service or Labor may be due.

Section 3.

1. New States may be admitted by the Congress into this Union; but no new State shall be formed or erected within the Jurisdiction of any other State; nor any State be formed by the Junction of two or more States, or Parts of States, without the Consent of the Legislatures of the States concerned as well as of the Congress.

2. The Congress shall have Power to dispose of and make all needful Rules and Regulations respecting the Territory or other Property belonging to the United States; and nothing in this Constitution shall be so construed as to Prejudice any Claims of the United States, or of any particular State.

Section 4.

The United States shall guarantee to every State in this Union a Republican Form of Government, and shall protect each of them against Invasion; and on Application of the Legislature, or of the Executive (when the Legislature cannot be convened) against domestic Violence.

ARTICLE V

The Congress, whenever two thirds of both Houses shall deem it necessary, shall propose Amendments to this Constitution, or, on the Application of the Legislatures of two thirds of the several States, shall call a Convention for proposing Amendments, which, in either Case, shall be valid to all Intents and Purposes, as Part of this Constitution, when ratified by the Legislatures of three fourths of the several States, or by Conventions in three fourths thereof, as the one or the other Mode of Ratification may be proposed by the Congress; Provided that no Amendment which may be made prior to the Year One thousand eight hundred and eight shall in any Manner affect the first and fourth Clauses in the Ninth section of the first Article; and that no State, without its Consent, shall be deprived of its equal Suffrage in the Senate.

ARTICLE VI

Section 1.

All Debts contracted and Engagements entered into, before the Adoption of this Constitution, shall be as valid against the United States under this Constitution, as under the Confederation.

Section 2.

This Constitution, and the Laws of the United States which shall be made in Pursuance thereof; and all Treaties made, or which shall be made, under the Authority of the United States, shall be the supreme Law of the Land; and the Judges in every State shall be bound thereby, anything in the constitution or Laws of any State to the Contrary notwithstanding.

Section 4. Guarantees to the States
The federal government guarantees that each state has the right to elect its leaders. The federal government will also protect the states from invasion and violent disorders.

11. There were only thirteen states when the Constitution was written. Do you think the framers expected the United States to grow in size? Why?

_____

_____

_____

_____

_____

Article 5 describes the two ways the Constitution can be amended. Two thirds of the Senate and House of Representatives can suggest an amendment, or two thirds of the state legislatures can have a special convention to suggest an amendment. Once an amendment has been suggested, three fourths of the state legislatures or three fourths of the special conventions must approve the amendment.

Article 6 deals with national law and the national debt. The federal government promises to pay all its debts and keep all agreements made under the Articles of Confederation.
The Constitution and federal laws are the highest laws in the land. If state laws disagree with them, the federal laws must be obeyed.

Section 3. Supporting the Constitution

Federal and state officials must promise to support the Constitution. A person's religion cannot disqualify him or her from holding office. Nine of the thirteen states must approve the Constitution for it to become the law of the land.

Article 7 deals with ratifying the Constitution. On September 17, 1787, twelve years after the Declaration of Independence, everyone at the Constitutional Convention agreed that the Constitution was complete.

The delegates to the Constitutional Convention signed their names below the Constitution to show they approved of it.

12. "The power under the Constitution will always be in the people," wrote George Washington in 1787. Explain what you think he meant.

_____

_____

_____

_____

_____

_____

_____

Section 3.

The Senators and Representatives before mentioned, and the Members of the several State legislatures, and all executive and judicial Officers, both of the United States and of the several States, shall be bound by Oath or Affirmation, to support this Constitution; but no religious Test shall ever be required as a Qualification to any Office or public Trust under the United States.

ARTICLE VII

The ratification of the Conventions of nine States, shall be sufficient for the Establishment of this Constitution between the States so ratifying the same.

Done in Convention by the Unanimous Consent of the States present the Seventeenth Day of September in the Year of our Lord one thousand seven hundred and Eighty-seven and of the Independence of the United States of America the twelfth. In witness whereof We have hereunto subscribed our Names.

Attest:
William Jackson,
  Secretary
George Washington,
  President and Deputy from Virginia

New Hampshire
John Langdon
Nicholas Gilman

Massachusetts
Nathaniel Gorham
Rufus King

Connecticut
William Samuel
  Johnson
Roger Sherman

New York
Alexander Hamilton

New Jersey
William Livingston
David Brearley
William Paterson
Jonathan Dayton

Pennsylvania
Benjamin Franklin
Thomas Mifflin
Robert Morris
George Clymer
Thomas FitzSimons
Jared Ingersoll
James Wilson
Gouverneur Morris

Delaware
George Read
Gunning Bedford, Jr.
John Dickinson
Richard Bassett
Jacob Broom

Maryland
James McHenry
Dan of St. Thomas
  Jenifer
Daniel Carroll

Virginia
John Blair
James Madison, Jr.

North Carolina
William Blount
Richard Dobbs
  Spaight
Hugh Williamson

South Carolina
John Rutledge
Charles
  Cotesworth Pinckney
Charles Pinckney
Pierce Butler

Georgia
William Few
Abraham Baldwin

AMENDMENTS
Amendment 1

Congress shall make no law respecting an establishment of religion, or prohibiting the free exercise thereof, or abridging the freedom of speech, or of the press; or the right of the people peaceably to assemble, and to petition the Government for a redress of grievances.

Amendment 2

A well-regulated Militia being necessary to the security of a free State, the right of the people to keep and bear Arms, shall not be infringed.

Amendment 3

No Soldier shall, in time of peace be quartered in any house, without the consent of the Owner, nor, in time of war, but in a manner to be prescribed by law.

Amendment 4

The right of the people to be secure in their persons, houses, papers, and effects, against unreasonable searches and seizures, shall not be violated, and no Warrants shall issue, but upon probable cause, supported by Oath or affirmation, and particularly describing the place to be searched, and the persons or things to be seized.

Amendment 5

No person shall be held to answer for a capital, or otherwise infamous crime, unless on a presentment or indictment of a Grand Jury, except in cases arising in the land or naval forces, or in the Militia, when in actual service in time of War, or public danger; nor shall any person be subject for the same offence to be twice put in jeopardy of life or limb; nor shall be compelled in any criminal case to be a witness against himself, nor be deprived of life, liberty, or property, without due process of law; nor shall private property be taken for public use, without just compensation.

The first ten amendments to the Constitution are called the Bill of Rights.

First Amendment—1791
Freedom of Religion and Speech
Congress cannot set up an official religion or stop people from practicing a religion. Congress cannot stop people or newspapers from saying what they want. People can gather peacefully to complain to the government.

Second Amendment—1791
Right to Have Firearms
People have the right to own and carry guns.

Third Amendment—1791
Right Not to House Soldiers
During peacetime, citizens do not have to house soldiers.

Fourth Amendment—1791
Search and Arrest Warrant
People or homes cannot be searched without reason. A search warrant is needed to search a house.

Fifth Amendment—1791
Rights of People Accused of Crimes
Only a grand jury can accuse people of a serious crime. No one can be tried twice for the same crime if found not guilty. People cannot be forced to testify against themselves.

13. Write the amendment number that protects each right.

_____ to speak freely

_____ to be protected against unreasonable searches

_____ to not be put on trial twice for the same crime

Sixth Amendment—1791
Right to a Jury Trial

People have the right to a fast trial by a jury and to hear the charges and evidence against them. They also have the right to a lawyer and to call witnesses in their own defense.

Seventh Amendment—1791
Right to a Jury Trial in a Civil Case

In a civil, or noncriminal case, a person also has the right to a trial by jury.

Eighth Amendment—1791
Protection From Unfair Punishment

A person accused of a crime cannot be forced to pay a very high bail. A person convicted of a crime cannot be asked to pay an unfairly high fine or be punished in a cruel or unusual way.

Ninth Amendment—1791
Other Rights

People have other rights that are not specifically mentioned in the Constitution.

Tenth Amendment—1791
Powers of the States and the People

Some powers are not given to the federal government or denied to states. These rights belong to the states or to the people.

Eleventh Amendment—1795
Limits on Rights to Sue States

People from another state or foreign country cannot sue a state.

Amendment 6

In all criminal prosecutions, the accused shall enjoy the right to a speedy and public trial, by an impartial jury of the State and district wherein the crime shall have been committed, which district shall have been previously ascertained by law, and to be informed of the nature and cause of the accusation; to be confronted with the witnesses against him; to have compulsory process for obtaining witnesses in his favor, and to have the Assistance of Counsel for his defense.

Amendment 7

In Suits at common law, where the value in controversy shall exceed twenty dollars, the right of trial by jury shall be preserved, and no fact tried by a jury, shall be otherwise re-examined in any Court of the United States, than according to the rules of the common law.

Amendment 8

Excessive bail shall not be required, nor excessive fines imposed, nor cruel and unusual punishment inflicted.

Amendment 9

The enumeration in the Constitution, of certain rights, shall not be construed to deny or disparage others retained by the people.

Amendment 10

The powers not delegated to the United States by the Constitution, nor prohibited by it to the States, are reserved to the States respectively, or to the people.

Amendment 11

The Judicial power of the United States shall not be construed to extend to any suit in law or equity, commenced or prosecuted against one of the United States by Citizens of another State, or by Citizens or Subjects of any Foreign State.

Amendment 12

The Electors shall meet in their respective States and vote by ballot for President and Vice President, one of whom, at least, shall not be an inhabitant of the same State with themselves; they shall name in their ballots the person voted for as President, and in distinct ballots the person voted for as Vice President, and they shall make distinct lists of all persons voted for as President, and of all persons voted for as Vice President, and of the number of votes for each, which lists they shall sign and certify, and transmit sealed to the seat of the government of the United States, directed to the President of the Senate;— The President of the Senate shall, in the presence of the Senate and the House of Representatives, open all the certificates and the votes shall then be counted;— the person having the greatest Number of votes for President shall be the President, if such number be a majority of the whole number of Electors appointed; and if no person have such a majority, then, from the persons having the highest numbers not exceeding three on the list of those voted for as President, the House of Representatives shall choose immediately, by ballot, the President. But in choosing the President, the votes shall be taken by States, the representation from each State having one vote; a quorum for this purpose shall consist of a member or members from two thirds of the States, and a majority of all the States shall be necessary to a choice. And if the House of Representatives shall not choose a President whenever the right of choice shall devolve upon them, before the fourth day of March next following, then the Vice President shall act as President, as in case of death or other constitutional disability of the President. The person having the greatest number of votes as Vice President, shall be the Vice President, if such number be a majority of the whole number of Electors appointed, and if no person have a majority, then from the two highest numbers on the list, the Senate shall choose the Vice President; a quorum for the purpose shall consist of two thirds of the whole number of Senators, a majority of the whole number shall be necessary to a choice. But no person constitutionally ineligible to the office of President shall be eligible to that of Vice-President of the United States.

Twelfth Amendment—1804
Election of President and Vice President

This amendment changed the way the Electoral College chooses the President and Vice President. Before this amendment, candidates for President and Vice President ran separately, and each elector had two votes—one for President and one for Vice President. The candidate receiving the most votes became President, and the runner-up became Vice President.

Under this amendment, a candidate for President and a candidate for Vice President must run together. Each elector has only one vote, and the pair of candidates that receives more than half the electoral votes become the President and Vice President. If no one receives a majority of the electoral votes, the House of Representatives votes for the President from a list of the top three vote getters. In this situation, each state has one vote, and the candidate must receive more than half of the votes to become President.

If the Representatives fail to elect a President by March 4 (later changed to January 20), the Vice President serves as President. If no candidate receives at least half the electoral votes for Vice President, the names of the two top vote getters are sent to the Senate. The Senators then vote on the names, and the person receiving more than half the votes becomes Vice President.

Thirteenth Amendment—1865
Abolition of Slavery

The United States outlaws slavery. Congress can pass any laws that are needed to carry out this amendment.

Fourteenth Amendment—1868
Rights of Citizens

People born in the United States are citizens of both the United States and of the state in which they live. States must treat their citizens equally. States cannot deny their citizens the rights outlined in the Bill of Rights.

This section of the amendment made former slaves citizens of both the United States and their home state.

Based on its population, each state has a certain number of Representatives in Congress. The number of Representatives from a state might be lowered, however, if the state does not let certain citizens vote.

This section tried to force states in the South to let former slaves vote.

14. Why would a state not want to have its number of Representatives in Congress cut?

_____

_____

_____

_____

_____

Amendment 13

Section 1. Neither slavery nor involuntary servitude, except as a punishment for crime whereof the party shall have been duly convicted, shall exist within the United States, or any place subject to their jurisdiction.

Section 2. Congress shall have power to enforce this article by appropriate legislation.

Amendment 14

Section 1. All persons born or naturalized in the United States and subject to the jurisdiction thereof, are citizens of the United States and of the State wherein they reside. No State shall make or enforce any law which shall abridge the privileges or immunities of citizens of the United States; nor shall any State deprive any person of life, liberty, or property, without due process of law; nor deny to any person within its jurisdiction the equal protection of the laws.

Section 2. Representatives shall be apportioned among the several States according to their respective numbers, counting the whole number of persons in each State, excluding Indians not taxed. But when the right to vote at any election for the choice of electors for President and Vice President of the United States, Representatives in Congress, the Executive and Judicial officers of a State, or the members of the Legislature thereof, is denied to any of the male inhabitants of such State, being twenty-one years of age and citizens of the United States, or in any way abridged, except for participation in rebellion, or other crime, the basis of representation therein shall be reduced in the proportion which the number of such male citizens shall bear to the whole number of male citizens twenty-one years of age in such State.

Section 3. No person shall be a Senator or Representative in Congress, or elector of President and Vice President, or hold any office, civil or military, under the United States, or under any State, who, having previously taken an oath, as a member of Congress, or as an officer of the United States, or as a member of any State legislature, or as an executive or judicial officer of any State, to support the Constitution of the United States, shall have engaged in insurrection or rebellion against the same, or given aid or comfort to the enemies thereof. But Congress may, by a vote of two thirds of each House, remove such disability.

Section 4. The validity of the public debt of the United States, authorized by law, including debts incurred for payment of pensions and bounties for services in suppressing insurrection or rebellion, shall not be questioned. But neither the United States nor any State shall assume or pay any debt or obligation incurred in aid of insurrection or rebellion against the United States, or any claim for the loss or emancipation of any slave; but all such debts, obligations and claims shall be held illegal and void.

Section 5. The Congress shall have power to enforce, by appropriate legislation, the provisions of this article.

Amendment 15

Section 1. The right of citizens of the United States to vote shall not be denied or abridged by the United States or by any State on account of race, color, or previous condition of servitude.

Section 2. The Congress shall have power to enforce this article by appropriate legislation.

Officials who took part in the Civil War against the United States cannot hold federal or state office. Congress can remove this provision by a two-thirds vote.

The United States will pay back the money it borrowed to fight the Civil War. The money that the South borrowed to fight the Civil War will not be paid back to lenders. The former owners of slaves will not be paid for the slaves that were set free. Congress can pass any necessary laws to enforce this article.

15. List two ways in which the Fourteenth Amendment tended to punish those who rebelled against the United States.

_____

_____

_____

_____

_____

_____

_____

_____

_____

Fifteenth Amendment—1870 Voting Rights
The federal and state government cannot stop people from voting based on race or color. Former slaves must be allowed to vote.

Sixteenth Amendment—1913
Income Tax
Congress has the power to collect an income tax regardless of the population of a state. (Originally, Section 9 of Article 1 had denied this power to Congress.)

Seventeenth Amendment—1913
Direct Election of Senators
The voters of each state will elect their Senators directly. (Originally, Article 1, Section 3 said state legislatures would elect Senators.)

A state can hold a special election to fill an empty Senate seat. Until then, the governor can appoint a Senator to fill an empty seat.

Eighteenth Amendment—1919
Prohibition
Making, importing, or selling alcoholic drinks is illegal in the United States. This was called Prohibition because the amendment prohibited, or outlawed, alcohol.

Congress and the states can make any laws to prohibit alcohol.

This amendment becomes part of the Constitution if it is approved within seven years.

This amendment was repealed, or cancelled, in 1933 by the Twenty-first Amendment.

16. Write the amendment number that did each of the following:

_____ let the Federal Government collect income tax

_____ guaranteed voting rights for African Americans

_____ outlawed the sale of alcohol

_____ abolished slavery

_____ let voters elect their Senators

Amendment 16
The Congress shall have power to lay and collect taxes on incomes, from whatever source derived, without apportionment among the several States, and without regard to any census or enumeration.

Amendment 17
The Senate of the United States shall be composed of two Senators from each State, elected by the people thereof, for six years; and each Senator shall have one vote. The electors in each State shall have the qualifications requisite for electors of the most numerous branch of the State legislatures.

When vacancies happen in the representation of any State in the Senate, the executive authority of such State shall issue writs of election to fill such vacancies: Provided, That the legislature of any State may empower the executive thereof to make temporary appointments until the people fill the vacancies by election as the legislature may direct.

This amendment shall not be so construed as to affect the election or term of any Senator chosen before it becomes valid as part of the Constitution.

Amendment 18
Section 1. After one year from the ratification of this article the manufacture, sale, or transportation of intoxicating liquors within, the importation thereof into, or the exportation thereof from the United States and all territory subject to the jurisdiction thereof for beverage purposes is hereby prohibited.

Section 2. The Congress and the several States shall have concurrent power to enforce this article by appropriate legislation.

Section 3. This article shall be inoperative unless it shall have been ratified as an amendment to the Constitution by the legislatures of the several States, as provided in the Constitution, within seven years of the date of the submission hereof to the States by Congress.

Amendment 19

The right of citizens of the United States to vote shall not be denied or abridged by the United States or by any State on account of sex.

Congress shall have power to enforce this article by appropriate legislation.

Amendment 20

Section 1. The terms of the President and Vice President shall end at noon on the 20th day of January, and the terms of Senators and Representatives at noon on the 3d day of January, of the years in which such terms would have ended if this article had not been ratified; and the terms of their successors shall then begin.

Section 2. The Congress shall assemble at least once in every year, and such meeting shall begin at noon on the 3d day of January, unless they shall by law appoint a different day.

Section 3. If, at the time fixed for the beginning of the term of the President, the President elect shall have died, the Vice President elect shall become President. If a President shall not have been chosen before the time fixed for the beginning of his term, or if the President-elect shall have failed to qualify, then the Vice President elect shall act as President until a President shall have qualified; and the Congress may by law provide for the case wherein neither a President elect nor a Vice President elect shall have qualified, declaring who shall then act as President, or the manner in which one who is to act shall be selected, and such person shall act accordingly until a President or Vice President shall have qualified.

Section 4. The Congress may by law provide for the case of the death of any of the persons from whom the House of Representatives may choose a President whenever the right of choice shall have devolved upon them, and for the case of the death of any of the persons from whom the Senate may choose a Vice President whenever the right of choice shall have devolved upon them.

Section 5. Sections 1 and 2 shall take effect on the 15th day of October following the ratification of this article.

Section 6. This article shall be inoperative unless it shall have been ratified as an amendment to the Constitution by the legislatures of three fourths of the several States within seven years from the date of its submission.

Nineteenth Amendment—1920
Women's Right to Vote

No government can stop people from voting because of their sex. Congress can pass necessary laws to carry out this amendment.

Twentieth Amendment—1933
Terms of Office

The term of a new President begins on January 20. This date is called Inauguration Day. Members of Congress take office on January 3. (Originally their terms began on March 4.)

Congress must meet at least once a year. They should first meet on January 3, unless they choose a different day.

If a candidate for President does not win a majority of votes in the Electoral College and dies while the election is being decided in the House, Congress has the power to pass laws to resolve the problem. Congress has similar power if a candidate for Vice President dies while the election is being decided in the Senate.

Sections 1 and 2 of this amendment take effect on the fifteenth day of October after the amendment becomes part of the Constitution. This amendment has to be approved by three fourths of the states within seven years.

Twenty-first Amendment—1933
Repeal of Prohibition

The Eighteenth Amendment, which outlawed alcohol, is no longer in effect.

Any state may pass laws to prohibit alcohol.

17. How long was the Eighteenth Amendment in effect in the United States?

_____

Twenty-second Amendment—1951
Limit on Terms of the President

A President can only be elected to the office for two terms (eight years). If a President serves more than two years of the last President's term, then the President may only be re-elected once.

18. Do you think a President should be limited to just two terms in office? Why or why not?

_____

_____

_____

_____

_____

_____

Amendment 21

Section 1. The eighteenth article of amendment to the Constitution of the United States is hereby repealed.

Section 2. The transportation or importation into any State, Territory, or possession of the United States for delivery or use therein of intoxicating liquors, in violation of the laws thereof, is hereby prohibited.

Section 3. This article shall be inoperative unless it shall have been ratified as an amendment to the Constitution by conventions in the several States, as provided in the Constitution, within seven years from the date of the submission hereof to the States by the Congress.

Amendment 22

Section 1. No person shall be elected to the office of the President more than twice, and no person who has held the office of President, or acted as President, for more than two years of a term to which some other person was elected President shall be elected to the office of the President more than once. But this Article shall not apply to any person holding the office of President, when this Article was proposed by the Congress, and shall not prevent any person who may be holding the office of President, or acting as President, during the term within which this Article becomes operative from holding the office of President or acting as President during the remainder of such term.

Section 2. This article shall be inoperative unless it shall have been ratified as an amendment to the Constitution by the legislatures of three fourths of the several states within seven years from the date of its submission to the States by the Congress.

Amendment 23

Section 1. The District constituting the seat of Government of the United States shall appoint in such manner as the Congress may direct:

A number of electors of President and Vice President equal to the whole number of Senators and Representatives in Congress to which the District would be entitled if it were a State, but in no event more than the least populous State; they shall be in addition to those appointed by the States, they shall be considered, for the purposes of the election of President and Vice President, to be electors appointed by a State; and they shall meet in the District and perform such duties as provided by the twelfth article of amendment.

Amendment 24

Section 1. The right of citizens of the United States to vote in any primary or other election for President or Vice President, for electors for President or Vice President, or for Senator or Representative in Congress, shall not be denied or abridged by the United States or any State by reason of failure to pay any poll tax or other tax.

Section 2. The Congress shall have power to enforce this article by appropriate legislation.

Amendment 25

Section 1. In case of the removal of the President from office or of his death or resignation, the Vice President shall become President.

Section 2. Whenever there is a vacancy in the office of the Vice President, the President shall nominate a Vice President who shall take office upon confirmation by a majority vote of both Houses of Congress.

Section 3. Whenever the President transmits to the President pro tempore of the Senate and the Speaker of the House of Representatives his written declaration that he is unable to discharge the powers and duties of his office, and until he transmits to them a written declaration to the contrary, such powers and duties shall be discharged by the Vice President as Acting President.

Twenty-third Amendment—1961 Presidential Elections for District of Columbia

People living in Washington, D.C., have the right to vote in presidential elections. Washington, D.C., can never have more electoral votes than the state with the smallest number of people.

Twenty-fourth Amendment—1964 Outlawing of Poll Tax

No one can be stopped from voting in a federal election because he or she has not paid a poll tax or any other kind of tax.

Congress can make laws to carry out this amendment.

Twenty-fifth Amendment—1967 Presidential Succession

If the President dies or resigns, the Vice President becomes President. If the office of Vice President is empty, the President appoints a new Vice President.

When the President is unable to carry out the duties of the office, Congress should be informed. The Vice President then serves as Acting President. The President may resume the duties of the office after informing Congress.

If the Vice President and half the President's top advisers, or Cabinet, inform Congress that the President cannot carry out his or her duties, the Vice President becomes Acting President. If the President informs Congress that he or she is able to carry out these duties, the President returns to office. However, after four days, if the Vice President and half the Cabinet again tell Congress that the President cannot carry out his or her duties, the President does not return to office. Instead, Congress must decide within 21 days whether the President is able to carry out his or her duties. If two thirds of Congress votes that the President cannot continue in office, the Vice President becomes Acting President. If two thirds do not vote in this way, the President remains in office.

19. Write the number of the amendment that:

_____ gave votes to women

_____ gave votes to citizens in Washington, D.C.

_____ gave votes to 18-year-old people

_____ outlawed taxes that blocked voting

Section 4. Whenever the Vice President and a majority of either the principal officers of the executive departments or of such other body as Congress may by law provide, transmit to the President pro tempore of the Senate and the Speaker of the House of Representatives their written declaration that the President is unable to discharge the powers and duties of his office, the Vice President shall immediately assume the powers and duties of the office as Acting President.

Thereafter, when the President transmits to the President pro tempore of the Senate and the Speaker of the House of Representatives his written declaration that no inability exists, he shall resume the powers and duties of his office unless the Vice President and a majority of either the principal officers of the executive department or of such other body as Congress may by law provide, transmit within four days to the President pro tempore of the Senate and the Speaker of the House of Representatives their written declaration that the President is unable to discharge the powers and duties of his office. Thereupon Congress shall decide the issue, assembling within forty-eight hours for that purpose if not in session. If the Congress, within twenty-one days after receipt of the latter written declaration, or, if Congress is not in session, within twenty-one days after Congress is required to assemble, determines by two-thirds vote of both Houses that the President is unable to discharge the powers and duties of his office, the Vice President shall continue to discharge the same as Acting President; otherwise, the President shall resume the powers and duties of his office.

Amendment 26

Section 1. The right of citizens of the United States, who are eighteen years of age or older, to vote shall not be denied or abridged by the United States or by any State on account of age.

Section 2. The Congress shall have the power to enforce this article by appropriate legislation.

Amendment 27

No law varying the compensation for the services of the Senators and Representatives, shall take effect, until an election of Representatives shall have intervened.

The United States of America, Political

Washington
★ Olympia

★ Salem

Oregon

Montana
★ Helena

North Dakota
★ Bismarck

Minne

St. P

★ Boise

Idaho

Wyoming

South Dakota
Pierre ★

Sacramento ★

Carson City ★

Salt Lake City ★

Cheyenne
★

Nebraska

Ia

Nevada

Utah

Denver ★

Lincoln ★

California

Colorado

Topeka ★

Kansas

Arizona

★ Phoenix

Santa Fe ★

New Mexico

Oklahoma
★ Oklahoma City

Texas

Austin
★

Alaska

Juneau ★

★ Honolulu

Hawaii

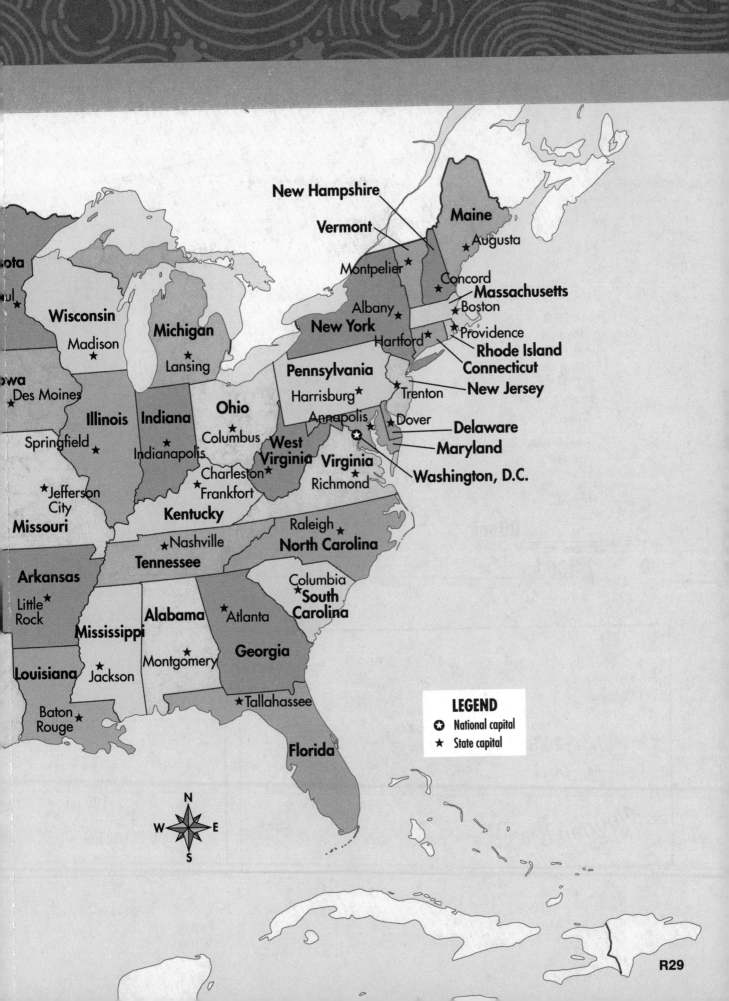

New Hampshire

Vermont

Maine
★ Augusta

Montpelier ★

Concord
Massachusetts
★ Boston

Albany
New York

Providence
Rhode Island
Hartford ★ Connecticut

Wisconsin

Madison ★

Michigan

Lansing ★

Pennsylvania

Harrisburg ★

Trenton
New Jersey

ota

ul
★

wa

Des Moines
★

Illinois

Indiana

Ohio

Columbus
★

Annapolis
Dover

Delaware
Maryland
Washington, D.C.

Springfield
★

Indianapolis ★

West
Virginia

Virginia

Charleston ★
Frankfort ★

Jefferson
City ★

Missouri

Kentucky

Nashville ★

Richmond ★

Raleigh ★
North Carolina

Arkansas

Tennessee

Little ★
Rock

Mississippi

Alabama

Atlanta ★

Columbia
★ South
Carolina

Louisiana

Jackson ★

Montgomery ★

Georgia

Baton ★
Rouge

Tallahassee ★

Florida

LEGEND

⊛ National capital

★ State capital

N
W   E
S

N
W E
S

LEGEND
Elevation

Feet	Meters
10,000	3,048
6,000	1,829
3,000	914
1,000	305
500	152
0	0

— National border
▲ Mountain

PACIFIC
OCEAN

Columbia R.
Snake R.
Great Salt Lake
Colorado R.

SIERRA NEVADA

ROCKY MOUNTAINS

0   400 mi
0   400 km

140°W
130°W
40°N
120°W
30°N

ARCTIC CIRCLE
160°W
Brooks Range
Denali
20,310 ft (6,190 m) ▲
Alaska Range
Bering Sea
Aleutian Islands
180°
60°N
140°W

0   300 mi
0   300 km

22°N
PAC
OC
20°N
160°W
Ha

0   100 mi
0   100 km

Missouri R.

Lake
Superior

Great Lakes

Lake
Ontario

Lake
Huron

Lake
Michigan

Lake Erie

Platte R.

G
R
E
A
T

P
L
A
I
N
S

CENTRAL
PLAINS

APPALACHIAN MOUNTAINS

Ohio R.

Red R.

C
O
A
S
T
A
L

P
L
A
I
N

ATLANTIC
OCEAN

Mississippi R.

80°W

70°W

Rio Grande

Gulf of Mexico

ACIFIC
CEAN

90°W

Hawaii

TROPIC OF CANCER

20°N

154°W

map
area

North America, Political

ARCTIC OCEAN

60° N

180°

Bering Strait

Bering Sea

Beaufort Sea

Viscount Melville Sound

GREENLAND (Denmark)

Baffin Bay

ALASKA (U.S.)

Fairbanks

Anchorage

Gulf of Alaska

Great Bear Lake

Great Slave Lake

Foxe Basin

Davis Strait

Labrador Sea

Juneau

Hudson Strait

CANADA

Lake Athabasca

Hudson Bay

James Bay

Gulf of St. Lawrence

ATLANTIC OCEAN

150° W

Edmonton

Calgary

Lake Winnipeg

Quebec

Vancouver

Puget Sound

Seattle

Regina

Winnipeg

Ottawa ✪ Montreal

Boston

Portland

Great Lakes

Toronto

Detroit

New York City

Philadelphia

Washington, D.C.

30° W

Great Salt Lake

Salt Lake City

Chicago

San Francisco

Denver

St. Louis

30° N

Las Vegas

UNITED STATES

Los Angeles

Phoenix

Atlanta

San Diego

Dallas

Savannah

60° W

TROPIC OF CANCER

San Antonio

New Orleans

BAHAMAS

DOMINICAN REPUBLIC

Houston

Miami

Nassau

PUERTO RICO (U.S.)

MEXICO

Gulf of Mexico

Havana

CUBA

Santo Domingo

PACIFIC OCEAN

Kingston

JAMAICA

HAITI

Port-au-Prince

Mexico City ✪

BELIZE

Belmopan

Caribbean Sea

GUATEMALA

HONDURAS

LEGEND
— National border
✪ National capital
• Other city

Guatemala City ✪

Tegucigalpa

San Salvador

Managua

EL SALVADOR

NICARAGUA

San José

Panama City

COSTA RICA

PANAMA

0° EQUATOR

120° W

90° W

North America, Physical

ARCTIC OCEAN

Bering Strait

Point Barrow

Viscount Melville Sound

Ellesmere Island

Greenland

Queen Elizabeth Islands

Baffin Bay

Melville I. Devon I.

Bering Sea

Beaufort Sea

Banks Island

Baffin Island

Davis Strait

Cape Farewell

Aleutian Islands

Denali 20,310 ft (6,190 m)

Brooks Range

Victoria Island

Foxe Basin

Labrador Sea

ATLANTIC OCEAN

Alaska Range

Yukon River

Mackenzie R.

Hudson Strait

Alaska Peninsula

Kodiak Island

Gulf of Alaska

Mt. Logan 19,524 ft (5,951 m)

Yukon Plateau

Great Bear Lake

Hudson Bay

Labrador

Newfoundland

Liard R.

Great Slave L.

Haida Qwaii (Queen Charlotte Islands)

Peace R.

Athabasca R.

Lake Athabasca

James Bay

Gulf of St. Lawrence

C A N A D I A N   S H I E L D

Saskatchewan R.

Lake Winnipeg

St. Lawrence R.

Nova Scotia

Vancouver Island

Puget Sound

Coast Mountains

Cascade Range

Coast Ranges

ROCKY MOUNTAINS

G R E A T   P L A I N S

Mississippi R.

Missouri R.

Great Lakes

APPALACHIAN MOUNTAINS

Bay of Fundy

Cape Cod

Long Island

Great Salt Lake

Snake R.

Black Hills

Platte R.

Arkansas

INTERIOR PLAINS

Ohio R.

Cape Hatteras

Sierra Nevada

GREAT BASIN

Colorado R.

Ozark Plateau

C O A S T A L   P L A I N

Mt. Whitney 14,495 ft (4,418 m)

Death Valley (lowest point in N.A.) −282 ft (−86 m)

Baja California

Sonoran Desert

Rio Grande

Gulf of Mexico

Bahamas

Puerto Rico

Lesser Antilles

TROPIC OF CANCER

Sierra Madre Occidental

Sierra Madre Oriental

Cuba

G r e a t e r   A n t i l l e s

Hispaniola

Yucatán Peninsula

Jamaica

Caribbean Sea

Citlaltépetl 18,701 ft (5,700 m)

Isthmus of Panama

Lake Nicaragua

PACIFIC OCEAN

ARCTIC CIRCLE

EQUATOR

60° N

60° N

30° N

30° N

30° W

30° W

60° W

150° W

120° W

90° W

180°

LEGEND

Elevation

Feet	Meters
10,000	3,048
6,000	1,829
3,000	914
1,000	305
500	152
0	0

▲ Peak

▼ Below sea level

R33

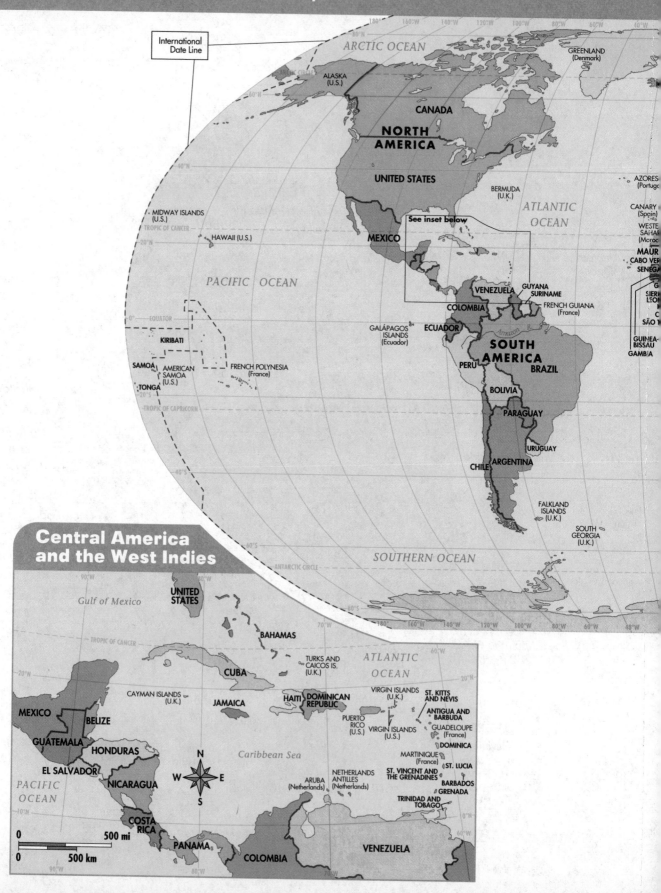

International Date Line

ARCTIC OCEAN

GREENLAND
(Denmark)

ALASKA
(U.S.)

CANADA

**NORTH
AMERICA**

UNITED STATES

BERMUDA
(U.K.)

ATLANTIC
OCEAN

AZORES
(Portuga

CANARY
(Spain)

WESTE
SAHAR
(Moroc

MIDWAY ISLANDS
(U.S.)

TROPIC OF CANCER

HAWAII (U.S.)

MEXICO

See inset below

MAUR
CABO VER
SENEGA

PACIFIC OCEAN

VENEZUELA
GUYANA
SURINAME

COLOMBIA
FRENCH GUIANA
(France)

SIERR
LEON

C
SÃO T

GALÁPAGOS
ISLANDS
(Ecuador)

ECUADOR

GUINEA-
BISSAU

GAMBIA

EQUATOR

KIRIBATI

**SOUTH
AMERICA**

PERU

BRAZIL

SAMOA
AMERICAN
SAMOA
(U.S.)

FRENCH POLYNESIA
(France)

BOLIVIA

TONGA

PARAGUAY

TROPIC OF CAPRICORN

URUGUAY

CHILE
ARGENTINA

FALKLAND
ISLANDS
(U.K.)

SOUTH
GEORGIA
(U.K.)

ANTARCTIC CIRCLE

SOUTHERN OCEAN

Central America and the West Indies

Gulf of Mexico

UNITED
STATES

TROPIC OF CANCER

BAHAMAS

CUBA

TURKS AND
CAICOS IS.
(U.K.)

ATLANTIC
OCEAN

MEXICO

CAYMAN ISLANDS
(U.K.)

JAMAICA

HAITI
DOMINICAN
REPUBLIC

VIRGIN ISLANDS
(U.K.)

ST. KITTS
AND NEVIS

ANTIGUA AND
BARBUDA

BELIZE

PUERTO
RICO
(U.S.)
VIRGIN ISLANDS
(U.S.)

GUADELOUPE
(France)

GUATEMALA

DOMINICA

HONDURAS

Caribbean Sea

MARTINIQUE
(France)
ST. LUCIA

EL SALVADOR

NICARAGUA

N
W   E
S

ARUBA
(Netherlands)

NETHERLANDS
ANTILLES
(Netherlands)

ST. VINCENT AND
THE GRENADINES

BARBADOS

GRENADA

PACIFIC
OCEAN

TRINIDAD AND
TOBAGO

COSTA
RICA

PANAMA

COLOMBIA

VENEZUELA

0   500 mi

0   500 km

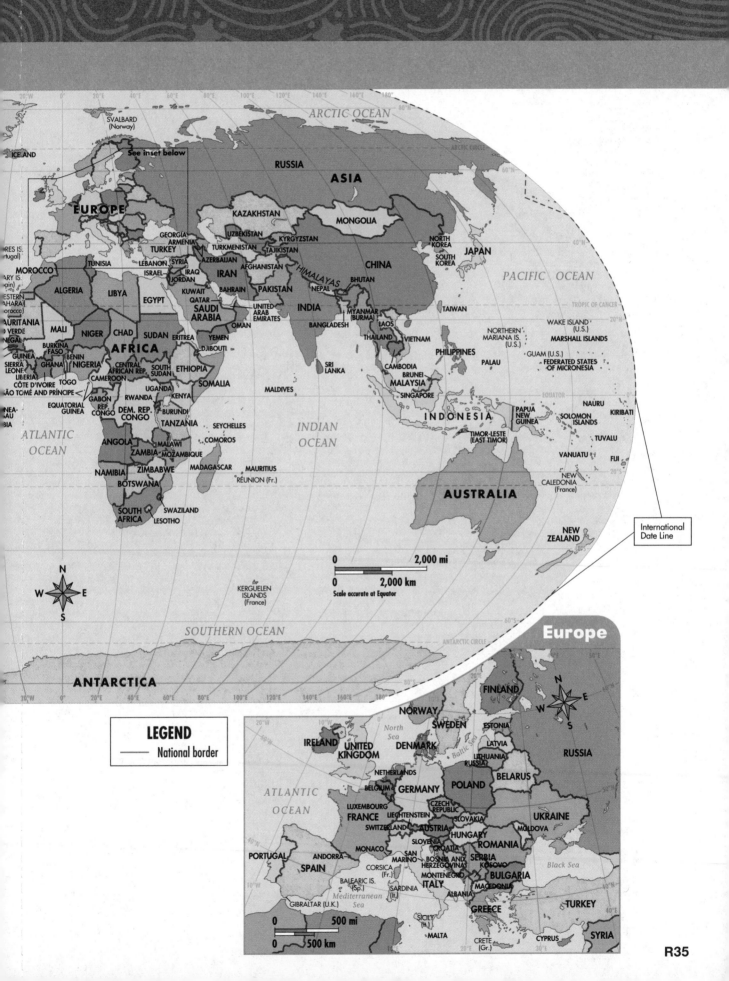

ARCTIC OCEAN

SVALBARD
(Norway)

ICELAND

See inset below

RUSSIA

ASIA

EUROPE

KAZAKHSTAN

MONGOLIA

GEORGIA
ARMENIA
TURKEY
TURKMENISTAN
UZBEKISTAN
KYRGYZSTAN
NORTH
KOREA
JAPAN

LEBANON SYRIA
AZERBAIJAN
TAJIKISTAN
SOUTH
KOREA

RES IS.
rtugal)

ARY IS.
pain)

ESTERN
AHARA
orocco)

TUNISIA
ISRAEL
IRAQ
JORDAN
IRAN
AFGHANISTAN
CHINA

MOROCCO

ALGERIA

LIBYA

EGYPT

KUWAIT
QATAR
BAHRAIN
SAUDI
ARABIA
UNITED
ARAB
EMIRATES
OMAN

PAKISTAN

HIMALAYAS
NEPAL

BHUTAN

INDIA

MYANMAR
(BURMA)

BANGLADESH

LAOS

TAIWAN

PACIFIC OCEAN

TROPIC OF CANCER

WAKE ISLAND
(U.S.)

NORTHERN
MARIANA IS.
(U.S.)

MARSHALL ISLANDS

AURITANIA

NEGAL

GUINEA
SIERRA
LEONE
LIBERIA
CÔTE D'IVOIRE
ÃO TOMÉ AND PRÍNCIPE

NEA-
SAU
BIA

MALI

NIGER

CHAD

SUDAN

ERITREA

YEMEN

DJIBOUTI

BURKINA
FASO
BENIN
GHANA NIGERIA
TOGO
CAMEROON
CENTRAL
AFRICAN REP.
SOUTH
SUDAN

AFRICA

ETHIOPIA

SOMALIA

THAILAND

VIETNAM

CAMBODIA

BRUNEI
MALAYSIA

SINGAPORE

PHILIPPINES

PALAU

GUAM (U.S.)
FEDERATED STATES
OF MICRONESIA

EQUATORIAL
GUINEA
GABON
REP.
CONGO

DEM. REP.
CONGO

UGANDA
RWANDA
BURUNDI

KENYA

TANZANIA

SEYCHELLES

MALDIVES

SRI
LANKA

INDONESIA

EQUATOR

NAURU

SOLOMON
ISLANDS

KIRIBATI

ATLANTIC
OCEAN

ANGOLA
ZAMBIA
MALAWI
MOZAMBIQUE

COMOROS

INDIAN
OCEAN

PAPUA
NEW
GUINEA

TIMOR-LESTE
(EAST TIMOR)

TUVALU

VANUATU

FIJI

NAMIBIA ZIMBABWE
BOTSWANA

MADAGASCAR

MAURITIUS

RÉUNION (Fr.)

AUSTRALIA

NEW
CALEDONIA
(France)

SOUTH
AFRICA

SWAZILAND

LESOTHO

N
W   E
S

KERGUELEN
ISLANDS
(France)

0   2,000 mi
0   2,000 km
Scale accurate at Equator

NEW
ZEALAND

International
Date Line

SOUTHERN OCEAN

ANTARCTIC CIRCLE

ANTARCTICA

LEGEND
—— National border

Europe

FINLAND

NORWAY
SWEDEN
ESTONIA

North
Sea
IRELAND UNITED
KINGDOM
DENMARK
LATVIA
LITHUANIA
RUSSIA
RUSSIA
BELARUS

Baltic Sea

NETHERLANDS

BELGIUM
GERMANY
POLAND

ATLANTIC
OCEAN

LUXEMBOURG
CZECH
REPUBLIC

UKRAINE

FRANCE
LIECHTENSTEIN
SLOVAKIA
MOLDOVA

SWITZERLAND
AUSTRIA
HUNGARY
ROMANIA

SLOVENIA
CROATIA

MONACO
SAN
MARINO
BOSNIA AND
HERZEGOVINA
SERBIA
KOSOVO

Black Sea

PORTUGAL
ANDORRA
CORSICA
(Fr.)
MONTENEGRO
BULGARIA

SPAIN
ITALY
MACEDONIA

BALEARIC IS.
(Sp.)
SARDINIA
(It.)
ALBANIA

GIBRALTAR (U.K.)

Mediterranean
Sea

GREECE

TURKEY

SICILY
(It.)

MALTA

CRETE
(Gr.)

CYPRUS

SYRIA

0   500 mi
0   500 km

Glossary

A

abolition (ab uh LIHSH un) The movement to end slavery.

abolitionist (ab uh LIHSH un ihst) A person who supported the movement to end slavery.

absolute location (AB suh loot loh KAY shun) The exact location of a place that does not change.

academy (uh KAD uh mee) A place for study or training.

according (uh KAWR ding) In agreement.

accumulate (uh KYOOM yoo layt) To gather an increasing amount of something.

accurately (AK yuh rut lee) Without errors or mistakes.

acknowledge (ak NAHL ihj) To recognize the authority of.

adapt (uh DAPT) To become adjusted to new conditions.

adviser (ad VYZ ur) A person who gives advice or guidance.

advocate (AD vuh kiht) A person who supports a particular cause.

agriculture (AG rih kul chur) The planting and raising of crops.

alliance (uh LY uns) An agreement or treaty.

ally (AL eye) A military partner.

amendment (uh MEND muh nt) A change or addition, especially to the U.S. Constitution.

anarchy (AN ur kee) Lawlessness; disorder caused by lack of rules.

ancestor (AN ses tur) A relative who lived in the past.

Anglican (ANG glih kun) Having a connection to the Church of England.

annex (uh NEKS) To take over a territory.

announce (uh NOUNS) To make known officially or publicly.

anthem (AN thum) A song.

Anti-Federalist (an ty FED ur ul ihst) A person who supported the Articles of Confederation.

Articles of Confederation (AHRT ih kulz uv kun fed ur AY shun) An agreement among the 13 original states that served as the first U.S. Constitution.

artifact (AHRT uh fakt) An object made and used by people that usually has historical or cultural interest.

artisan (AHRT uh zuhn) A person specialized in one type of work or trade.

aspect (AS pekt) A part of something.

assassinate (uh SAS un neyt) To murder someone famous or powerful, usually for political reasons.

assemble (uh SEM bul) To meet together.

astrolabe (AS troh layb) An instrument used in navigation that measures the sun and stars.

authority (uh THOR uh tee) The power to give orders or make decisions.

autobiography (aht oh by AH gruh fee) The account of a person's life written by that person.

B

barter (BAHR tur) To trade one good for another.

Bill of Rights (bihl uv ryts) The first ten amendments to the U.S. Constitution, which guarantees basic rights of all citizens.

biography (by AH gruh fee) A book about a person's life that is written by someone else.

black codes (blak kohdz) A group of laws passed in the late 1800s that denied African American men the right to vote, kept African Americans from owning guns or taking certain types of jobs.

blockade (blah KEYD) A barrier of troops or ships to keep people and supplies from moving in or out of an area.

boundary (BOUN dree) A line that divides an area.

boycott (BOI kaht) The refusal to buy a product as part of a protest.

C

Cabinet (KAB uh niht) A group of advisors that usually advise a president or other leader.

canal (kuh NAL) A human-made waterway.

capable (KAY puh bul) Having the necessary ability.

caravan (KAR uh van) A group of families that would move west together.

caravel (KAR uh vel) A small, fast sailing ship.

carpetbaggers (KAHR pit bag erz) Northern people who moved South to start businesses after the Civil War.

cash crop (kash krahp) Crops that are sold instead of being used by a farmer.

challenge (CHAL unj) A difficult situation.

checks and balances (cheks and BAL un ses) A system where each branch of government has ways of limiting the powers of the other branches.

civilization (sihv ul ih ZAY shun) A society in which there are organized systems of government, religion, and learning.

class (KLAHS) A ranking in society based on wealth or importance.

class system (clas SIS tuhm) A method of ranking people, often by race, power, or wealth.

climate (KLY mut) The weather in a place over time.

colony (KAHL uh nee) A country or area under the control of another country.

Columbian Exchange (kuh LUM bee un eks CHAYNJ) The movement of people, animals, plants, and cultures between the Eastern and Western hemispheres.

commerce (KAHM urs) The business or trade between countries or states.

commodity (kuh MAHD uh tee) A trade good that is a raw material and not manufactured.

compromise (KAHM pruh myz) People on both sides of an issue giving up something to reach an agreement.

condition (kun DIHSH un) The physical state of something.

Confederacy (kun FED ur uh see) Another name for the Confederate States of America, the southern states during the U.S. Civil War.

confederacy (kun FED ur uh see) A group whose members share the same goals and usually have a written or oral form of an alliance or agreement.

confine (kun FYN) To prevent from leaving; imprison.

congress (KAHN grus) A lawmaking body.

conquistador (kahn KEES tuh door) A conqueror, especially one of the Spanish conquerors in North or South America in the 1500s.

constitution (kahn stuh TOO shuyn) A plan of government, usually written, but may be oral.

constitutional republic (kahn stuh TOO shuh nul rih PUB lihk) A government in which officials are elected to represent the people, and then govern according to a constitution.

construct (kun STRUKT) To build.

consult (kun SULT) To look for information or advice from something or someone.

Continental Army (KAHNT un ent ul AHR mee) During the American Revolution, the army authorized by the Continental Congress in 1775 and led by George Washington.

convince (kun VIHNS) To make someone believe something is true.

coordinate (koh ORD uh nayt) To bring different things together; to place in proper order.

council (KOUN sul) A decision-making body that could be made up of a group's single leader or a small group of leaders.

create (kree EYT) To design or invent something.

crucial (KROO shul) Of great importance.

currency (KUR un see) Money.

current events (KUR unt ih VENTS) Events that are in the news.

custom (KUS tum) Ways of life that are done on a regular basis.

customs (KUS tumz) Taxes on products coming into a country.

D

debt (det) A sum of money that is owed.

declare (dee KLAYR) To make known to the public.

defend (dih FEND) To protect from harm or danger.

delegate (DEL uh giht) A person who represents others, often an elected official.

demolish (dih MAHL ihsh) To destroy.

determine (dee TUR mun) To decide.

discrimination (dih skrihm ih NAY shun) Unfair treatment of people, often based on race, gender, or age.

display (dihs PLAY) To show.

distinct (dih STIHNKT) Different.

distribute (dih STRIHB yoot) To spread out.

diverse (duh VURS) Showing a great deal of variety.

domestic tranquility (doh MES tihk trang KWIHL uh tee) Peace within a nation.

drought (drout) A long period of low or no rainfall.

E

economy (ih KAHN uh mee) The system by which a group makes, shares, and uses goods.

ecosystem (EE koh sihs tum) All living things that share and interact with each other in a distinct environment.

Electoral College (ee LEK tur ul KAH lihj) A group of people chosen by people in each state to choose the U.S. President and Vice President.

elevation (el uh VAY shun) The distance or height of land above sea level.

elevation map (el uh VAY shun map) A map that compares and contrasts the elevations of different areas.

eliminate (ee LIHM uh nayt) To remove.

emancipation (ih man suh PEY shuh n) The setting free of enslaved African Americans.

emerge (ee MURJ) To develop.

empire (EM pyr) A large group of states or countries.

enable (en AY bul) To let happen.

encomienda (en koh mee EN duh) A system granted from the Spanish government that gives Spanish settlers the right to take land and control local American Indians on that land.

enforce (en FOHRS) To make people obey a law or rule.

enlist (en LIHST) To join the military.

enormous (ee NOR mus) Very large or great in size.

entrepreneur (ahn truh pruh NOOR) Someone who takes risks to start a business.

epidemic (ep uh DEM ihk) A widespread disease.

equality (ee KWAW luh tee) The condition of having the same rights as everyone else.

equator (ee KWAYT ur) The imaginary line that runs around the center of Earth.

establish (uh STAB lihsh) To set up or organize something permanent.

eventually (ee VEN choo ul ee) After a period of time.

examine (eg ZAM un) To inspect in detail.

executive (eg ZEK yoo tihv) The branch of government that carries out the laws.

exhibit (eg ZIB it) A collection of items put out so that people can see them.

expedition (eks puh DIHSH un) A journey or voyage.

export (EKS port) A product sold to other countries.

F

famine (FAM ihn) A severe shortage of food.

Federalist (FED ur ul ihst) A person who supported the new U.S. Constitution.

finance (FY nans) To provide money for something.

folklore (FOHK lor) Traditional customs, beliefs, and stories.

foreign policy (FOR un PAHL uh see) Policies of one country in its dealings with other countries.

foundation (foun DAY shun) The base or support of something.

frontier (frun TEER) The edge of the wilderness.

G

geography (jee AHG ruh fee) The land and bodies of water of a place.

globe (glohb) A model of Earth.

gold rush (gohld rush) A rapid flood of people into an area where gold has been discovered.

government (GUV urn munt) A system for making rules and decisions, to help a group or nation.

H

hemisphere (HEM ih sfeer) Half of the sphere of Earth.

historical map (hihs TAWR ih kul map) A map that shows a particular time from the past.

horrific (haw RIF ik) Having the power to horrify; frightening or shocking.

House of Burgesses (hous uv BUR jihs ez) The first representative legislative body in North America; established in the colony of Virginia.

hunter-gatherer (HUNT ur GATHH ur ur) An early person who lived by hunting animals and gathering nuts, seeds, and fruit.

I

impeachment (im PEECH muh nt) The process by which charges of wrongdoing are brought against an elected official.

import (IHM port) A product brought from other countries.

impressment (ihm PRES munt) The practice of capturing foreign soldiers and forcing them to work for country besides their own.

inauguration (ihn aw gyuh RAY shun) A ceremony to mark the beginning of something.

indentured servant (ihn DEN churd SUR vunt) A person who agrees to work without pay for certain period ot time in exchange for food, clothing, and shelter, and the promise of land.

independence (ihn dee PEN duns) Freedom.

indicate (IHN dih kayt) To point out; show.

inflation (ihn FLAY shun) When the price of goods increases while the value of money decreases.

influence (IHN floo uns) To help produce an effect.

innovation (ihn uh VAY shun) The introduction of something new.

insert (ihn SURT) To put inside.

inspect (ihn SPEKT) To look at something closely.

interact (in ter AKT) To talk or work with others.

interpreter (ihn TUR pruh tur) A person who translates foreign languages.

investigate (ihn VES tuh gayt) To study carefully.

irrigation (ihr uh GAY shun) The use of technology to bring water to crops.

J

judicial (joo DIHSH ul) The branch of government, made up of courts and judges, that decides what laws mean.

Juneteenth (joon-teenth) The name of a celebration for the day enslaved African Americans in Texas learned of the Emancipation Proclamation.

K

King Philip's War (kihng FIHL ihps wor) A war between the colonists and American Indians in 1637; led by Metacom, also known as King Philip.

L

landform (LAND form) A natural feature of Earth, such as mountains and deserts.

latitude (LAT uh tood) Evenly spaced lines on a map that extend around the globe both north and south of the equator.

league (leeg) A group whose members share the same goals.

legislative (LEJ ihs lay tihv) The branch of government that makes laws.

levy (LEV ee) To collect or impose.

longitude (LAHN juh tood) Evenly spaced lines on a map that extend north and south between the North Pole and the South Pole.

Loyalist (LOI ul ihst) A person who remained loyal to Great Britain during the American Revolution.

M

maintain (mayn TAYN) To keep something going or continuing without changing.

Manifest Destiny (MAN uh fest DES tuh nee) The idea, popular in the 1800s, that the United States had a right to add territory until it reached the Pacific Ocean.

martial law (MAR shul law) Placing the military in charge of a government.

mass production (mas pruh DUK shun) A system of making many of the same item at one time.

massacre (MAS uh kur) The purposeful killing of many people.

Mayflower Compact (MAY flou ur KAHM pakt) An agreeement made by the Pilgrims to govern themselves.

mercantilism (MUR kun tihl iz um) An economic idea popular in the 1600s and 1700s, which suggested that governments should limit imports but increase manufacturing and exports, especially to colonies.

mercenary (MUR suh ner ee) A soldier hired by a foreign country.

merchant (MUR chunt) A person who buys and sells goods for profit.

method (METH ud) A way of doing something.

Middle Passage (MIHD ul PAS ij) The forced voyage of enslaved Africans on ships across the Atlantic Ocean from West Africa to the West Indies as part of the triangular trade route from the 1500s to the mid-1800s.

migrate (MY grayt) To move from one place to another.

militia (muh LIHSH uh) Local armies of colonists.

missionary (MIHSH un air ee) A person who is sent to another country to convince others to believe in a particular religion.

monopoly (muh NAHP uh lee) Exclusive control over trade in a certain area.

Monroe Doctrine (mun ROH DAHK trun) U.S. foreign policy established by President James Monroe in 1823, warning European leaders not to establish colonies in the Western Hemisphere.

N

nationalism (NASH un ul ihz um) A feeling of pride for your country.

navigation (nav uh GAY shun) The process of planning a route and finding one's location.

negotiate (nih GOH shee ayt) To discuss something in order to come to an agreement.

neutral (NOO trul) Not taking a side in a conflict.

nomad (NOH mad) A person who moves within a specific region to follow herds of animals and collect food.

Northwest Passage (NORTH west PAS ihj) A northern sea route from the Atlantic to the Pacific oceans that would shorten the route between Europe and Asia.

O

obtain (uh b TEYN) To get or acquire.

ordinance (ORD uh nuns) A law.

organized (OR guh nyzd) Formal or arranged.

overwhelm (oh ver HWELM) Beaten or vanquished.

P

Patriot (PAY tree ut) A colonist who opposed Britain's actions and policies before and during the American Revolution.

patron (PAY trun) A person who supports another financially.

peninsula (puh NIHN suh luh) A piece of land almost surrounded by water, but still attached to the mainland.

persecution (pur suh KYOO shun) Unfair treatment because of race or political or religious beliefs.

persuade (pur SWAYD) To convince.

physical map (FIHZ ih kul map) A map that shows information such as landforms and bodies of water.

pilgrim (PIHL grum) Someone who makes a long journey, usually for religious reasons.

pioneer (py uh NEER) A person who built a home on the edge of the wilderness.

plain (playn) An open area of flat land.

plantation (plan TAY shun) A large farm on which a single crop is usually grown.

political party (puh LIHT ih kul PAHR tee) A group of people with the same general political opinions.

polluted (puh LOOT ihd) Impure, dirty.

Pony Express (POH nee ek SPRES) A system of carrying mail by horse used in the western United States from 1860 to 1861.

popular sovereignty (PAHP yoo lur SAHV run tee) The idea that the government gets its power from the people and needs their consent to make laws.

prairie schooner (PRAIR ee SKOO nur) A common wagon on the westward trail, named after a type of sailing ship.

Preamble (PREE am bul) An introduction.

primary source (PRY mair ee sors) A source that is written or created by someone who witnessed an event.

prime meridian (prym muh RIHD ee un) The line of longitude marked as 0 degrees.

process (PRAH ses) A system by which something is done.

proclamation (prok luh MEY shuhn) An official announcement, usually by the government.

profit (PRAHF iht) The money a business earns after its debts have been paid.

profiteering (prahf ih TEER ing) Charging extra high prices for goods.

proposal (pruh POHZ ul) A plan or suggestion laid out for others to consider.

propose (pruh POHZ) To suggest.

proprietor (pruh PRY uh tur) Someone who owns land or property.

prove (proov) Find out something is difficult or a problem.

Puritan (PYOOR ih tun) Someone who wanted to change the Church of England and came to North America to worship freely in the 1600s.

Q

quarter (KWAR tur) To shelter.

R

ratified (RAT uh fyd) Signed, or made official.

raw material (raw muh TEER ee uhl) A resource that can be made into other products.

Reconstruction (ree kuh n STRUHK shuh n) The name of the plan by President Lincoln to help rebuild and heal the country after the Civil War.

recover (rih KUV ur) To get back; regain.

reflected (rih FLEKT ihd) Shown.

reform (rih FORM) To change.

region (REE jun) An area that shares physical or human characteristics.

regions map (REE junz map) A map that shows areas that share similar physical or human characteristics.

regulate (REG yoo layt) To control or adjust.

reinforcements (ree ihn FORS muntz) More people, supplies, or weapons.

relationship (rih LAY shun) A way in which people or things are connected.

relative location (REL uh tihv loh KAY shun) A description of a place in relation to another place.

relief (rih LEEF) The use of colors and shading on a map to show high and low places.

representative (rep ruh ZEN tuh tihv) A person elected to act for others.

responsible (rih SPAHN suh bul) Able to do what is right or expected.

retain (rih TAYN) To keep.

retreat (rih TREET) The movement of soldiers away from the enemy.

rigid (RIHJ ihd) Unchanging.

royal charter (ROI ul CHAR tur) A document from a king or queen that gave permission to set up and govern a colony.

royal province (ROI ul PRAHV ihns) An area controlled and governed by a king or queen.

rule of law (rool uv law) The idea that all citizens must follow the laws and that they will be protected from government abuse of power.

S

satellite (SAT ul eyt) A device that is placed in orbit around Earth in order to relay radio, television, and telephone signals.

scarcity (SKAIR suh tee) A lack of necessary supplies.

secede (sih SEED) Break away from.

secession (sih SESH uhn) To formally stop being part of something.

secondary source (SEK un dair ee sors) A source that is written or created by someone who did not witness an event.

segregation (seg ri GEY shuh n) The separation of groups of people, usually by race.

separation of powers (sep uh RAY shun uv POU urz) The idea that the powers and duties of government are divided among separate branches.

sharecropping (SHAIR krop ing) A system in which someone who owns land rents the land to others in exchange for some of the crops raised on the land.

siege (seej) A military blockade designed to make a city surrender.

significant (sihg NIHF uh kunt) Important.

slave trade (slayv trayd) Getting, transporting, and selling human beings as slaves.

slavery (SLAY vur ee) The act of buying and selling people.

Sons of Liberty (sunz uv LIHB ur tee) A group of colonial men who protested the unjust taxes of the British.

Stamp Act (stamp akt) A law passed by the British government that taxed all of the paper used by the colonists.

strategy (STRAT i jee) A thought-out plan to accomplish a goal over a long time.

style (stahyl) A distinctive, particular, or characteristic of acting or way of moving.

states' rights (steyts ryts) The right of each U.S. state to make its own local laws.

sufficient (suh FIHSH unt) Good enough.

suffrage (SUF rihj) The right to vote.

survey (SUR vay) A very detailed record of a geographical feature.

symbol (SIHM bul) An action or object that represents an idea or feeling.

T

tariff (TAIR ihf) Taxes on products coming into a country.

technology (tek NAHL uh jee) The use of scientific knowledge or tools to do work.

tolerance (TAHL ur uns) A fair attitude toward those whose opinions, beliefs, practices, and race differ from your own.

Townshend Acts (TOUN zend akts) A series of acts that placed taxes on products being sold to the colonists.

total war (TOHT l wawr) A method of warfare that seeks to destroy civilian as well as military targets to force a surrender.

trading network (TRAYD ing NET wurk) A system of trade routes that connected different areas.

tradition (truh DIHSH un) A custom or belief that is passed on from one generation to the next.

Trail of Tears (trayl uv teerz) The journey of American Indians from their homes in the east to the Indian Territory.

treason (TREE zun) The act of attempting to overthrow one's government.

treaty (TREE tee) An agreement, usually between nations.

Treaty of Paris (TREE tee uv PAR ihs) The peace treaty between Great Britain and the United States in 1783 that ended the American Revolution.

triangular trade (try ANG gyuh lur trayd) A pattern of trade that developed during the 1600s and 1700s that had three parts and linked the 13 colonies with Europe, Africa, and the West Indies.

U

Underground Railroad (UHN der GROUND REYL rohd) A secret organization that helped escaped enslaved African Americans to get to the North or to Canada.

unify (YOO nih fy) To bring together.

Union (YOON yuhn) Another name for the United States, especially the northern states during the Civil War.

unite (yoo NYT) To join together to achieve a common goal.

uprising (UP ryz ing) A revolt.

V

vaquero (vah KER oh) A Mexican cowboy.

veto (VEE toh) A refusal to sign a bill into law.

viceroy (VYS roi) Someone sent by a king or queen to rule a colony.

violate (VY uh layt) To do something that is against the law.

W

wagon train (WAG un trayn) A line of wagons traveling as a group.

Glosario

A

abolition/abolición Movimiento para terminar con la esclavitud.

abolitionist/abolicionista Persona que apoyaba el movimiento para poner fin a la esclavitud.

absolute location/ubicación absoluta La ubicación exacta de un lugar que no cambia.

academy/academia Lugar para estudio o entrenamiento.

according/según Conforme a.

accumulate/acumular Reunir una cantidad cada vez mayor de algo.

accurately/con precisión Sin equivocaciones ni errores.

acknowledge/reconocer Admitir la autoridad de alguien.

adapt/adaptarse Acostumbrarse a nuevas condiciones.

adviser/asesor Persona que da consejos o indicaciones.

advocate/defensor Persona que apoya una causa.

agriculture/agricultura La plantación y el cultivo para obtener cosechas.

alliance/alianza Acuerdo o pacto.

ally/aliado Socio militar.

amendment/enmienda Cambio o incorporación, especialmente a la Constitución de los Estados Unidos.

anarchy/anarquía Falta de ley; desorden causado por no haber reglas.

ancestor/ancestro Pariente que vivió en el pasado.

Anglican/anglicano Relacionado con la Iglesia de Inglaterra.

annex/anexar Ocupar un territorio.

announce/anunciar Dar a conocer de forma oficial o pública.

anthem/himno Una canción.

Anti-Federalist/antifederalista Persona que apoyaba los Artículos de la Confederación.

Articles of Confederation/Artículos de la Confederación Acuerdo entre los 13 estados originales que sirvió como la primera Constitución de los Estados Unidos.

artifact/artefacto Objeto hecho y usado por personas que suele tener interés histórico o cultural.

artisan/artesano Persona especializada en un tipo de trabajo o comercio.

aspect/aspecto Una parte de algo.

assassinate/asesinar Matar a alguien famoso o poderoso, generalmente por razones políticas.

assemble/congregarse Reunirse.

astrolabe/astrolabio Instrumento usado en navegación que mide la posición del sol y las estrellas.

authority/autoridad El poder de dar órdenes o tomar decisiones.

autobiography/autobiografía El relato de la vida de una persona escrito por esa misma persona.

B

barter/hacer un trueque Intercambiar un bien por otro.

Bill of Rights/Carta de Derechos Las diez primeras enmiendas de la Constitución de los Estados Unidos, que garantizan derechos básicos a todos sus ciudadanos.

biography/biografía Libro acerca de la vida de una persona escrito por otra persona.

black codes/códigos negros Conjunto de leyes aprobadas a finales del siglo XIX que les negaban el derecho a votar a los hombres afroamericanos y les impedían poseer armas y tomar ciertos tipos de empleo.

blockade/bloqueo Barrera de tropas o barcos colocada con el fin de evitar que las personas y los suministros entren o salgan de una zona.

boundary/límite Línea que divide un área de otra.

boycott/boicot El rechazo a comprar un producto como parte de una protesta.

C

Cabinet/Gabinete Grupo de asesores que suelen aconsejar al presidente o a otro líder.

canal/canal Vía de navegación hecha por el hombre.

capable/capaz Que tiene la habilidad necesaria.

caravan/caravana Grupo de familias que se trasladaban juntas al Oeste.

caravel/carabela Barco pequeño y veloz.

carpetbaggers/*carpetbaggers* Norteños que iban al Sur después de la Guerra Civil para empezar negocios.

cash crop/cultivo comercial Cultivos que se venden en lugar de ser usados por el agricultor.

challenge/desafío Situación difícil.

checks and balances/sistema de controles y equilibrios Sistema donde cada poder del gobierno tiene maneras de limitar las capacidades de los otros poderes.

civilization/civilización Sociedad que tiene sistemas organizados de gobierno, religión y enseñanza.

class/clase Rango en una sociedad basado en riqueza o importancia.

class system/sistema de clases Método para clasificar a las personas, a menudo según su raza, poder o riqueza.

climate/clima El estado del tiempo habitual a lo largo del tiempo en un lugar.

colony/colonia País o zona que está bajo el control de otro país.

Columbian Exchange/intercambio colombino El movimiento de personas, animales, plantas y culturas entre el hemisferio oriental y el occidental.

commerce/comercio Los negocios o transacciones entre países o estados.

commodity/bien de consumo Bien de comercio que es una materia prima y no algo manufacturado.

compromise/acuerdo Situación donde las personas de los dos lados de una disputa renuncian a algo para llegar a un acuerdo.

condition/condición El estado físico de algo.

Confederacy/Confederación Otro nombre para los Estados Confederados de América, los estados sureños durante la Guerra Civil.

confederacy/confederación Grupo en el que todos los miembros comparten las mismas metas; suelen tener una forma escrita u oral de alianza o pacto.

confine/recluir Impedir la salida de alguien; encarcelar.

congress/congreso Cuerpo de gobierno para la creación de leyes.

conquistador/conquistador Alguien que conquista un territorio, especialmente los españoles en América del Norte y América del Sur en el siglo XVI.

constitution/constitución Plan de gobierno, generalmente escrito, pero puede ser oral.

constitutional republic/república constitucional Gobierno en el que los funcionarios son elegidos para representar al pueblo y luego gobiernan según una constitución.

construct/construir Fabricar.

consult/consultar Buscar información o consejo en algo o pidiéndolo a alguien.

Continental Army/Ejército Continental Durante la Guerra de Independencia, el ejército autorizado por el Congreso Continental en 1775 y liderado por George Washington.

convince/convencer Hacer que alguien crea que algo es cierto.

coordinate/coordinar Unir cosas diferentes; poner en el orden correcto.

council/consejo Cuerpo de gobierno que toma decisiones y puede estar formado solo por el líder de un grupo o por un pequeño grupo de líderes.

create/crear Diseñar o inventar algo.

crucial/crucial De gran importancia.

currency/moneda corriente Dinero.

current events/sucesos actuales Sucesos que están en las noticias.

custom/costumbre Formas de vida que se practican a menudo.

customs/tasa de aduana Impuestos a los productos que llegan a un país.

D

debt/deuda Cantidad de dinero que se debe.

declare/declarar Dar a conocer al público.

defend/defender Proteger de daño o peligro.

delegate/delegado Persona que representa a otros; suele ser un funcionario elegido por el voto.

demolish/demoler Destruir.

determine/determinar Decidir.

discrimination/discriminación Tratamiento injusto a las personas; suele estar basado en raza, género o edad.

display/exhibir Mostrar.

distinct/distinto Diferente.

distribute/distribuir Dividir algo entre varias personas.

diverse/diverso Que tiene mucha variedad.

domestic tranquility/tranquilidad doméstica Paz dentro de una nación.

drought/sequía Período de tiempo largo con poca lluvia o sin lluvia.

E

economy/economía El sistema con el que un grupo produce, comparte y usa bienes.

ecosystem/ecosistema Todos los seres vivos que comparten un entorno e interactúan en él.

Electoral College/Colegio Electoral Grupo de personas elegidas por el pueblo en cada estado con el fin de que elijan a su vez al Presidente y al Vicepresidente de los Estados Unidos.

elevation/altitud Distancia o altura de la tierra sobre el nivel del mar.

elevation map/mapa de altitud Mapa que compara y contrasta las elevaciones de diferentes áreas.

eliminate/eliminar Quitar.

emancipation/emancipación La liberación de los afroamericanos esclavizados.

emerge/surgir Aparecer.

empire/imperio Un gran grupo de estados o países.

enable/permitir Dejar que algo ocurra.

encomienda/encomienda Sistema establecido por el gobierno español que daba a los colonos españoles el derecho a tomar tierras y controlar a los indígenas americanos en esa tierra.

enforce/hacer cumplir Hacer que las personas obedezcan una ley or regla.

enlist/alistarse Unirse al ejército.

enormous/enorme De gran tamaño.

entrepreneur/empresario Alguien que toma riesgos para crear una empresa.

epidemic/epidemia Una enfermedad muy difundida.

equality/igualdad La condición de tener los mismos derechos que todos los demás.

equator/ecuador Línea imaginaria que corre alrededor del centro de la Tierra.

establish/fundar Crear u organizar algo que es permanente.

eventually/con el tiempo Después de que pase un tiempo.

examine/examinar Inspeccionar en detalle.

executive/ejecutivo Poder del gobierno que ejecuta las leyes.

exhibit/exhibición Colección de objetos que se muestra para que las personas la vean.

expedition/expedición Un viaje.

export/exportación Producto que es vendido a otros países.

F

famine/hambruna Una falta extrema de alimentos.

Federalist/federalista Persona que apoyó la nueva Constitución de los Estados Unidos.

finance/financiar Dar dinero para algo.

folklore/folklore Costumbres, creencias y cuentos tradicionales.

foreign policy/política exterior Políticas de un país para tratar con otros países.

foundation/fundamento La base o el apoyo de algo.

frontier/frontera El límite con las tierras vírgenes.

G

geography/geografía La tierra y las masas de agua de un lugar.

globe/globo terráqueo Un modelo de la Tierra.

gold rush/fiebre del oro Una repentina masa de personas que llega a un área donde se descubrió oro.

government/gobierno Un sistema para crear reglas y tomar decisiones para ayudar a un grupo o una nación.

H

hemisphere/hemisferio La mitad de la esfera de la Tierra.

historical map/mapa histórico Mapa que muestra un punto particular del pasado.

horrific/horrible Tener el poder de causar horror; espantoso o estremecedor.

House of Burgesses/Cámara de los Burgueses El primer cuerpo legislativo representativo de América del Norte; fundado en la colonia de Virginia.

hunter-gatherer/cazador-recolector Personas antiguas que vivían de la caza de animales y la recolección de nueces, semillas y frutas.

I

impeachment/juicio político Proceso por el cual cargos son presentados contra un funcionario.

import/importación Producto traído de otro país.

impressment/reclutamiento forzado La práctica de capturar soldados extranjeros y obligarlos a trabajar para un país que no es el suyo.

inauguration/inauguración Ceremonia que marca el comienzo de algo.

indentured servant/siervo por contrato Persona que acepta trabajar sin pago durante cierto período de tiempo a cambio de comida, ropa y vivienda con la promesa de recibir tierras.

independence/independencia Libertad.

indicate/indicar Señalar, mostrar.

inflation/inflación Cuando los precios de los bienes aumentan y el valor del dinero disminuye.

influence/influir Ayudar a producir un efecto.

innovation/innovación La introducción de algo nuevo.

insert/insertar Meter.

inspect/inspeccionar Mirar algo con detenimiento.

interact/interactuar Hablar o trabajar con otros.

interpreter/intérprete Persona que traduce idiomas extranjeros.

investigate/investigar Estudiar con mucha atención.

irrigation/irrigación El uso de tecnología para llevar agua a los cultivos.

judicial/judicial Poder del gobierno que está formado por cortes y jueces, y decide lo que significan las leyes.

Juneteenth/fiesta del 19 de junio Nombre de la celebración del día en que afroamericanos esclavizados en Texas supieron sobre la Proclamación de Emancipación.

King Philip's War/Guerra del Rey Philip Guerra entre los colonos y los indígenas norteamericanos en 1637, llevada a cabo por Metacom, también conocido como Rey Philip.

landform/accidente geográfico Característica natural de la Tierra, como las montañas y los desiertos.

latitude/latitud Líneas en un mapa separadas por distancias regulares que se extienden alrededor del globo al norte y al sur del ecuador.

league/liga Grupo cuyos miembros comparten las mismas metas.

legislative/legislativo Poder del gobierno que crea las leyes.

levy/imponer Recaudar u obligar a algo.

longitude/longitud Líneas en un mapa separadas por distancias regulares que se extienden hacia el norte y hacia el sur entre el Polo Norte y el Polo Sur.

Loyalist/leal al rey Persona que se mantuvo leal a Inglaterra durante la Guerra de Independencia.

maintain/mantener Continuar con algo o hacerlo seguir sin cambios.

Manifest Destiny/destino manifiesto La idea, muy popular en el siglo XIX, de que Estados Unidos tenía el derecho a adquirir territorio hasta llegar al Océano Pacífico.

martial law/ley marcial Colocar al ejército a cargo del gobierno.

mass production/producción en masa Sistema para producir una gran cantidad del mismo artículo al mismo tiempo.

massacre/masacre La matanza intencional de muchas personas.

Mayflower Compact/Pacto del Mayflower Acuerdo hecho por los peregrinos para gobernarse a sí mismos.

mercantilism/mercantilismo Idea económica popular en los siglos XVII y XVIII, que sugería que los gobiernos deberían limitar las importaciones pero aumentar la fabricación y las exportaciones, especialmente a las colonias.

mercenary/mercenario Soldado contratado por un país extranjero.

merchant/comerciante Persona que compra y vende bienes para obtener una ganancia.

method/método Una manera de hacer algo.

Middle Passage/travesía intermedia El viaje forzado de africanos esclavizados en barco a través del océano Atlántico desde África Occidental hasta el Caribe, desde el siglo XVI hasta mediados del siglo XIX, como parte de la ruta de comercio triangular.

migrate/migrar Trasladarse desde un lugar a otro.

militia/milicia Ejércitos locales formados por colonos.

missionary/misionero Persona enviada a otro país para convencer a otros de que crean en una religión.

monopoly/monopolio Control exclusivo del comercio en un área determinada.

Monroe Doctrine/Doctrina Monroe Política exterior de los Estados Unidos creada por el presidente James Monroe en 1823, que advertía a los líderes europeos que no establecieran colonias en el hemisferio occidental.

N

nationalism/nacionalismo Sentimiento de orgullo por tu país.

navigation/navegación El proceso de planificar una ruta y encontrar la propia ubicación.

negotiate/negociar Discutir algo para llegar a un acuerdo.

neutral/neutral Que no se pone de uno de los lados en un conflicto.

nomad/nómada Persona que viaja por una región específica para seguir grupos de animales y recoger comida.

Northwest Passage/paso del noroeste Ruta de navegación al norte desde el océano Atlántico hasta el océano Pacífico que acortaría el trayecto entre Europa y Asia.

O

obtain/obtener Conseguir o adquirir.

ordinance/decreto Ley.

organized/organizado Formal u ordenado.

overwhelmed/asolado Dominado o vencido.

P

Patriot/patriota Colono que estaba en contra de las acciones y políticas de Inglaterra antes y durante la Guerra de Independencia.

patron/patrocinador Persona que da apoyo financiero a otra.

peninsula/península Porción de tierra rodeada por agua casi por completo pero unida al continente.

persecution/persecución Trato injusto a causa de raza o creencias políticas o religiosas.

persuade/persuadir Convencer.

physical map/mapa físico Mapa que muestra información como accidentes geográficos y masas de agua.

pilgrim/peregrino Alguien que hace un viaje muy largo, generalmente por motivos religiosos.

pioneer/pionero Persona que construye una casa en el límite con las tierras vírgenes.

plain/llanura Zona abierta o tierra plana.

plantation/plantación Granja de gran tamaño en la que se suele cultivar solo un tipo de planta.

political party/partido político Grupo de personas que tienen las mismas opiniones políticas en general.

polluted/contaminado Impuro, sucio.

Pony Express/Pony Express Sistema de transporte de correo a caballo usado en el oeste de los Estados Unidos desde 1860 a 1861.

popular sovereignty/soberanía popular La idea de que el gobierno obtiene su poder del pueblo y necesita su consentimiento para crear leyes.

prairie schooner/goleta de la pradera Un tipo de carreta común en el camino hacia el oeste; su nombre viene de un tipo de barco.

Preamble/preámbulo Introducción.

primary source/fuente primaria Fuente que fue escrita o creada por alguien que fue testigo de un suceso.

prime meridian/primer meridiano Línea de longitud marcada como 0 grados.

process/proceso Sistema con el que se hace algo.

proclamation/proclamación Anuncio oficial, generalmente del gobierno.

profit/ganancia Dinero que gana una empresa después de que sus deudas fueron pagadas.

profiteering/ganancias excesivas Cobrar precios demasiado altos por bienes.

proposal/propuesta Plan o sugerencia que se presenta ante otros para que lo consideren.

propose/proponer Sugerir.

proprietor/propietario Alguien que posee tierra o propiedad.

prove/validar Encontrar que algo tiene particular valor o mérito.

Puritan/puritano Alguien que quería cambiar la Iglesia de Inglaterra y se trasladó a América del Norte para practicar su religión libremente en el siglo XVII.

Q

quarter/alojar Dar albergue.

R

ratified/ratificado Firmado o hecho oficial.

raw material/materia prima Recurso que se usa para hacer otros productos.

Reconstruction/Reconstrucción Nombre del plan del presidente Lincoln para ayudar a reconstruir y sanar el país después de la Guerra Civil.

recover/recuperar Volver a tener algo, recobrar.

reflected/reflejado Mostrado.

reform/reformar Cambiar.

region/región Zona donde existen las mismas características físicas o humanas.

regions map/mapa de regiones Mapa que muestra zonas donde existen las mismas características físicas o humanas.

regulate/regular Controlar o ajustar.

reinforcements/refuerzos Más personas, provisiones o armas.

relationship/relación Manera en la que personas o cosas están conectadas.

relative location/ubicación relativa Descripción de un lugar en relación con otro lugar.

relief/relieve Uso de colores y sombras en un mapa para mostrar lugares altos y bajos.

representative/representante Persona elegida para actuar en nombre de otros.

responsible/responsable Capaz de hacer lo correcto o lo que se espera.

retain/retener Conservar.

retreat/retirada Movimiento de soldados para alejarse del enemigo.

rigid/rígido Que no cambia.

royal charter/carta real Documento de un rey o una reina que daba permiso para fundar y gobernar una colonia.

royal province/provincia real Zona controlada y gobernada por un rey o una reina.

rule of law/imperio de la ley La idea de que todos los ciudadanos deben obedecer las leyes y serán protegidos del abuso de poder por parte del gobierno.

S

satellite/satélite Artefacto que entra en órbita alrededor de la Tierra para transmitir señales de radio, televisión y teléfono.

scarcity/escasez Falta de provisiones necesarias.

secede/separarse Apartarse o retirarse de algo.

secession/secesión Acto de separarse formalmente de algo.

secondary source/fuente secundaria Fuente que fue escrita o creada por alguien que no fue testigo de un suceso.

segregation/segregación Separación de un grupo de personas, generalmente por su raza.

separation of powers/separación de poderes La idea de que las capacidades y las obligaciones de un gobierno se dividen en poderes separados.

sharecroppping/aparcería Sistema en el que alguien que posee tierras se las alquila a otros a cambio de parte de sus cultivos.

siege/sitio Bloqueo militar diseñado para hacer que una ciudad se rinda.

significant/significativo Importante.

slave trade/comercio de esclavos Obtener, transportar y vender seres humanos como esclavos.

slavery/esclavitud La acción de comprar y vender esclavos.

Sons of Liberty/Hijos de la Libertad Grupo de colonos que protestaban por los impuestos injustos que debían pagar a los ingleses.

Stamp Act/Ley del Timbre Ley aprobada por el gobierno inglés que establecía un impuesto a todo el papel usado por los colonos.

strategy/estrategia Plan bien pensado para alcanzar una meta durante un largo período de tiempo.

style/estilo Manera distintiva, particular o característica de actuar o moverse.

states' rights/derechos de los estados Derecho de cada estado de los Estados Unidos a crear sus propias leyes locales.

sufficient/suficiente Tan bueno como es necesario.

suffrage/sufragio Derecho al voto.

survey/agrimensura Un registro muy detallado de una característica geográfica.

symbol/símbolo Acción u objeto que representa una idea o un sentimiento.

T

tariff/arancel Impuestos a productos que entran en un país.

technology/tecnología Uso de conocimiento o instrumentos científicos para hacer un trabajo.

tolerance/tolerancia Actitud justa hacia personas cuyas opiniones, creencias y raza son distintas de las tuyas.

Townshend Acts/Leyes Townshend Una serie de actas que establecían impuestos sobre los productos que eran vendidos a los colonos.

total war/guerra total Método de guerra que busca destruir objetivos civiles y militares por igual para obligar al enemigo a rendirse.

trading network/red de comercio Sistema de rutas de rutas de comercio que conectaban zonas diferentes.

tradition/tradición Costumbre o creencia que se transmite de una generación a la siguiente.

Trail of Tears/Camino de Lágrimas El viaje de los indígenas norteamericanos desde sus hogares en el este hasta el territorio indígena.

treason/traición La acción de intentar derrocar el gobierno del país propio.

treaty/tratado Un acuerdo, generalmente entre naciones.

Treaty of Paris/Tratado de París Tratado de paz entre Inglaterra y los Estados Unidos en 1783 que terminó con la Guerra de Independencia.

triangular trade/comercio triangular Un patrón de comercio que se desarrolló en los siglos XVII y XVIII que tenía tres partes y unía las 13 colonias con Europa, África y el Caribe.

U

Underground Railroad/Tren Clandestino Organización secreta que ayudó a afroamericanos esclavizados a escapar y llegar al Norte o a Canadá.

unify/unificar Unir.

Union/Unión Otro nombre para los Estados Unidos, especialmente los estados norteños durante la Guerra Civil.

unite/unirse Lograr un acuerdo para alcanzar un objetivo común.

uprising/levantamiento Revuelta.

V

vaquero/vaquero Pastor de vacas mexicano.

veto/veto Rechazo a firmar un proyecto de ley.

viceroy/virrey Alguien que es enviado por un rey o una reina para gobernar una colonia.

violate/transgredir Hacer algo en contra de la ley.

W

wagon train/caravana de carretas Una fila de carretas que viajaban en grupo.

Index

This index lists the pages on which topics appear in this book. Page numbers followed by *m* refer to maps. Page numbers followed by *p* refer to photographs. Page numbers followed by *c* refer to charts or graphs. Page numbers followed by *t* refer to timelines. The terms *See* and *See also* direct the reader to alternate entries.

Stock Photo; 116: George Bernard/Science Source; 118L: Photo Researchers, Inc/Alamy Stock Photo; 118R: Lebrecht Music and Arts Photo Library/Alamy Stock Photo; 119: Robert Stanton/AFP/Getty Images; 121: North Wind Picture Archives/Alamy Stock Photo; 122: American Swedish Historical Museum; 125: Alexey Smolyanyy/Shutterstock; 126B: Branislavpudar/Shutterstock; 126T: Sarin Images/Granger, NYC

Chapter 04

132-133: Dennis Tarnay, Jr./Alamy Stock Photo; 134: Philip Scalia/Alamy Stock Photo; 135BL: North Wind Picture Archives/Alamy Stock Photo; 135BR: Interfoto/Personalities/Alamy Stock Photo; 135TL: North Wind Picture Archives/Alamy Stock Photo; 135TR: North Wind Picture Archives/Alamy Stock Photo; 137: Syda Productions/Shutterstock; 138-139: Mira/Alamy Stock Photo; 141: David Persson/Shutterstock; 143: JG Photography/Alamy Stock Photo; 145: North Wind Picture Archives; 146: Ad Oculos/Shutterstock; 147: African Americans picking cotton on a southern plantation. 1883/Universal History Archive/UIG/Bridgeman Art Library; 149: Mark Summerfield/Alamy Stock Photo; 153: Pat & Chuck Blackley/Alamy Stock Photo; 154: North Wind Picture Archives/Alamy Stock Photo; 155: North Wind Picture Archives/Alamy Stock Photo; 158: Pictorial Press Ltd/Alamy Stock Photo; 158: World History Archive/Alamy Stock Photo; 160: North Wind Picture Archives; 161: Photo Researchers, Inc/Alamy Stock Photo; 162: North Wind Picture Archives/Alamy Stock Photo; 163: Music Alan King/Alamy Stock Photo; 164: Nat Turner (1800-31) with fellow insurgent slaves during the Slave Rebellion of 1831 (coloured engraving 1863), Darley, Felix Octavius Carr (1822-88) (after)/Private Collection/Peter Newark American Pictures/Bridgeman Art Library; 166: Pictorial Press Ltd/Alamy Stock Photo; 168: North Wind Picture Archives/Alamy Stock Photo; 170-171: Michael Runkel Appalacheans/Alamy Stock Photo; 172: North Wind Picture Archives/Alamy Stock Photo; 175: Richard Nowitz/National Geographic Creative/Alamy Stock Photo; 177: North Wind Picture Archives/Alamy Stock Photo; 178: North Wind Picture Archives; 180B: Stock Montage/Archive Photos/Getty Images; 180T: Wim Wiskerke/Alamy Stock Photo

Chapter 05

186-187: Nancy Carter/North Wind Picture Archives/Alamy Stock Photo; 188: Daniel Dempster Photography/Alamy Stock Photo; 189BL: Photo Researchers, Inc/Alamy Stock Photo; 189BR: James Lafayette Armistead (engraving), Martin, John (1789-1854)/Virginia Historical Society, Richmond, Virginia, USA/Bridgeman Art Library; 189TL: GraphicaArtis/Archive Photos/Getty Images; 189TR: SuperStock/Getty Images; 192-193: Niday Picture Library/Alamy Stock Photo; 194B: Bettmann/Getty Images; 194T: JT Vintage/Glasshouse Images/Alamy Stock Photo; 195: Benjamin Franklin/Library of Congress Prints and Photographs Division[LC-USZC4-5315]; 196:

North Wind Picture Archives/Alamy Stock Photo; 200: Niday Picture Library/Alamy Stock Photo; 201B: North Wind Picture Archives/Alamy Stock Photo; 201T: Carol M. Highsmith/Library of Congress Prints and Photographs Division[LC-DIG-highsm-09900]; 203: Bettmann/Getty Images; 204L: John Singleton Copley/De Agostini Picture Library/Getty Images; 204R: Thomas Hutchinson (1711-80) 1741 (oil on canvas), Truman, Edward (18th century)/Massachusetts Historical Society, Boston, MA, USA/Bridgeman Art Library; 205: VCG Wilson/Fine Art/Corbis Historical/Getty Images; 206: North Wind Picture Archives/Alamy Stock Photo; 210: Barney Burstein/Corbis Historical/VCG/Getty Images; 212: Bettmann/Getty Images; 214: Fine Art Images/Heritage Images/Hulton Archive/Getty Images; 215: Universal History Archive/Universal Images Group/Getty Images; 216: Culture Club/Hulton Archive/Getty Images; 218B: EvgeniyQ/iStock/Getty Images; 218T: Stock Montage/Archive Photos/Getty Images; 220: North Wind Picture Archives/Alamy Stock Photo; 222: North Wind Picture Archives/Alamy Stock Photo; 224: VCG Wilson/Fine Art/Corbis Historical/Getty Images; 227C: Universal History Archive/Universal Images Group/Getty Images; 227L: Photo Researchers, Inc/Alamy Stock Photo; 227R: Lebrecht Authors/Lebrecht Music and Arts Photo Library/Alamy Stock Photo; 228: North Wind Picture Archives/Alamy Stock Photo; 229: Fotosearch/Archive Photos/Getty Images; 230: Edmund P. Restein/Ludwig Restein/Library of Congress Prints and Photographs Division[LC-DIG-pga-02468]; 233: World History Archive/Alamy Stock Photo; 235: Everett Collection Historical/Alamy Stock Photo; 236: North Wind Picture Archives/Alamy Stock Photo; 238B: JacobH/E+/Getty Images; 238T: Photos.com/Getty Images; 243: Kevin Dodge/Corbis/Getty Images

Chapter 06

244: Tim Mainiero/Shutterstock; 246: Kickstand/E+/Getty Images; 247BL: North Wind Picture Archives/Alamy Stock Photo; 247BR: North Wind Picture Archives/Alamy Stock Photo; 247TL: National Portrait Gallery, Smithsonian Institution/Art Resource; 247TR: Everett Historical/Shutterstock; 249: Tom Grill/JGI/Blend Images/Getty Images; 250-251: The Artchives/Alamy Stock Photo; 254: North Wind Picture Archives/Alamy Stock Photo; 258: Kali Nine LLC/E+/Getty Images; 260-261: GraphicaArtis/Archive Photos/Getty Images; 262: World History Archive/Alamy Stock Photo; 264: Kickstand/E+/Getty Images; 266: Peter Gridley/Stockbyte/Getty Images; 269: Mark Wilson/Getty Images; 270: Duplessis, Joseph-Siffrède/Library of Congress Prints and Photographs Division[LC-USZC4-7214]; 273L: Albert Knapp/Alamy Stock Photo; 273R: Everett Collection Historical/Alamy Stock Photo; 274: Everett Historical/Shutterstock; 275: Niday Picture Library/Alamy Stock Photo; 276: Brooks Kraft/Corbis Historical/Getty Images; 277B: Max Herman/SIPPL Sipa USA/AP Images; 277T: Jim West/Alamy Stock Photo; 280L: Pictorial Press Ltd/Alamy Stock

Photo; 280R: Bettmann/Getty Images; 282: Justin Sullivan/ Getty Images; 284: Chuck Place/Alamy Stock Photo; 285: Omersukrugoksu/E+/Getty Images; 286: Francis Miller/The LIFE Picture Collection/Getty Images; 287: SU Archives/ Everett Collection Inc/Alamy Stock Photo; 288: Keystone Pictures USA/Alamy Stock Photo; 290B: Michael Neelon (tourism)/Alamy Stock Photo; 290T: Everett Historical/ Shutterstock; 295: Asiseeit/E+/Getty Images

Chapter 07

296-297: Rudi1976/Alamy Stock Photo; 298: Picsbyst/ Shutterstock; 299BL: North Wind Picture Archives/Alamy Stock Photo; 299BR: Niday Picture Library/Alamy Stock Photo; 299TL: Lewis and Clark with Sacagawea(colour litho)(detail), Paxson,Edgar Samuel (1852-1915)/Private Collection/Peter Newark American Pictures/Bridgeman Art Library; 299TR: B. Christopher/Alamy Stock Photo; 302-303: First in War,First in Peace and First in the Hearts of His Countrymen (colour litho), American School, (19th century) /©Collection of the New-York Historical Society, USA/Bridgeman Art Library.; 304: North Wind Picture Archives/Alamy Stock Photo; 305: Amble Design/ Shutterstock; 307: Nikreates/Alamy Stock Photo; 308: North Wind Picture Archives/Alamy Stock Photo; 310: Bettmann/Getty Images; 312: North Wind Picture Archives; 314: North Wind Picture Archives/Alamy Stock Photo; 316: North Wind Picture Archives/Alamy Stock Photo; 318: Andrew Molinaro/Alamy Stock Photo; 319: North Wind Picture Archives/Alamy Stock Photo; 320: GL Archive/ Alamy Stock Photo; 321L: North Wind Picture Archives/ Alamy Stock Photo; 321R: Backyard Productions/Alamy Stock Photo; 323: Niday Picture Library/Alamy Stock Photo; 324B: XAOC/Shutterstock; 324T: Bettmann/Getty Images; 325: World History Archive/Alamy Stock Photo; 326: A Hundred Years Peace, the signing of the Treaty of Ghent between Great Britain and the US Dec. 24, 1814, to end the War of 1812.Painting by Amedee Forestier (1854-1930) made in 1914, oil on canvas, 71.4 x102 cm.Belgium,19th century/De Agostini Picture Library/Bridgeman Art Library.; 328: Sarin Images/Granger, NYC; 329: Print Collector/ Hulton Archive/Getty Images; 330: North Wind Picture Archives; 333: Jackson slaying the many headed monster', 1828 (colour litho), American School, (19th century)/ Private Collection/Peter Newark American Pictures/ Bridgeman Art Library.; 334: Niday Picture Library/Alamy Stock Photo; 336: Granger, NYC; 337: North Wind Picture Archives/Alamy Stock Photo; 338: Aldo Liverani/Andia/ Alamy Stock Photo; 339: Everett Collection Historical/ Alamy Stock Photo; 340: North Wind Picture Archives/ Alamy Stock Photo; 342T: The Great Famine of Ireland in 1849 (gouache on paper), Nicolle, Pat (Patrick)(1907-95)/ Private Collection/Look and Learn/Bridgeman Art Library.; 344BL: Shutterstock; 344BR: Everett Collection Inc/Alamy Stock Photo; 344T: Encyclopaedia Britannica, Inc./Library of Congress/Universal Images Group North America LLC/ Alamy Stock Photo; 345: Pictorial Press Ltd/Alamy Stock Photo; 346: Everett Historical/Shutterstock; 347: Bettmann/

Getty Images; 348: Niday Picture Library/Alamy Stock Photo; 350: Niday Picture Library/Alamy Stock Photo; 351BC: IanDagnall Computing/Alamy Stock Photo; 351BL: World History Archive/Alamy Stock Photo; 351BR: Everett Collection Historical/Alamy Stock Photo; 351TC: IanDagnall Computing/Alamy Stock Photo; 351TL: Collection/Active Museum/Alamy Stock Photo; 351TR: Niday Picture Library/ Alamy Stock Photo; 642B: North Wind Picture Archives/ Alamy Stock Photo

Chapter 08

356-357: Charles Phelps Cushing/ClassicStock/ Archive Photos/Getty Images; 358: George Ostertag/Age Fotostock; 359BL: Everett Collection Historical/Alamy Stock Photo; 359BR: Fotosearch/Archive Photos/Getty Images; 359TL: Stock Montage/Hulton Archive/Archive Photos/ Getty Images; 359TR: Narcissa Whitman (1808-47) (litho) (see also 268168)0, American School, (19th century)/ Private Collection/Peter Newark American Pictures/ Bridgeman Art Library; 362: Photo Researchers, Inc/Alamy Stock Photo; 364: North Wind Picture Archives; 365: North Wind Picture Archives; 367: North Wind Picture Archives/ Alamy Stock Photo; 369: Bettmann/Getty Images; 372: Ricardo Reitmeyer/Shutterstock; 373: Bettmann/Getty Images; 376B: Ed Vebell/Archive Photos/Getty Images; 376T: T. Lesia/Shutterstock; 378: Bettmann/Getty Images; 379: Plan-B/Shutterstock; 383B: MPI/Archive Photos/ Getty Images; 383T: Gary Crabbe/Enlightened Images/ Alamy Stock Photo; 385: Presbyterian Historical Society; 386: North Wind Picture Archives/Alamy Stock Photo; 387: North Wind Picture Archives/Alamy Stock Photo; 390: Kali9/iStock/Getty Images; 391: Nata-Lunata/Shutterstock; 392: North Wind Picture Archives/Alamy Stock Photo; 393: Bettmann/Getty Images; 394: Gold prospectors using a 'long tom' sluice at Spanish Flat, California, 1852 (b/w photo), American Photographer, (19th century)/ Private Collection/Peter Newark American Pictures/ Bridgeman Art Library; 395: Granger, NYC; 396: Chinese Immigrants working on the gold fields, 1849 (coloured engraving), American School, (19th century)/Private Collection/Peter Newark American Pictures/Bridgeman Art Library; 398: George A. Crofutt/Library of Congress Prints and Photographs Division[LC-DIG-ppmsca-09855]; 400:Peter Stackpole/The Life Picture Collection/Getty Images; 401BCL: Ed Vebell/Archive Photos/Getty Images; 401BCR: MPI/Archive Photos/Getty Images; 401BR: Plan-B/ Shutterstock; 401TC: T. Lesia/Shutterstock; 401TL: North Wind Picture Archives/Alamy Stock Photo; 401TR: North Wind Picture Archives/Alamy Stock Photo

Chapter 09

408 Juanmonino/E+/Getty Images; 406-407 Karen Bleier/ AFP/Getty Images; 409TL Stocktrek Images, Inc./Alamy Stock Photo; 409TR Bettmann/Getty Images; 409BL Pictorial Press Ltd/Alamy Stock Photo; 409BR Stocktrek Images, Inc./Alamy Stock Photo; 412 North Wind Picture Archives/Alamy Stock Photo; 416T PF-(bygone1)/Alamy